FAIRY TAIL

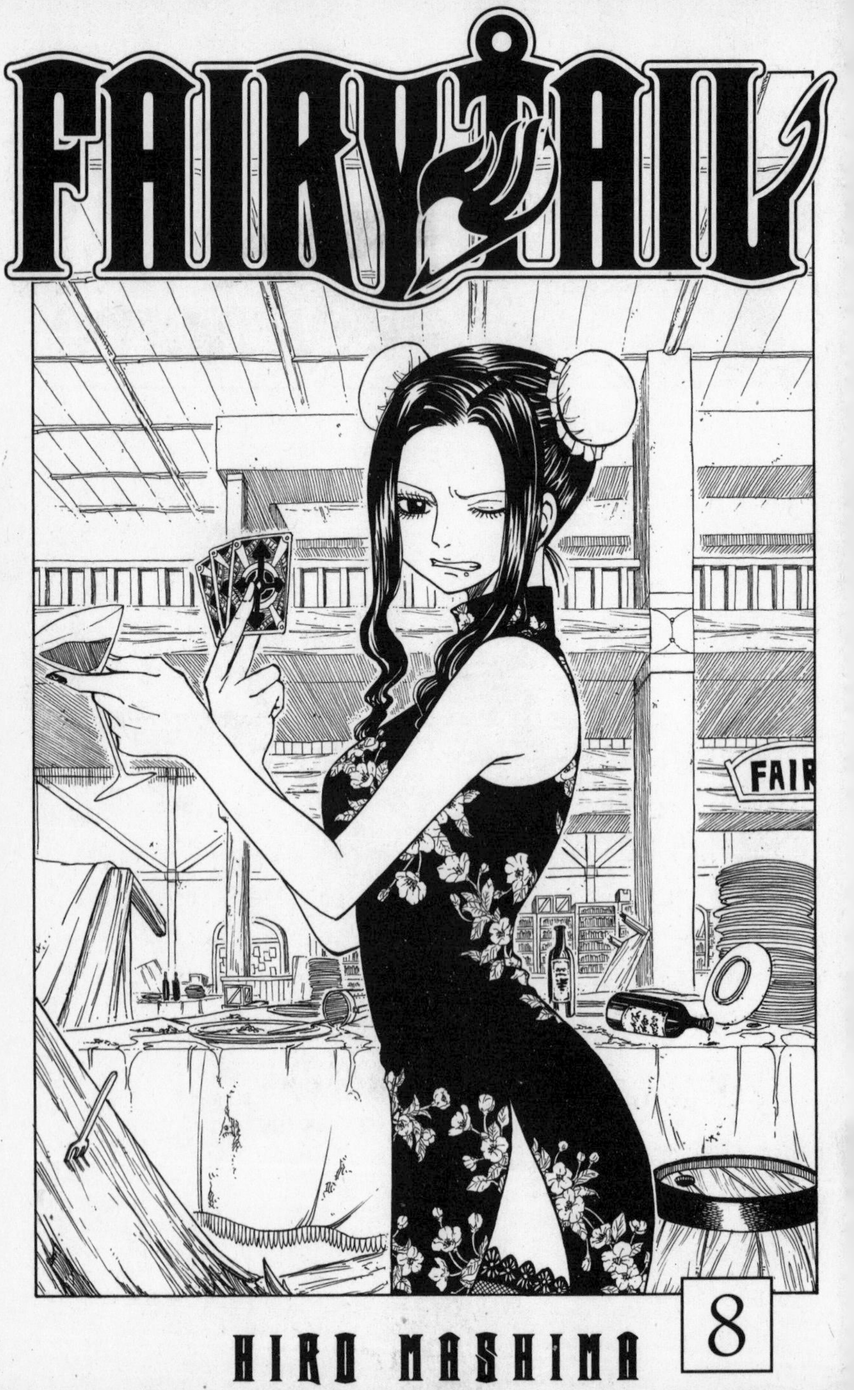
FAIR

8

HIRO MASHIMA

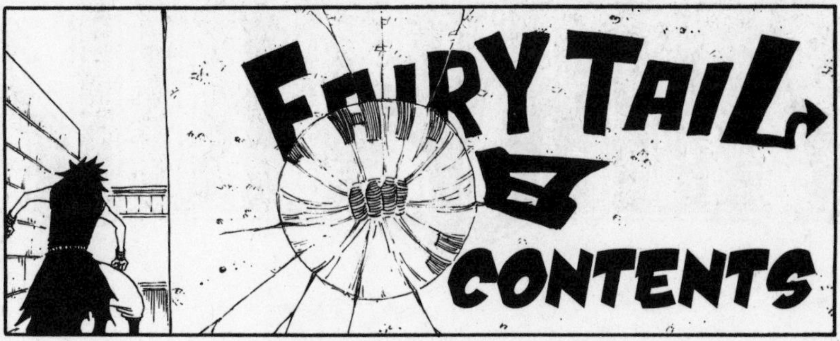
FAIRY TAIL
8
CONTENTS

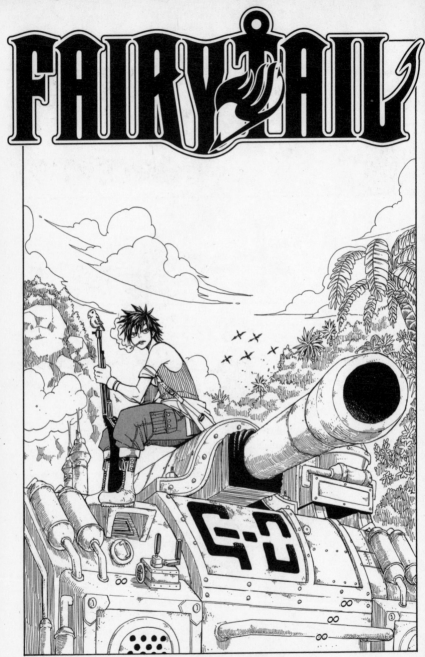

Chapter 57:
Fair-Weather Charm

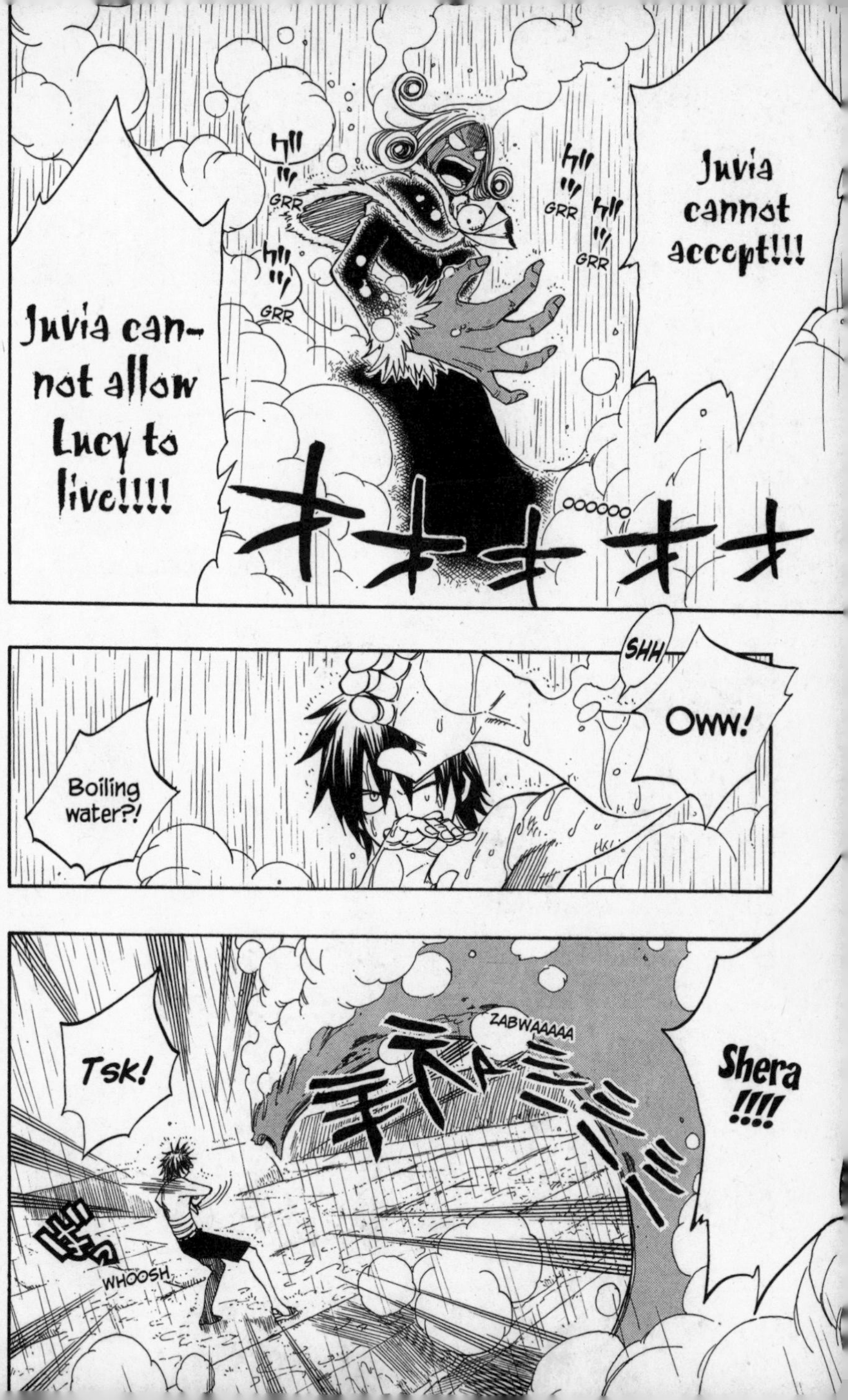
Juvia cannot accept!!!
GRR
GRR
GRR
GRR
Juvia cannot allow Lucy to live!!!!
OOOOOO
SHH
Oww!
Boiling water?!
Shera!!!!
ZABWAAAAA
Tsk!
WHOOSH

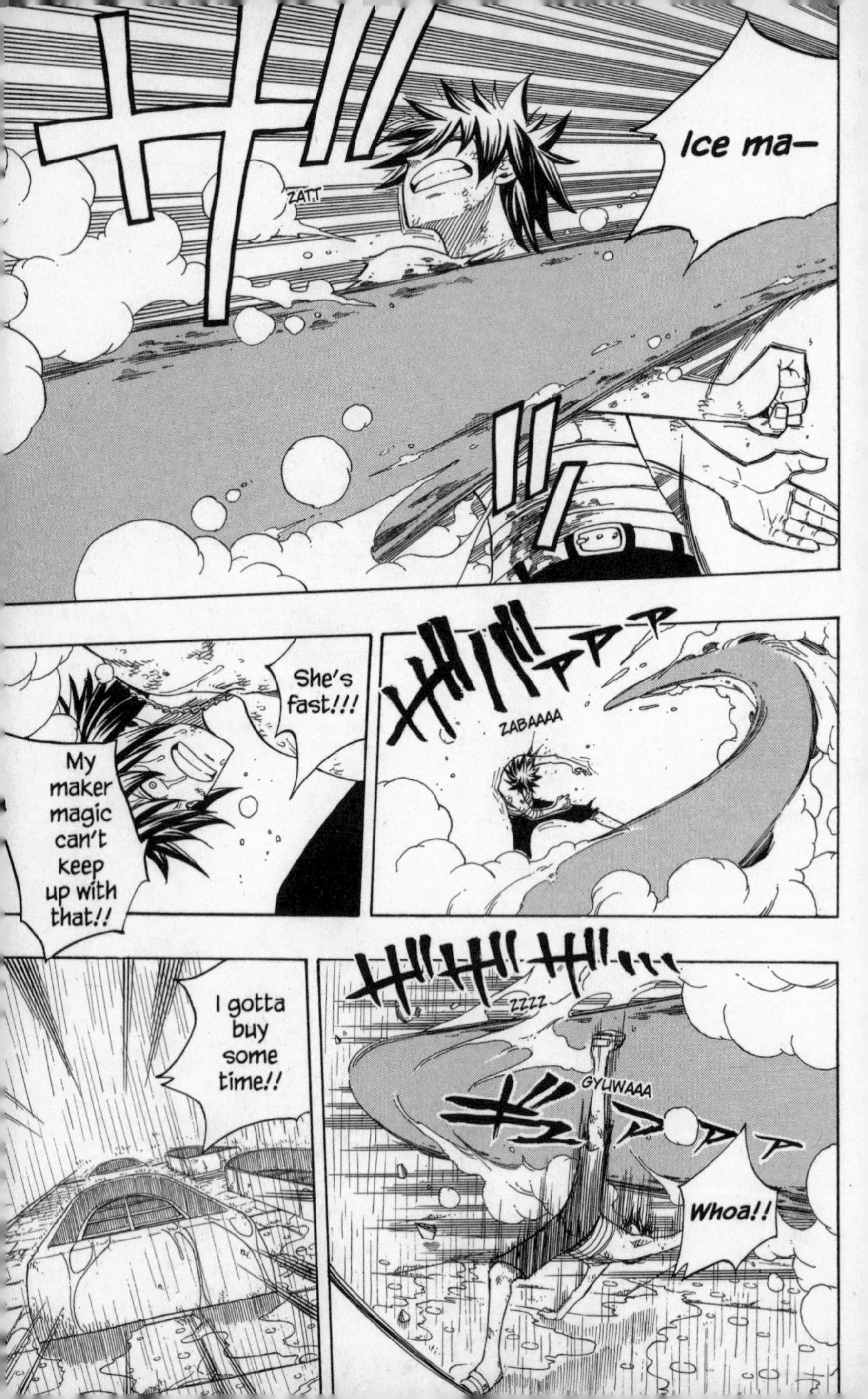
Ice ma—
ZATT
ZABAAAA
She's fast!!!
My maker magic can't keep up with that!!
ZZZZ
GYUWAAA
Whoa!!
I gotta buy some time!!

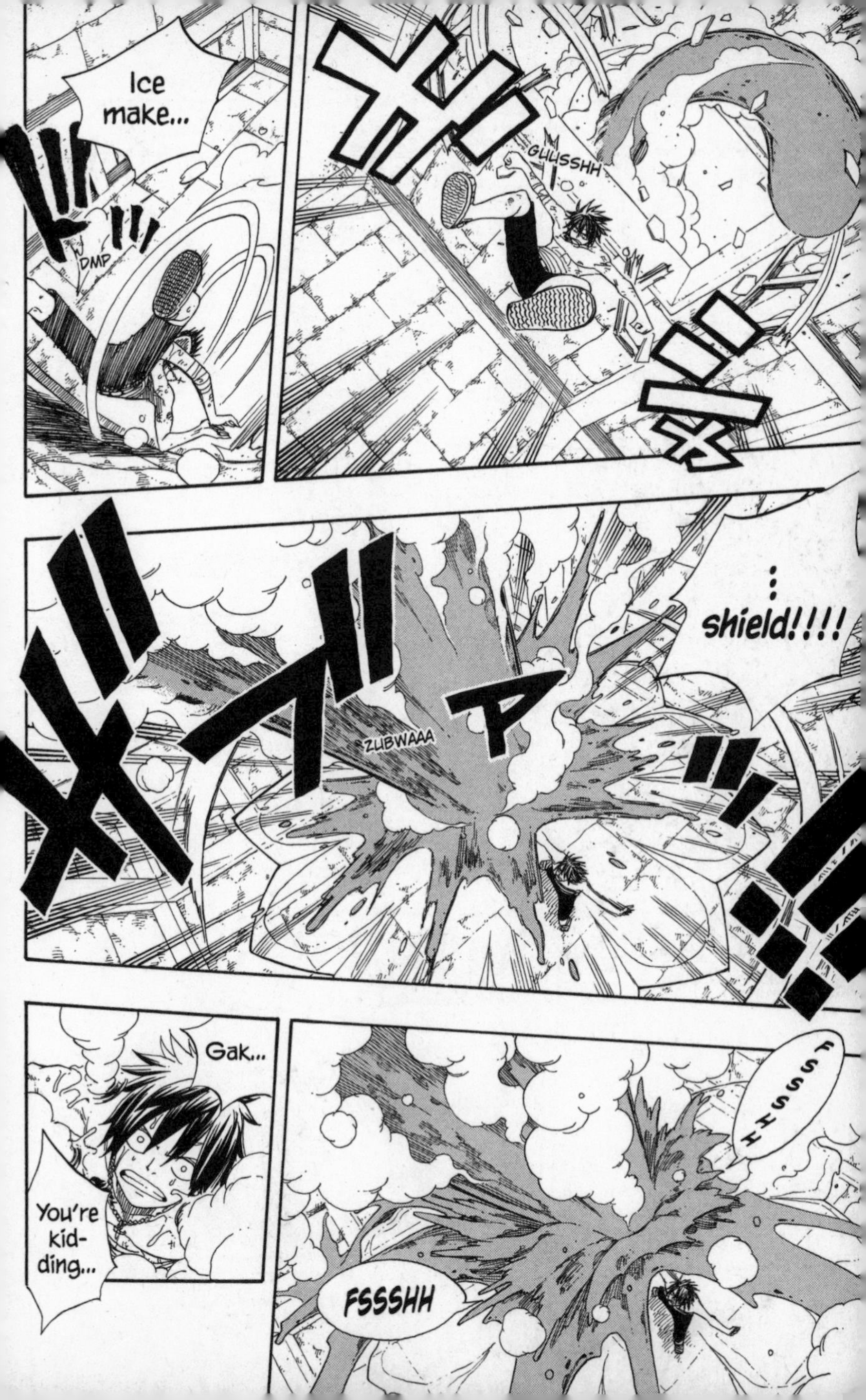
GUUSSHH
Ice make...
DMP
...shield!!!!
ZUBWAAA
FSSSHH
FSSSHH
Gak...
You're kid-ding...

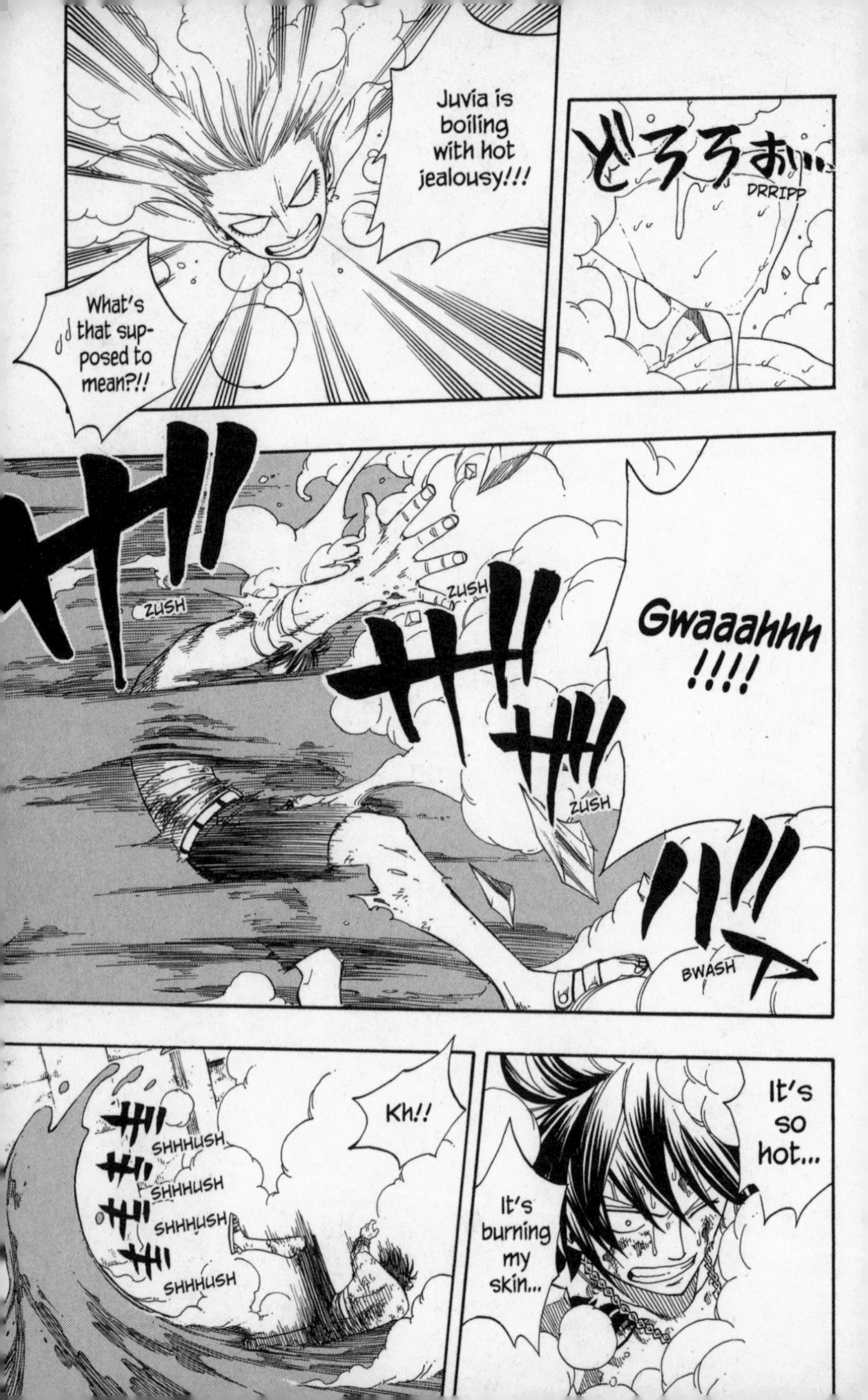
DRRIPP
Juvia is boiling with hot jealousy!!!
What's that supposed to mean?!!
Gwaaahhh!!!!
ZUSH
ZUSH
ZUSH
BWASH
It's so hot...
It's burning my skin...
Kh!!
SHHHUSH
SHHHUSH
SHHHUSH
SHHHUSH

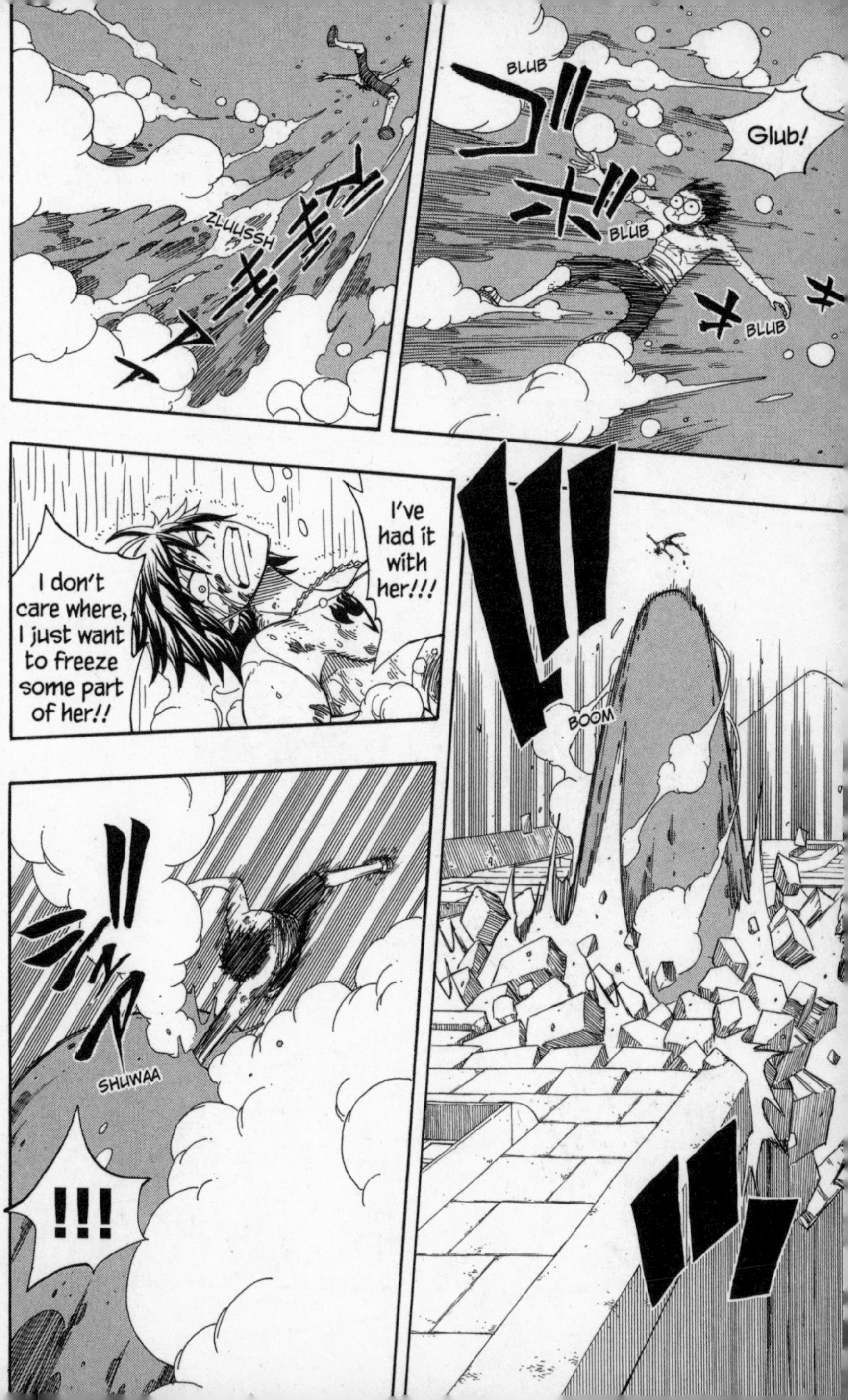
Glub!
BLUB
BLUB
BLUB
ZLUUSSH
BOOM
I've had it with her!!!
I don't care where, I just want to freeze some part of her!!
SHUWAA
!!!

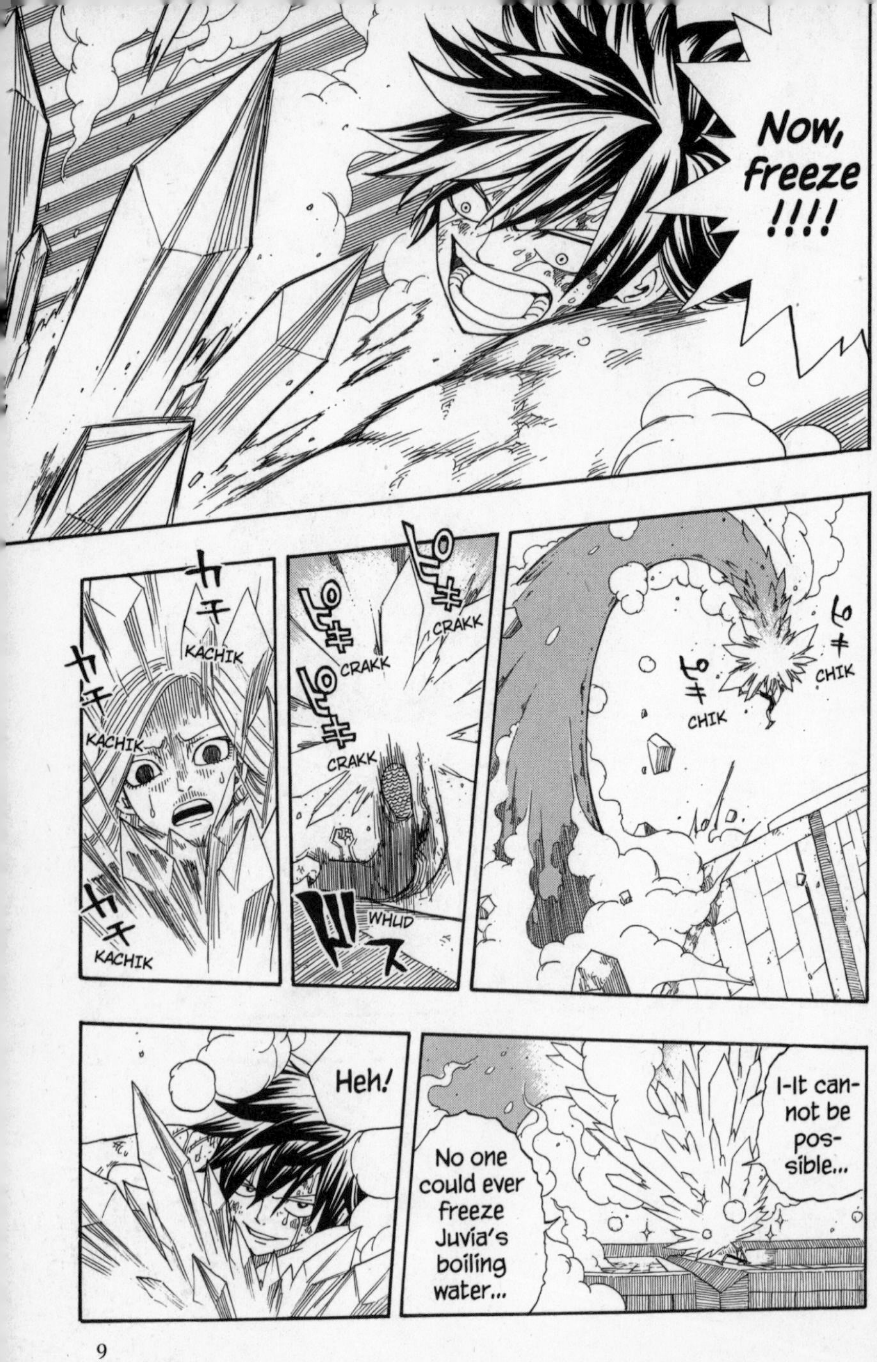
Now, freeze !!!!
ピキ
CHIK
ピキ
CHIK
ピキ
CRAKK
ピキ
CRAKK
ピキ
CRAKK
ドス
WHUD
カチ
KACHIK
カチ
KACHIK
カチ
KACHIK
I-It cannot be possible...
No one could ever freeze Juvia's boiling water...
Heh!

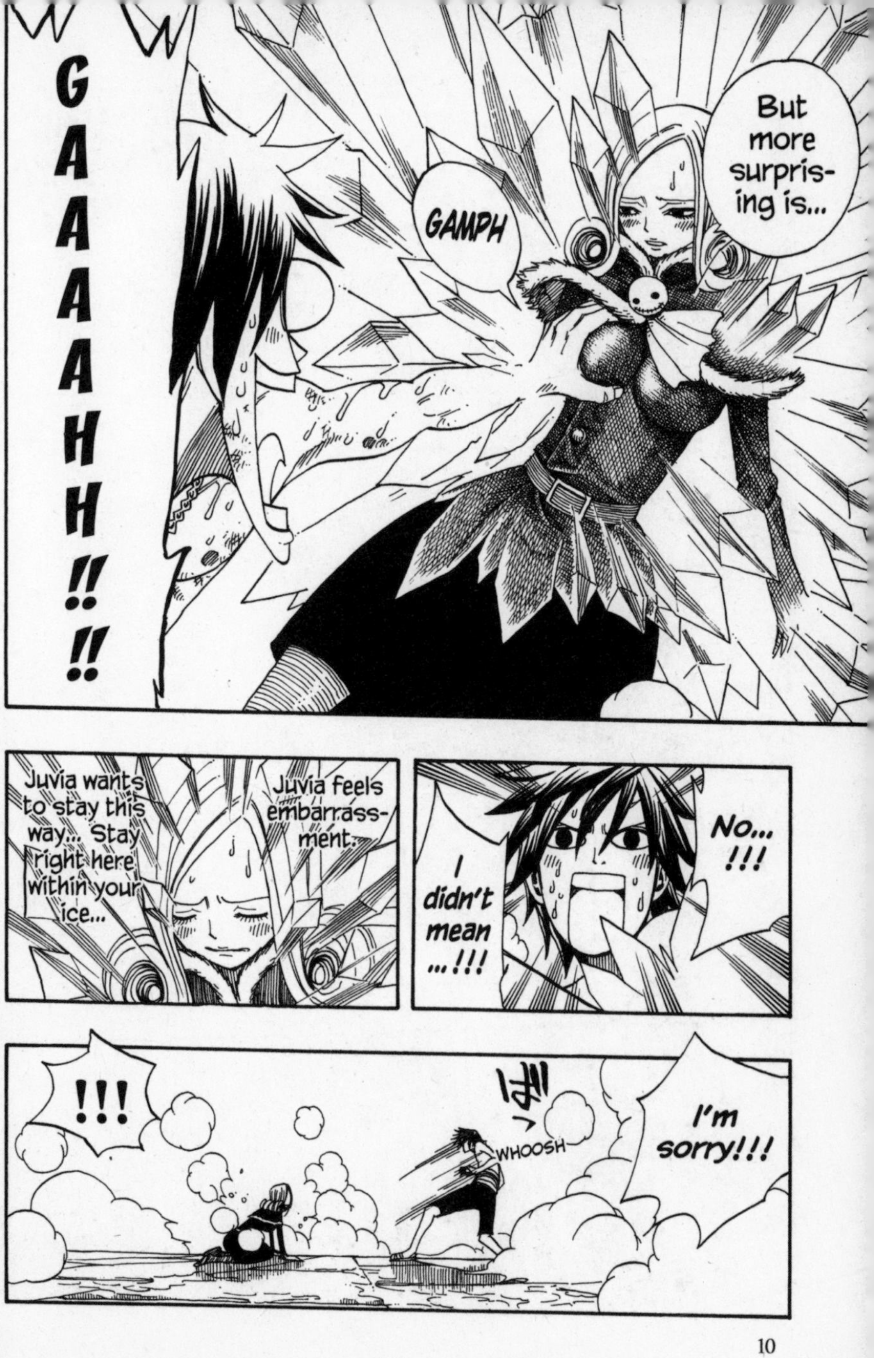
But more surprising is...
GAMPH
GAAAAHH!!!!
No...!!!
I didn't mean...!!!
Juvia feels embarrassment.
Juvia wants to stay this way... Stay right here within your ice...
I'm sorry!!!
ば
WHOOSH
!!!

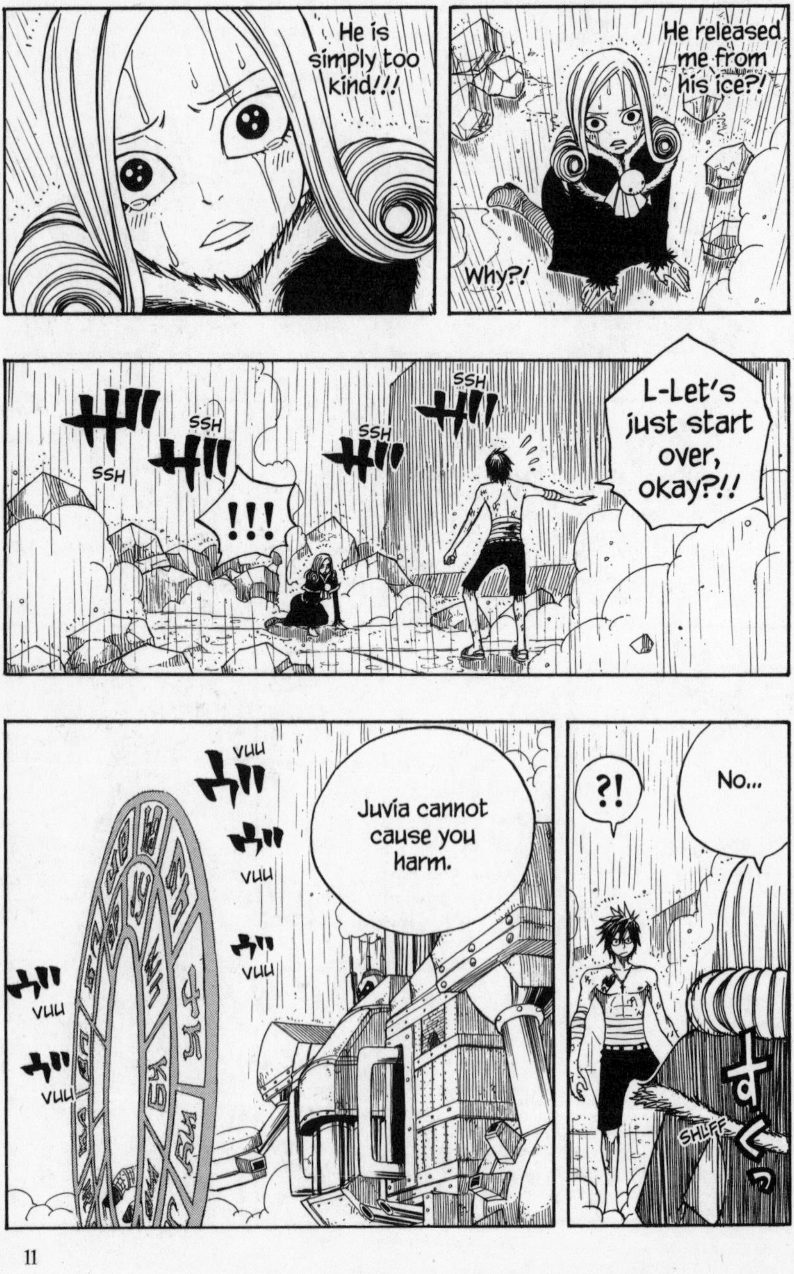
He released me from his ice?!
Why?!
He is simply too kind!!!
L-Let's just start over, okay?!!
SSH
SSH
SSH
SSH
!!!
No...
?!
SHLFF
Juvia cannot cause you harm.
VUU
VUU
VUU
VUU
VUU

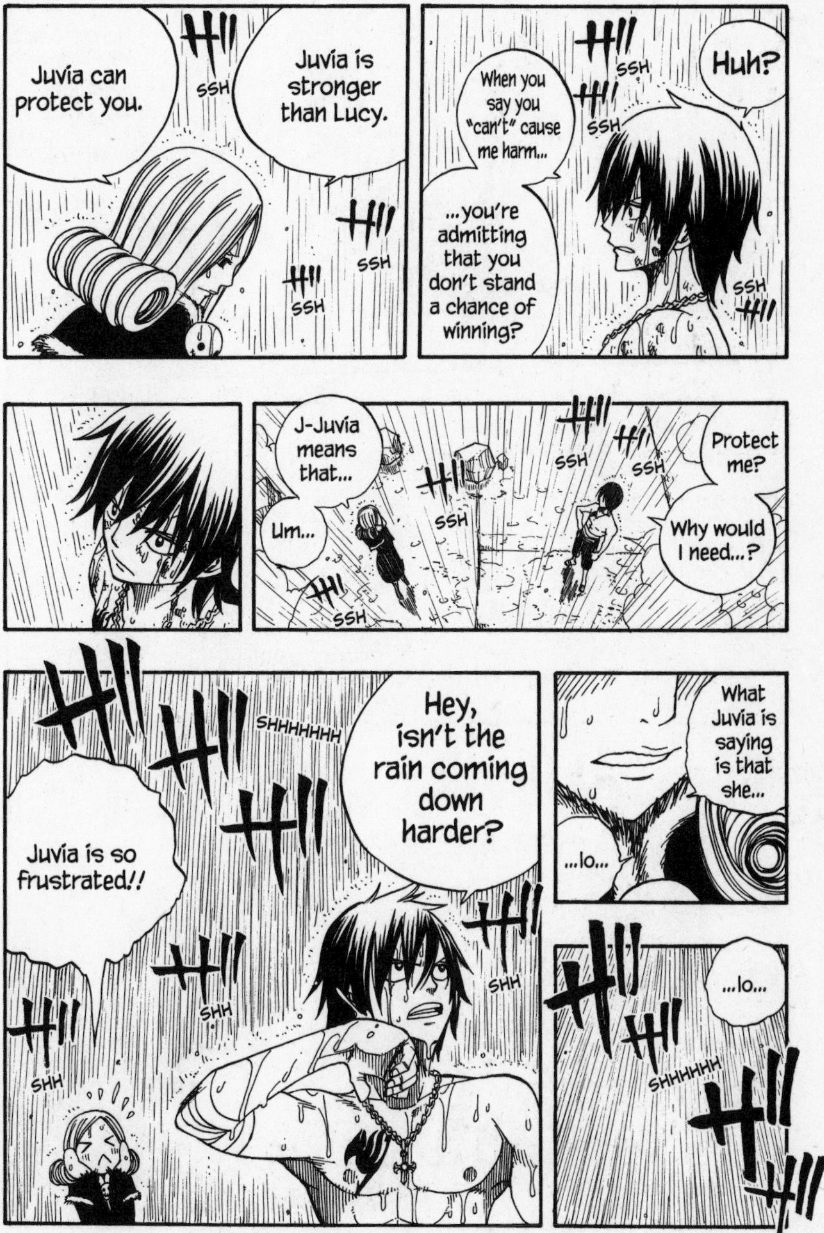
Huh?
SSH
SSH
When you say you "can't" cause me harm...
...you're admitting that you don't stand a chance of winning?
SSH
SSH
Juvia is stronger than Lucy.
Juvia can protect you.
SSH
SSH
Protect me?
Why would I need...?
SSH
SSH
SSH
J-Juvia means that...
Um...
SSH
What Juvia is saying is that she...
...lo...
...lo...
SHHHHHH
SHHHHHHH
Hey, isn't the rain coming down harder?
SHH
Juvia is so frustrated!!
SHH
SHH

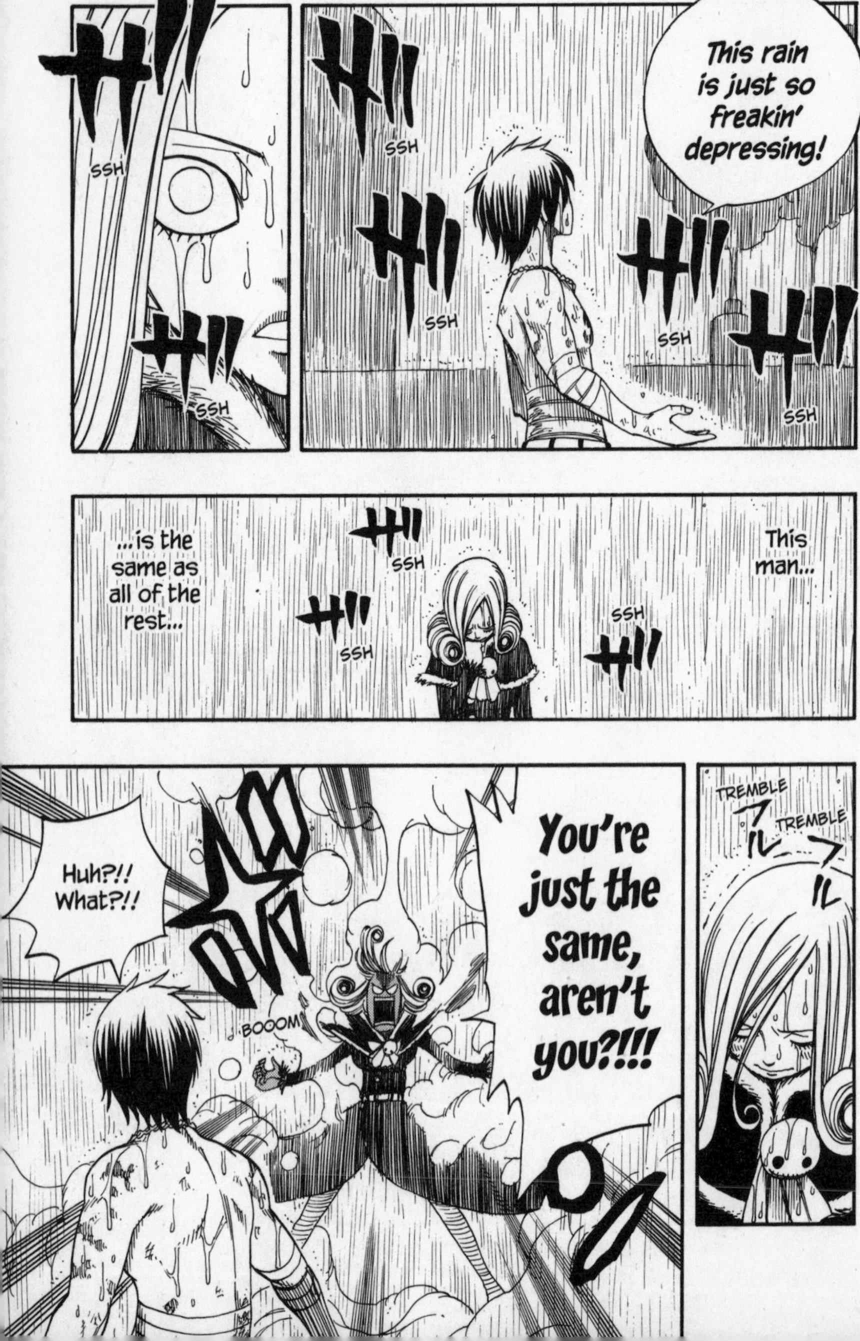
This rain is just so freakin' depressing!
SSH
SSH
SSH
SSH
SSH
SSH
This man...
...is the same as all of the rest...
SSH
SSH
SSH
TREMBLE
TREMBLE
You're just the same, aren't you?!!!
BOOOM
Huh?!! What?!!

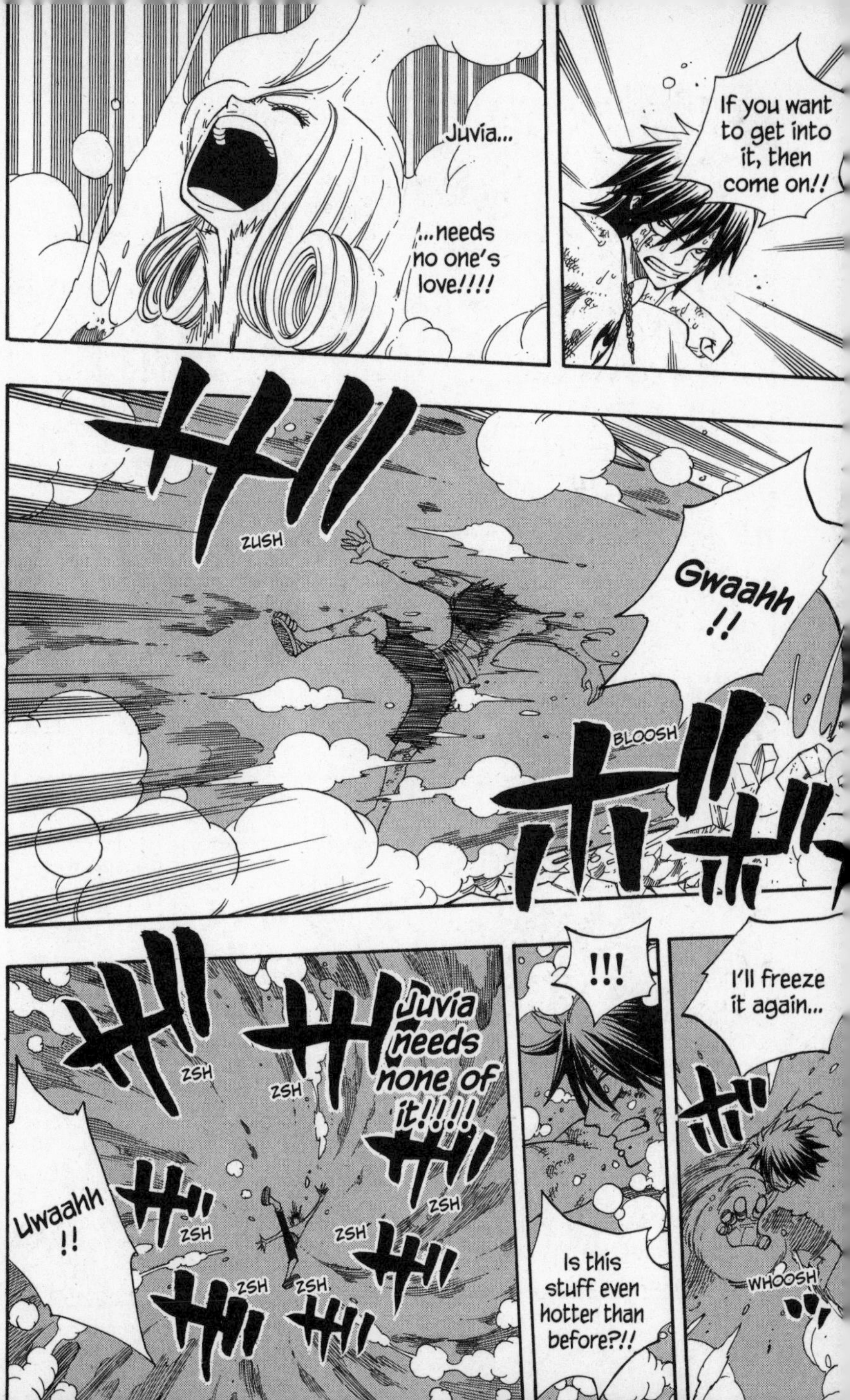
If you want to get into it, then come on!!
Juvia...
...needs no one's love!!!!
Gwaahh !!
BLOOSH
ZUSH
I'll freeze it again...
WHOOSH
!!!
Is this stuff even hotter than before?!!
Juvia needs none of it!!!!
ZSH
ZSH
ZSH
ZSH
ZSH
ZSH
ZSH
Uwaahh !!

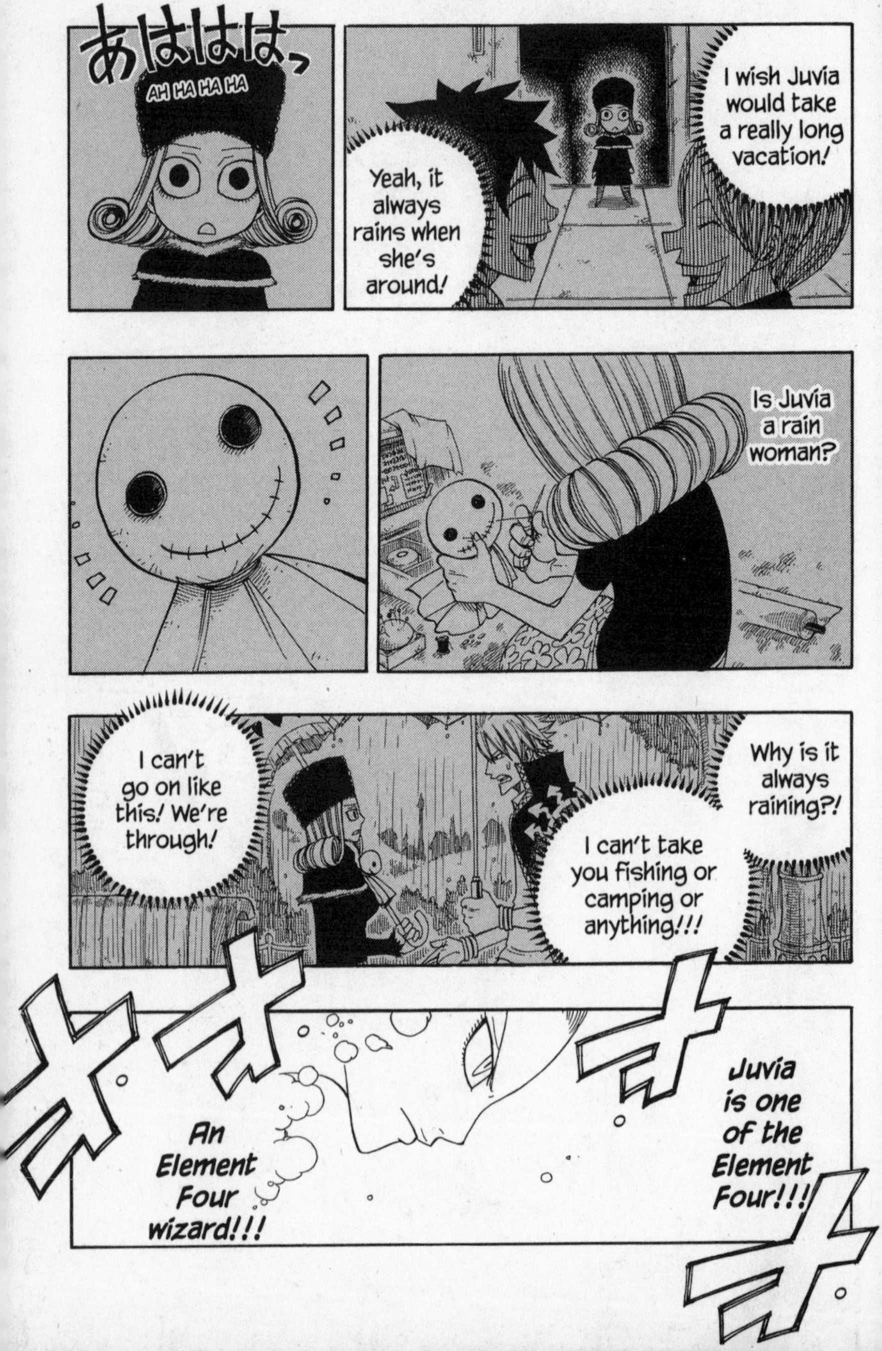
I wish Juvia would take a really long vacation!
Yeah, it always rains when she's around!
あははは
AH HA HA HA
Is Juvia a rain woman?
Why is it always raining?!
I can't take you fishing or camping or anything!!!
I can't go on like this! We're through!
Juvia is one of the Element Four!!!
An Element Four wizard!!!

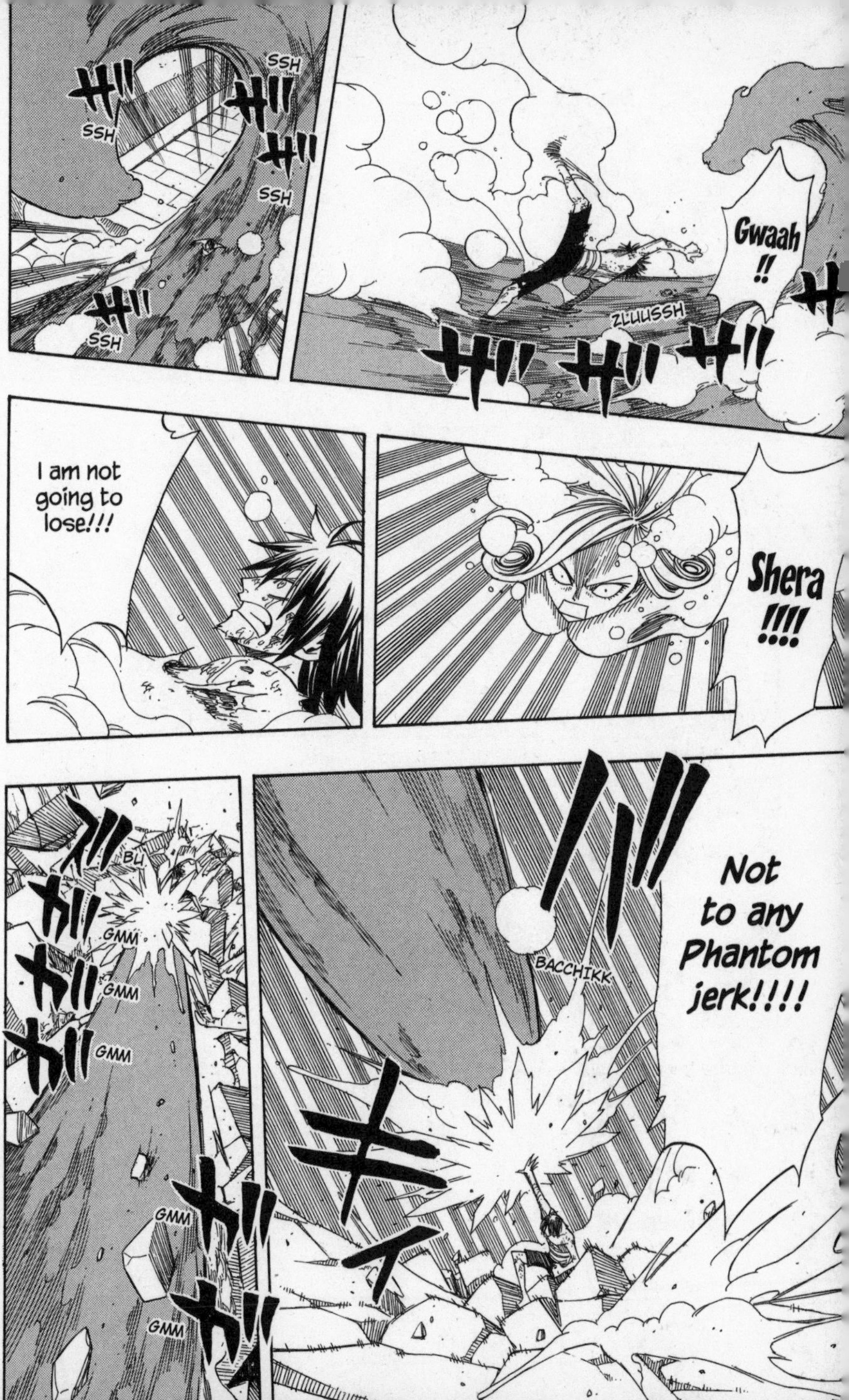
Gwaah!!
ZLUUSSH
SSH
SSH
SSH
SSH
Shera!!!!
I am not going to lose!!!
Not to any Phantom jerk!!!!
BACCHIKK
BU
GMM
GMM
GMM
GMM
GMM

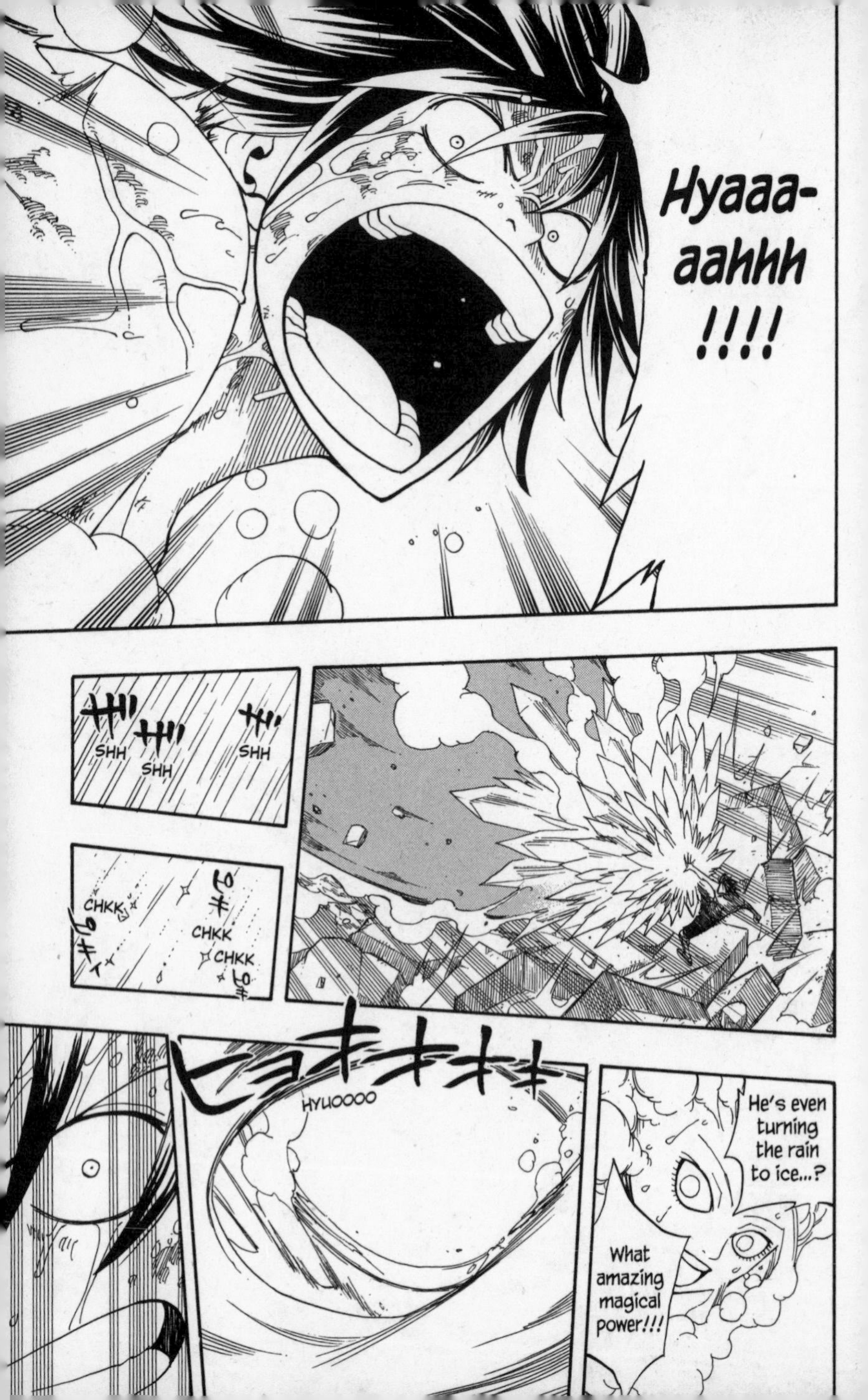

Hyaaa-aahhh!!!!
SHH SHH SHH
CHKK CHKK CHKK
He's even turning the rain to ice...?
What amazing magical power!!!
HYUOOOO

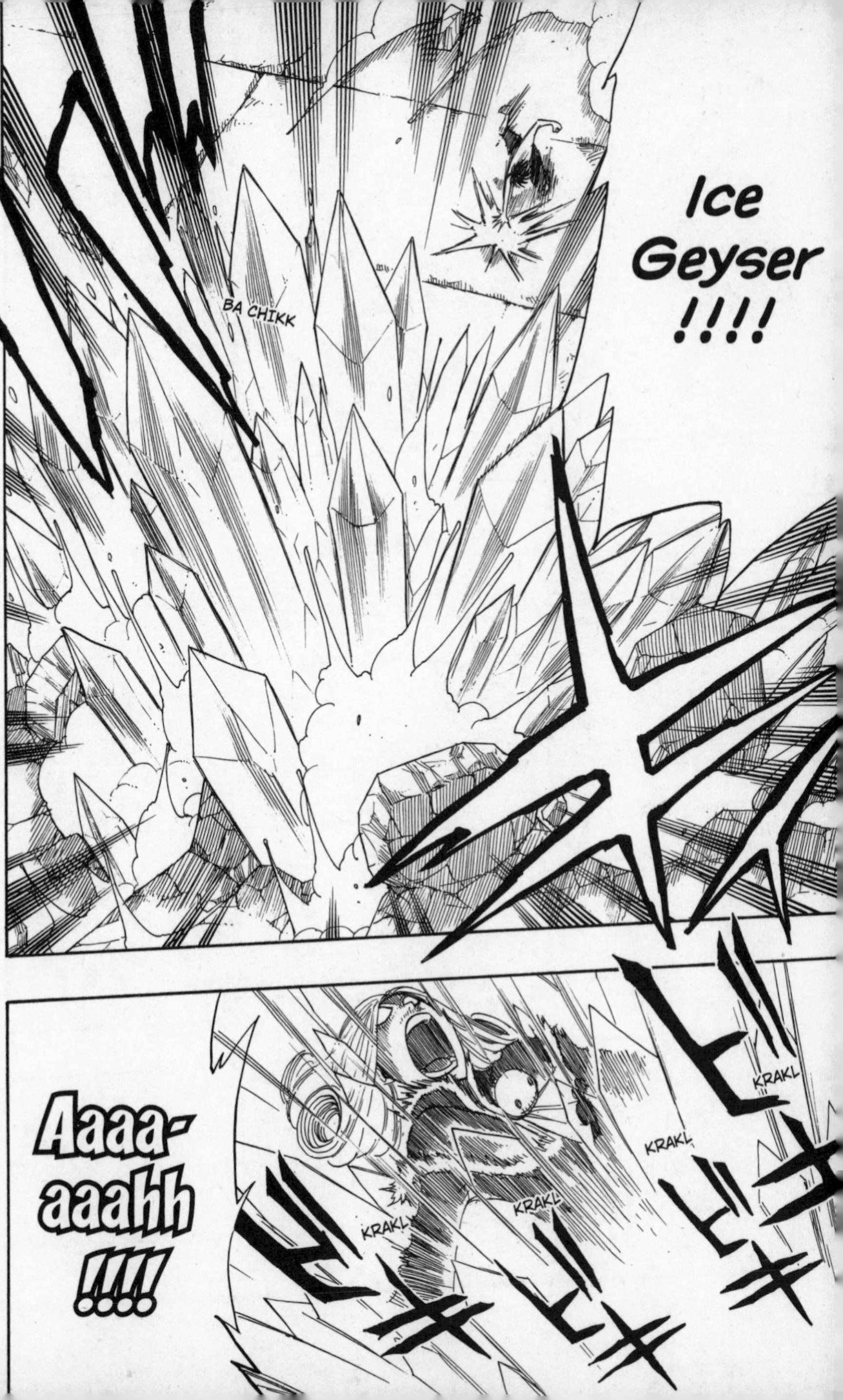
Ice Geyser !!!!
BA CHIKK
KRAKL
KRAKL
KRAKL
KRAKL
Aaaa-aaahh !!!!

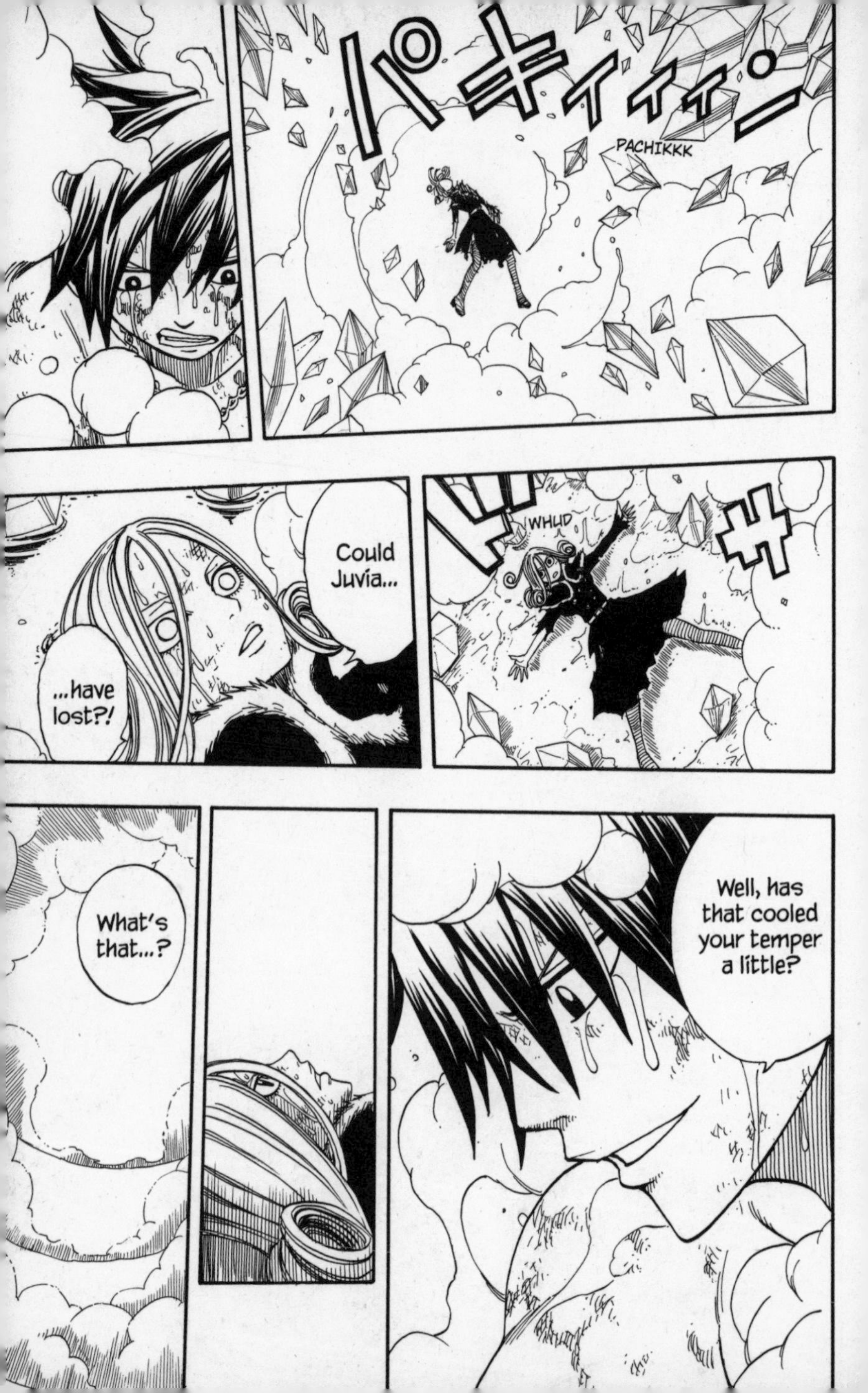
パキィィーン
PACHIKKK
WHUD
Could Juvia...
...have lost?!
Well, has that cooled your temper a little?
What's that...?

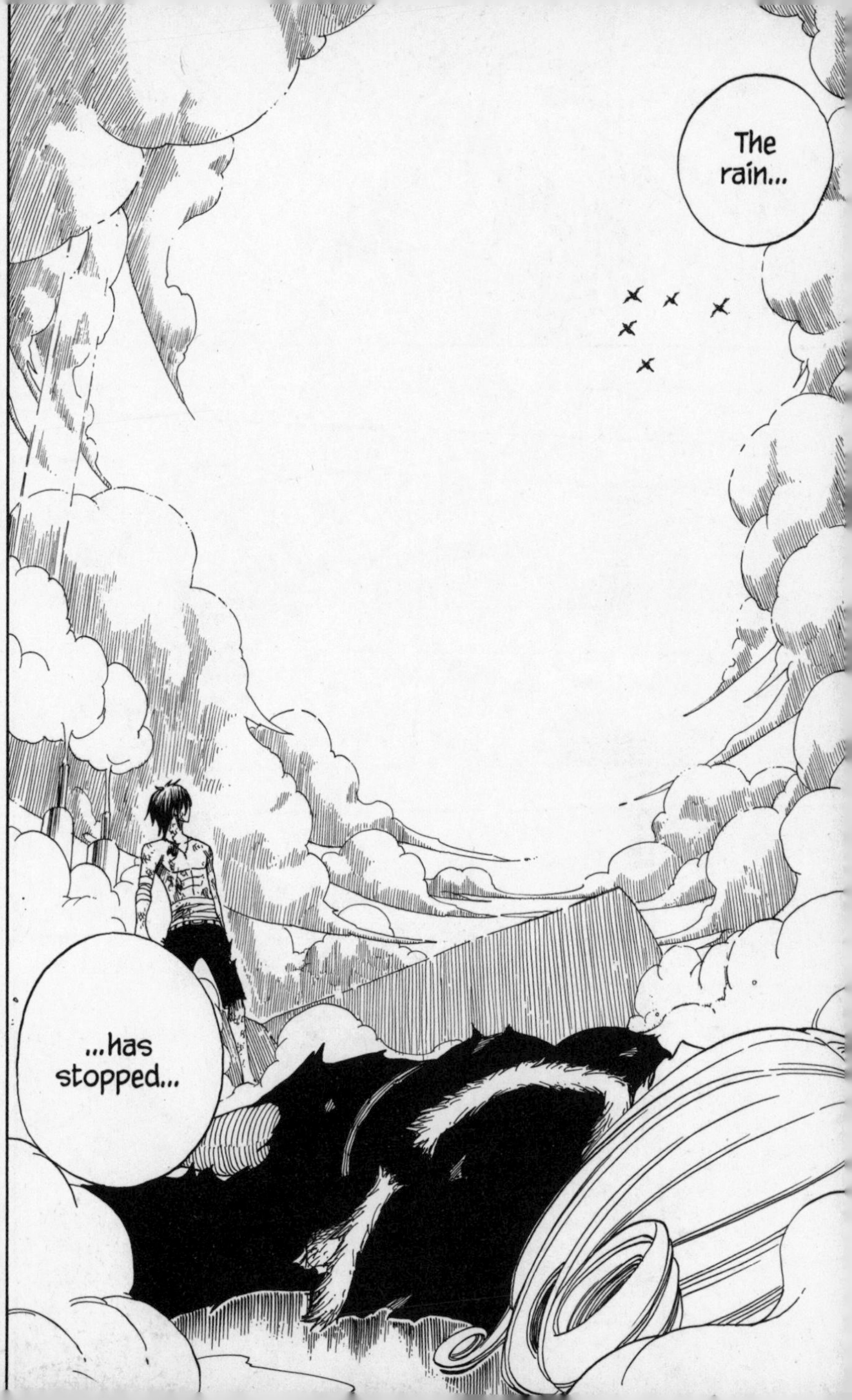
The rain...
...has stopped...

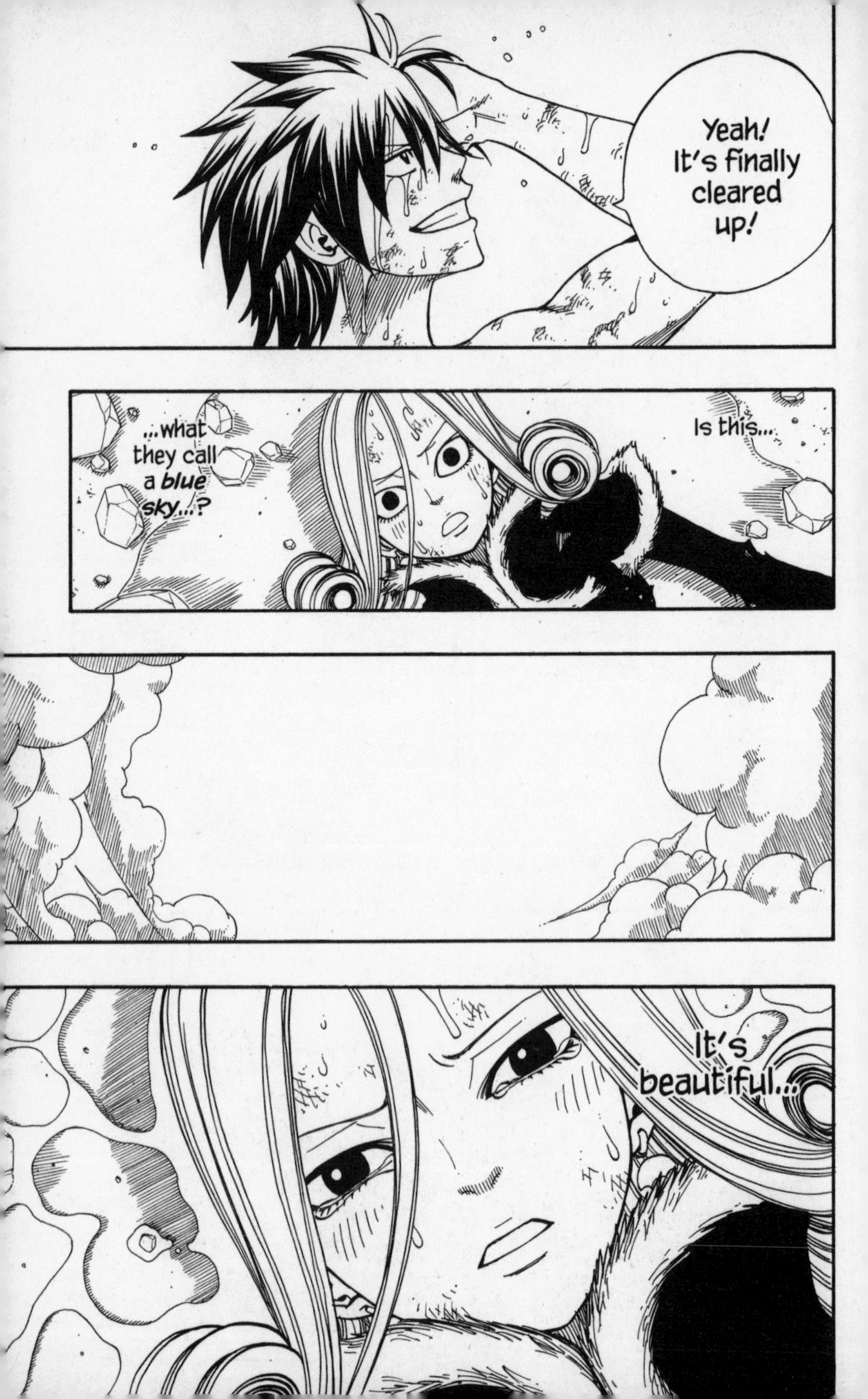
Yeah! It's finally cleared up!
Is this...
...what they call a *blue sky*...?
It's beautiful...

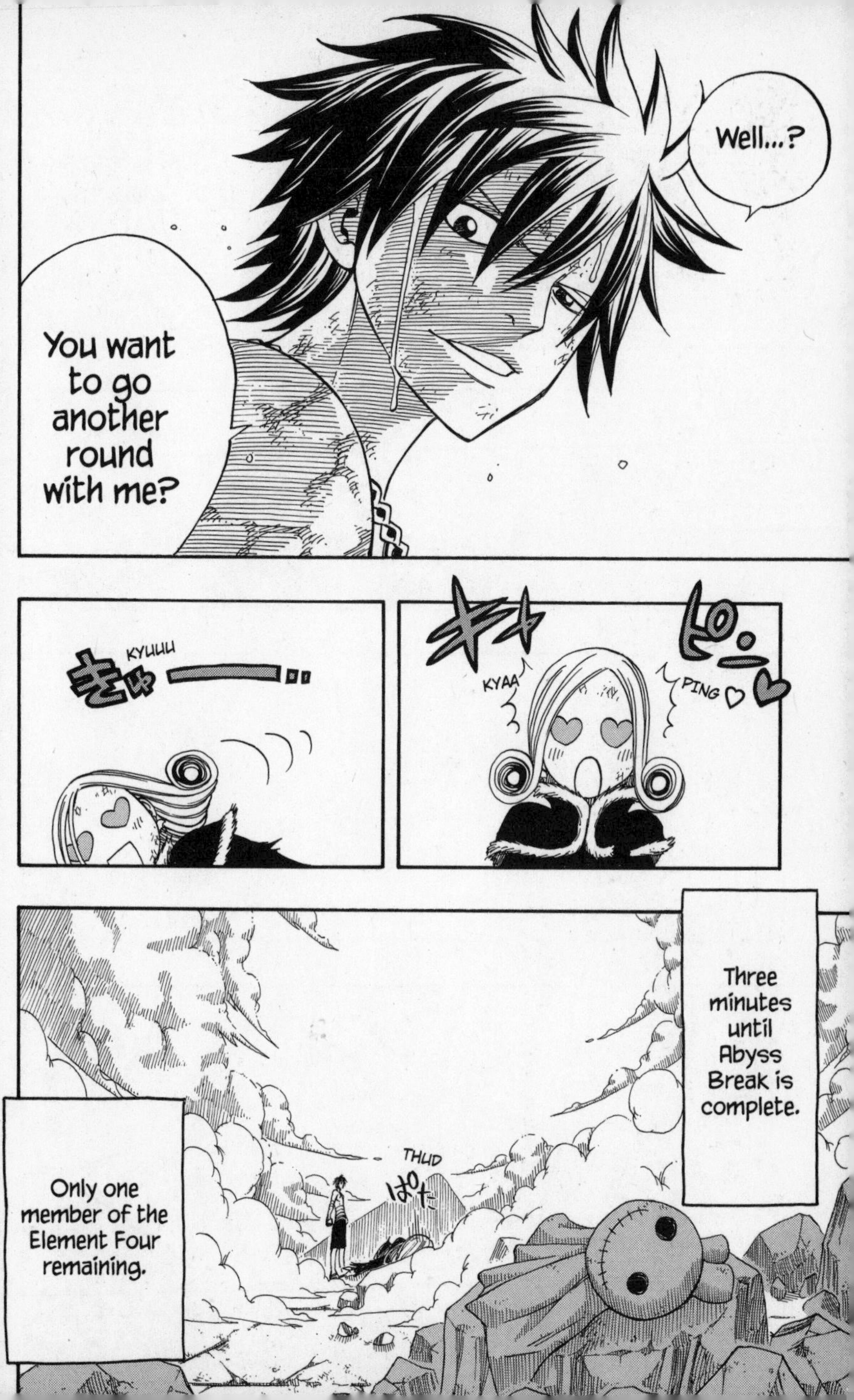
Well...?
You want to go another round with me?
KYAA
PING ♡
きゅ
KYUUU
Three minutes until Abyss Break is complete.
THUD
Only one member of the Element Four remaining.

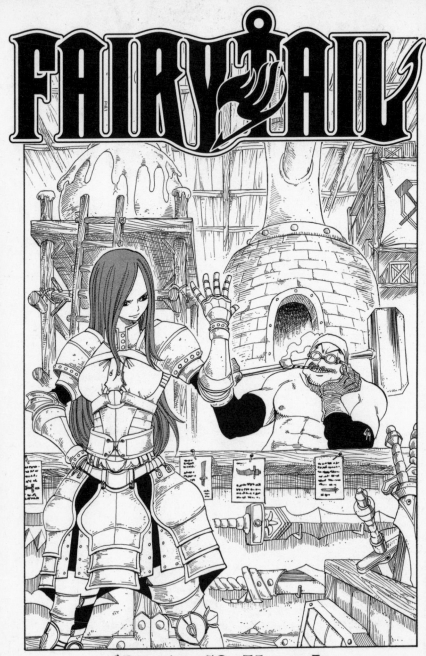

Chapter 58: There Is
Always Someone Better

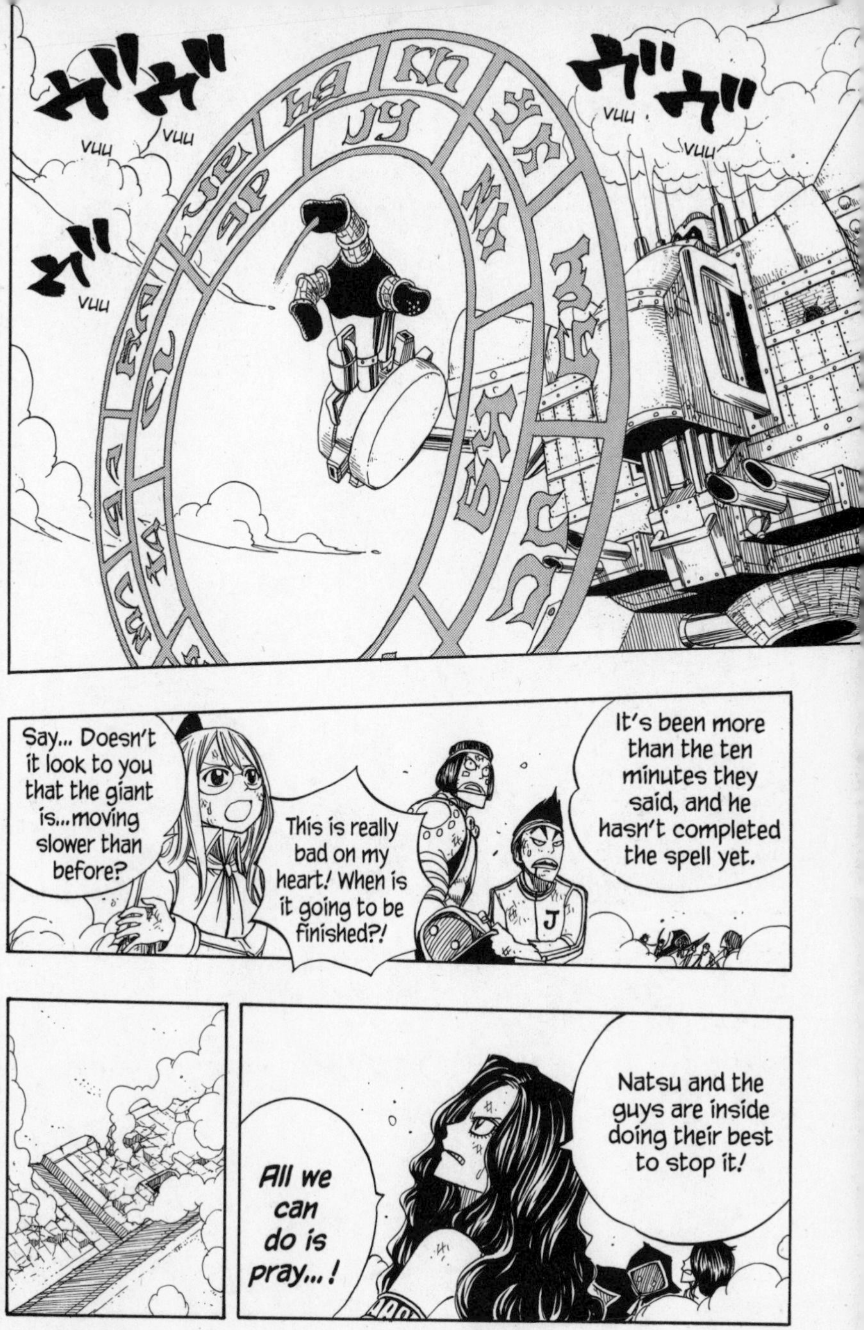
VUU
VUU
VUU
VUU
VUU
It's been more than the ten minutes they said, and he hasn't completed the spell yet.
This is really bad on my heart! When is it going to be finished?!
Say... Doesn't it look to you that the giant is...moving slower than before?
Natsu and the guys are inside doing their best to stop it!
All we can do is pray...!

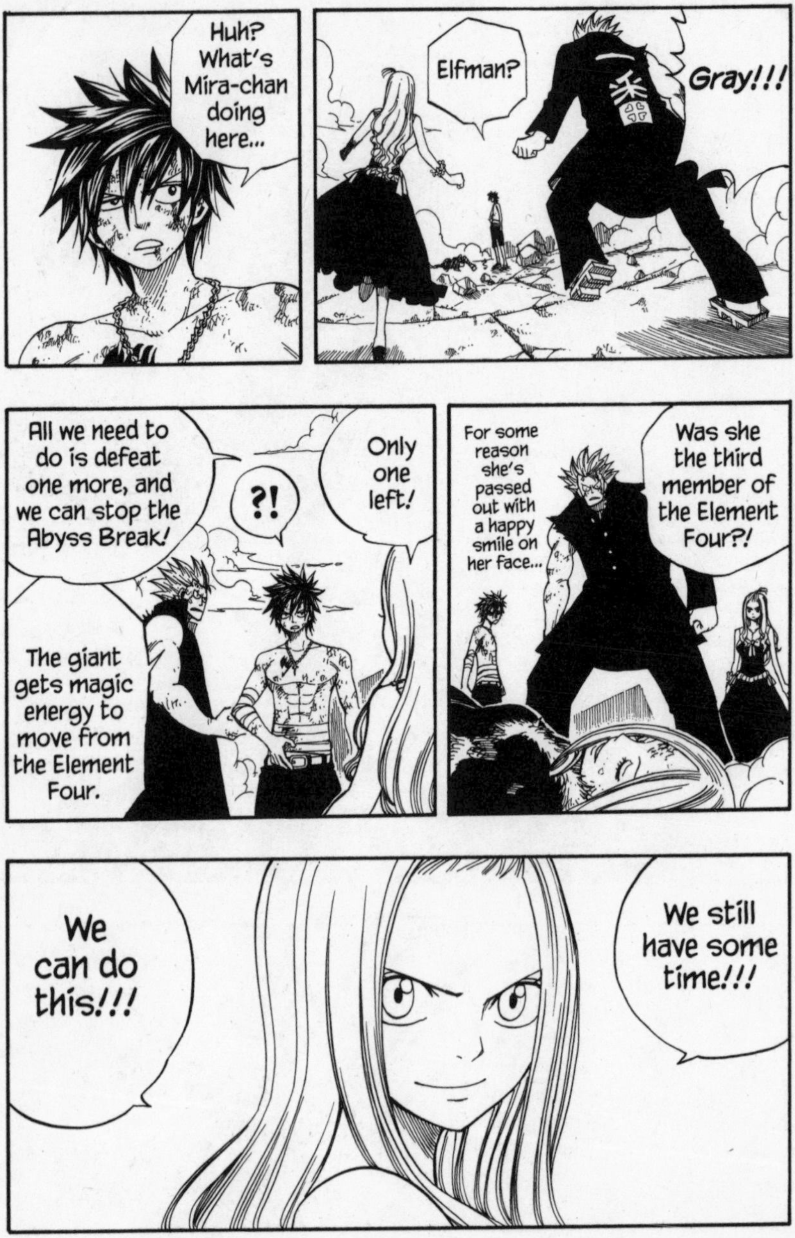
Gray!!!
Elfman?
Huh? What's Mira-chan doing here...
Was she the third member of the Element Four?!
For some reason she's passed out with a happy smile on her face...
Only one left!
?!
All we need to do is defeat one more, and we can stop the Abyss Break!
The giant gets magic energy to move from the Element Four.
We still have some time!!!
We can do this!!!

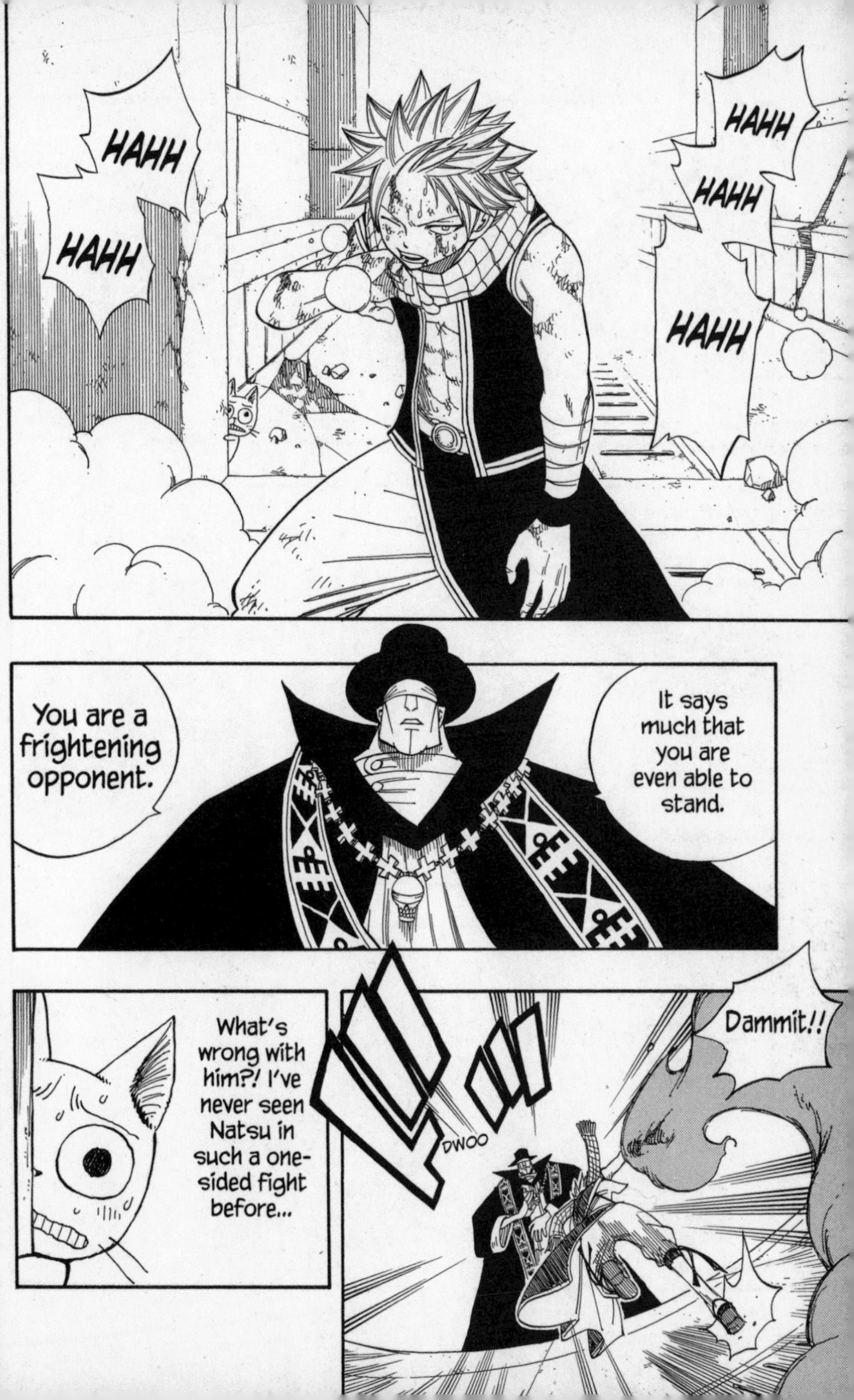
HAHH
HAHH
HAHH
HAHH
HAHH
It says much that you are even able to stand.
You are a frightening opponent.
Dammit!!
DWOO
What's wrong with him?! I've never seen Natsu in such a one-sided fight before...

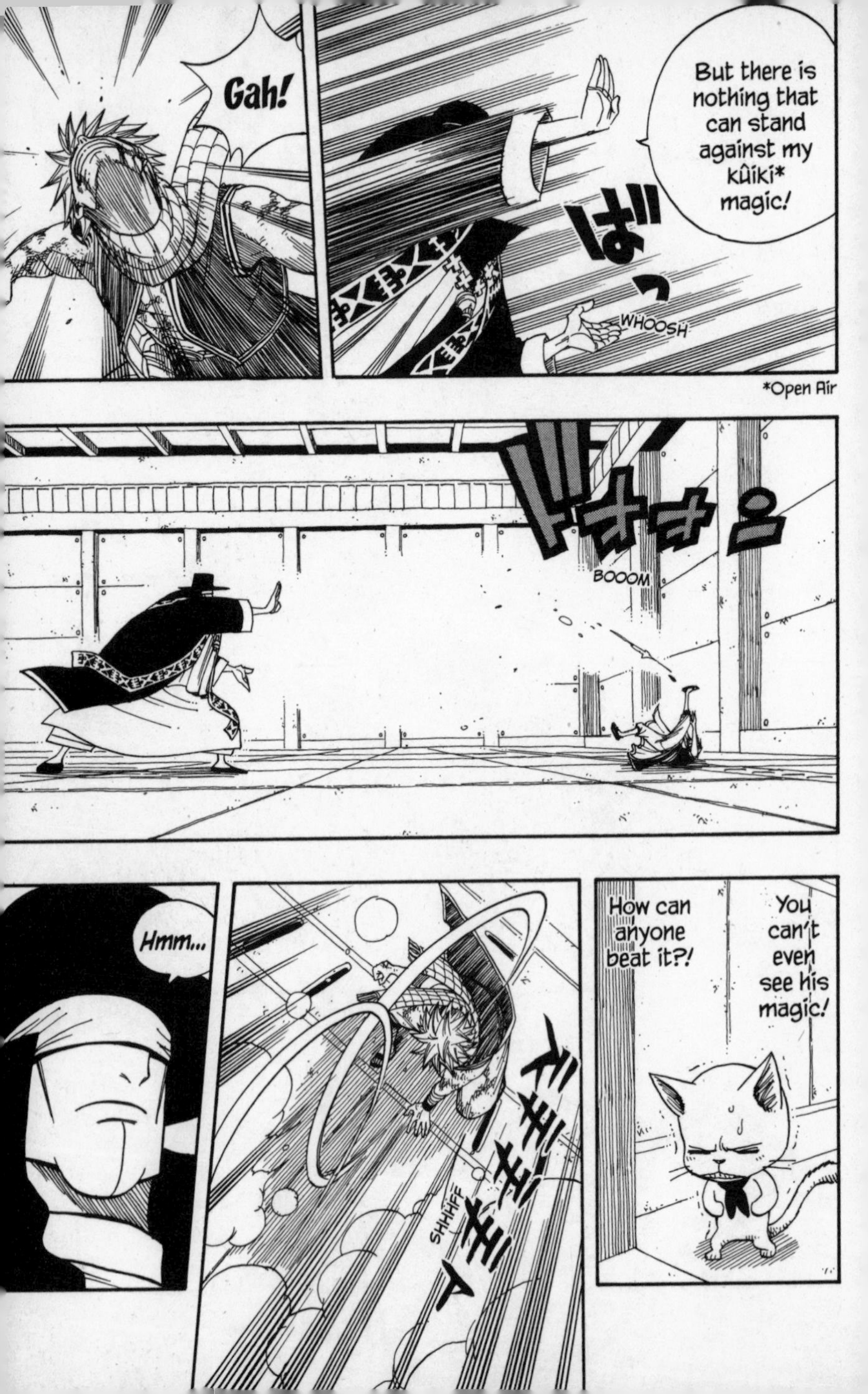
But there is nothing that can stand against my kûiki* magic!
ばっ
WHOOSH
Gah!
BOOOM
You can't even see his magic!
How can anyone beat it?!
SHHHFF
Hmm...
*Open Air

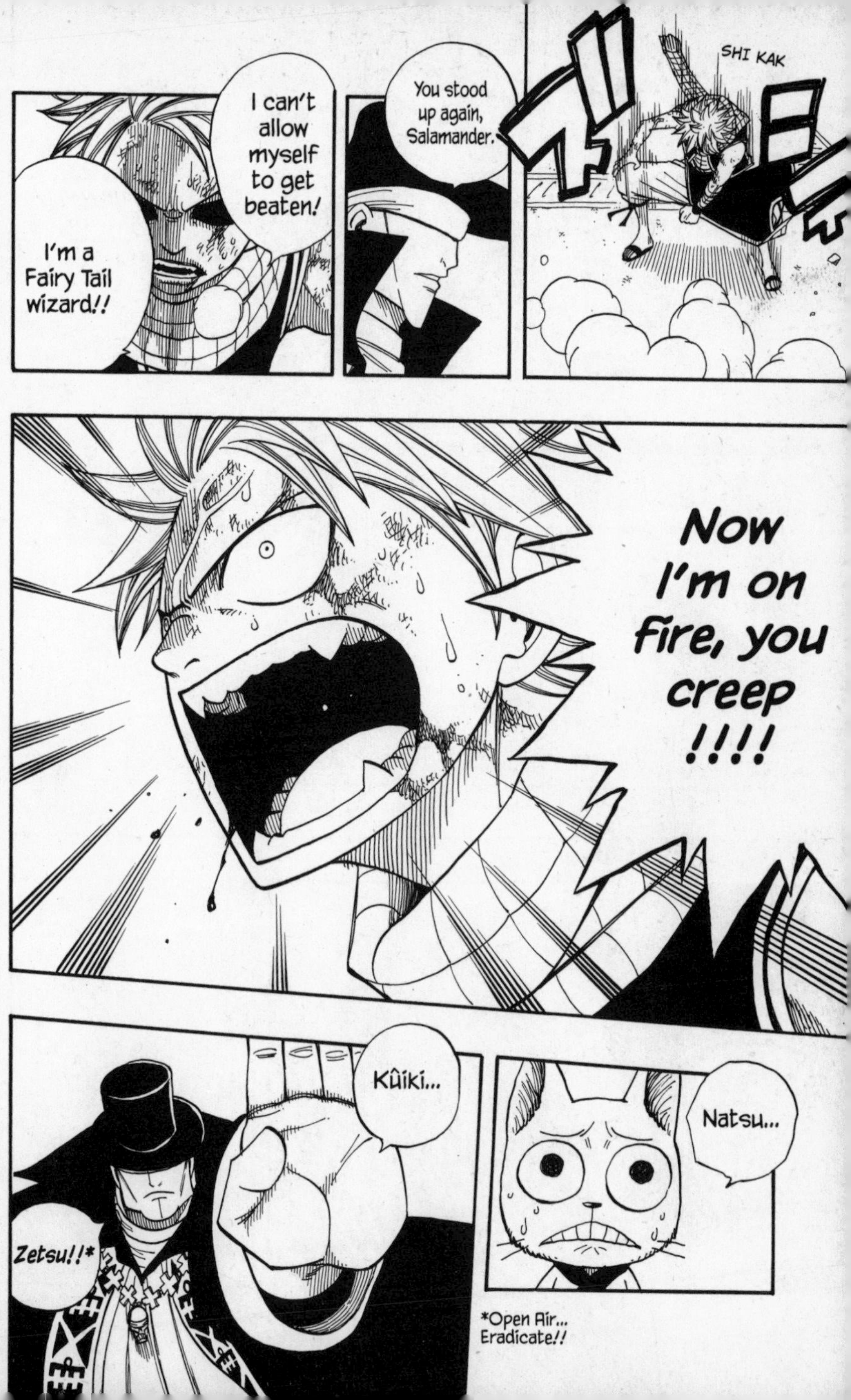
SHI KAK
You stood up again, Salamander.
I can't allow myself to get beaten!
I'm a Fairy Tail wizard!!
Now I'm on fire, you creep!!!!
Natsu...
Kûiki...
Zetsu!!*

*Open Air... Eradicate!!

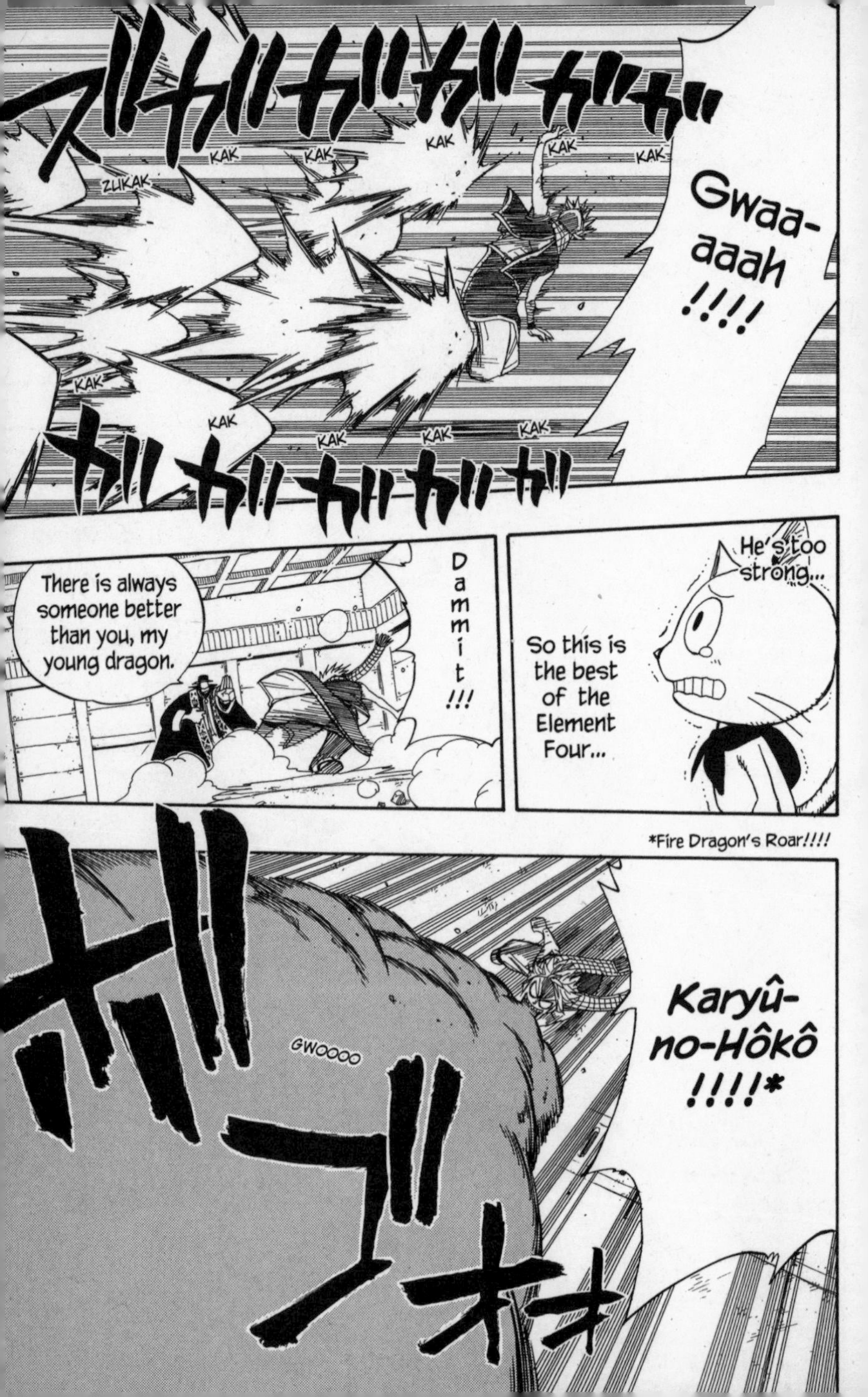
Gwaa-aaah!!!!
KAK
KAK
KAK
KAK
KAK
ZUKAK
KAK
KAK
KAK
KAK
KAK
He's too strong...
So this is the best of the Element Four...
Dammit!!!
There is always someone better than you, my young dragon.
Karyû-no-Hôkô!!!!*
GWOOOO
*Fire Dragon's Roar!!!!

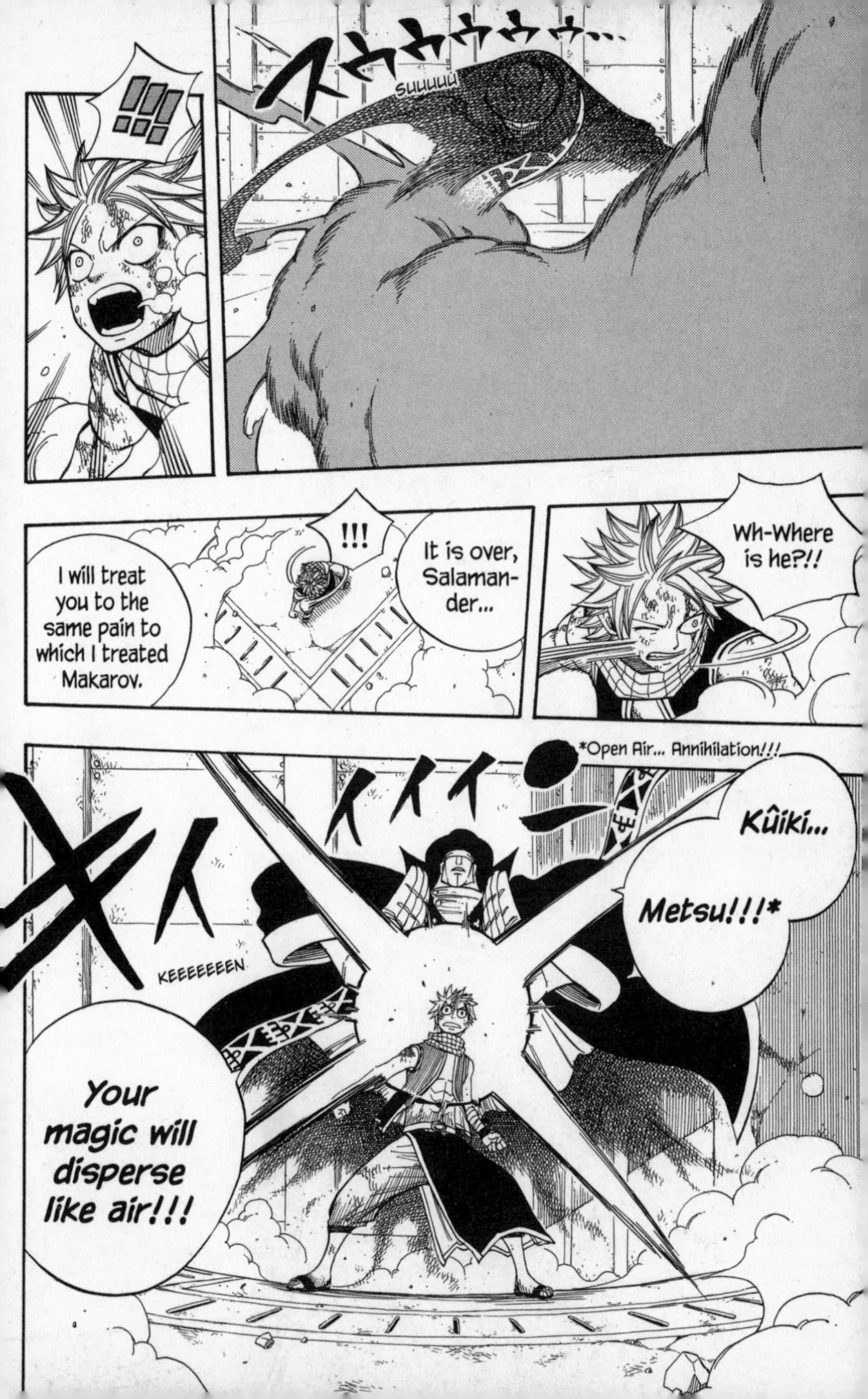
SUUUUU
!!!
Wh-Where is he?!!
!!!
It is over, Salamander...
I will treat you to the same pain to which I treated Makarov.
Kûiki...
Metsu!!!*
*Open Air... Annihilation!!!
KEEEEEEEN
Your magic will disperse like air!!!

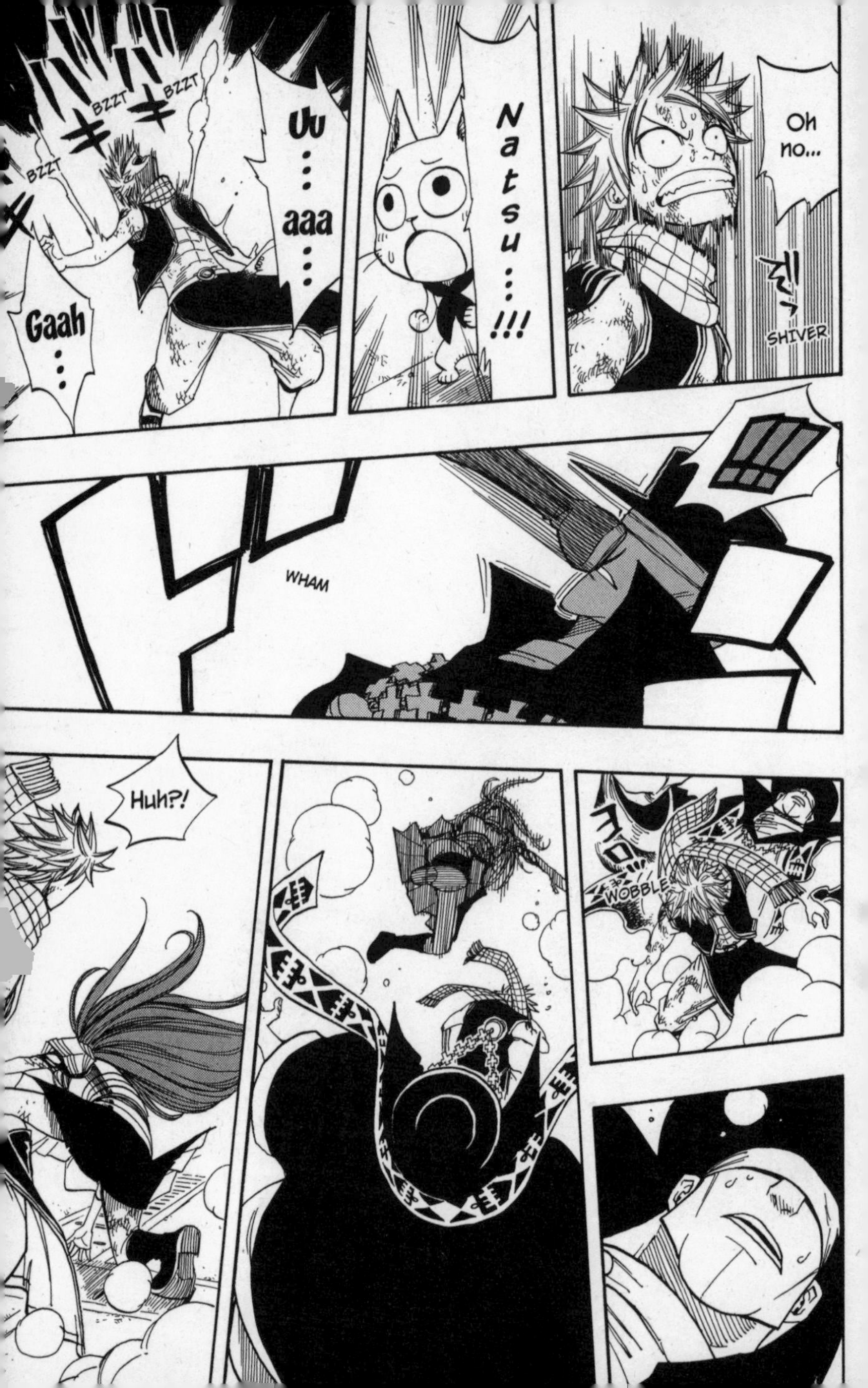
Oh no...
SHIVER
Natsu...!!!
Uu... aaa...
BZZT
BZZT
BZZT
Gaah...
!!!
WHAM
WOBBLE
Huh?!

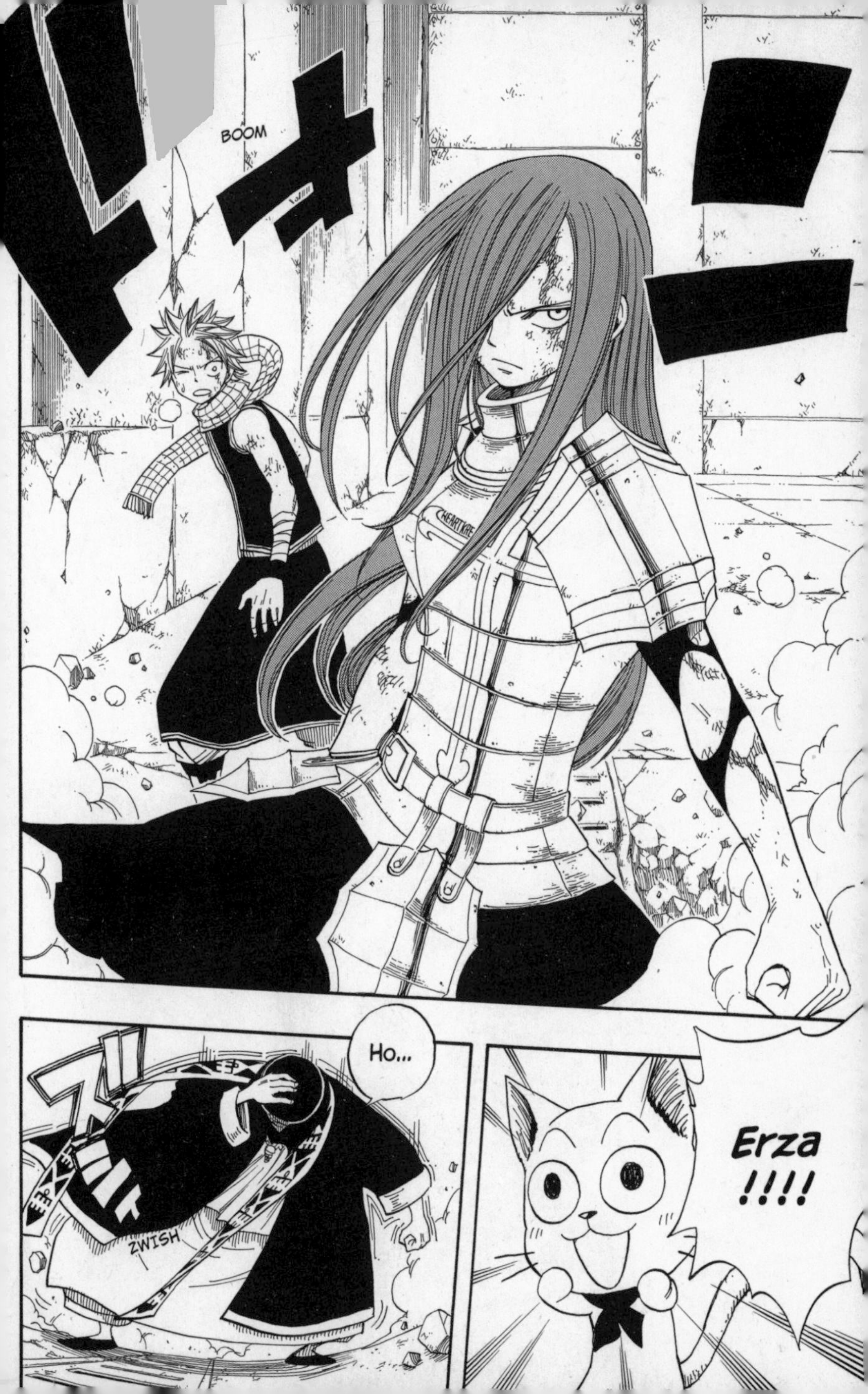
BOOM
Erza !!!!
Ho...
ZWISH

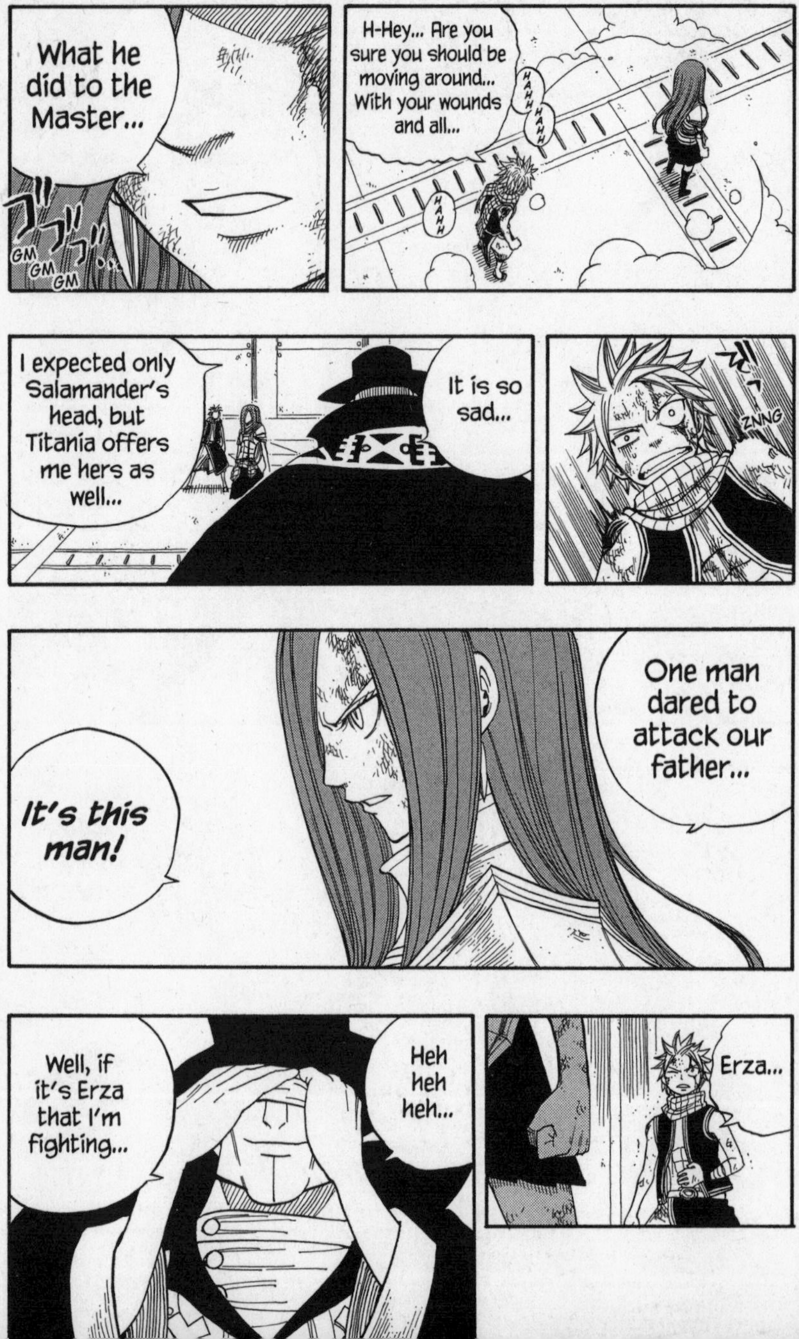
H-Hey... Are you sure you should be moving around... With your wounds and all...
HAHH
HAHH
HAHH
What he did to the Master...
GM GM GM
ZNNG
It is so sad...
I expected only Salamander's head, but Titania offers me hers as well...
One man dared to attack our father...
It's this man!
Erza...
Heh heh heh...
Well, if it's Erza that I'm fighting...

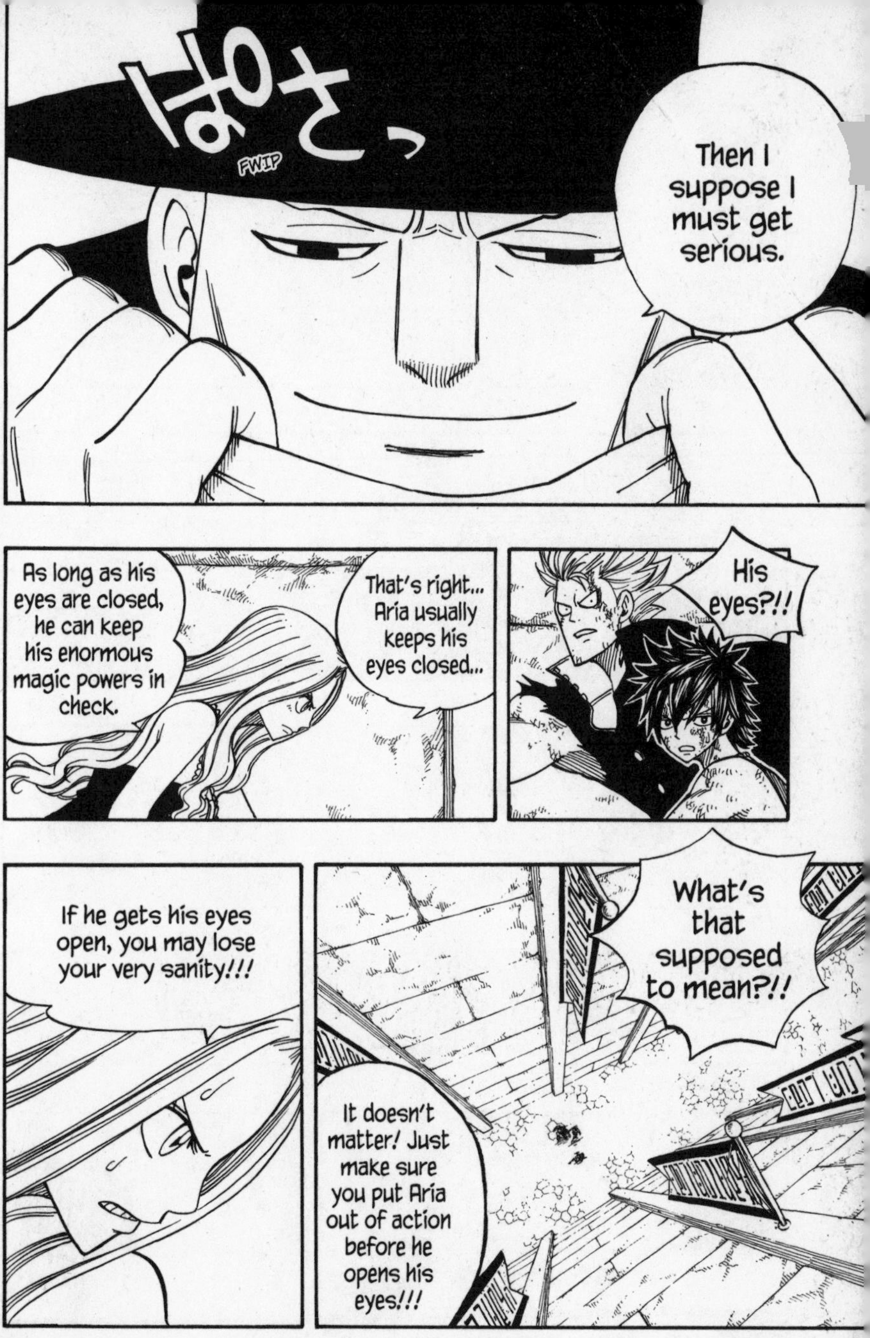

ばさっ
FWIP
Then I suppose I must get serious.
His eyes?!!
That's right... Aria usually keeps his eyes closed...
As long as his eyes are closed, he can keep his enormous magic powers in check.
What's that supposed to mean?!!
It doesn't matter! Just make sure you put Aria out of action before he opens his eyes!!!
If he gets his eyes open, you may lose your very sanity!!!

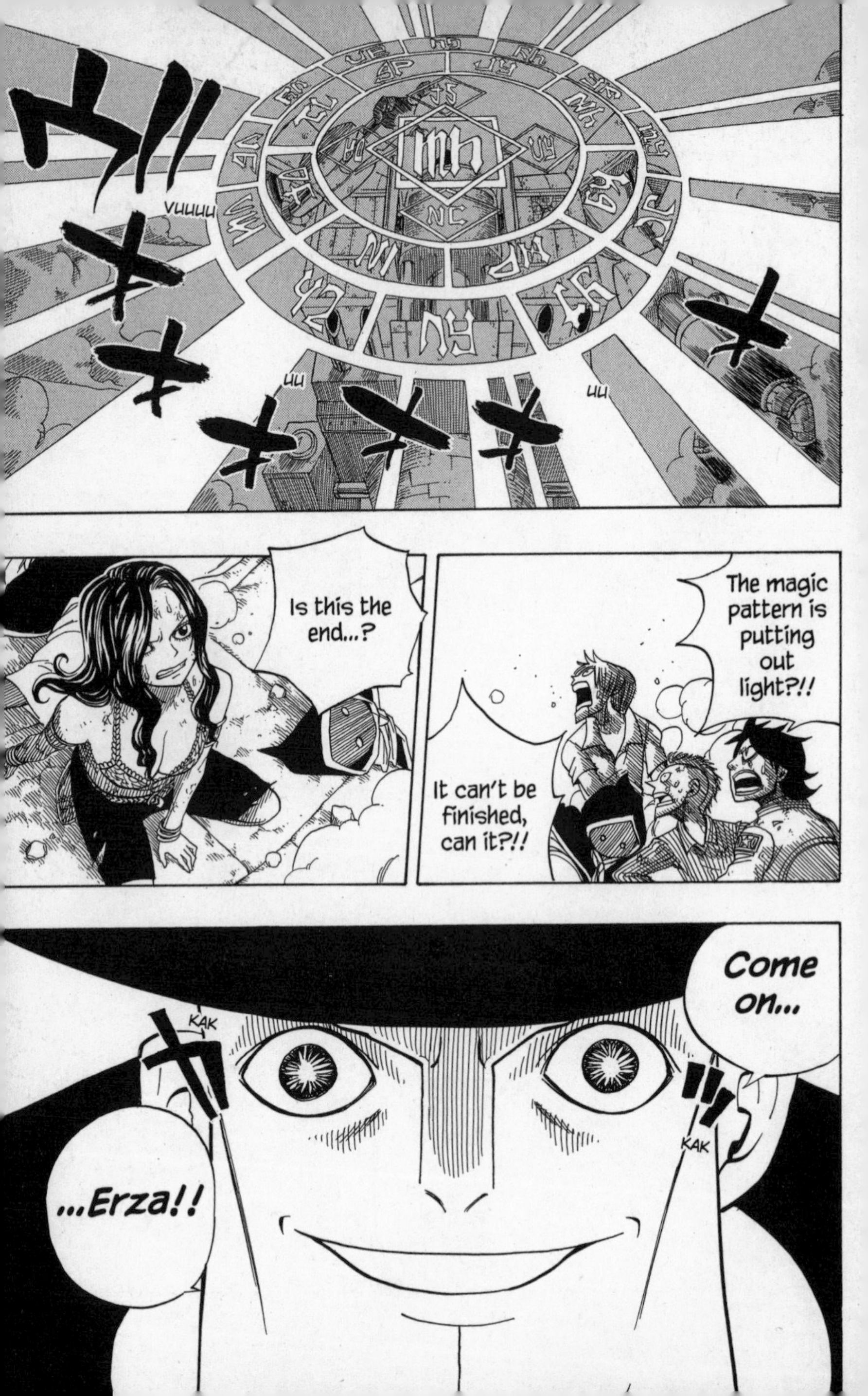
VUUUU
UU
UU
The magic pattern is putting out light?!!
It can't be finished, can it?!!
Is this the end...?
Come on...
KAK
KAK
...Erza!!

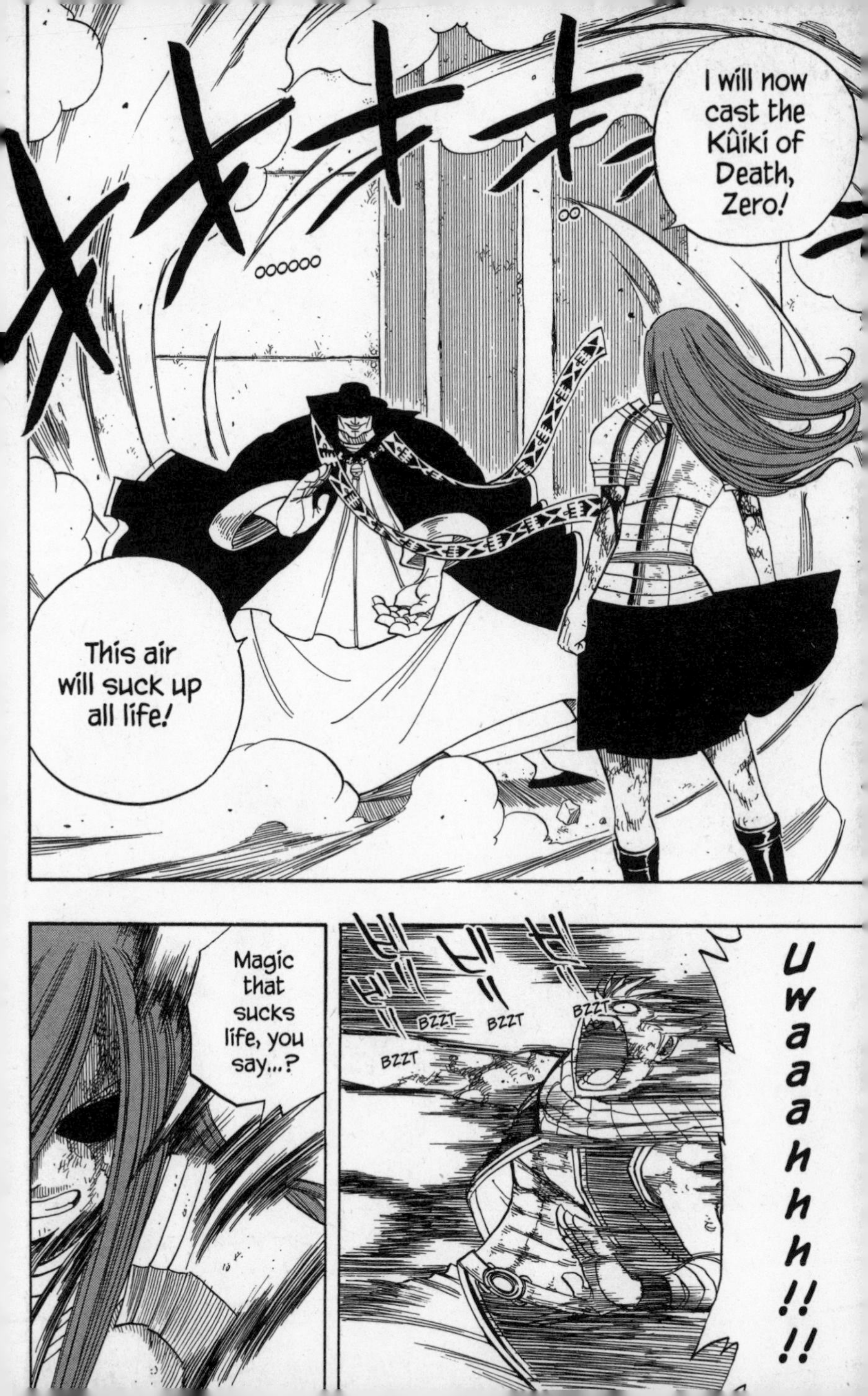
I will now cast the Kûiki of Death, Zero!
oooooo
This air will suck up all life!
Uwaaaahhhh!!!!
BZZT
BZZT
BZZT
BZZT
Magic that sucks life, you say...?

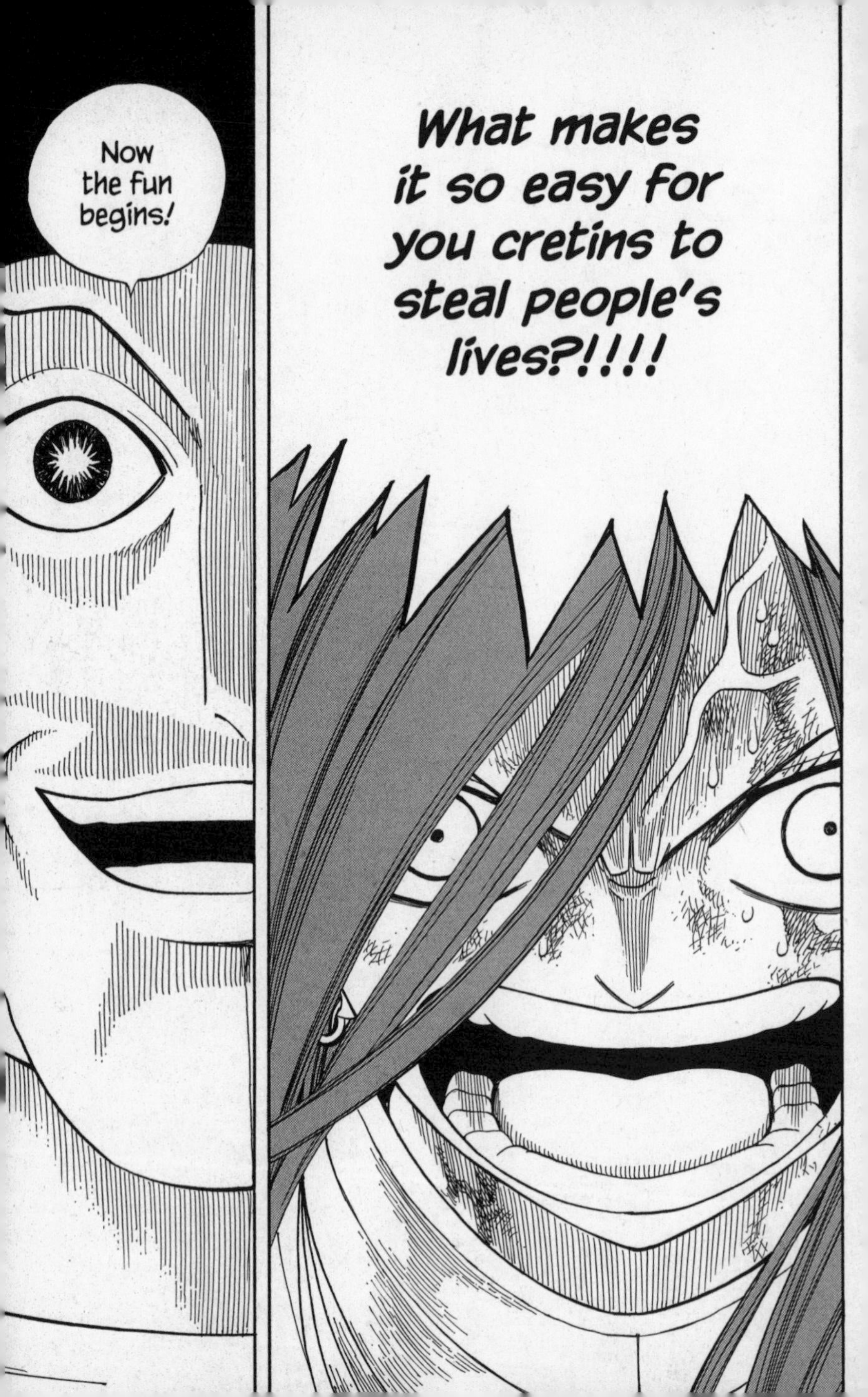
What makes it so easy for you cretins to steal people's lives?!!!!
Now the fun begins!

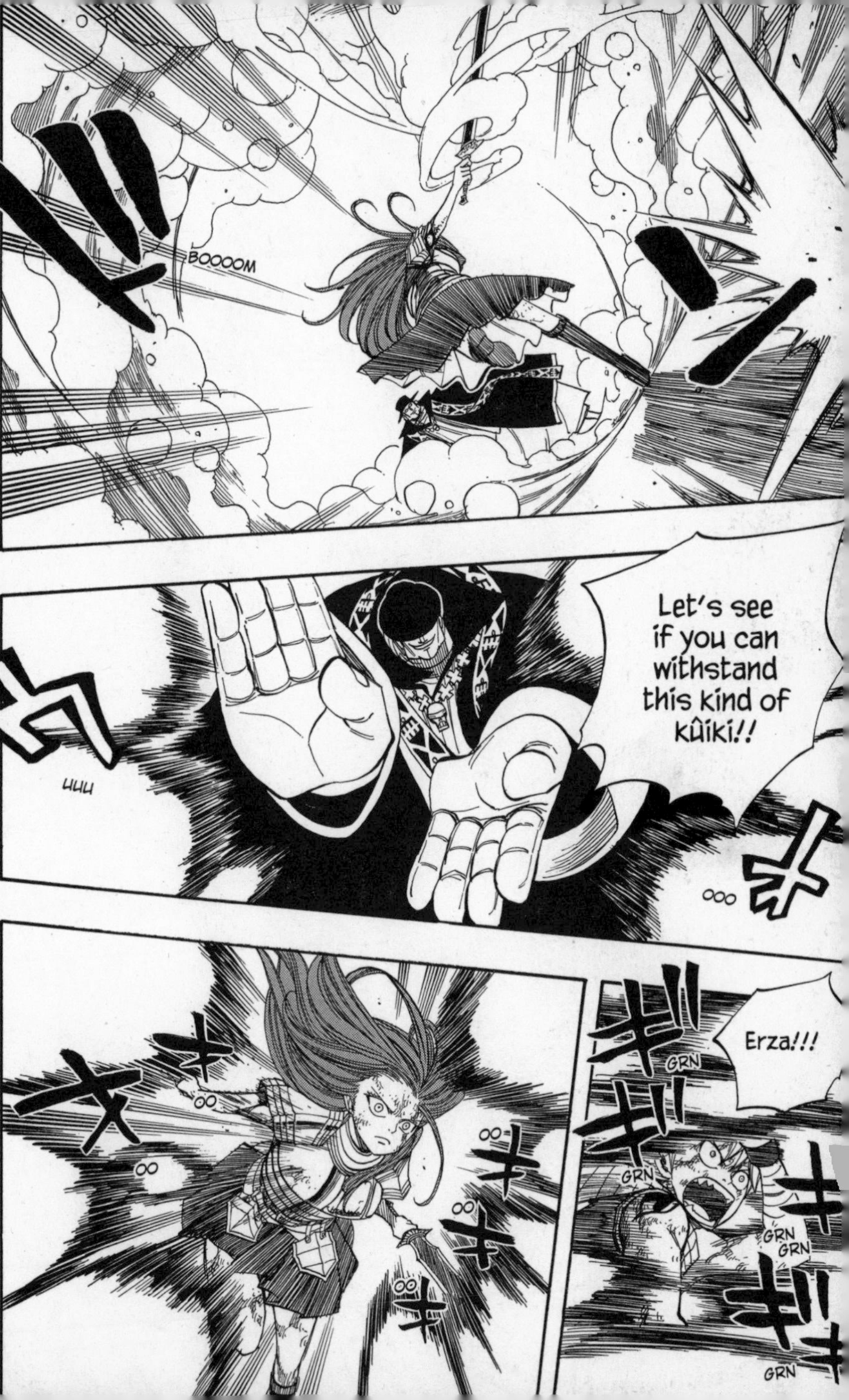
BOOOOM
Let's see if you can withstand this kind of kûiki!!
UUU
OOO
Erza!!!
GRN
GRN
GRN
GRN
GRN

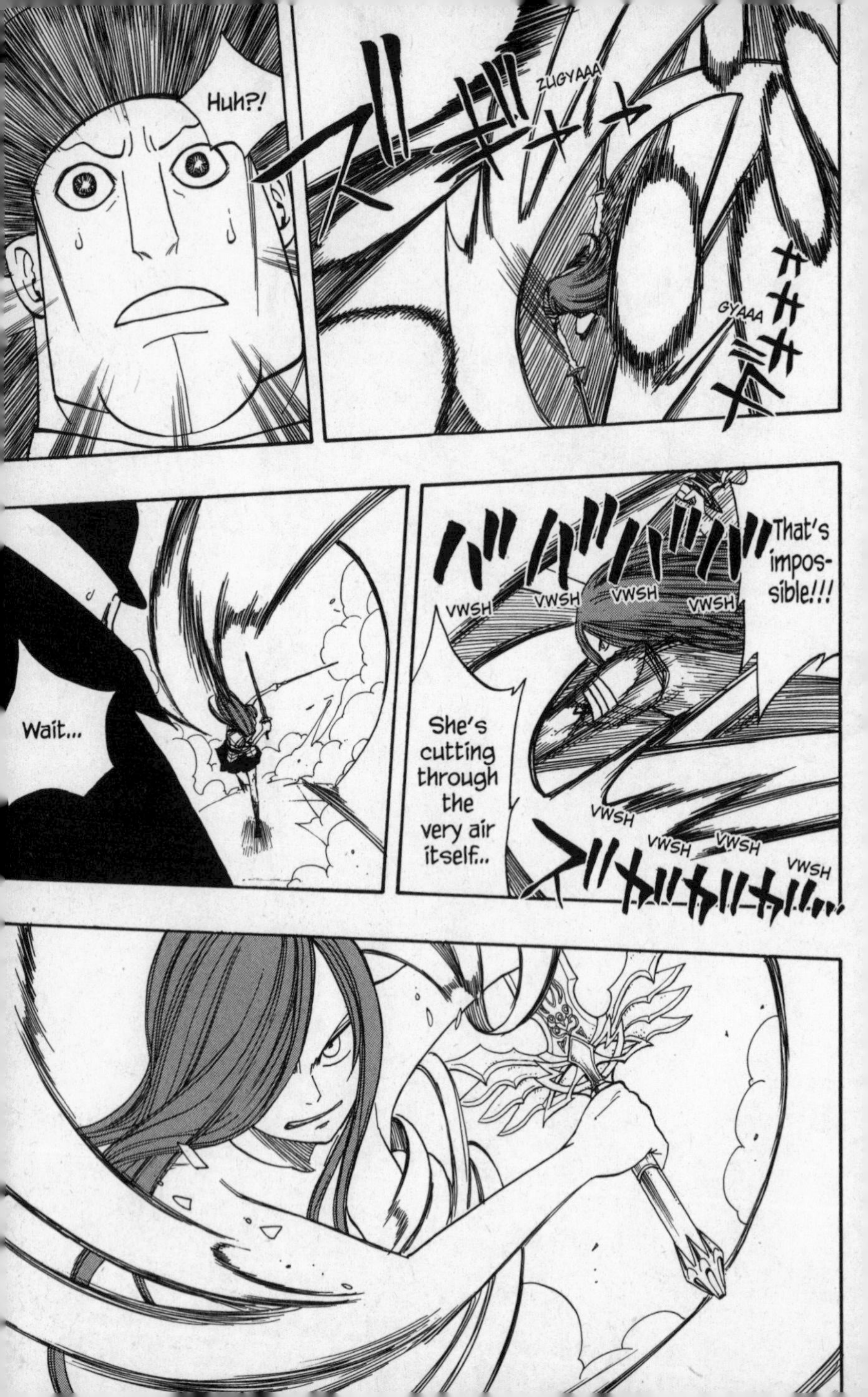
ZUGYAAA
GYAAA
Huh?!
That's impos-sible!!!
VWSH VWSH VWSH VWSH
She's cutting through the very air itself...
VWSH VWSH VWSH VWSH
Wait...

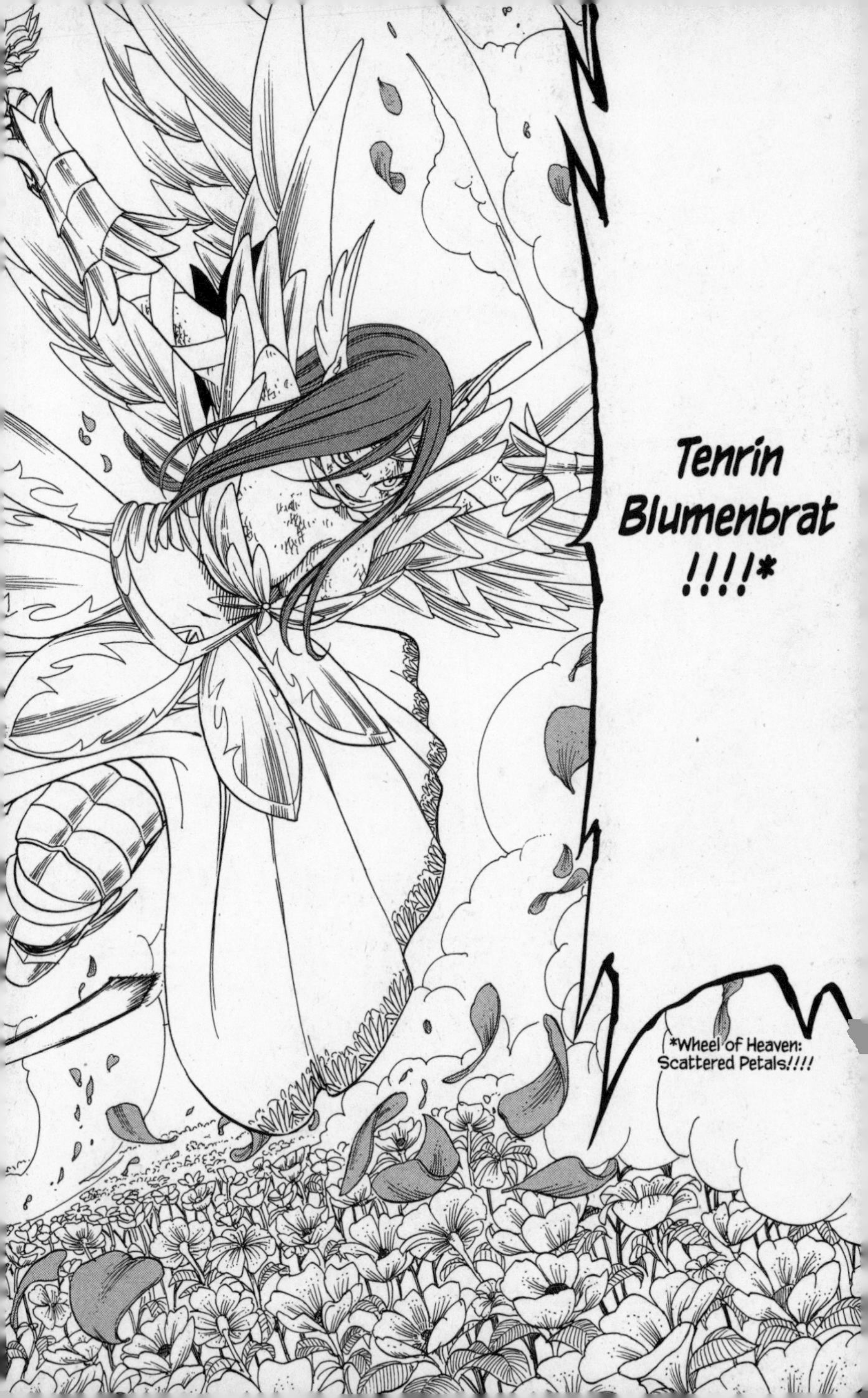
Tenrin Blumenbrat !!!!*
*Wheel of Heaven: Scattered Petals!!!!

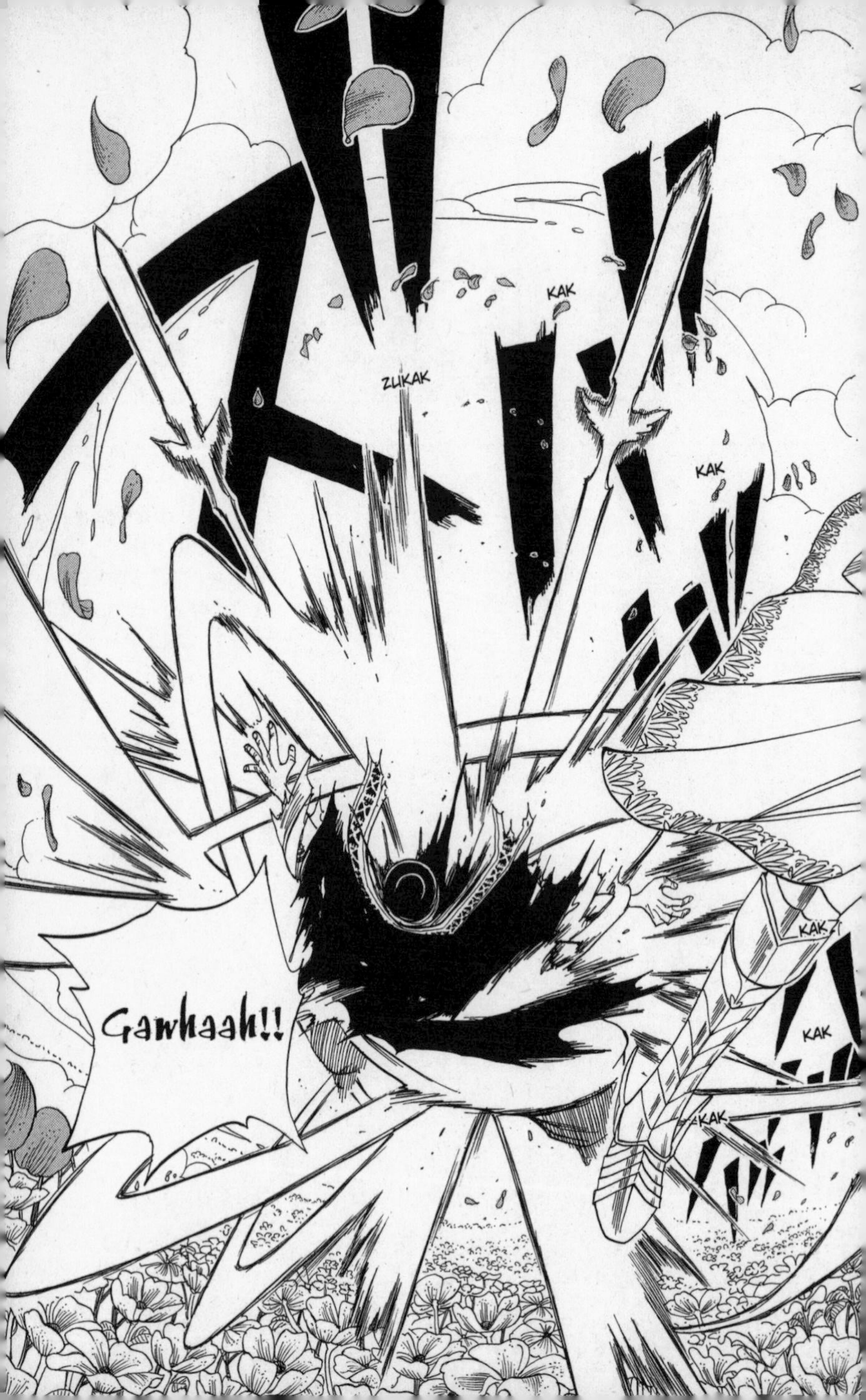
KAK
ZUKAK
KAK
KAK
KAK
KAK
Gawhaah!!

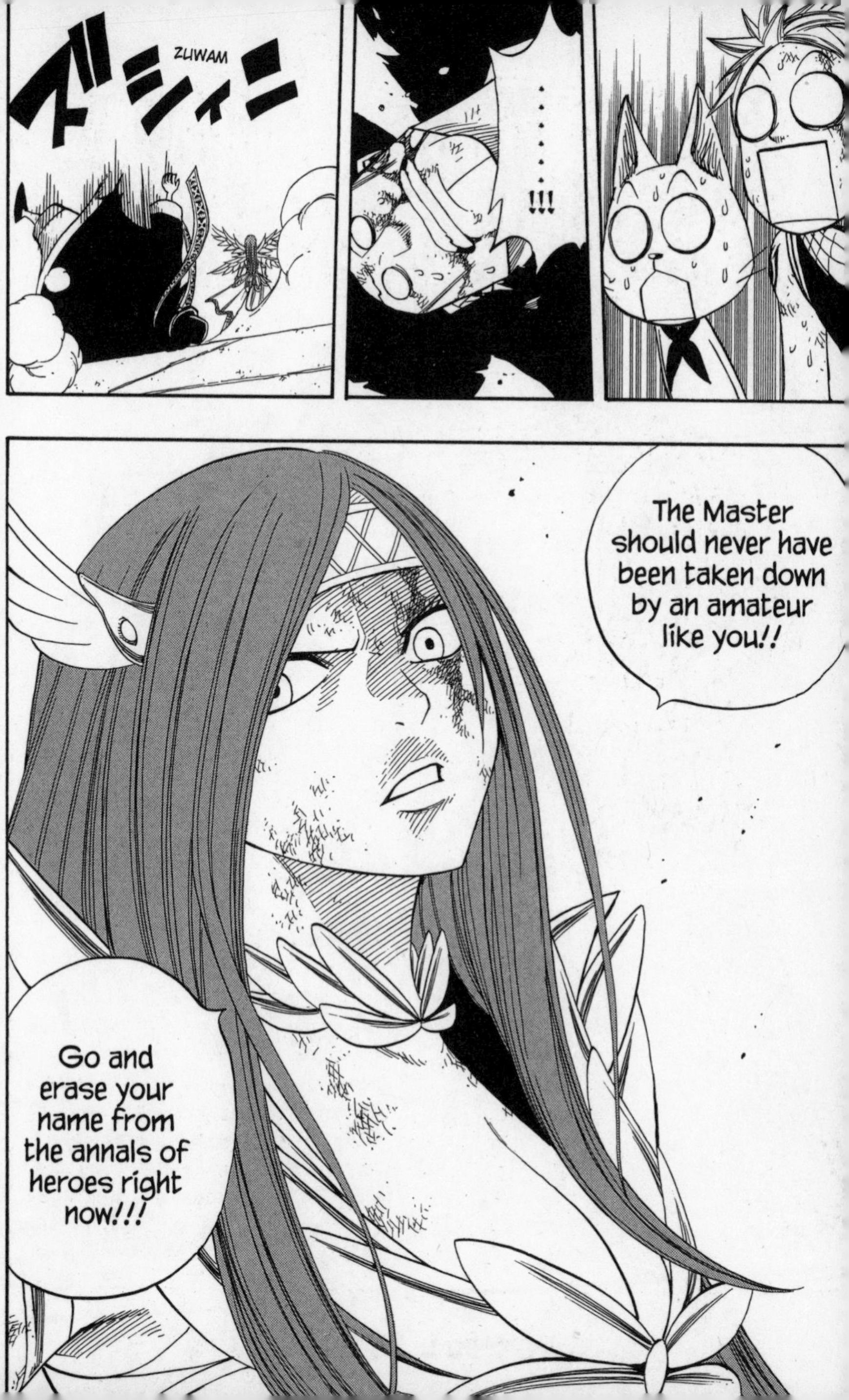
......!!!
ZUWAM
The Master should never have been taken down by an amateur like you!!
Go and erase your name from the annals of heroes right now!!!

FAIRY TAIL

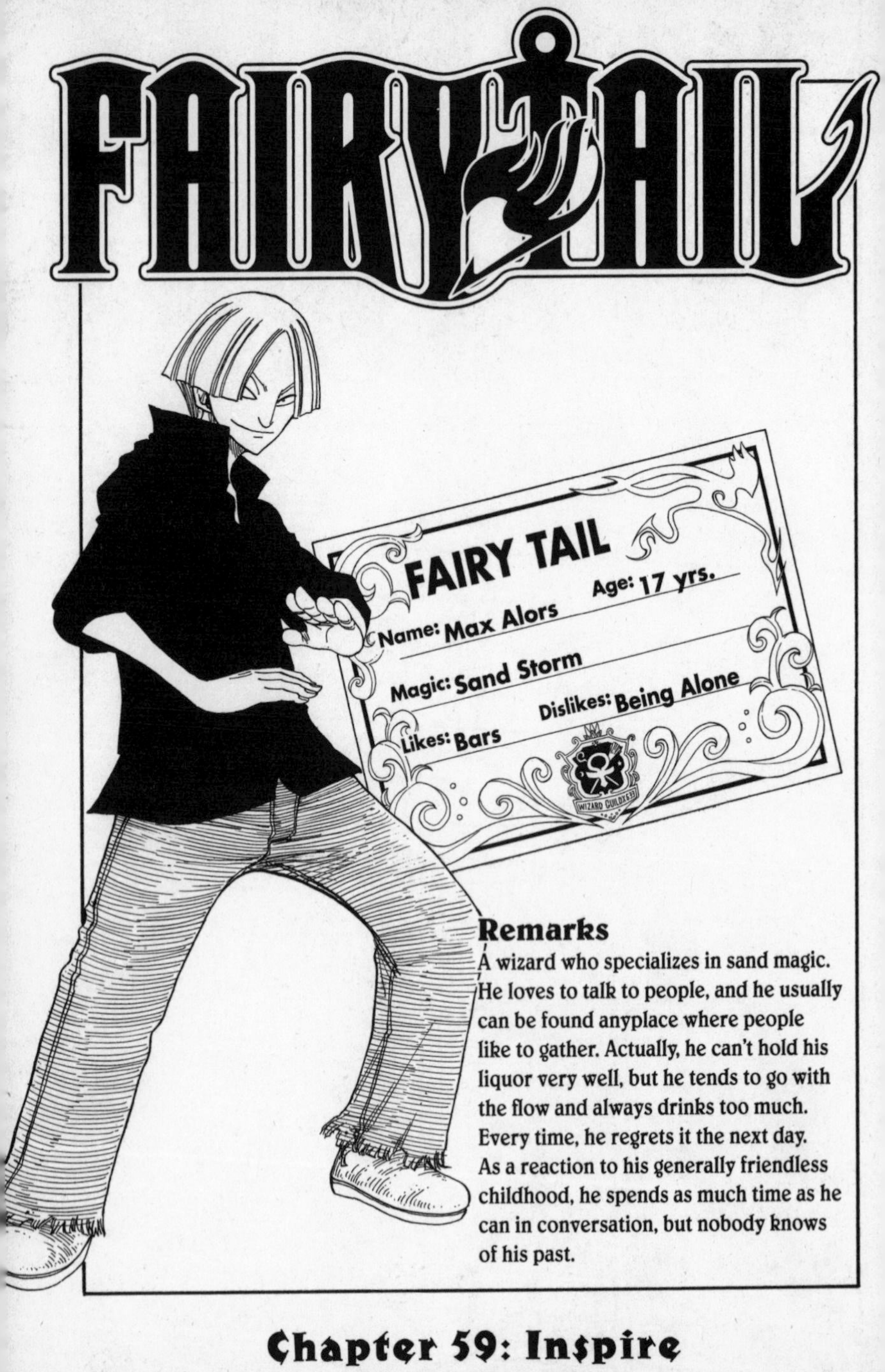

FAIRY TAIL
Name: Max Alors
Age: 17 yrs.
Magic: Sand Storm
Likes: Bars
Dislikes: Being Alone
WIZARD GUILD X633

Remarks

A wizard who specializes in sand magic. He loves to talk to people, and he usually can be found anyplace where people like to gather. Actually, he can't hold his liquor very well, but he tends to go with the flow and always drinks too much. Every time, he regrets it the next day. As a reaction to his generally friendless childhood, he spends as much time as he can in conversation, but nobody knows of his past.

Chapter 59: Inspire

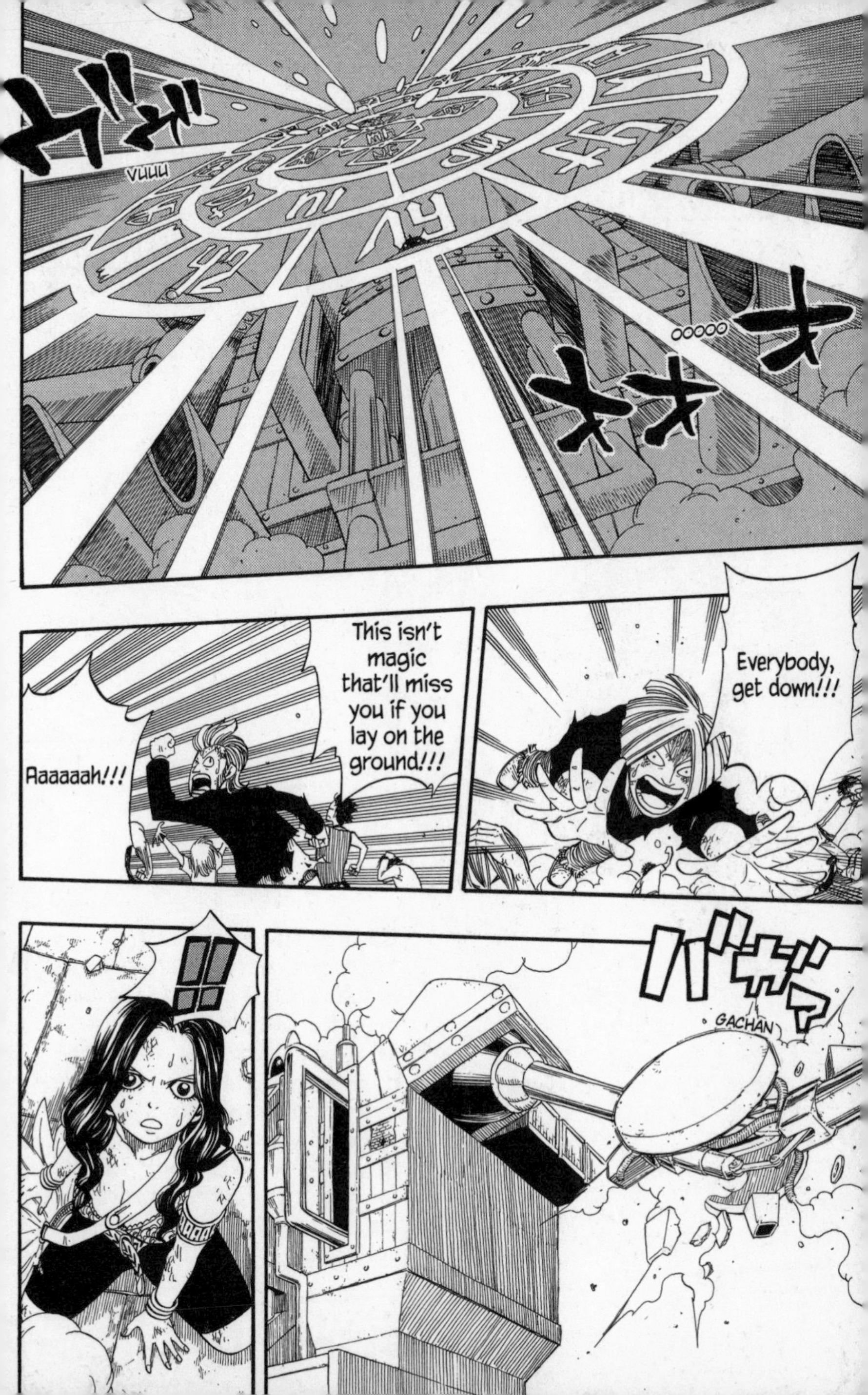
VUUU
Everybody, get down!!!
This isn't magic that'll miss you if you lay on the ground!!!
Aaaaaah!!!
GACHAN

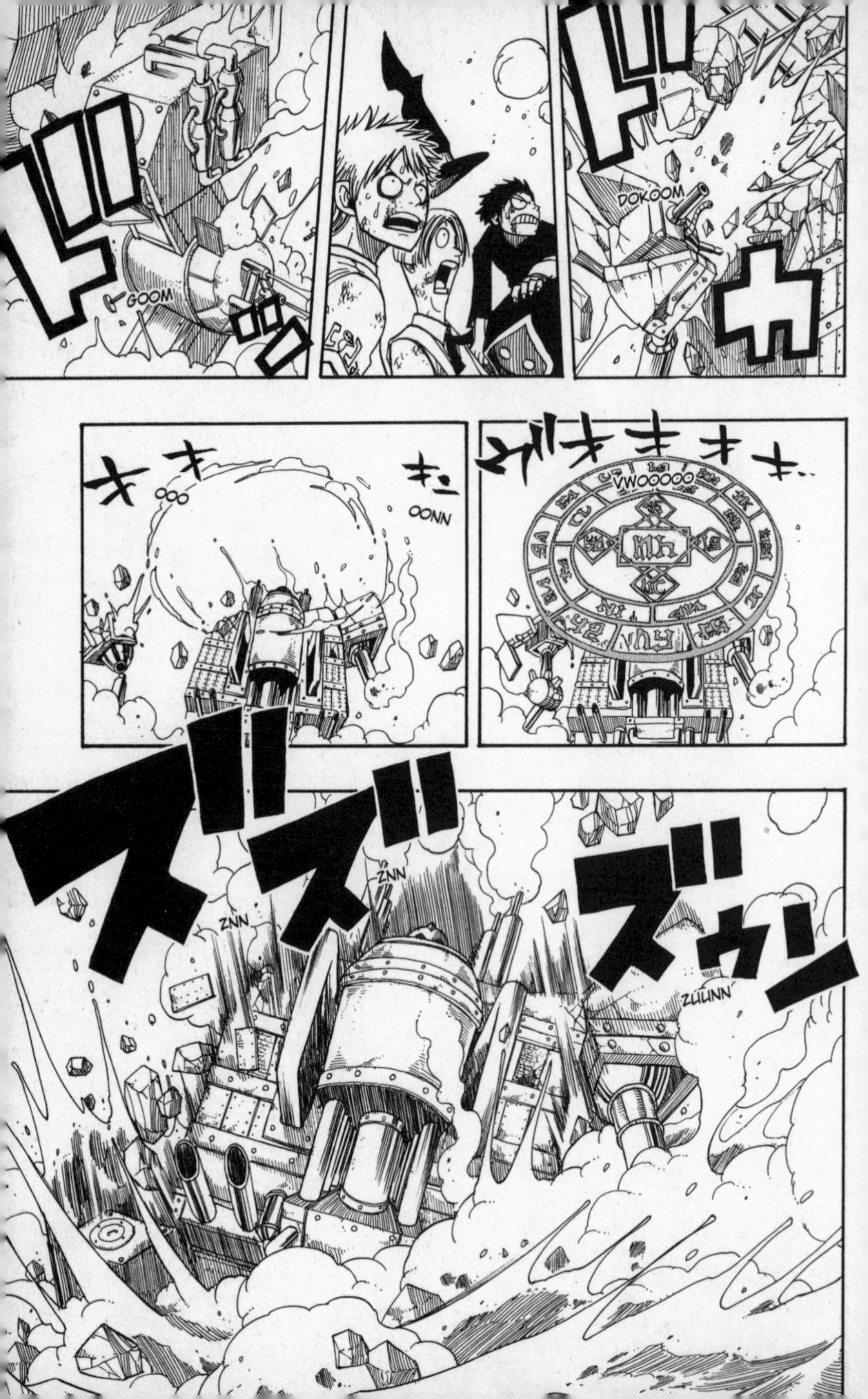
DOKOOM
GOOM
VWOOOOO
OONN
ZNN
ZNN
ZUUNN

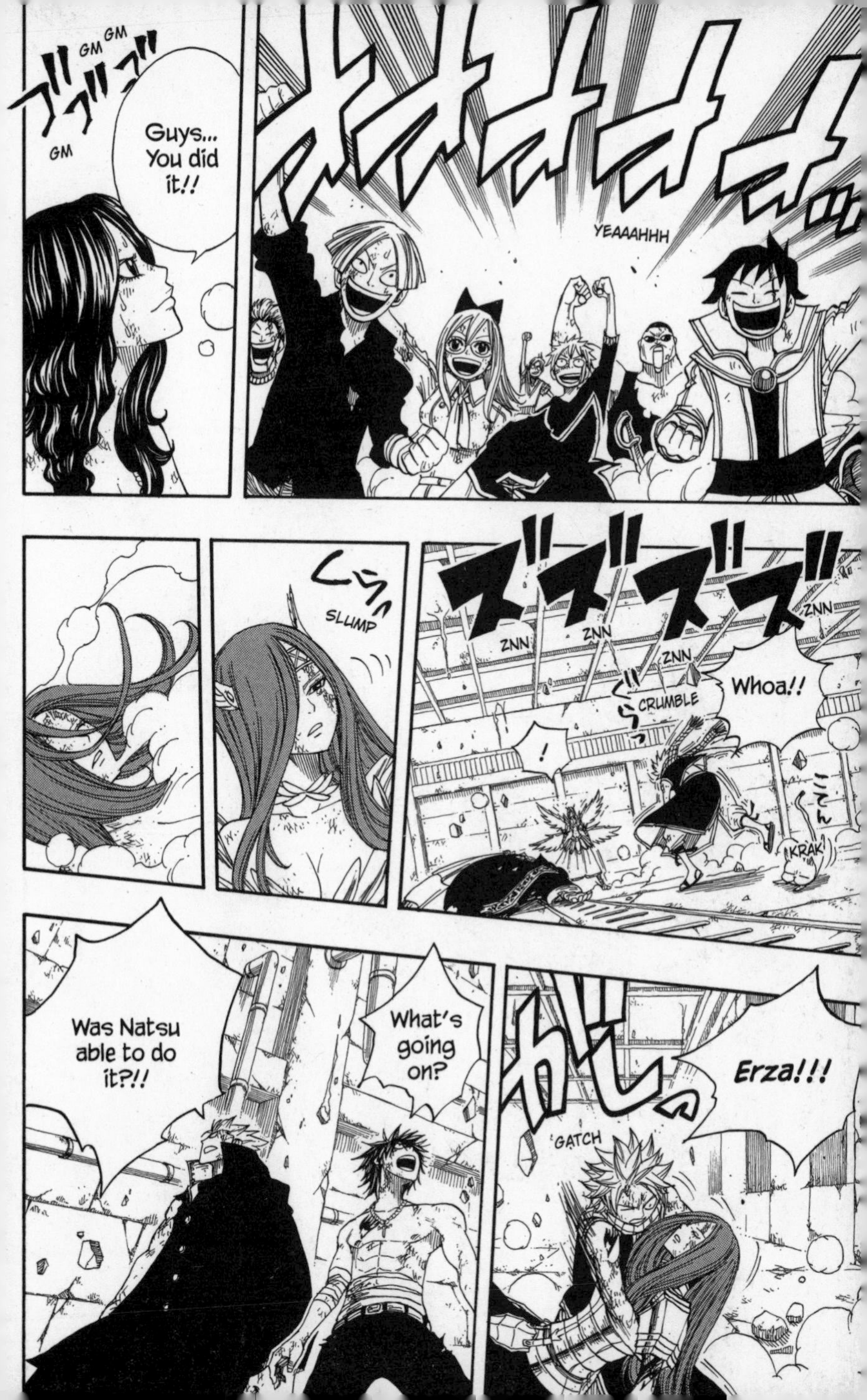
YEAAAHHH
GM GM GM
GM
Guys... You did it!!
ズズズズ
ZNN
ZNN
ZNN
ZNN
CRUMBLE
Whoa!!
!
KRAK
SLUMP
GATCH
Erza!!!
What's going on?
Was Natsu able to do it?!!

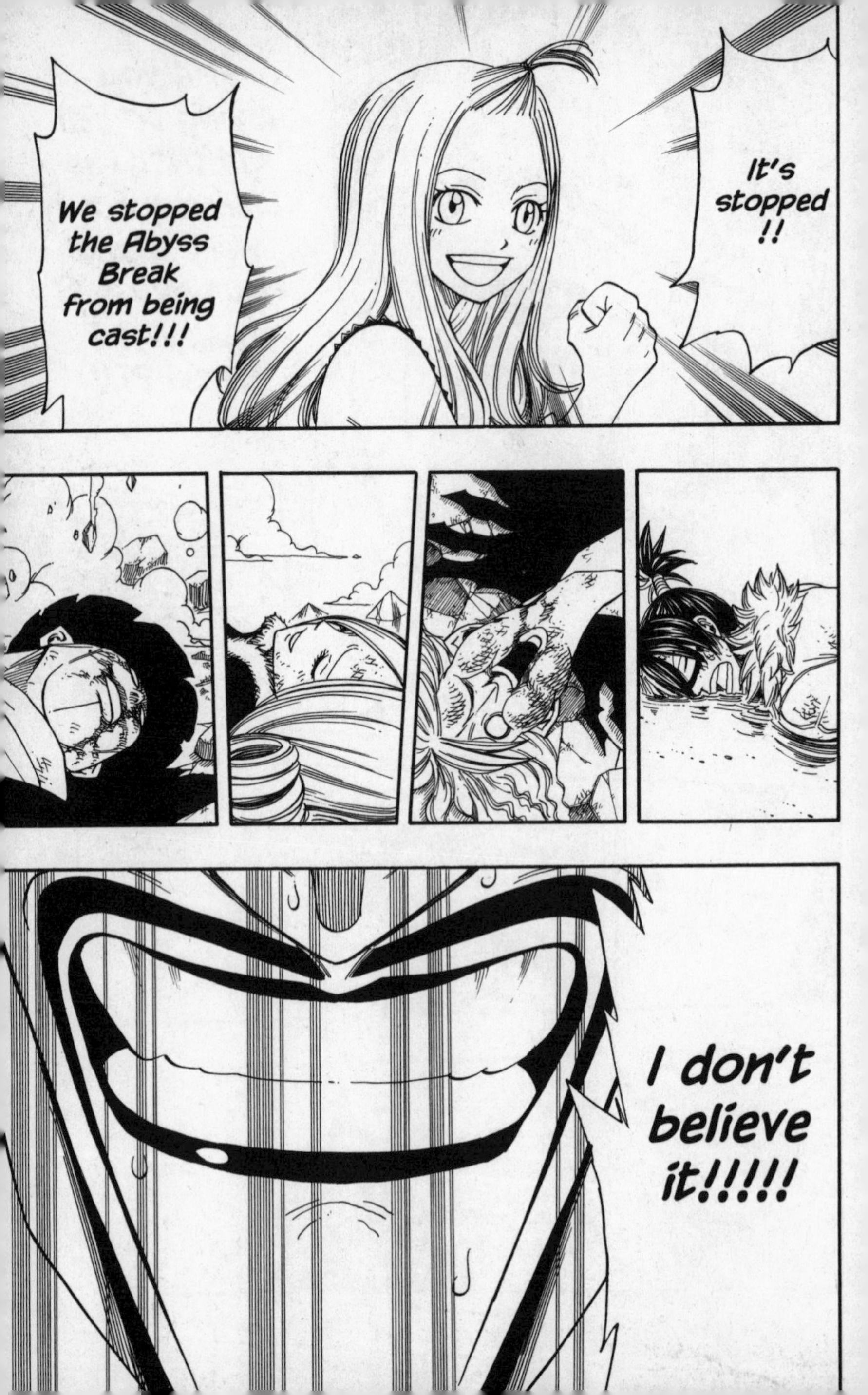
It's stopped!!
We stopped the Abyss Break from being cast!!!
I don't believe it!!!!!

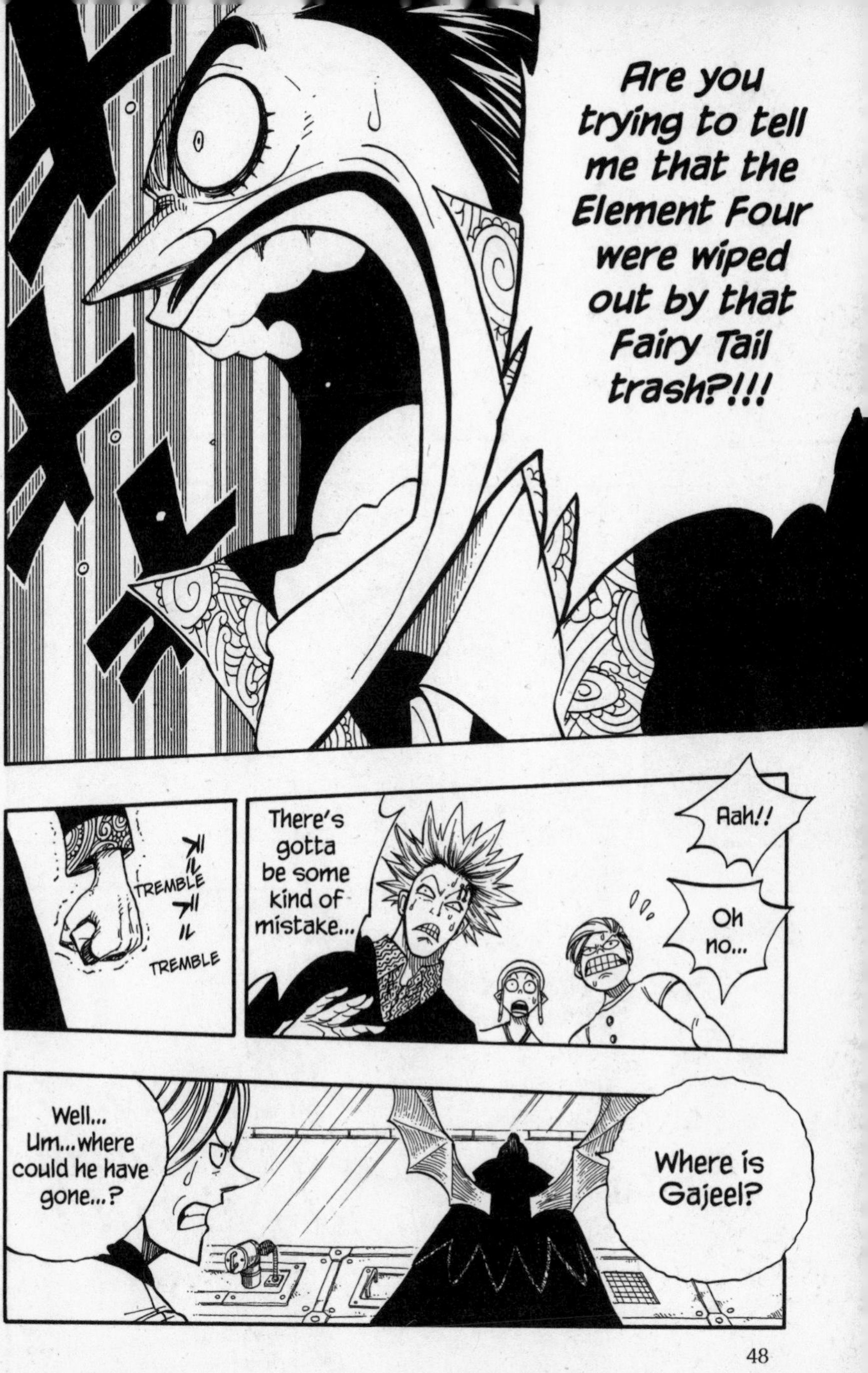
Are you trying to tell me that the Element Four were wiped out by that Fairy Tail trash?!!!
Aah!!
Oh no...
There's gotta be some kind of mistake...
TREMBLE
TREMBLE
Where is Gajeel?
Well... Um...where could he have gone...?

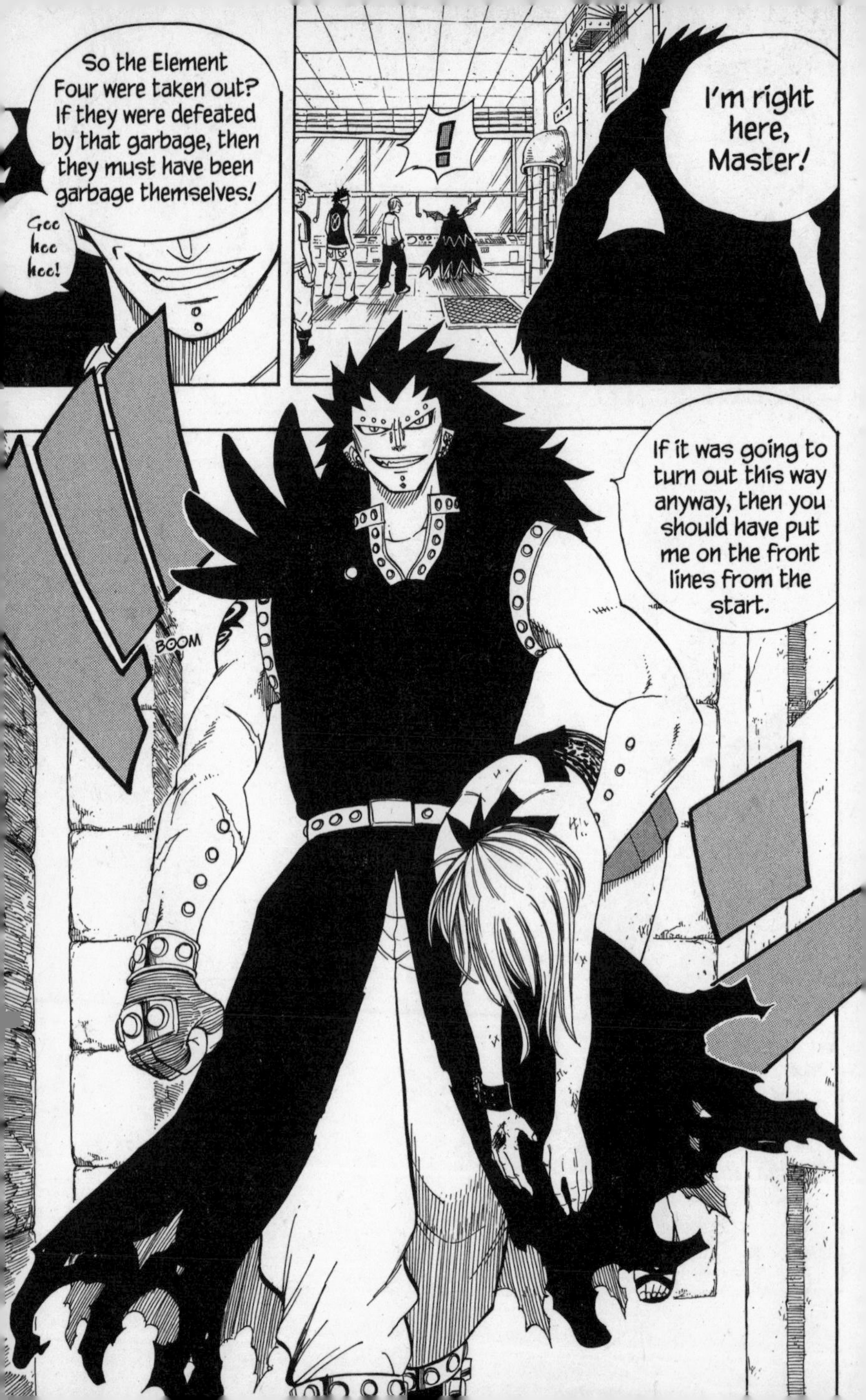
I'm right here, Master!
!
So the Element Four were taken out? If they were defeated by that garbage, then they must have been garbage themselves!
Goo hee hee!
If it was going to turn out this way anyway, then you should have put me on the front lines from the start.
BOOM

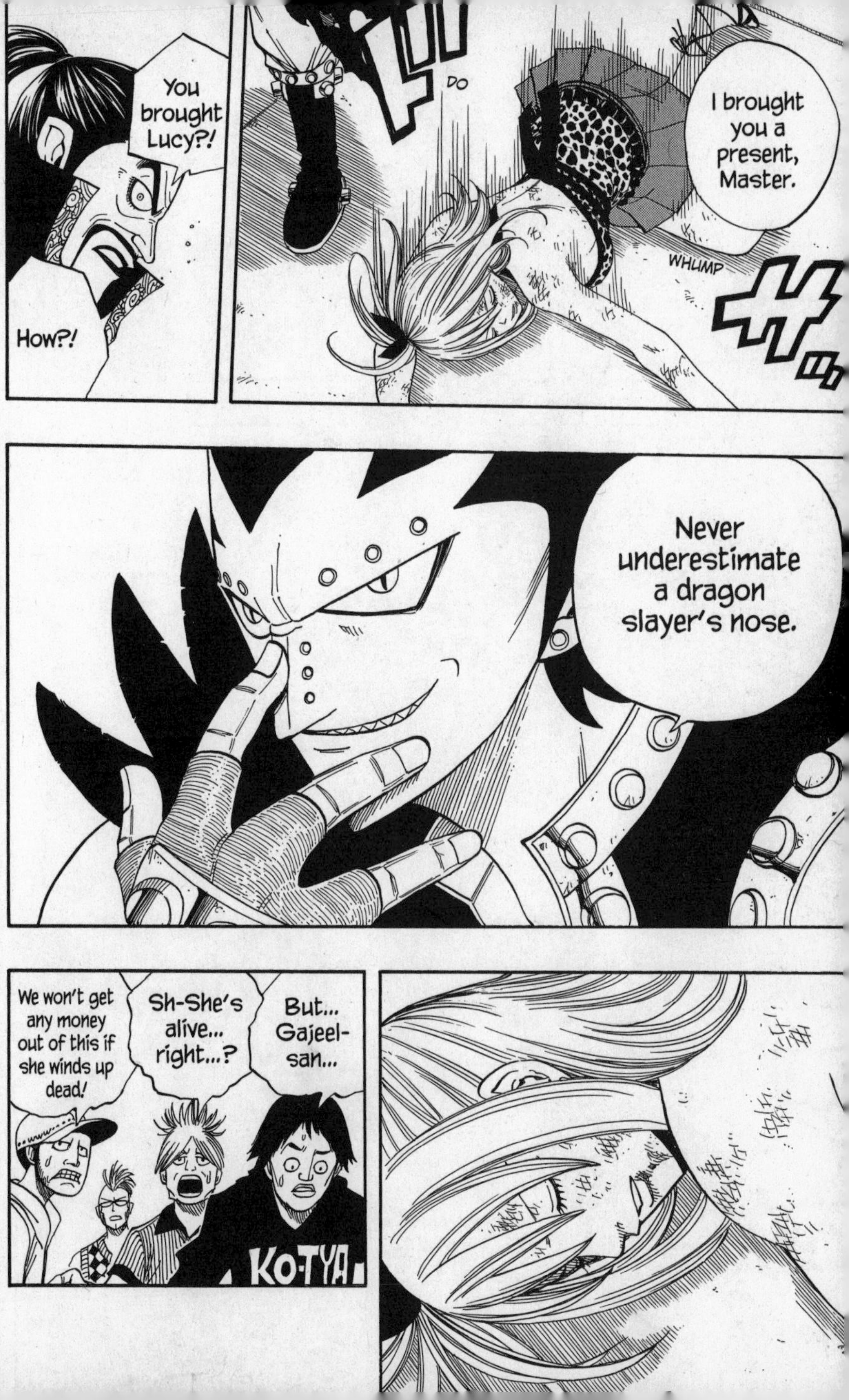
I brought you a present, Master.
DO
WHUMP
You brought Lucy?!
How?!
Never underestimate a dragon slayer's nose.
But... Gajeel-san...
Sh-She's alive... right...?
We won't get any money out of this if she winds up dead!
KO-TYA

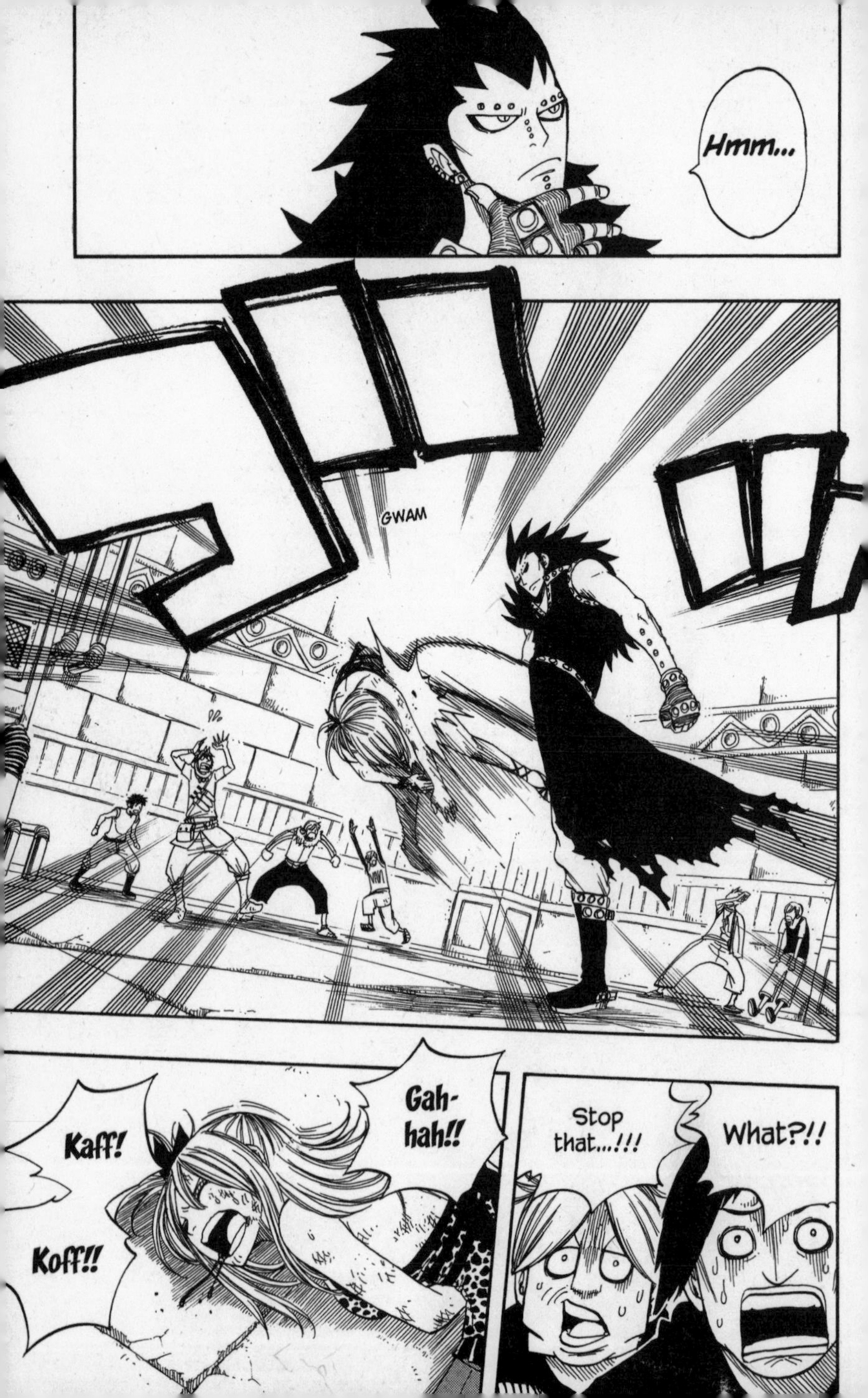
Hmm...
GWAM
What?!!
Stop that...!!!
Gah-hah!!
Kaff!
Koff!!

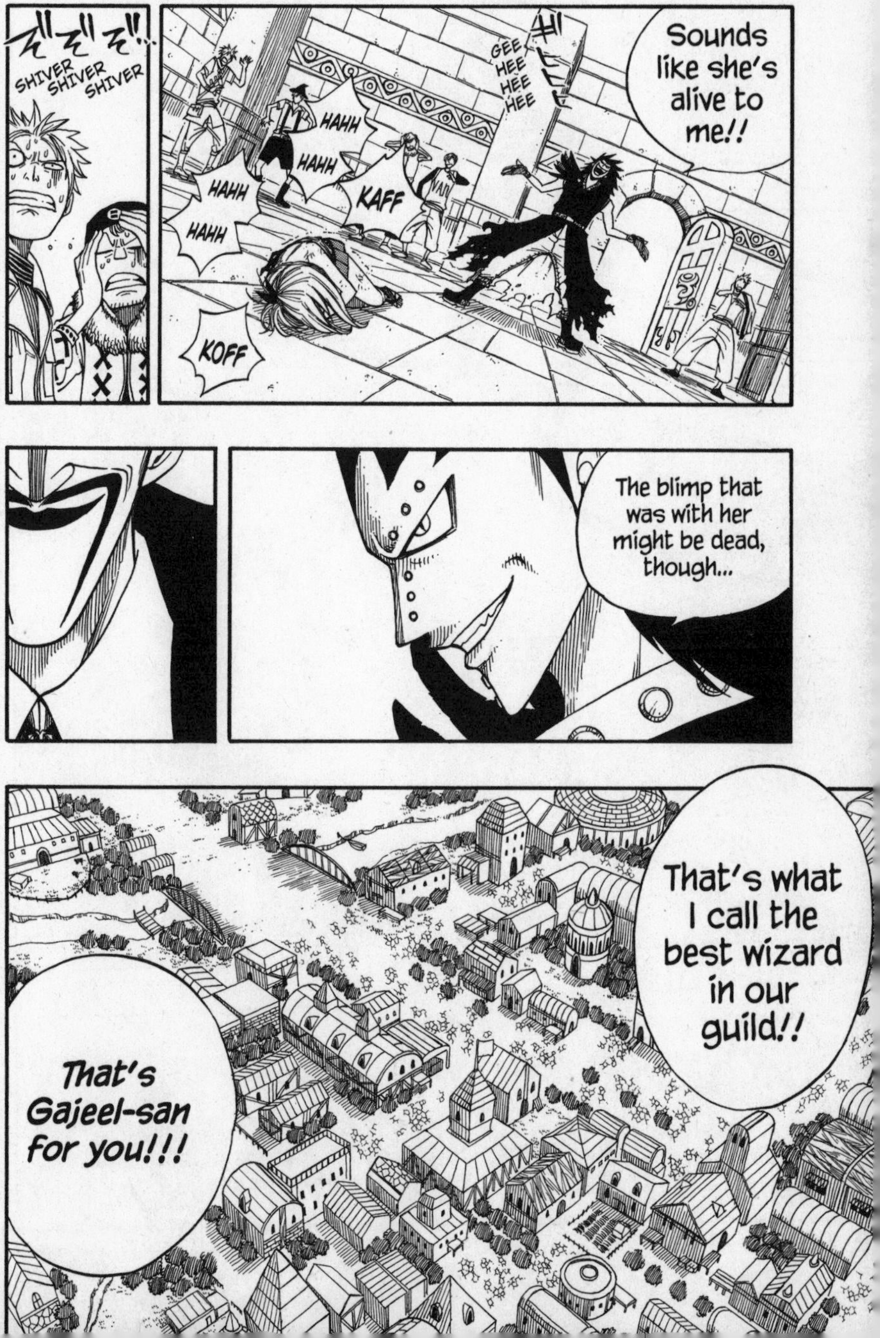
Sounds like she's alive to me!!
GEE HEE HEE HEE
HAHH
HAHH
KAFF
HAHH
HAHH
KOFF
SHIVER SHIVER SHIVER
The blimp that was with her might be dead, though...
That's what I call the best wizard in our guild!!
That's Gajeel-san for you!!!

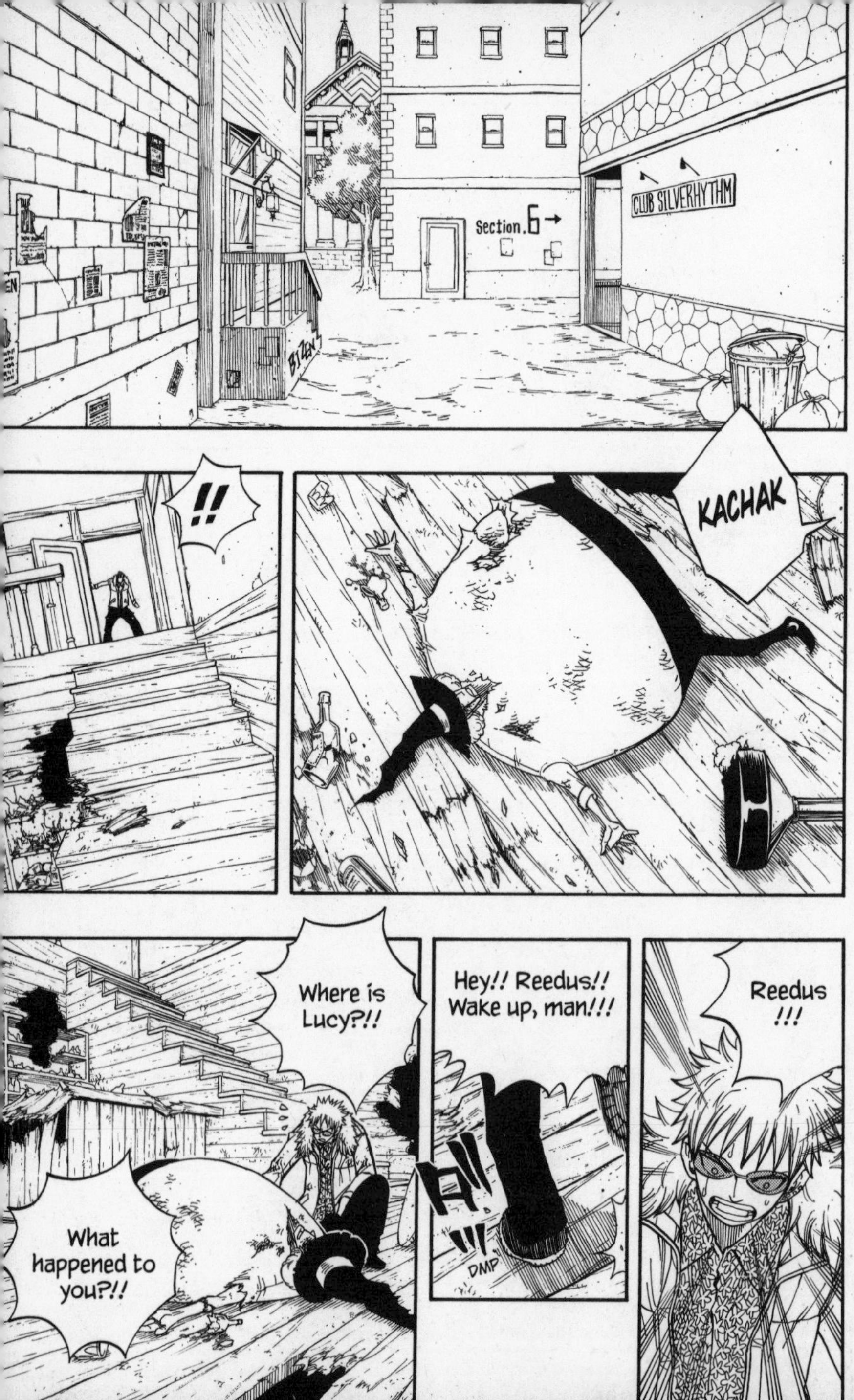
CLUB SILVERHYTHM
Section.6 →
BIZEN
KACHAK
!!
Reedus !!!
Hey!! Reedus!! Wake up, man!!!
DMP
Where is Lucy?!!
What happened to you?!!

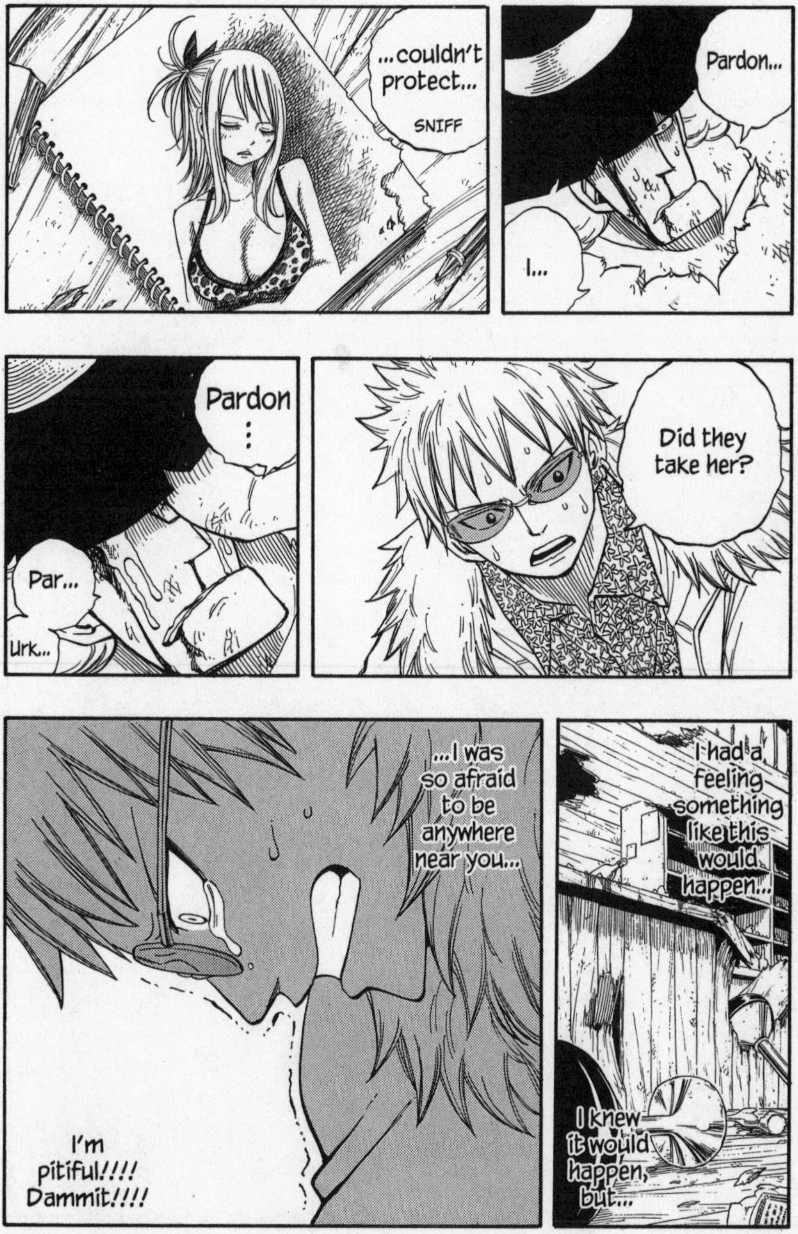
Pardon...
I...
...couldn't protect...
SNIFF
Did they take her?
Pardon
...
Par...
Urk...
I had a feeling something like this would happen...
I knew it would happen, but...
...I was so afraid to be anywhere near you...
I'm pitiful!!!! Dammit!!!!

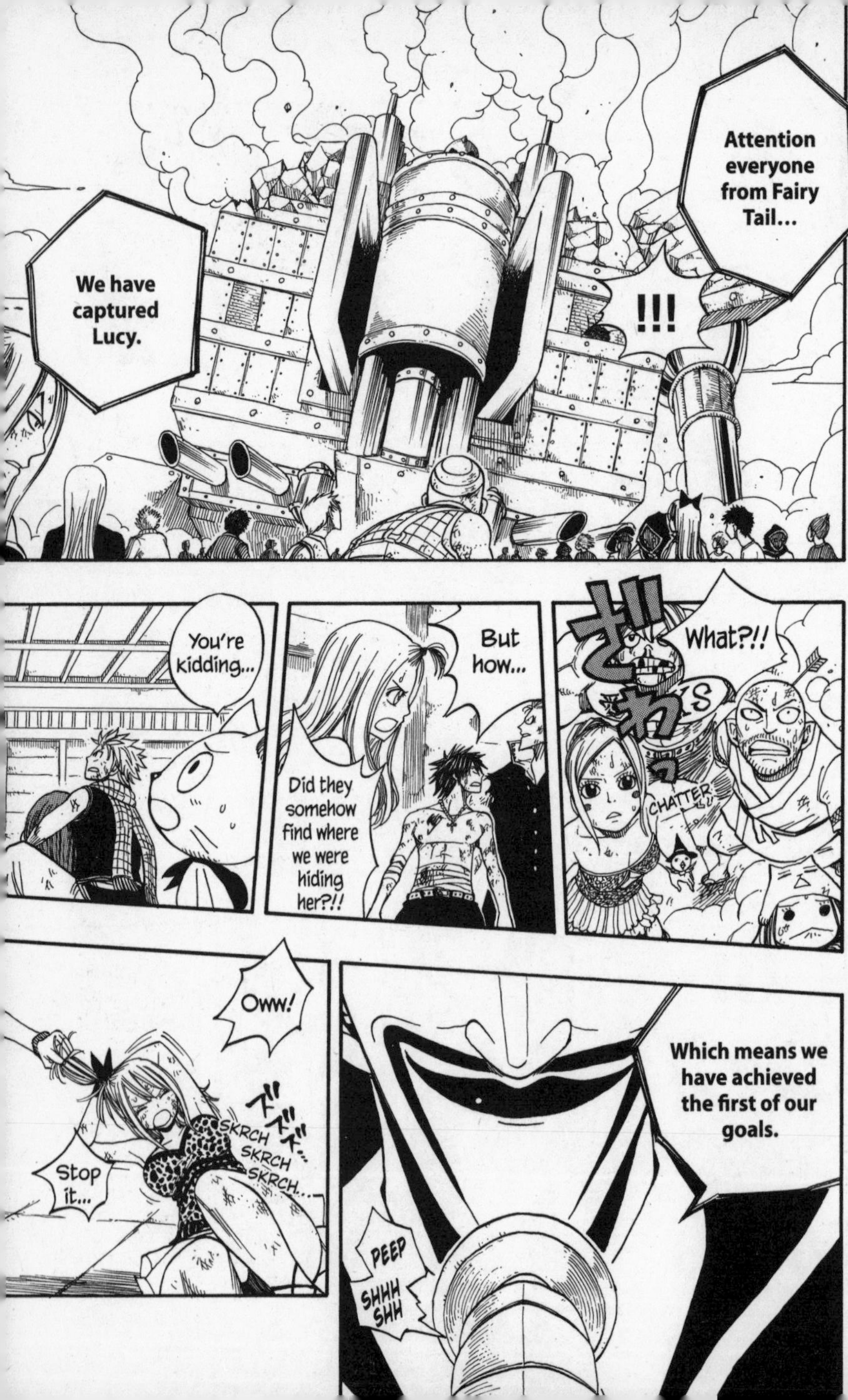
Attention everyone from Fairy Tail...
!!!
We have captured Lucy.
What?!!
ざわっ
CHATTER
But how...
Did they somehow find where we were hiding her?!!
You're kidding...
Which means we have achieved the first of our goals.
PEEP
SHHH SHH
Oww!
ズズズ...
SKRCH SKRCH SKRCH...
Stop it...

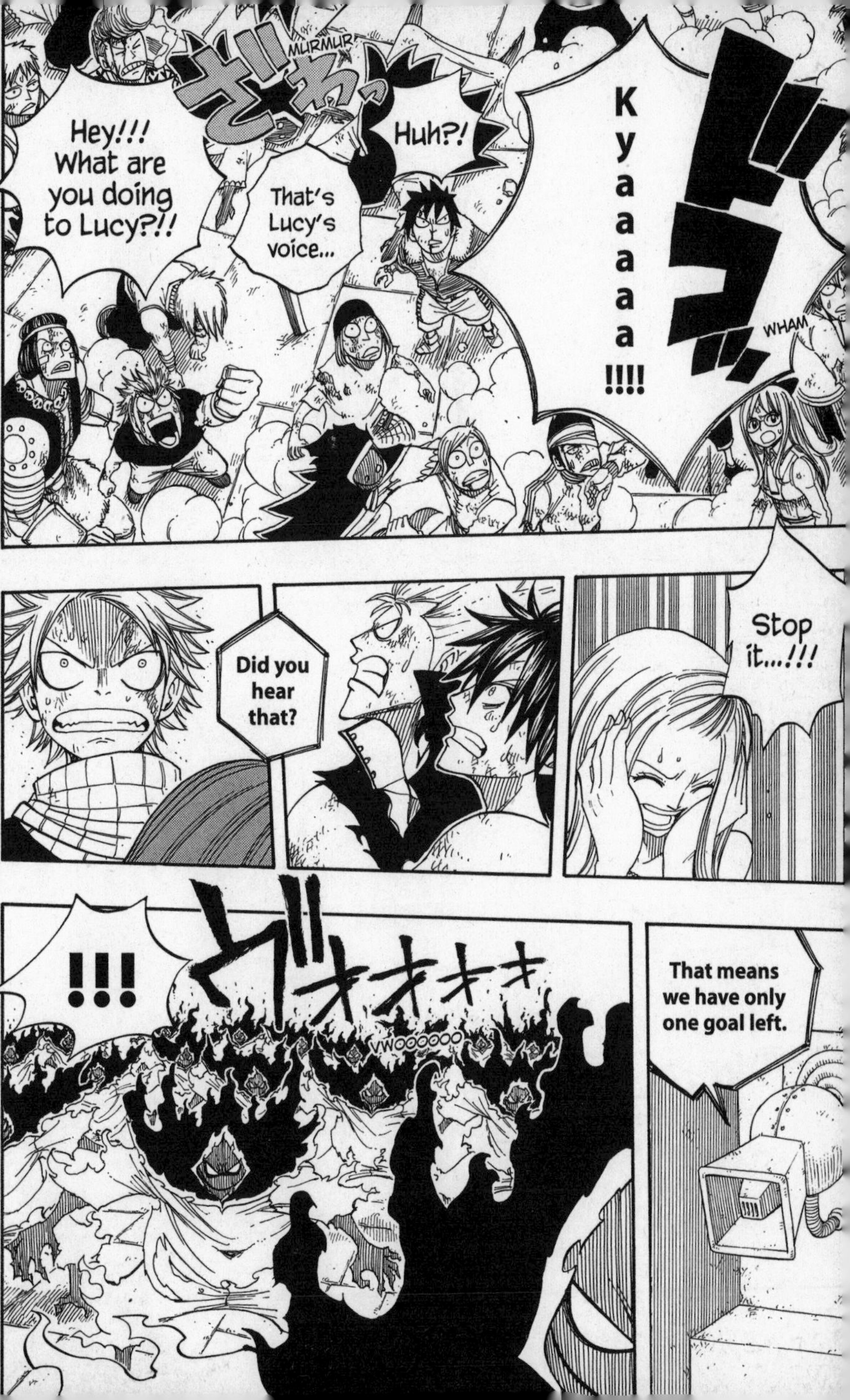
WHAM
Kyaaaaa!!!!
Huh?!
MURMUR
That's Lucy's voice...
Hey!!! What are you doing to Lucy?!!
Stop it...!!!
Did you hear that?
That means we have only one goal left.
VWOOOOOO
!!!

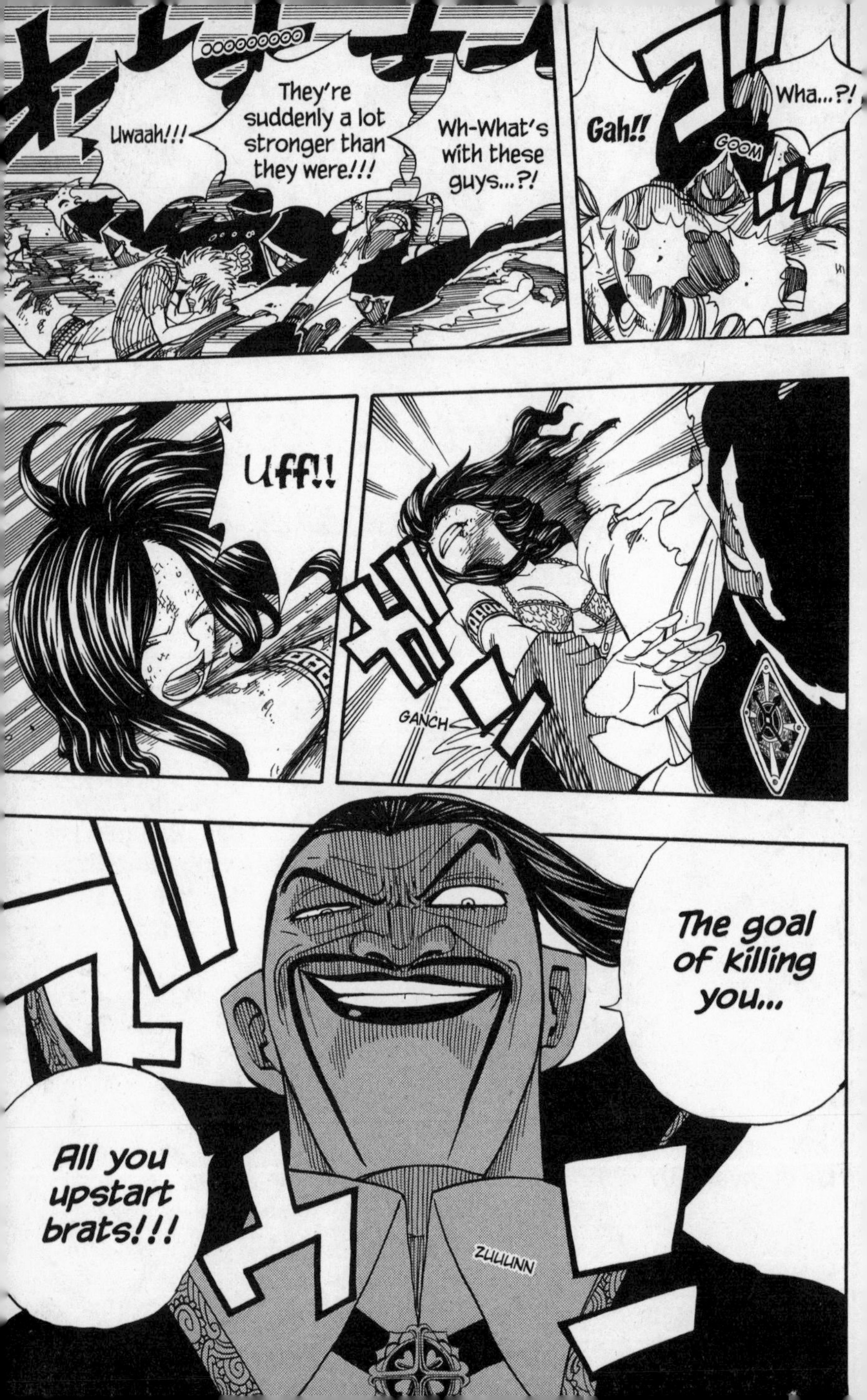

Wha...?!
Gah!!
GOOM
Wh-What's with these guys...?!
They're suddenly a lot stronger than they were!!!
Uwaah!!!
GANCH
Uff!!
The goal of killing you...
All you upstart brats!!!
ZHUUNN

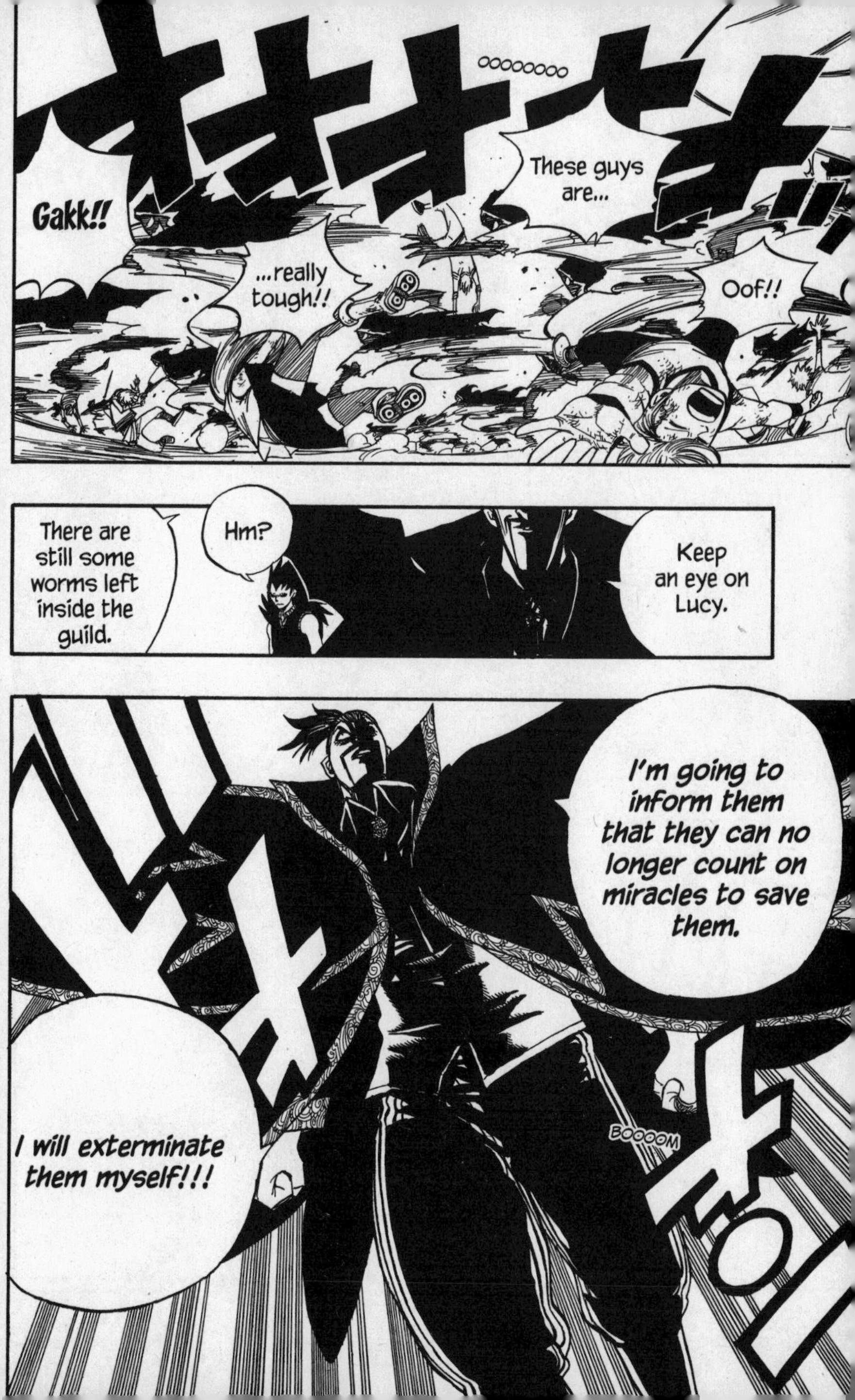
oooooooo
These guys are...
Oof!!
...really tough!!
Gakk!!
Keep an eye on Lucy.
Hm?
There are still some worms left inside the guild.
I'm going to inform them that they can no longer count on miracles to save them.
BOOOOM
I will exterminate them myself!!!

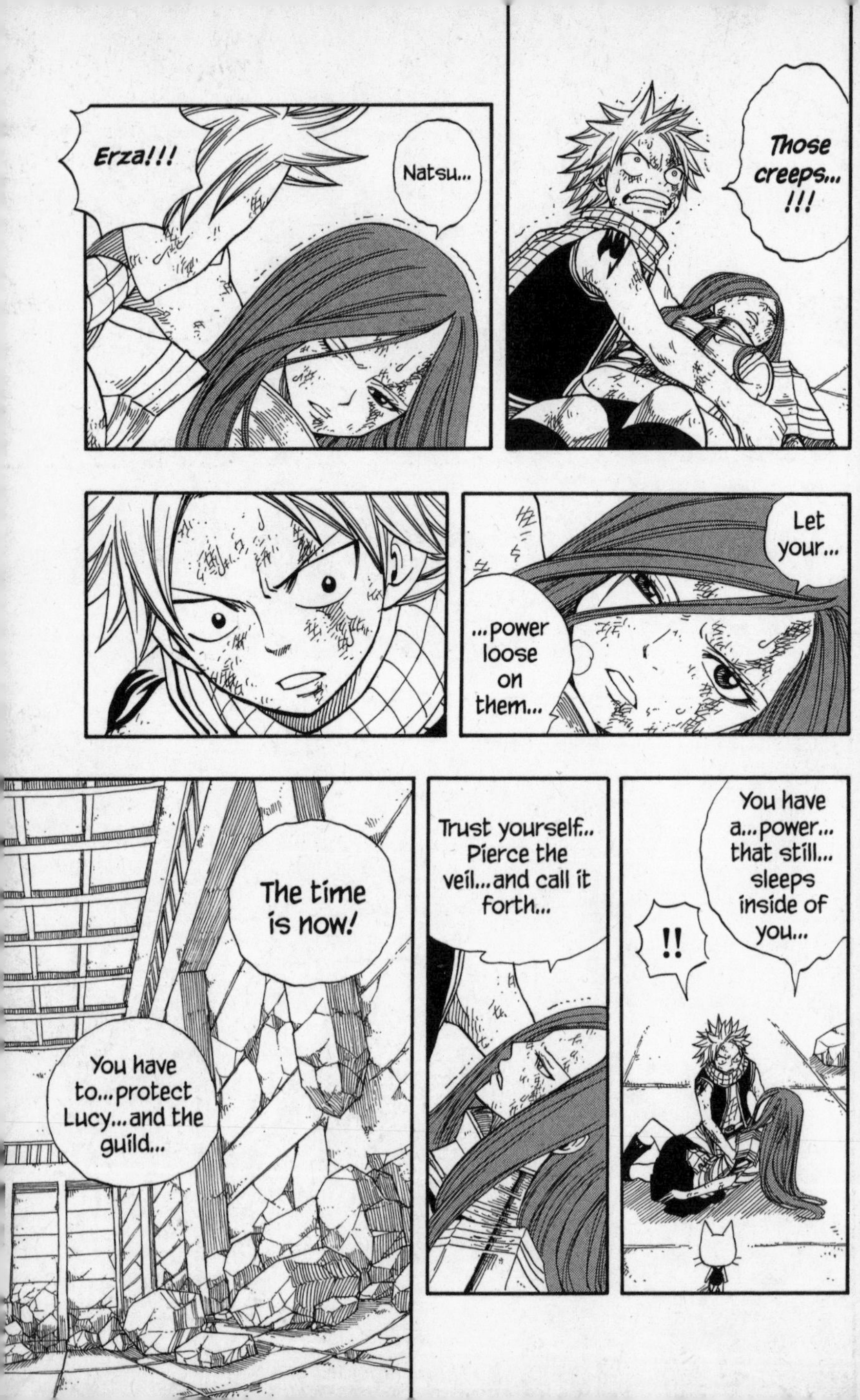
Those creeps... !!!
Natsu...
Erza!!!
Let your...
...power loose on them...
You have a...power... that still... sleeps inside of you...
!!
Trust yourself... Pierce the veil...and call it forth...
The time is now!
You have to...protect Lucy...and the guild...

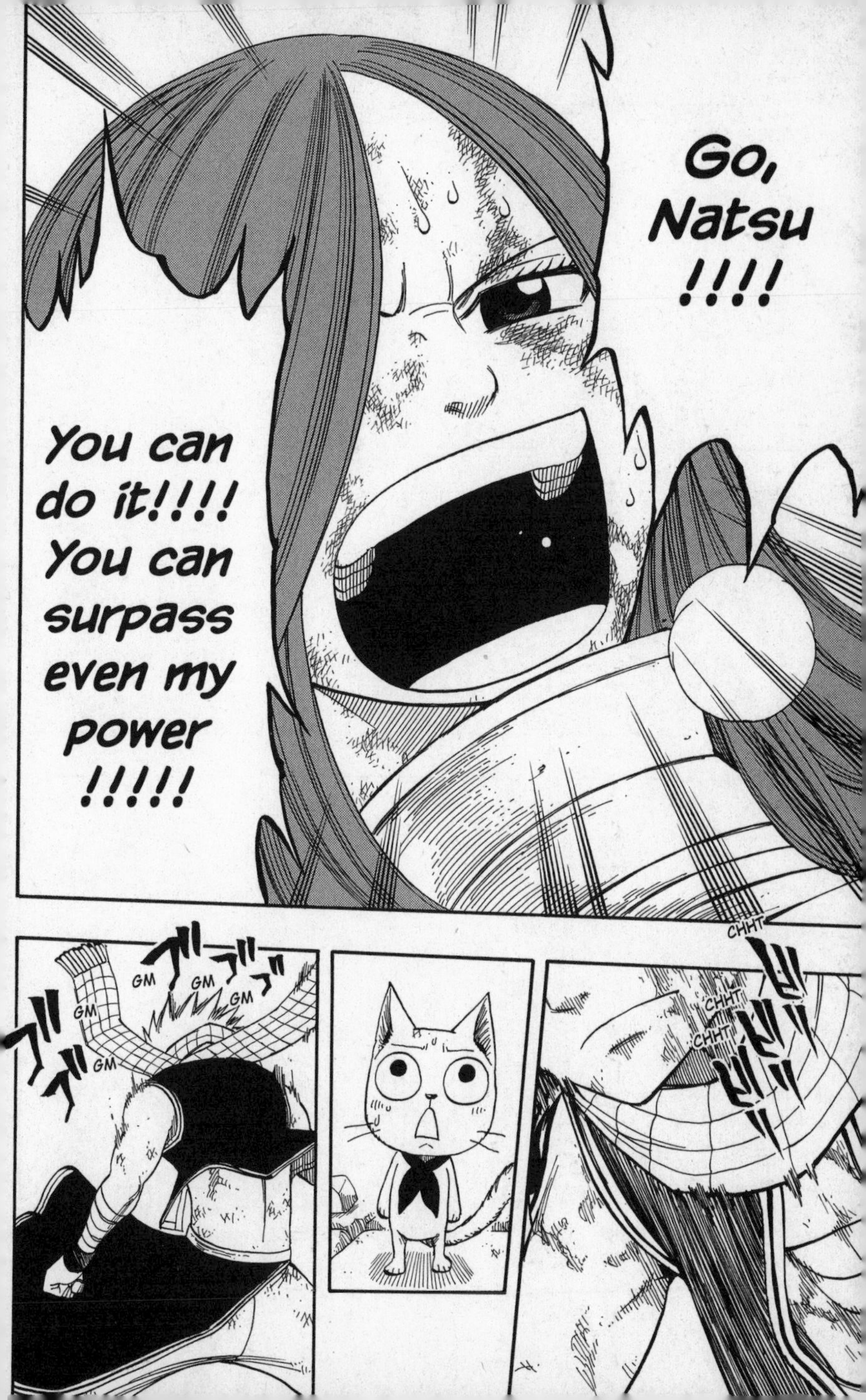
Go, Natsu !!!!
You can do it!!!! You can surpass even my power !!!!!
CHHT
CHHT
CHHT
GM
GM
GM
GM
GM

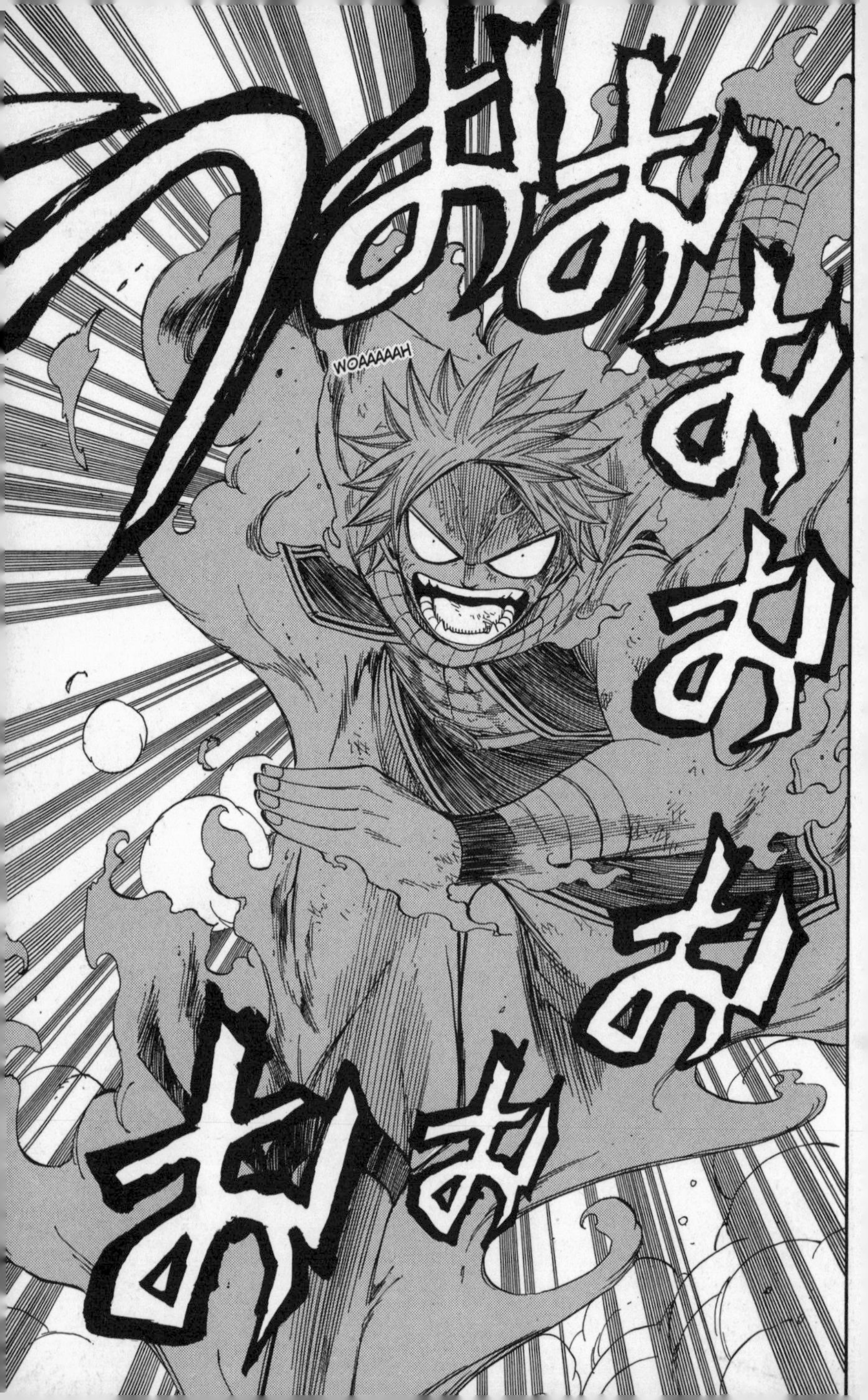
WOAAAAAH

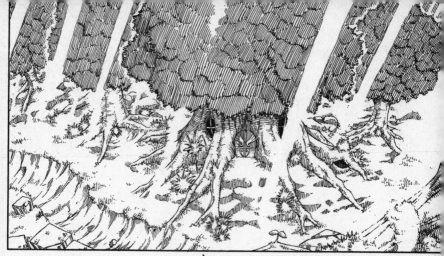

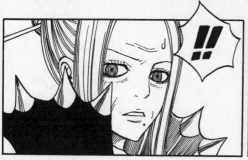

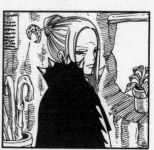

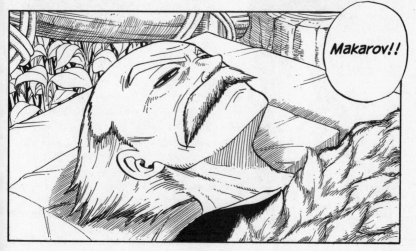

Makarov!!

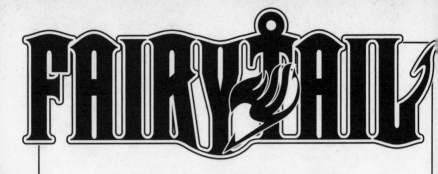

FAIRY TAIL

Chapter 60:
Wings of Fire

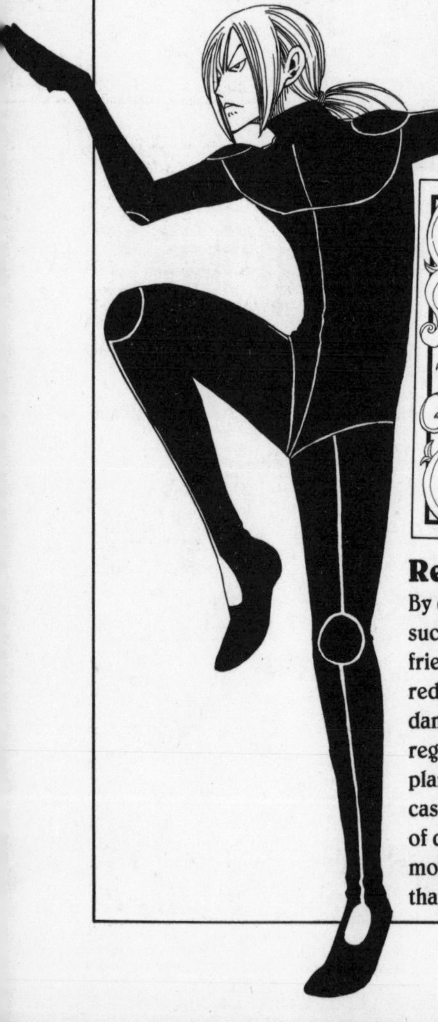

FAIRY TAIL

Name: Vijeeter Ecor   Age: 16 yrs.

Magic: Dance

Likes: Dance   Dislikes: Fermented soybeans

Remarks

By dancing particular dances, he can do things
such as boost the fighting power of all of his
friends within a ten-meter radius or, similarly,
reduce the fighting power of enemies with his
dance magic. He's always loved dance, and can
regularly be seen dancing within the guild. His
plan for the future seems to be to save up his
cash and go study at Minstrel, the cultural capital
of dance. But he never can seem to save any
money. As a side note, he has a hundred suits
that all look alike.

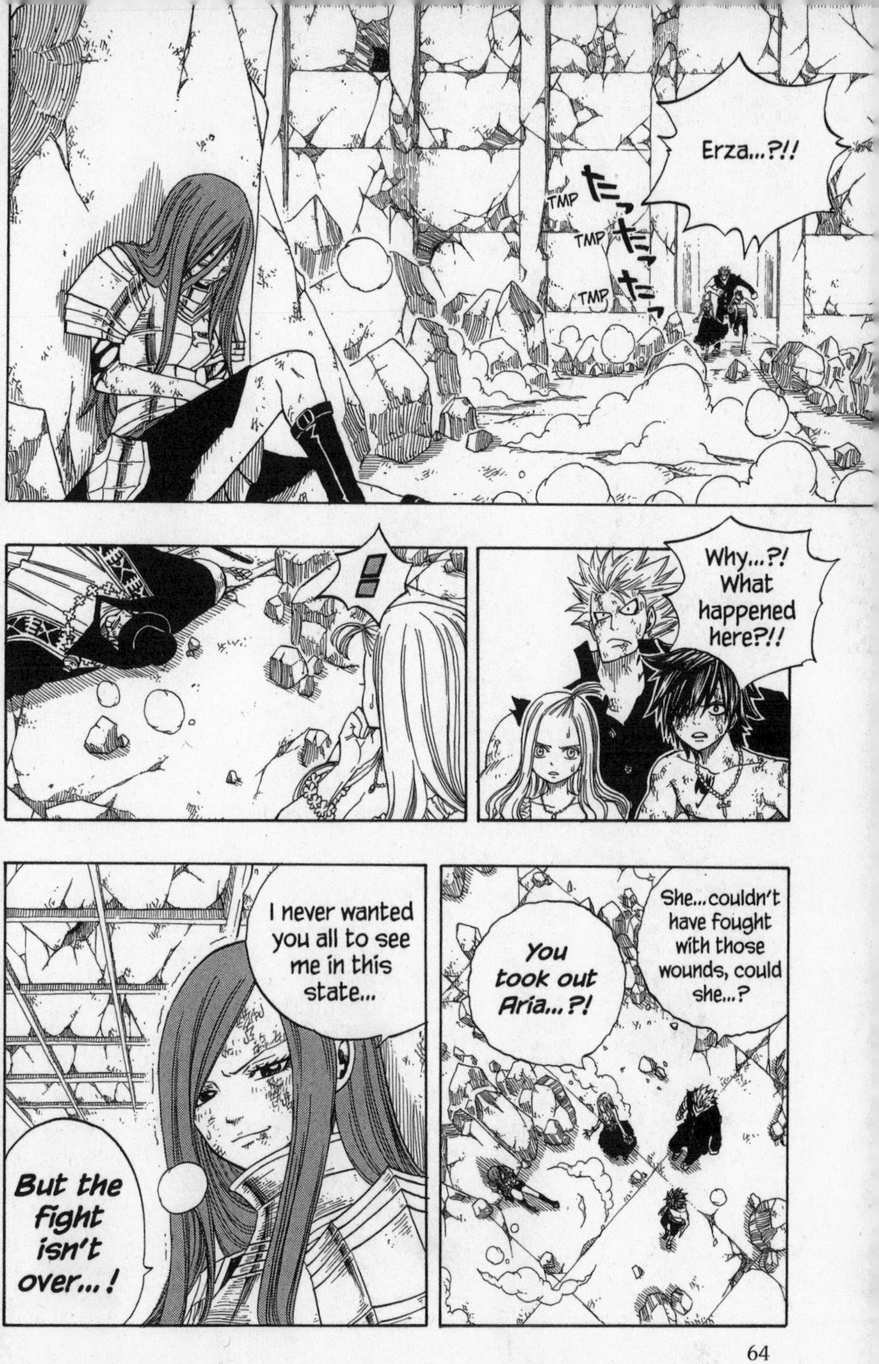
Erza...?!!
TMP
TMP
TMP
Why...?! What happened here?!!
!!
She...couldn't have fought with those wounds, could she...?
You took out Aria...?!
I never wanted you all to see me in this state...
But the fight isn't over...!

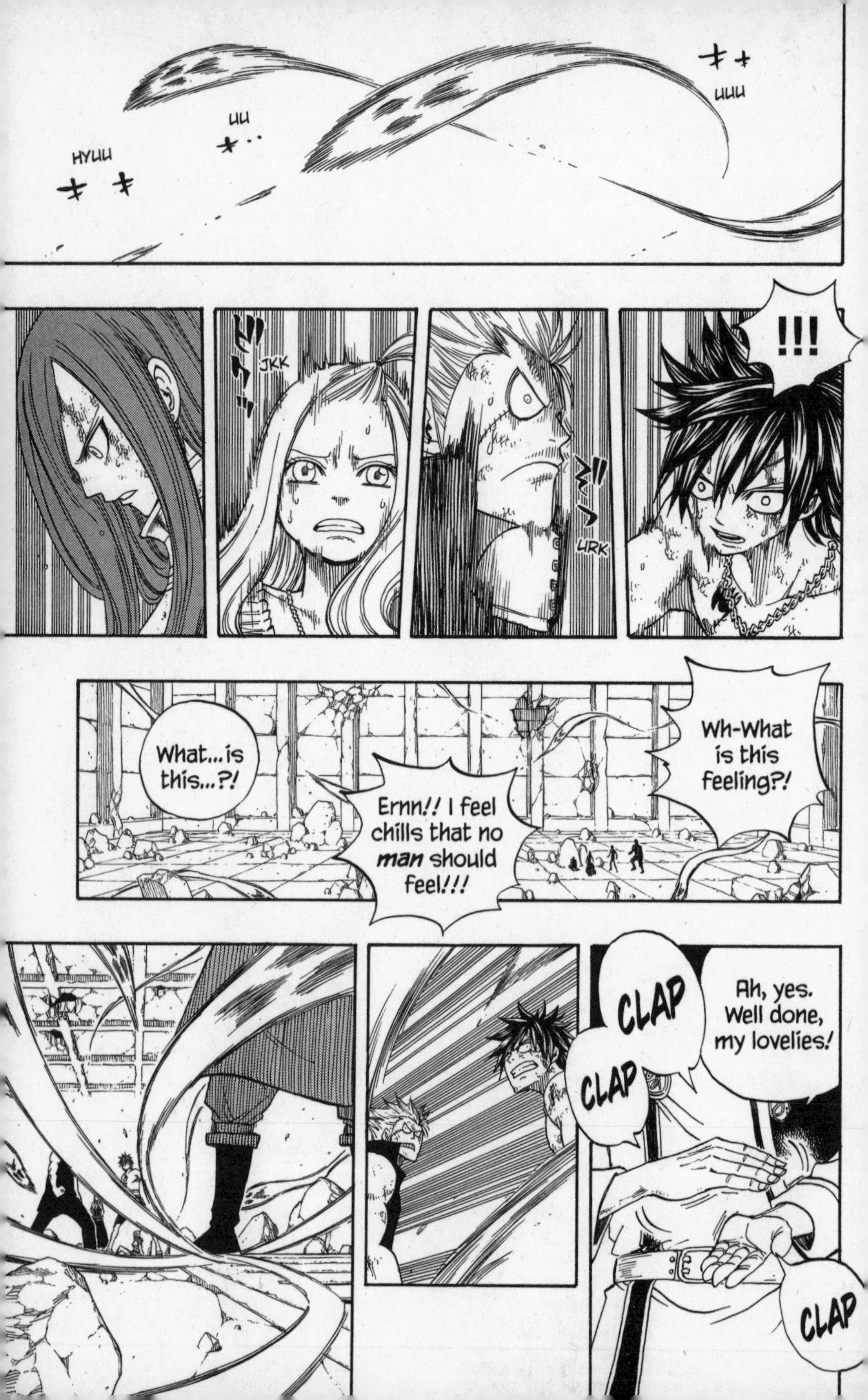
uuu
uu
HYUU
!!!
URK
JKK
Wh-What is this feeling?!
Ernn!! I feel chills that no *man* should feel!!!
What...is this...?!
Ah, yes. Well done, my lovelies!
CLAP
CLAP
CLAP

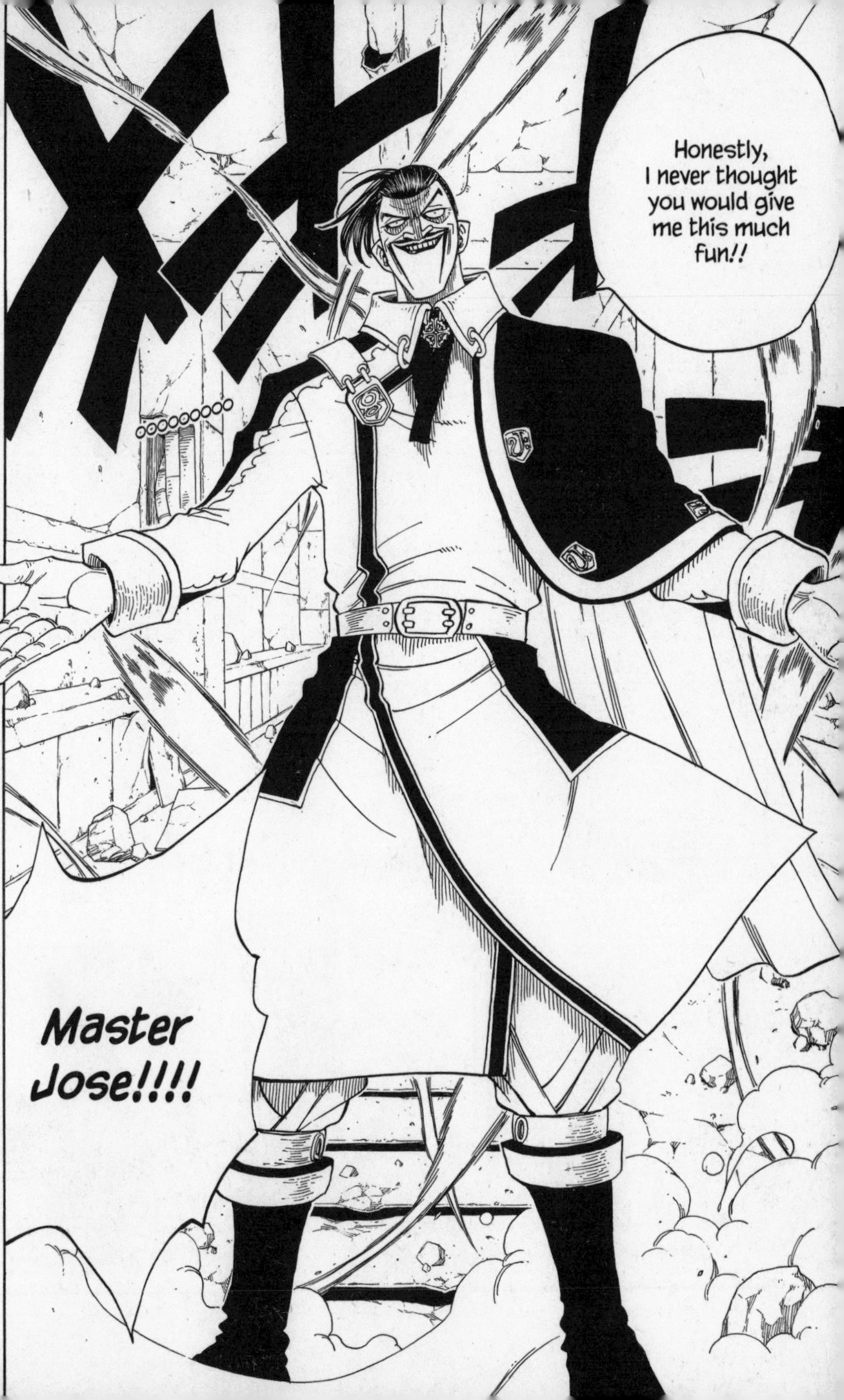
Honestly, I never thought you would give me this much fun!!
Master Jose!!!!

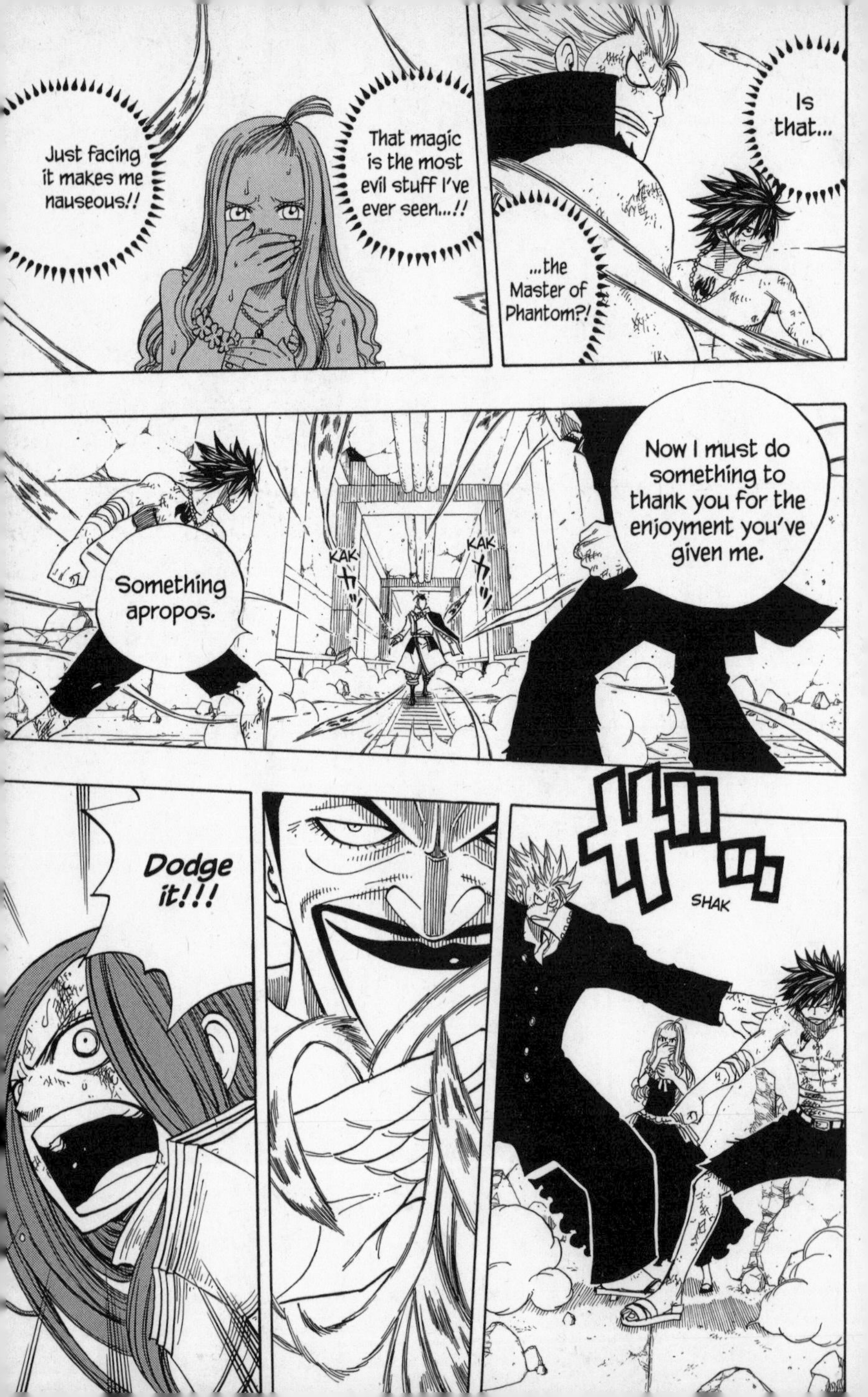
Is that...
...the Master of Phantom?!
That magic is the most evil stuff I've ever seen...!!
Just facing it makes me nauseous!!
Now I must do something to thank you for the enjoyment you've given me.
KAK
KAK
Something apropos.
SHAK
Dodge it!!!

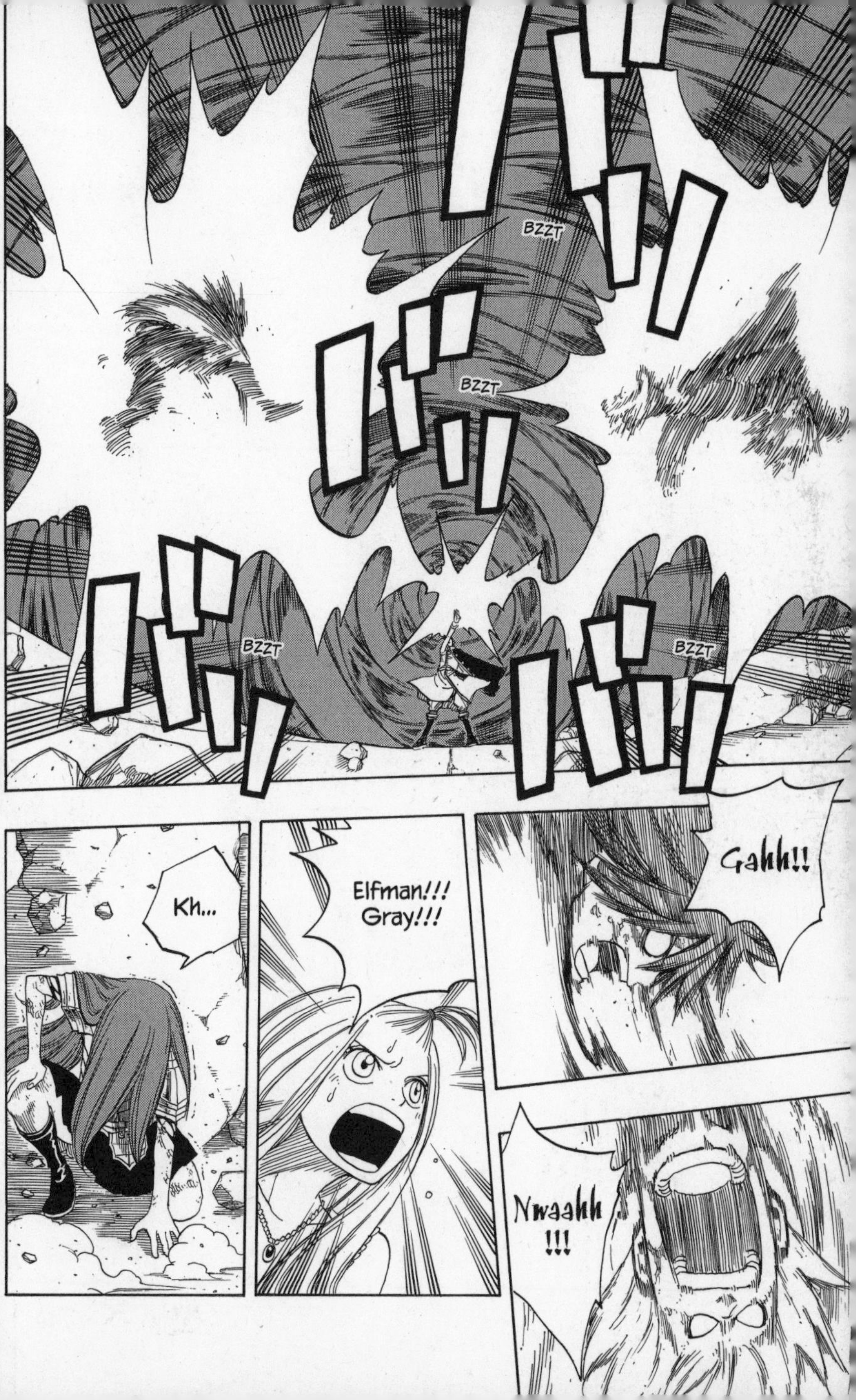
BZZT
BZZT
BZZT
BZZT
Gahh!!
Nwaahh !!!
Elfman!!! Gray!!!
Kh...

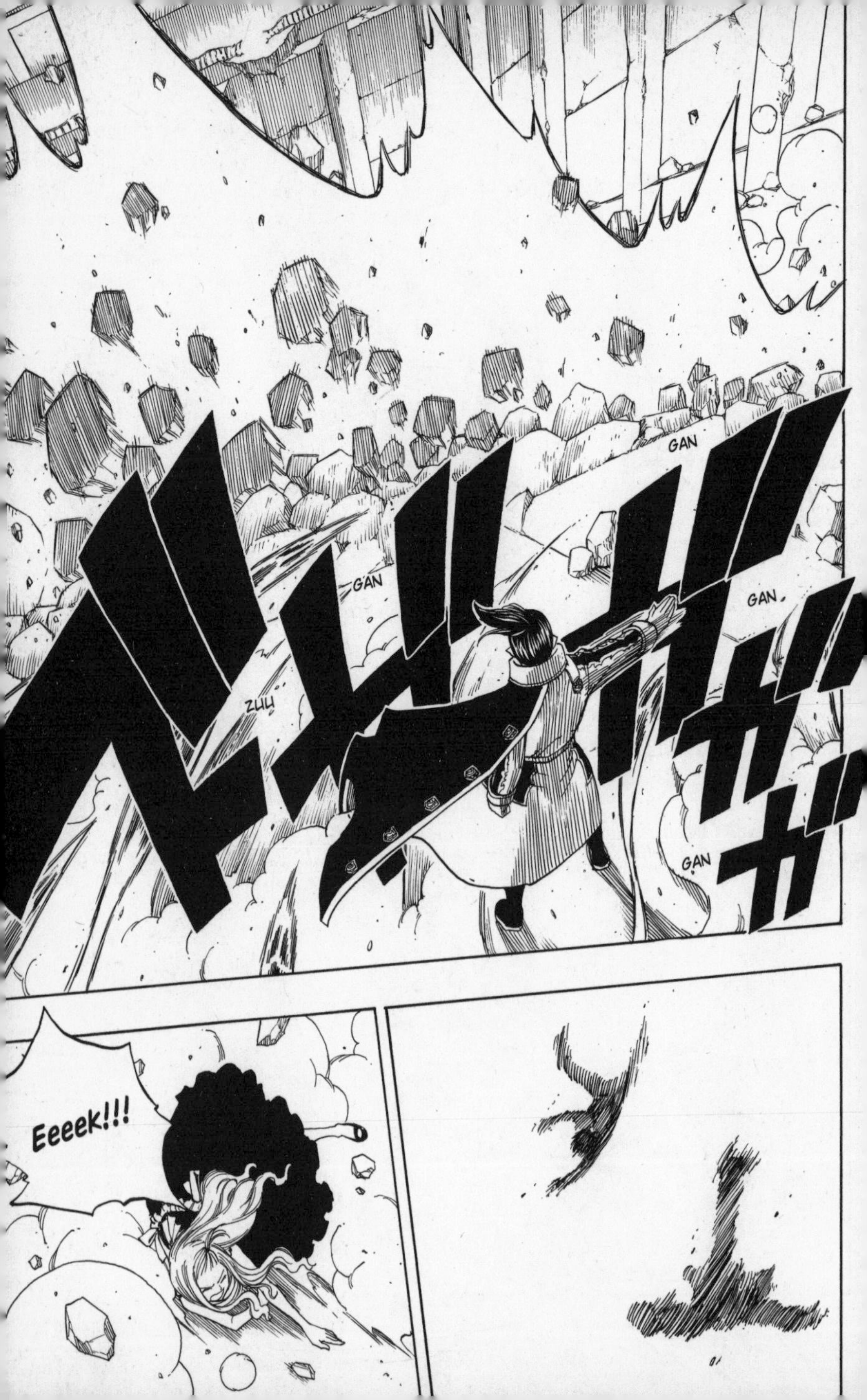
GAN
GAN
GAN
ZUU
GAN
Eeeek!!!

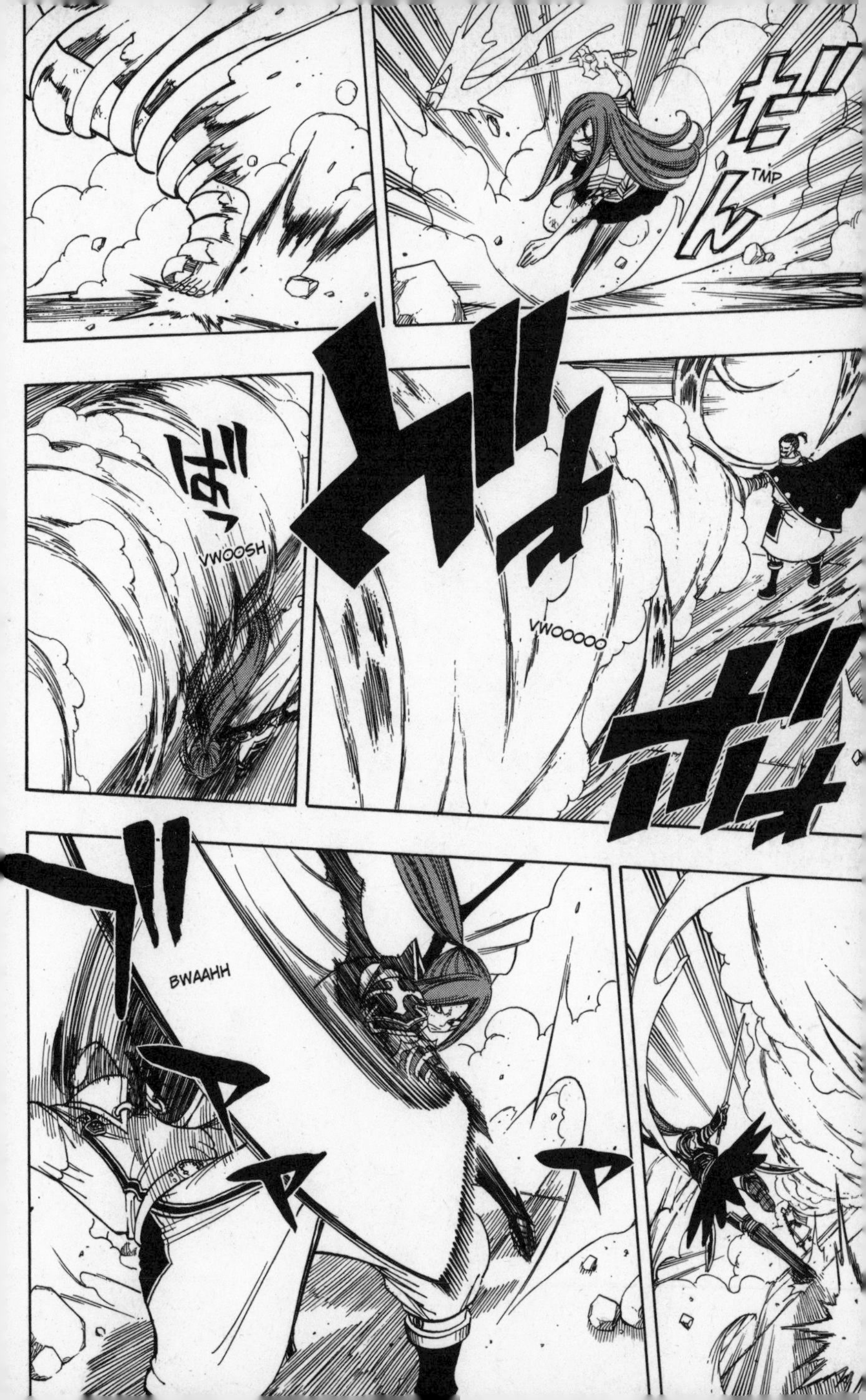
だん
TMP
VWOOOOO
ばっ
VWOOSH
BWAAHH

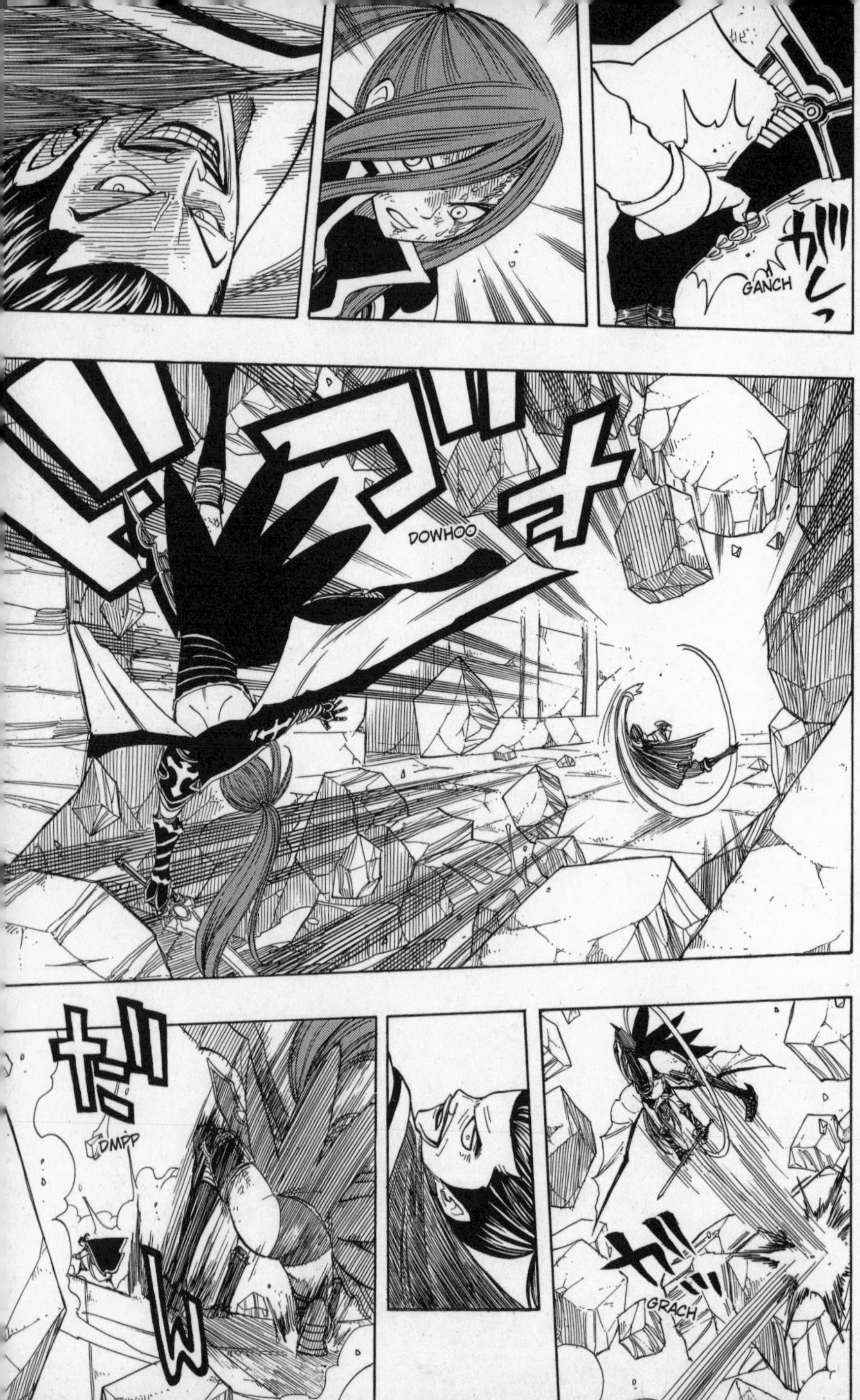
GANCH
DOWHOO
GRACH
DMPP

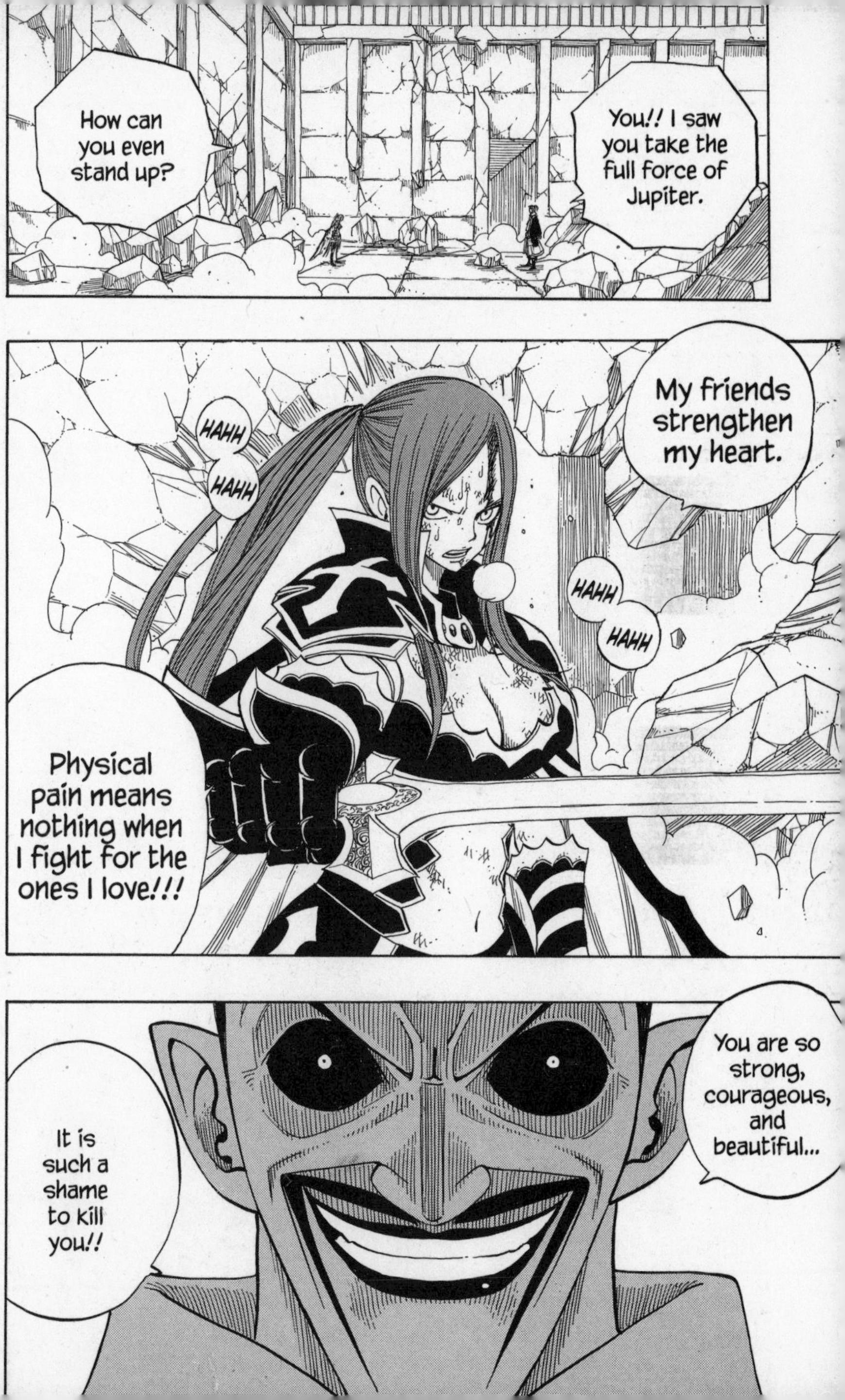
You!! I saw you take the full force of Jupiter.
How can you even stand up?
My friends strengthen my heart.
HAHH
HAHH
HAHH
HAHH
Physical pain means nothing when I fight for the ones I love!!!
You are so strong, courageous, and beautiful...
It is such a shame to kill you!!

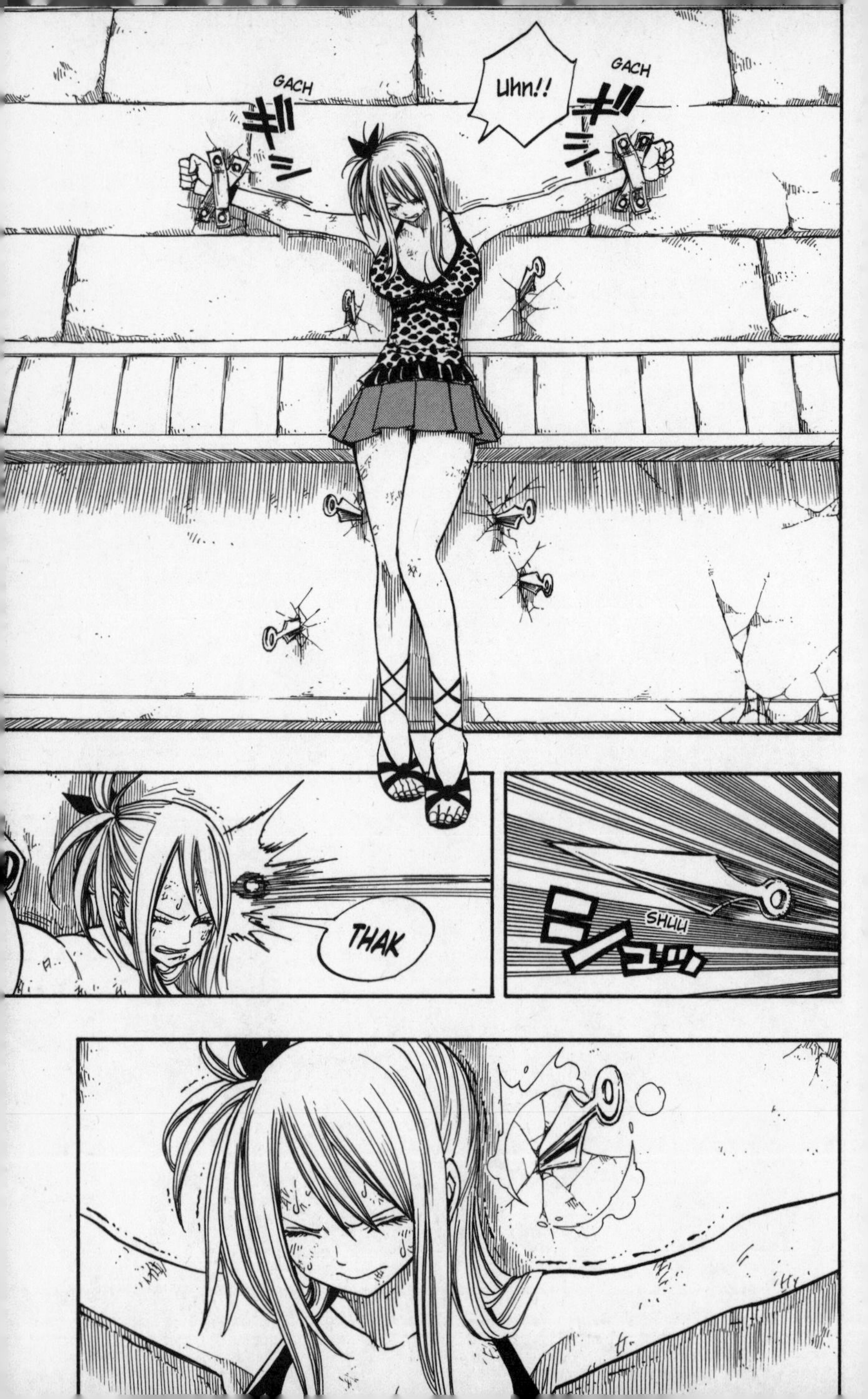

GACH
Uhn!!
GACH
SHUU
THAK

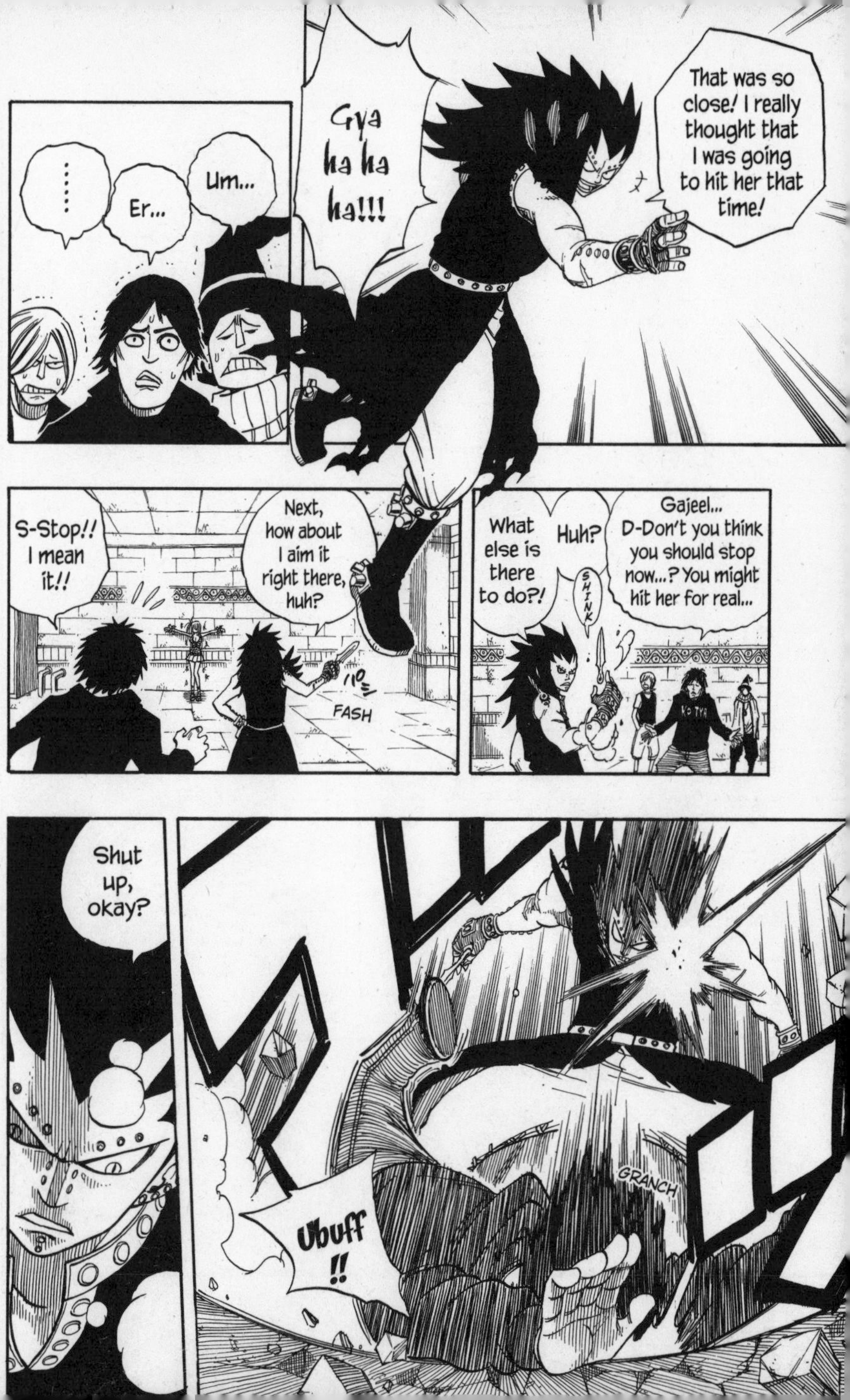
That was so close! I really thought that I was going to hit her that time!
Gya ha ha ha!!!
Um...
Er...
......
Gajeel... D-Don't you think you should stop now...? You might hit her for real...
Huh?
What else is there to do?!
SHINK
Next, how about I aim it right there, huh?
FASH
S-Stop!! I mean it!!
GRANCH
Ubuff!!
Shut up, okay?

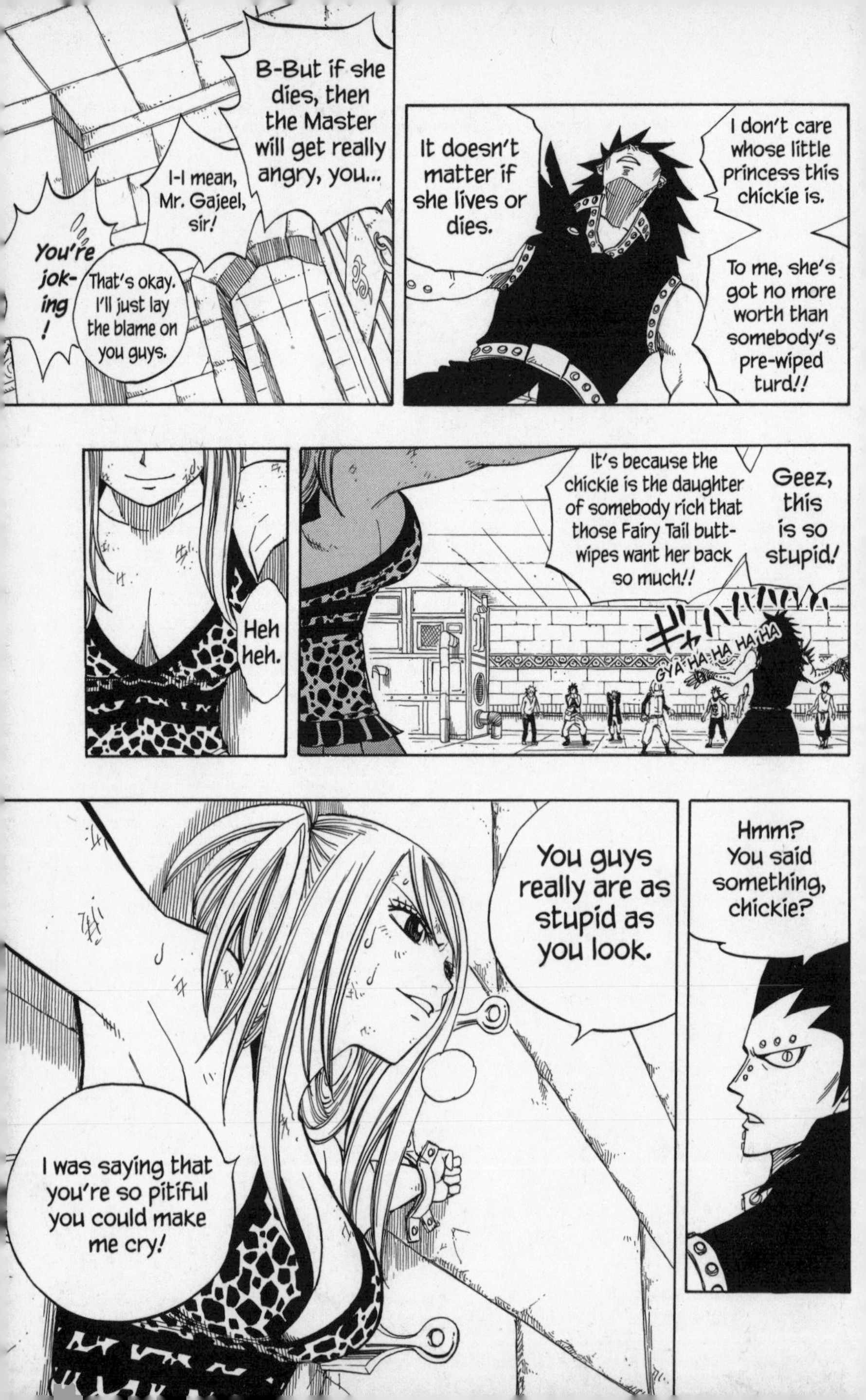
I don't care whose little princess this chickie is.
It doesn't matter if she lives or dies.
To me, she's got no more worth than somebody's pre-wiped turd!!
B-But if she dies, then the Master will get really angry, you...
I-I mean, Mr. Gajeel, sir!
You're jok-ing!
That's okay. I'll just lay the blame on you guys.
Geez, this is so stupid!
It's because the chickie is the daughter of somebody rich that those Fairy Tail butt-wipes want her back so much!!
ギャハハハハ
GYA HA HA HA HA
Heh heh.
Hmm? You said something, chickie?
You guys really are as stupid as you look.
I was saying that you're so pitiful you could make me cry!

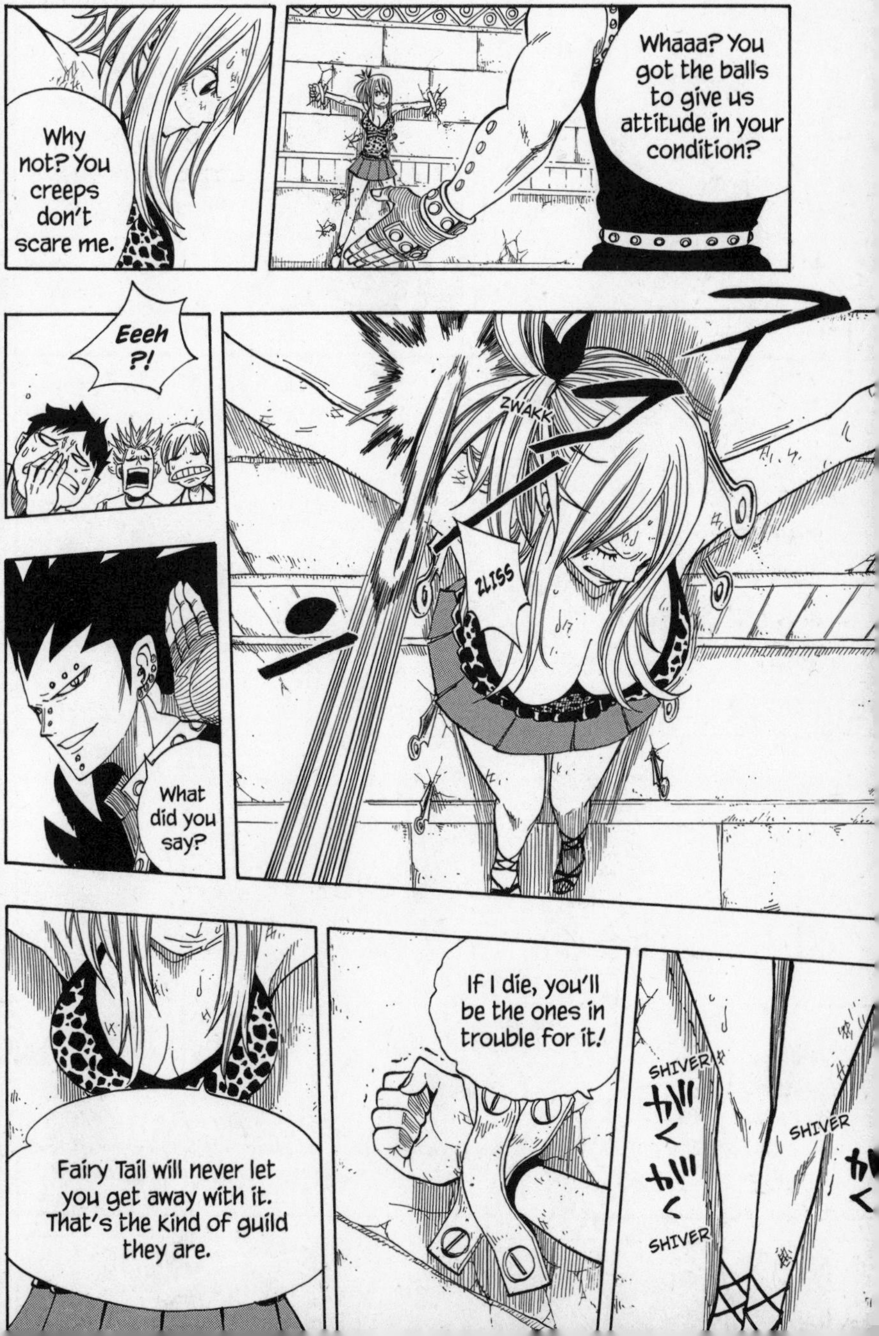
Whaaa? You got the balls to give us attitude in your condition?
Why not? You creeps don't scare me.
ZWAKK
ZLISS
Eeeh ?!
What did you say?
SHIVER
SHIVER
SHIVER
If I die, you'll be the ones in trouble for it!
Fairy Tail will never let you get away with it. That's the kind of guild they are.

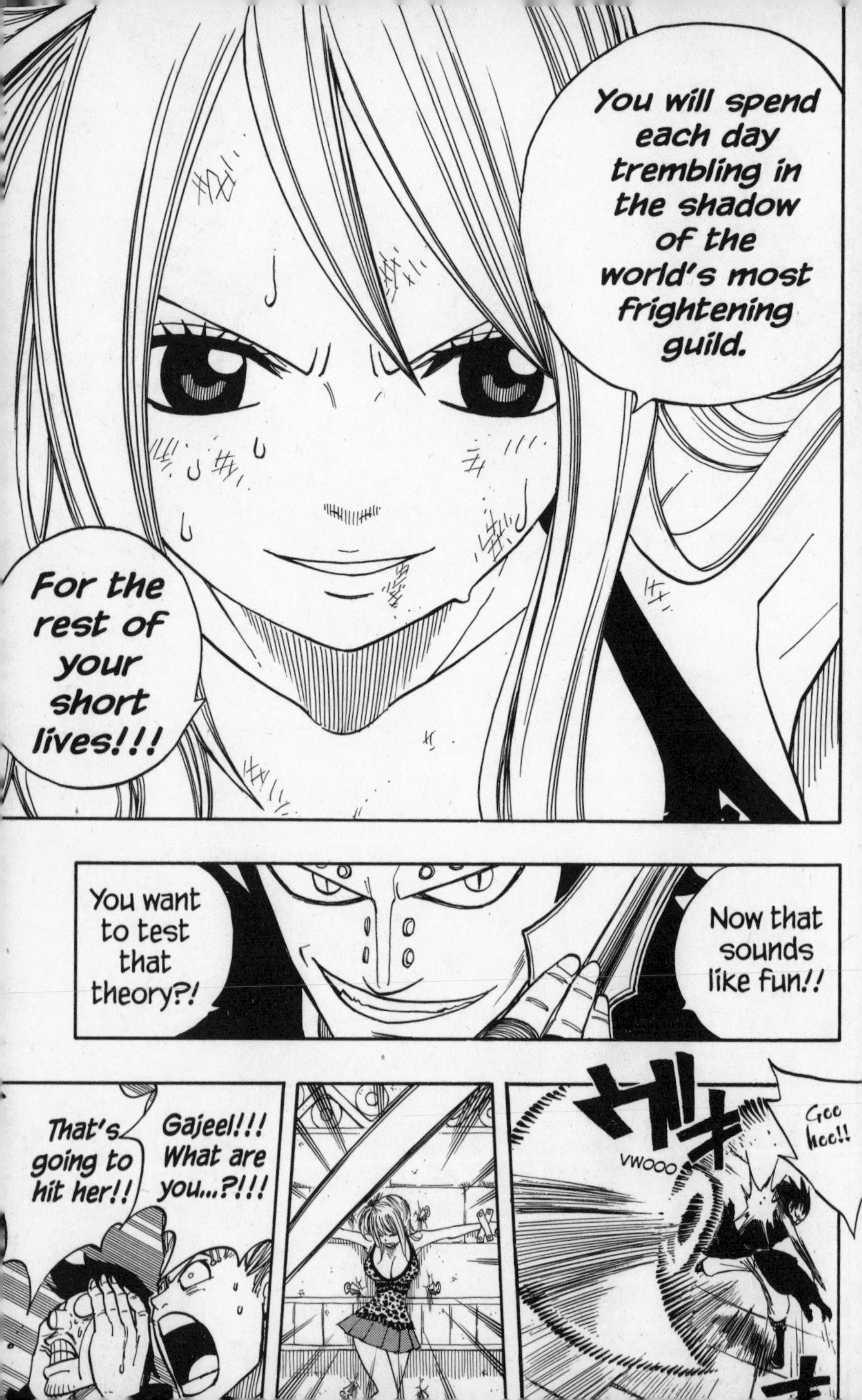
You will spend each day trembling in the shadow of the world's most frightening guild.
For the rest of your short lives!!!
Now that sounds like fun!!
You want to test that theory?!
Gee hee!!
VWOOO
Gajeel!!! What are you...?!!!
That's going to hit her!!

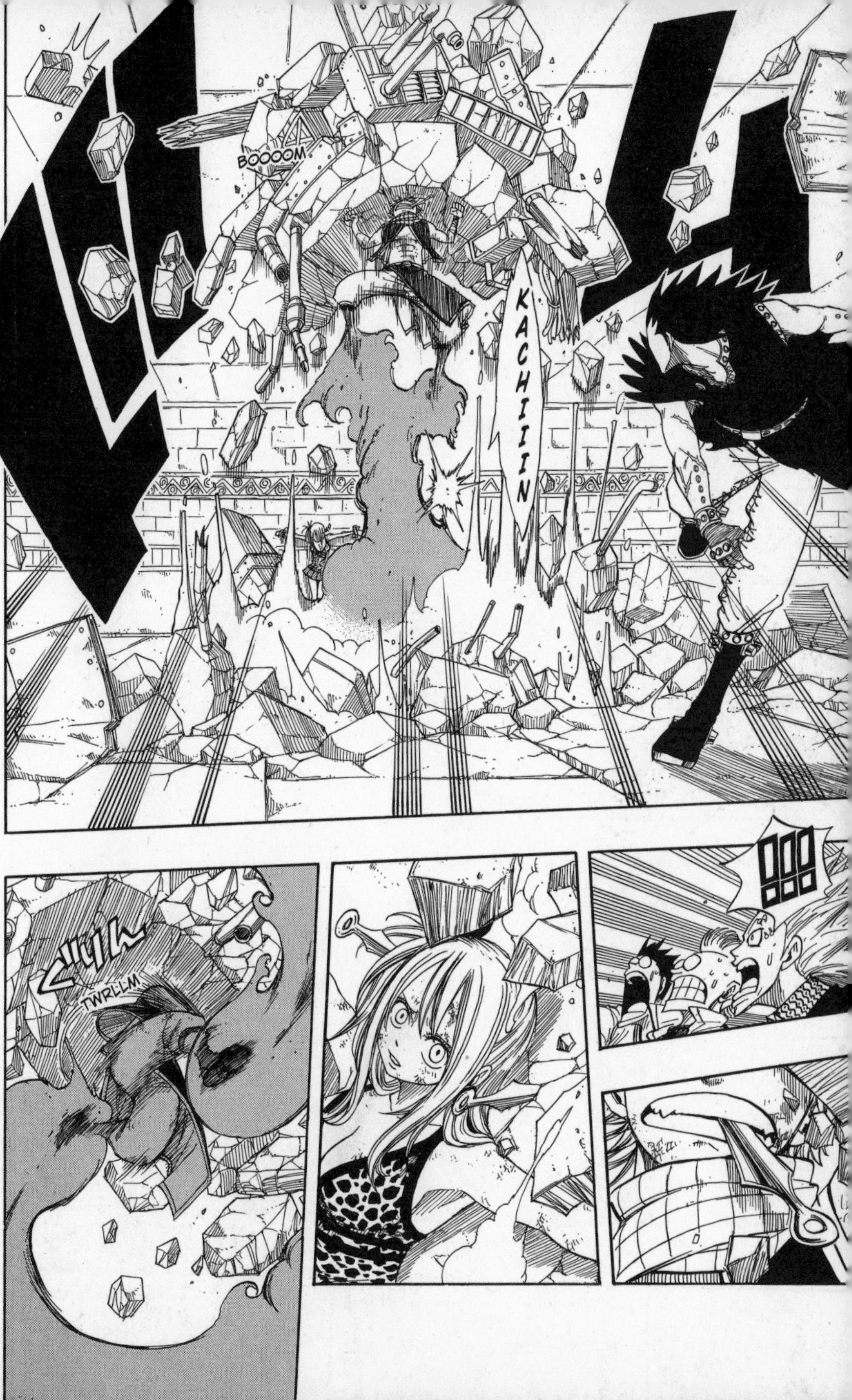
BOOOOM
KACHIIIIN
TWRLLM

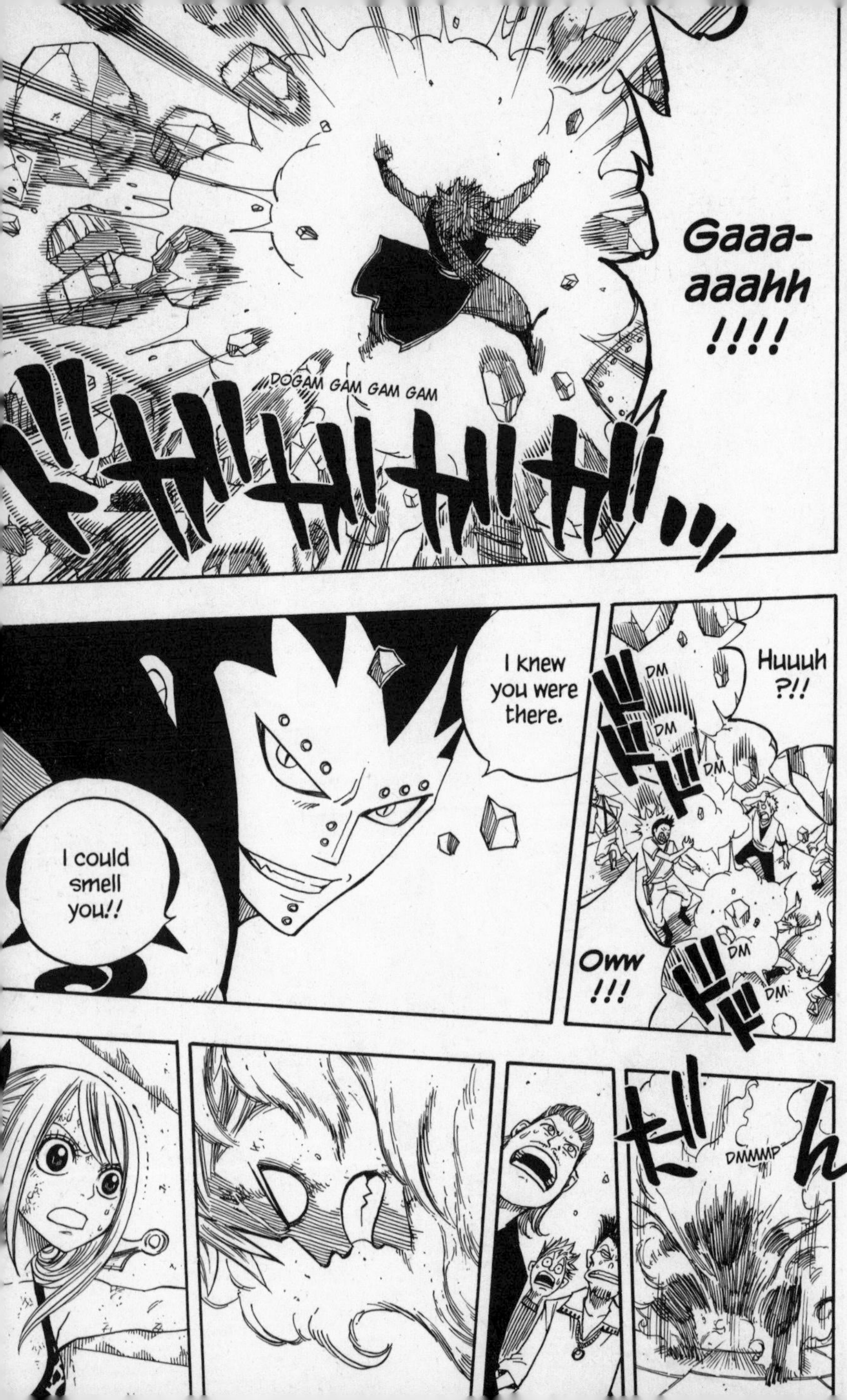
Gaaa-aaahh!!!!
DOGAM GAM GAM GAM
Huuuh?!!
DM
DM
DM
Oww!!!
DM
DM
I knew you were there.
I could smell you!!
DMMMP

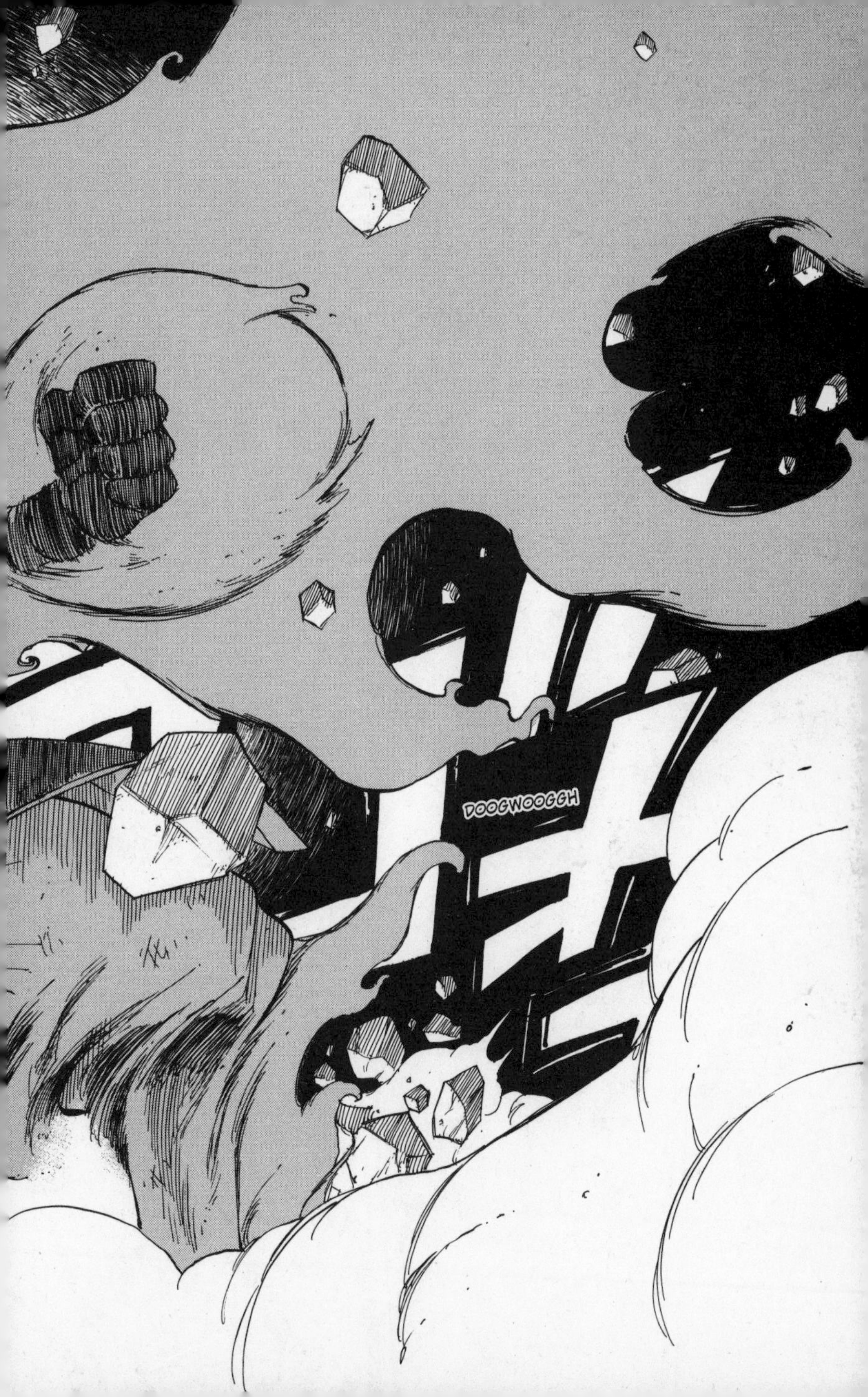
DOOGWOOGGH

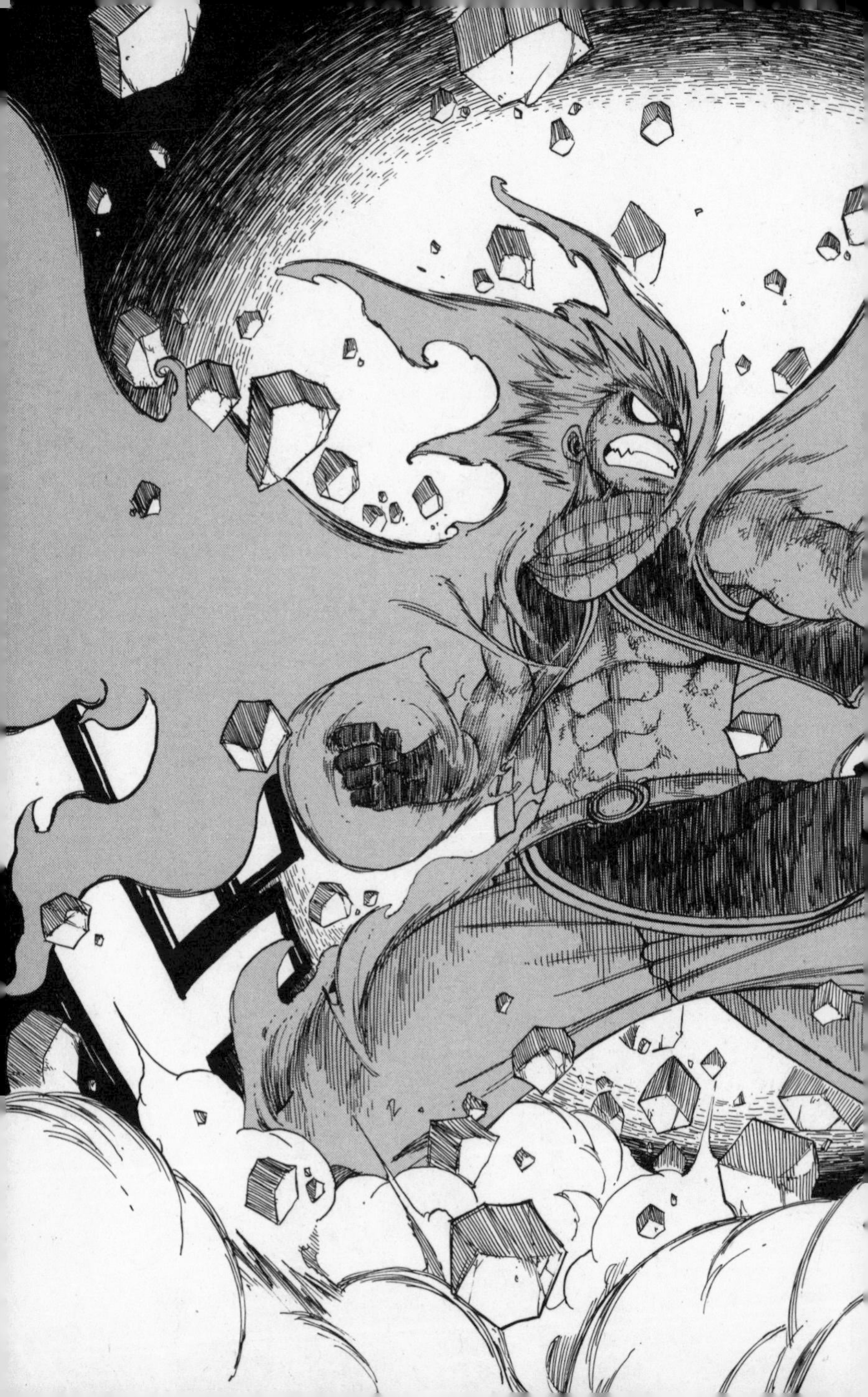

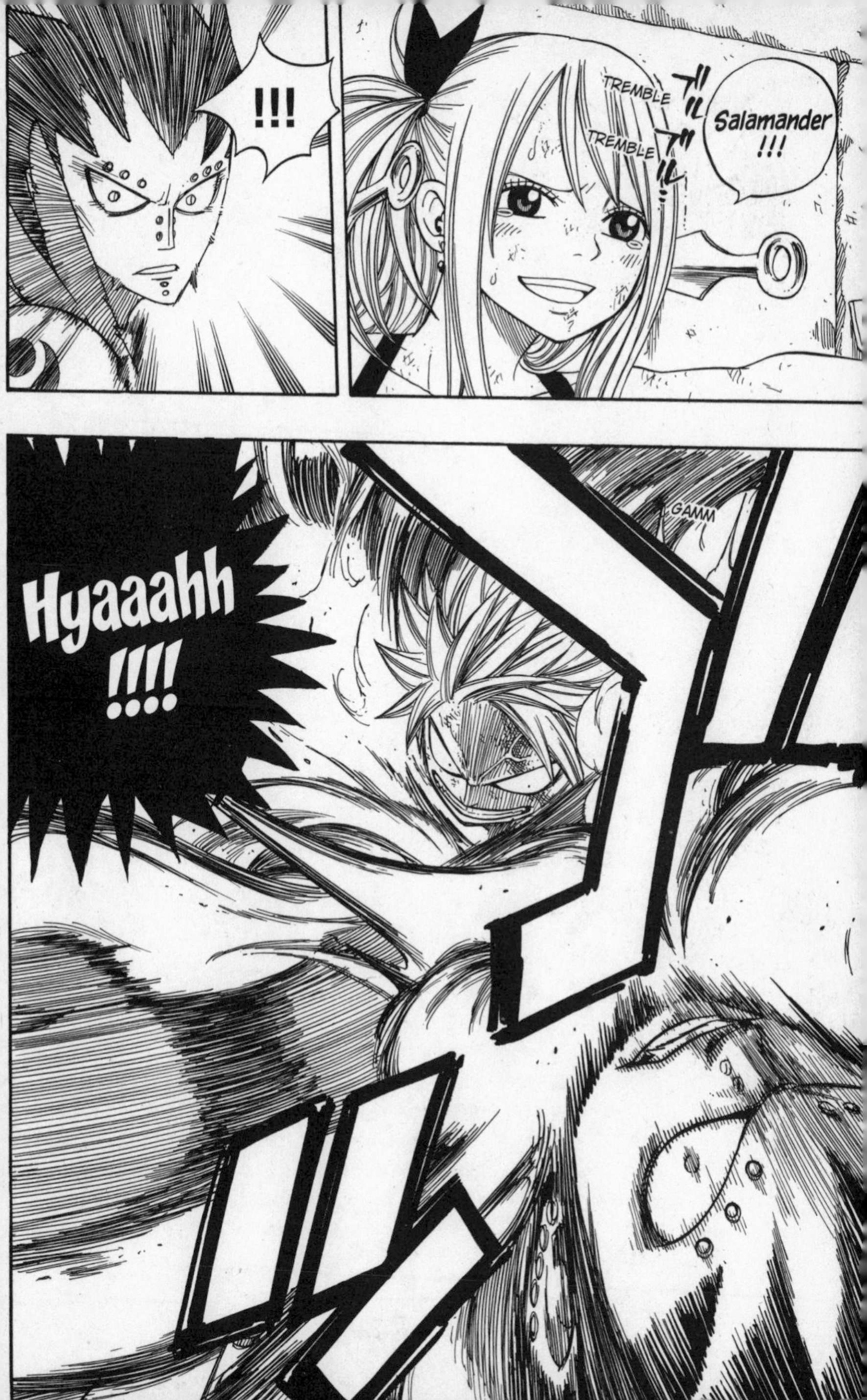
Salamander !!!
TREMBLE
TREMBLE
!!!
GAMM
Hyaaahh !!!!

FAIRY TAIL

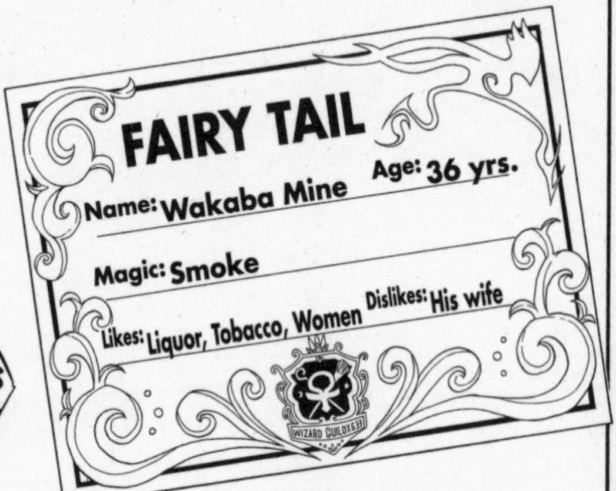

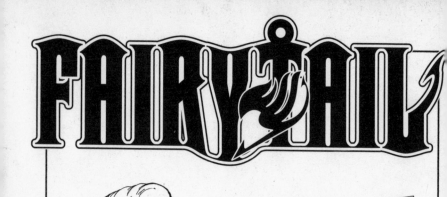

FAIRY TAIL
Name: Wakaba Mine
Age: 36 yrs.
Magic: Smoke
Likes: Liquor, Tobacco, Women
Dislikes: His wife
WIZARD GUILD X633

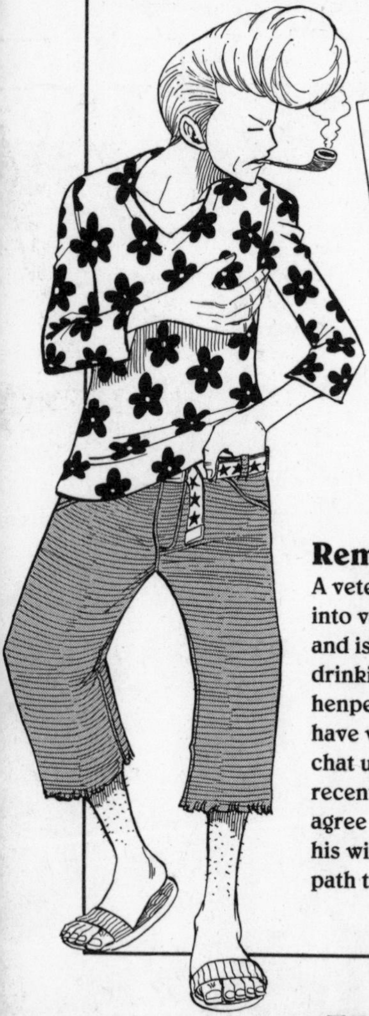

Remarks

A veteran wizard who can fight by shaping smoke into various forms. He has much the same history and is the same age as Macao, so at times they are drinking buddies, and at other times, rivals. He is henpecked by his wife, so even when he doesn't have work, you can find him at the guild trying to chat up the pretty young guild employees. His most recent target was Mirajane, saying that if she would agree to go out with him, he would break it off with his wife. She turned him down flat. He's well on the path to mastering the art of being a creepy old guy.

Chapter 61: The Two Dragon Slayers

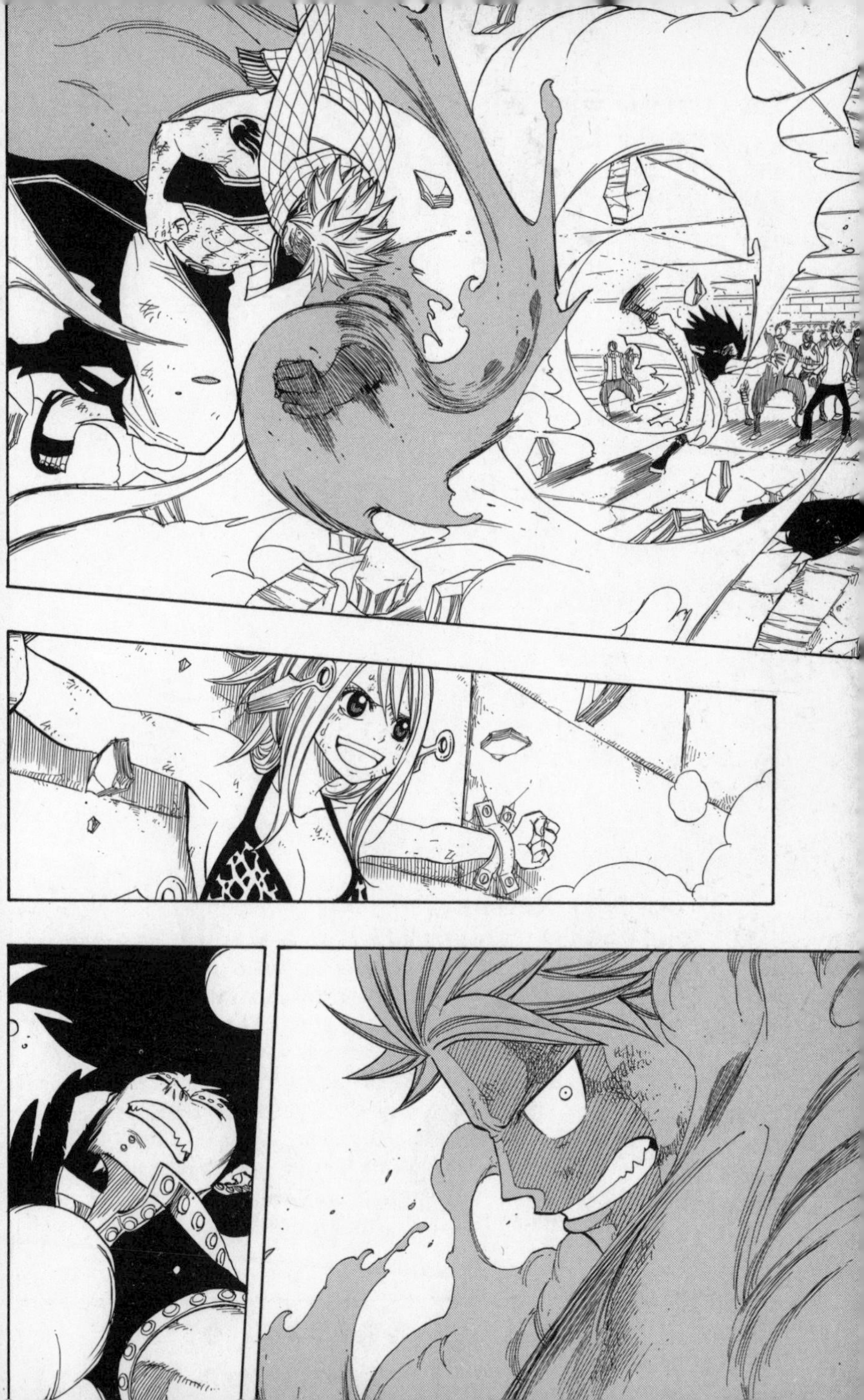

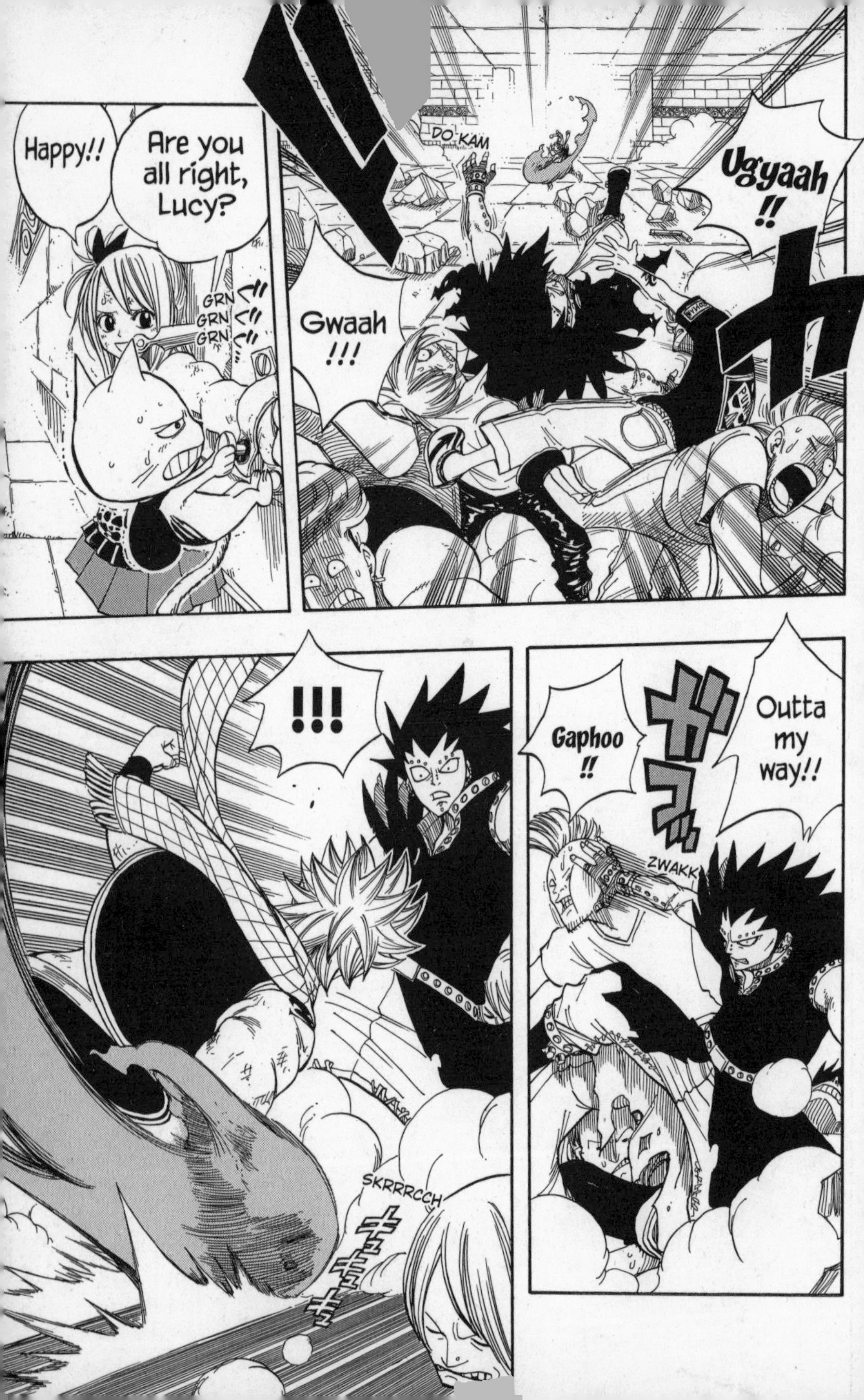
DO KAM
Ugyaah!!
Gwaah!!!
Happy!!
Are you all right, Lucy?
GRN GRN GRN
Outta my way!!
Gaphoo!!
ZWAKK
!!!
SKRRRCCH

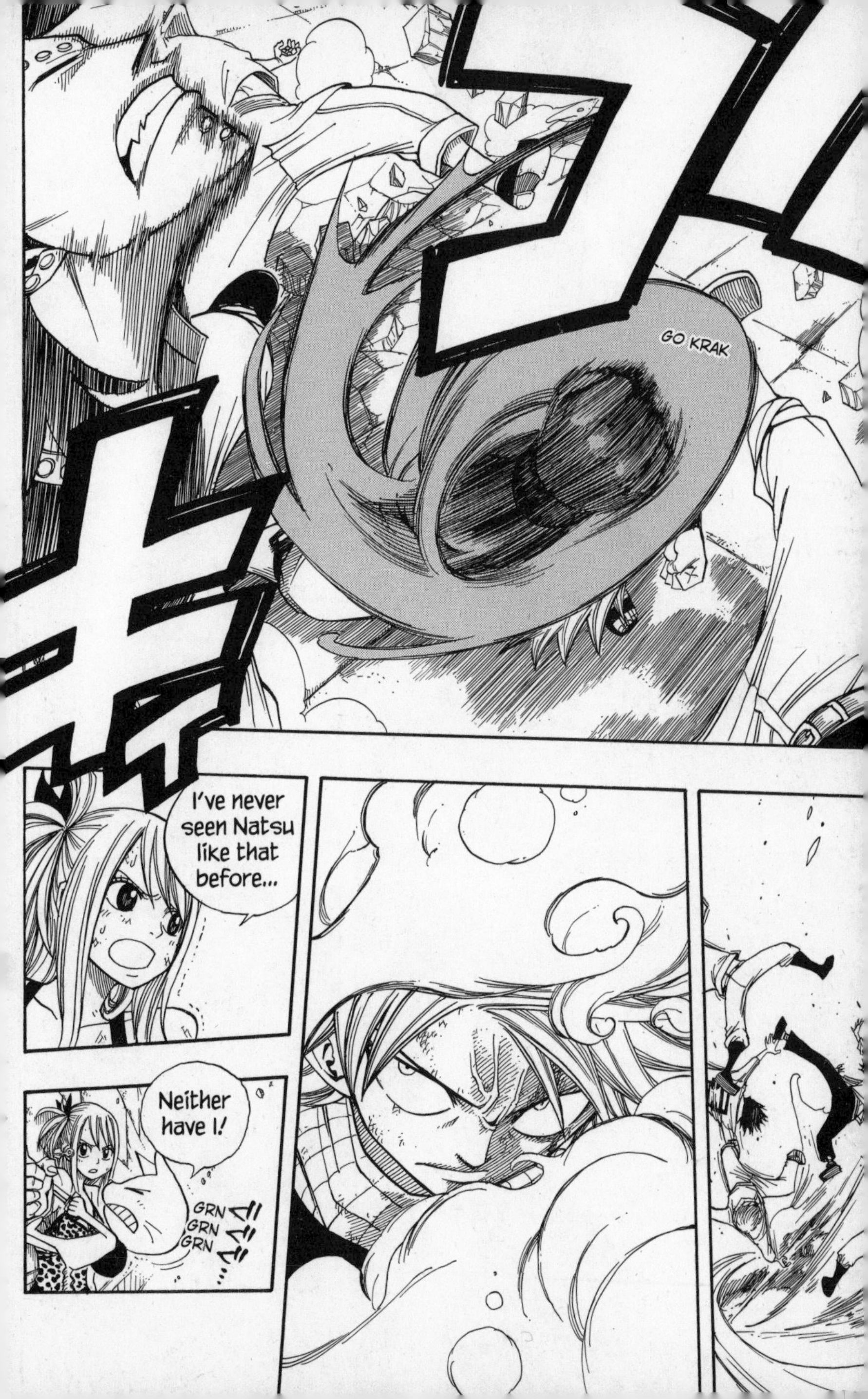
GO KRAK
I've never seen Natsu like that before...
Neither have I!
GRN GRN GRN
...!!!

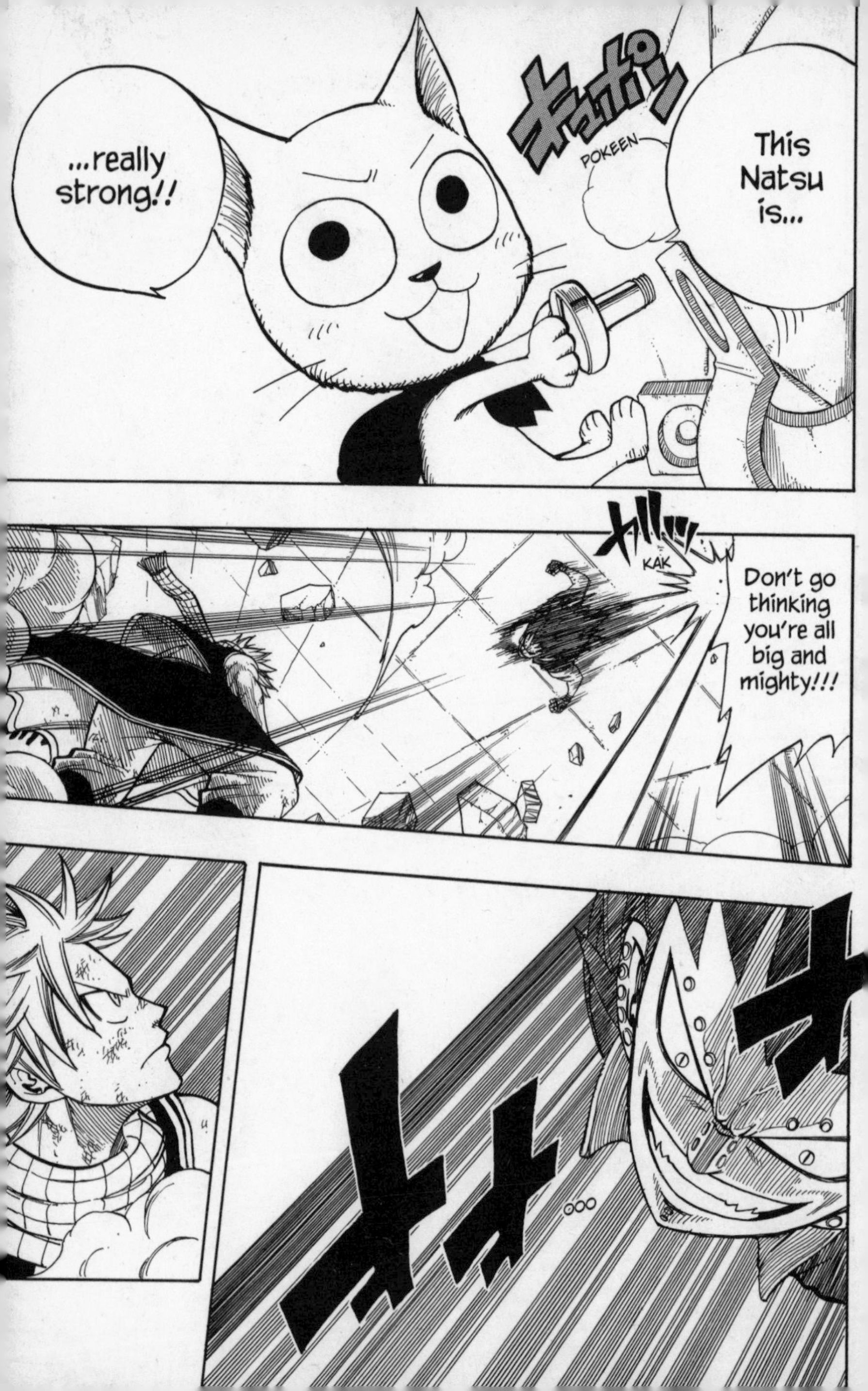
POKEEN
This Natsu is...
...really strong!!
KAK
Don't go thinking you're all big and mighty!!!

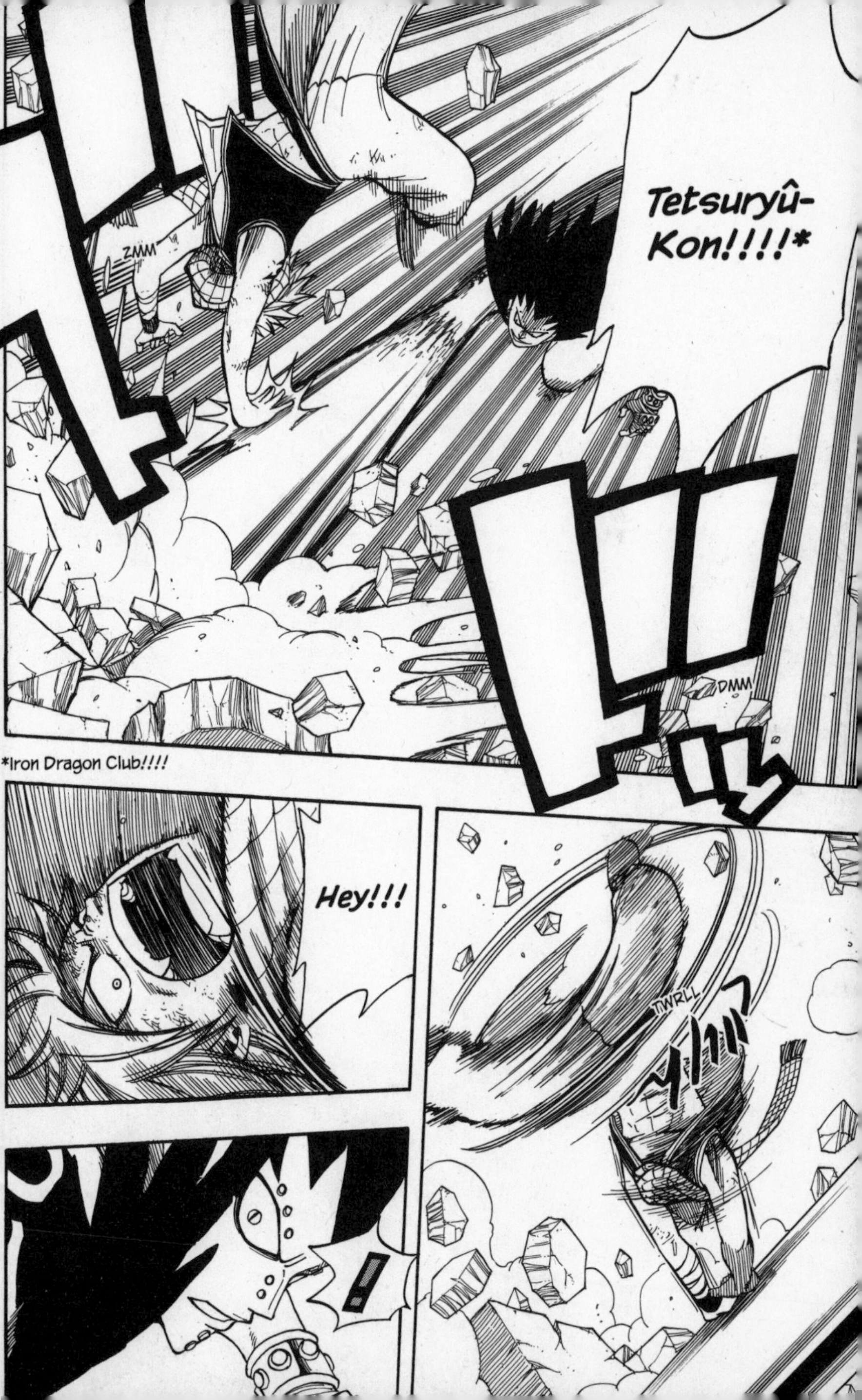
Tetsuryû-Kon!!!!*
ZMM
DMM
*Iron Dragon Club!!!!
TWRLL
Hey!!!

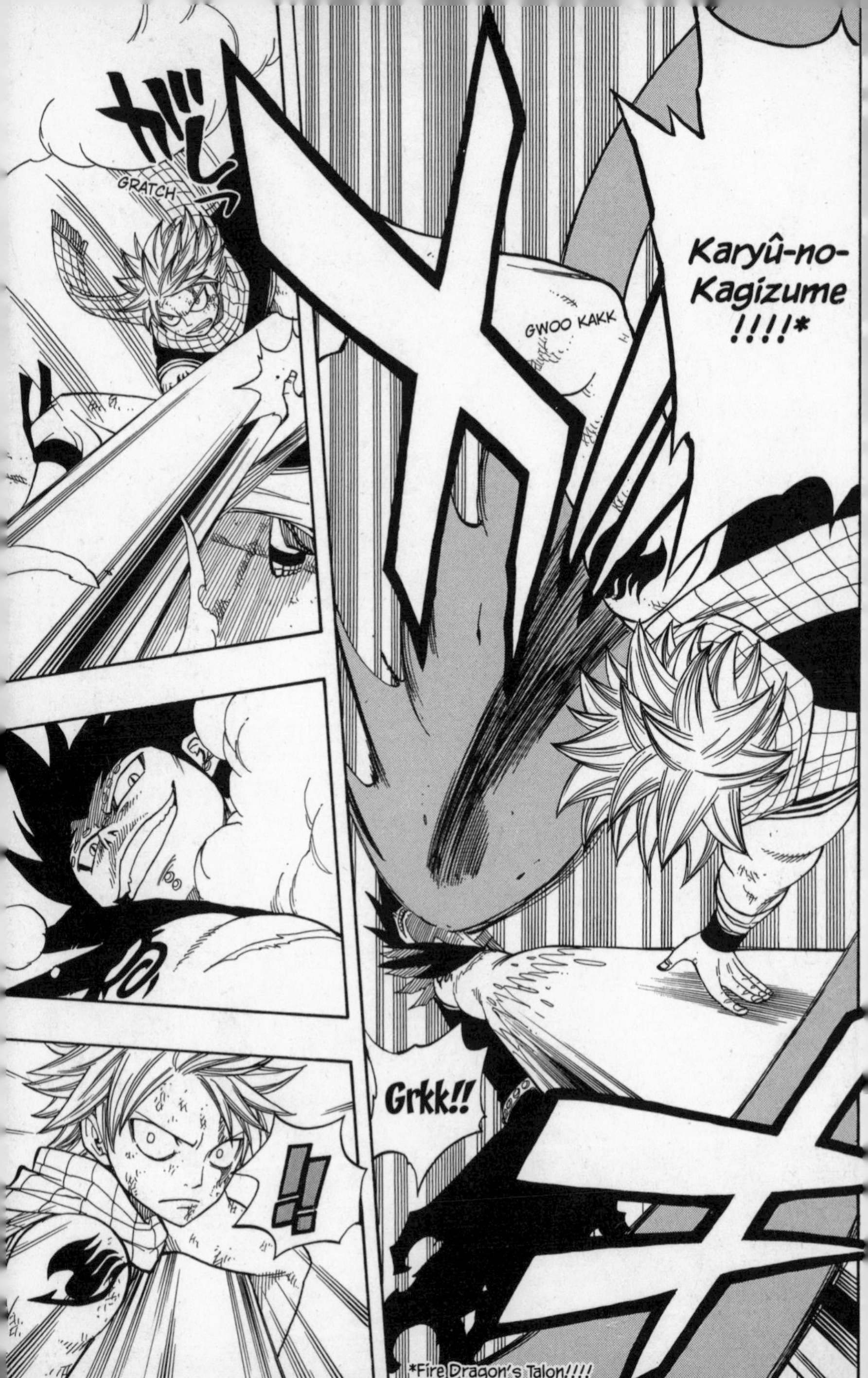
Karyû-no-Kagizume !!!!*
GWOO KAKK
Grkk!!
GRATCH

*Fire Dragon's Talon!!!!

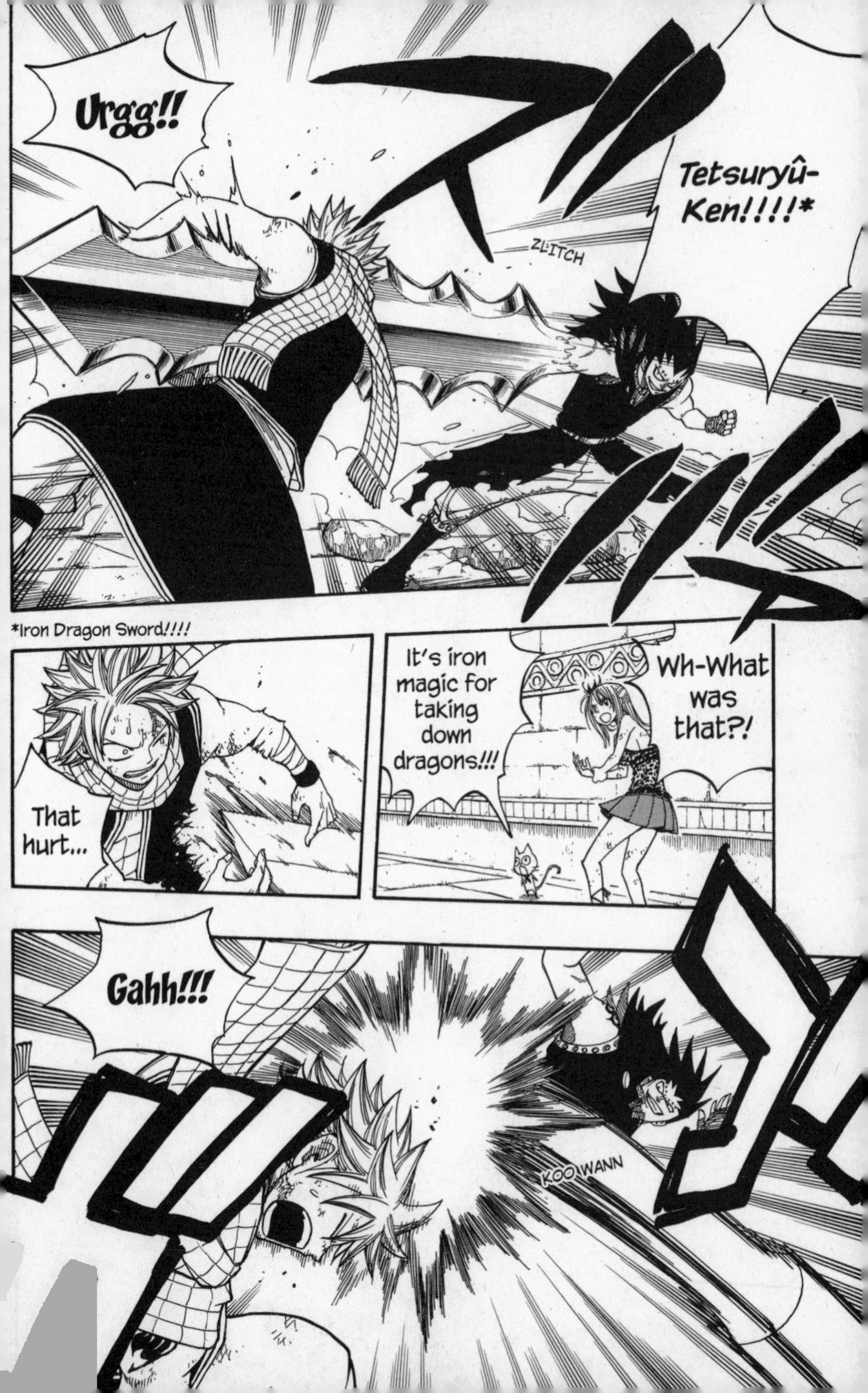
Tetsuryû-Ken!!!!*
ZLITCH
Urgg!!
*Iron Dragon Sword!!!!
Wh-What was that?!
It's iron magic for taking down dragons!!!
That hurt...
KOO WANN
Gahh!!!

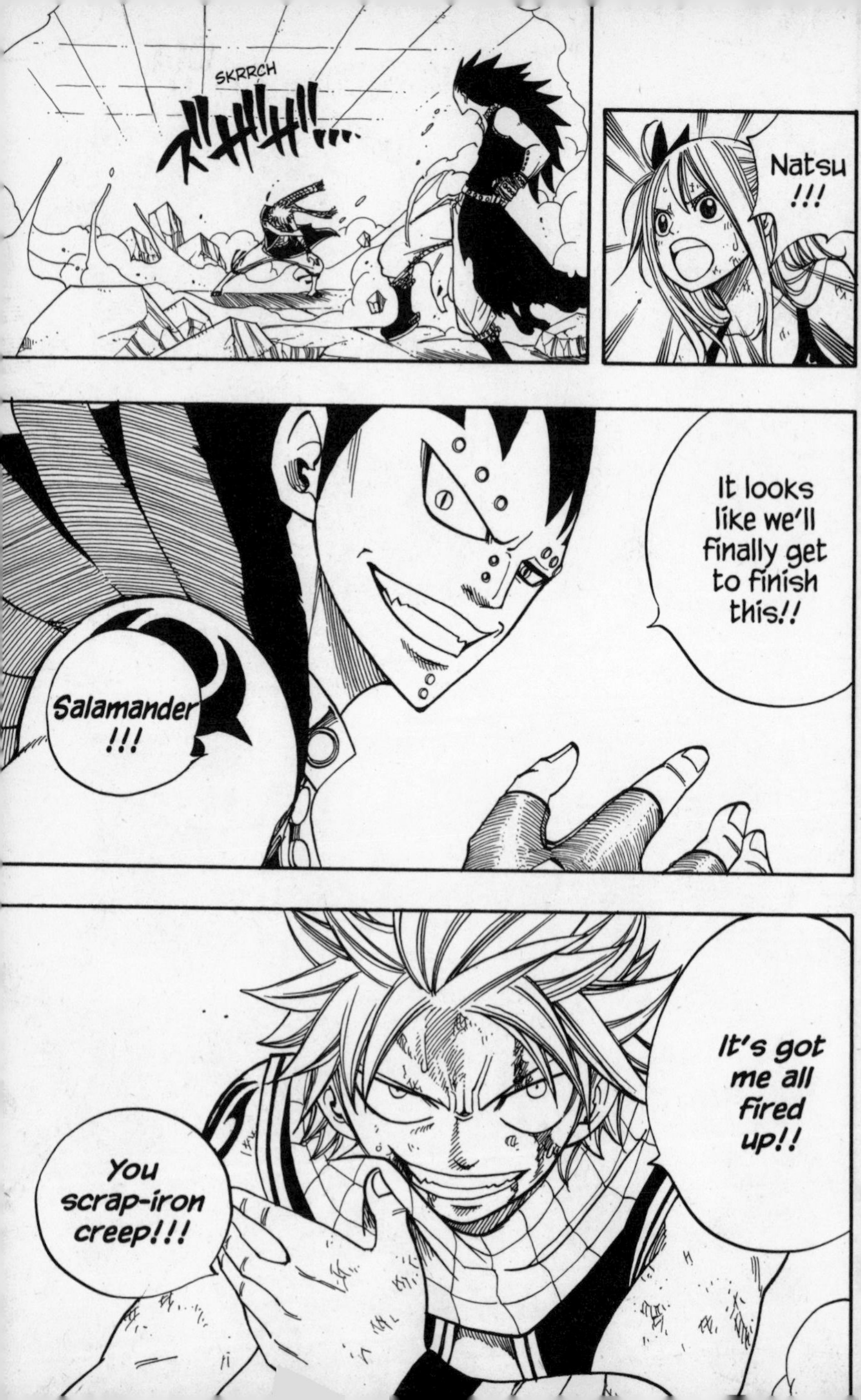
Natsu!!!
SKRRCH
It looks like we'll finally get to finish this!!
Salamander!!!
It's got me all fired up!!
You scrap-iron creep!!!

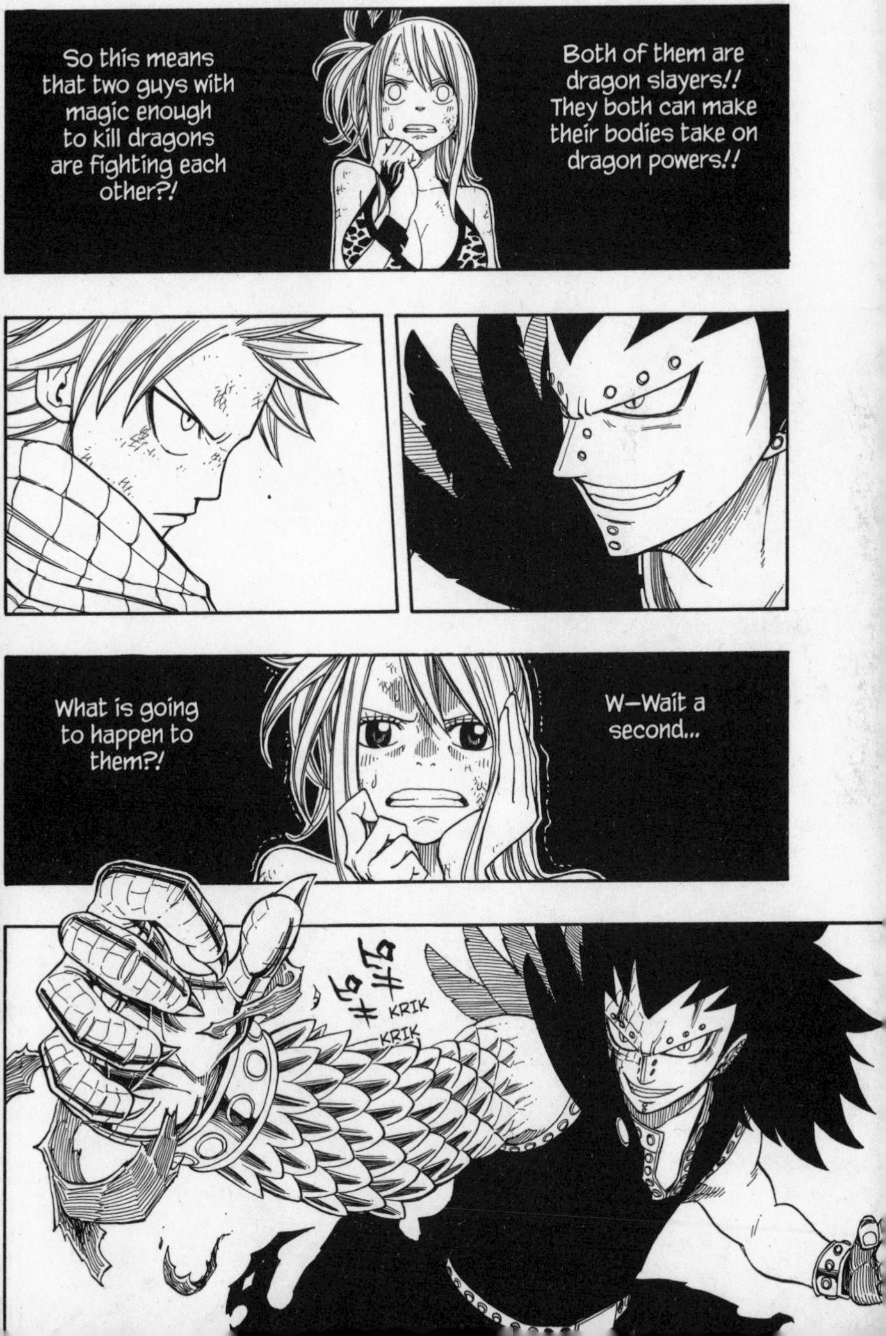
Both of them are dragon slayers!! They both can make their bodies take on dragon powers!!
So this means that two guys with magic enough to kill dragons are fighting each other?!
W-Wait a second...
What is going to happen to them?!
KRIK
KRIK

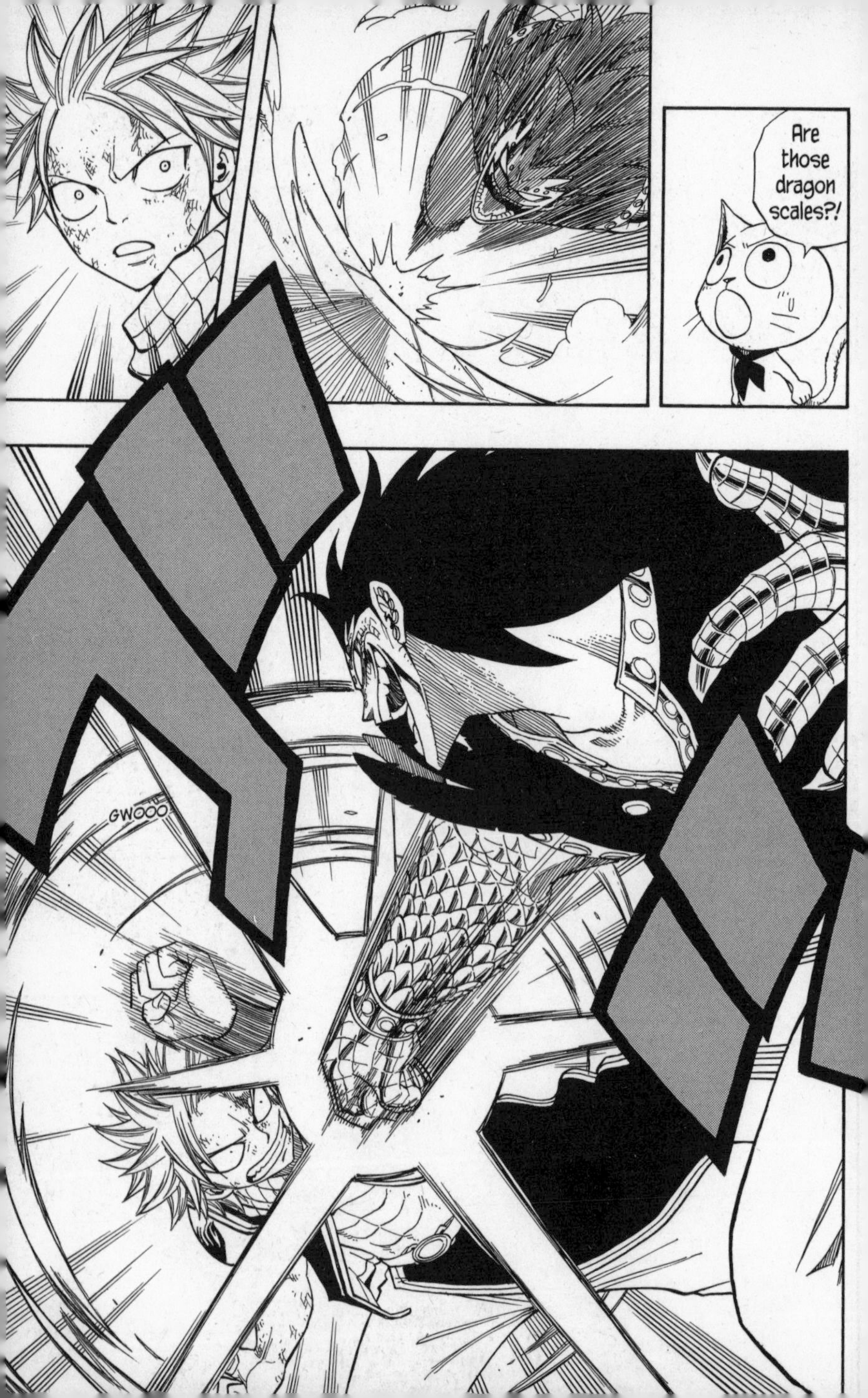
Are those dragon scales?!
GWOOO

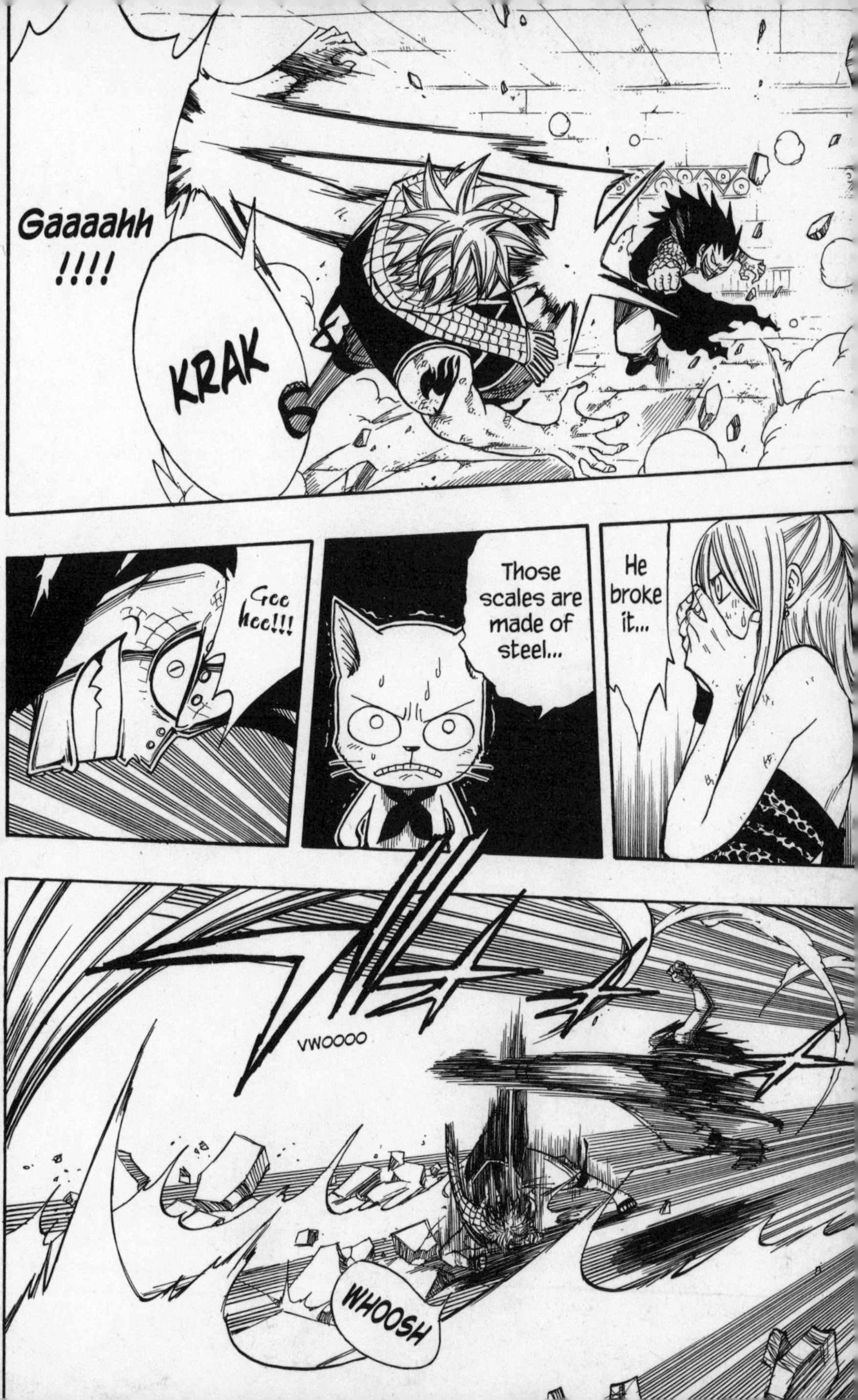
Gaaaaahh!!!!
KRAK
He broke it...
Those scales are made of steel...
Gee hee!!!
VWOOOO
WHOOSH

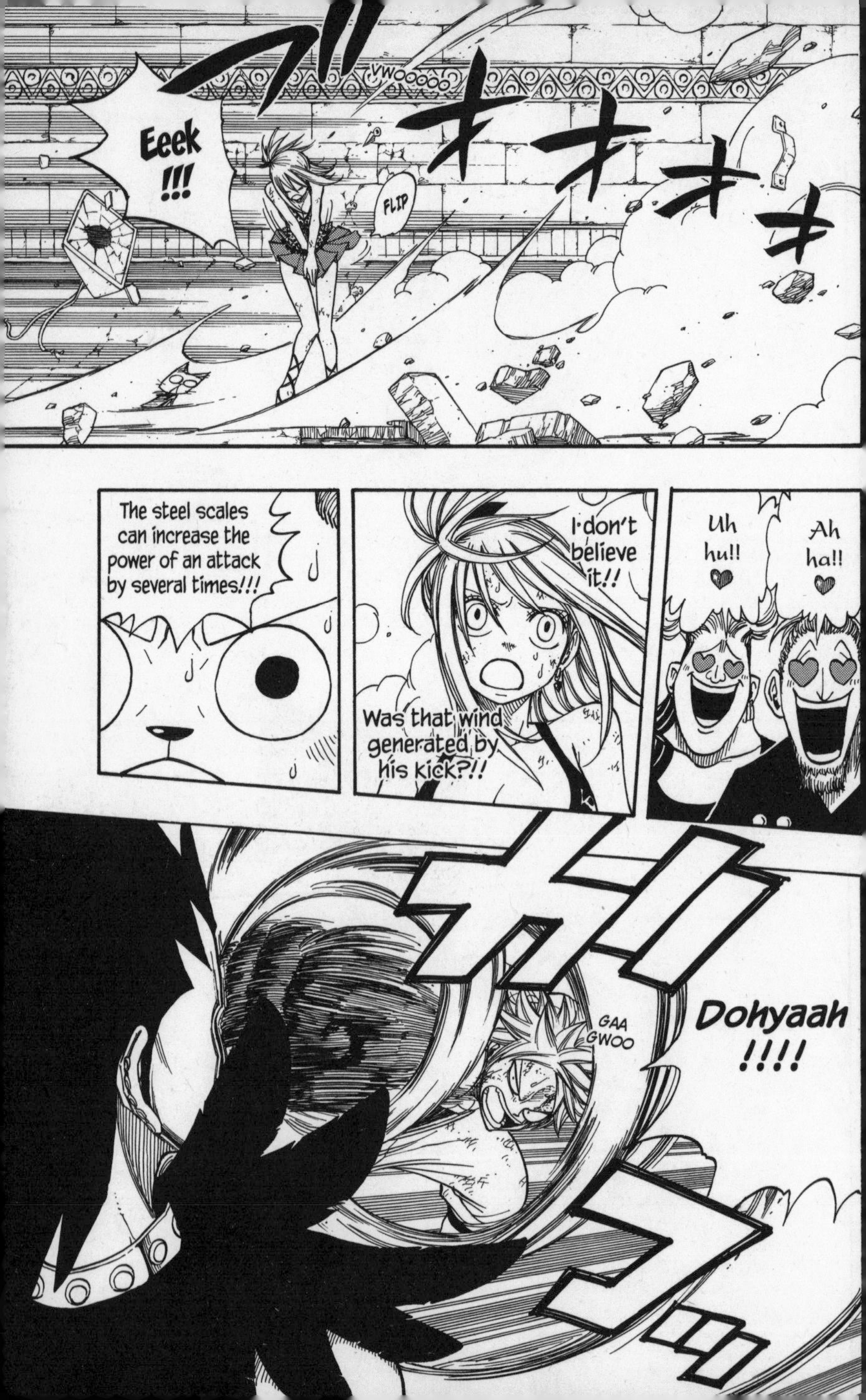
VWOOOOOO
FLIP
Eeek !!!
Uh hu!!
Ah ha!!
I don't believe it!!
Was that wind generated by his kick?!!
The steel scales can increase the power of an attack by several times!!!
Dohyaah !!!!
GAA GWOO

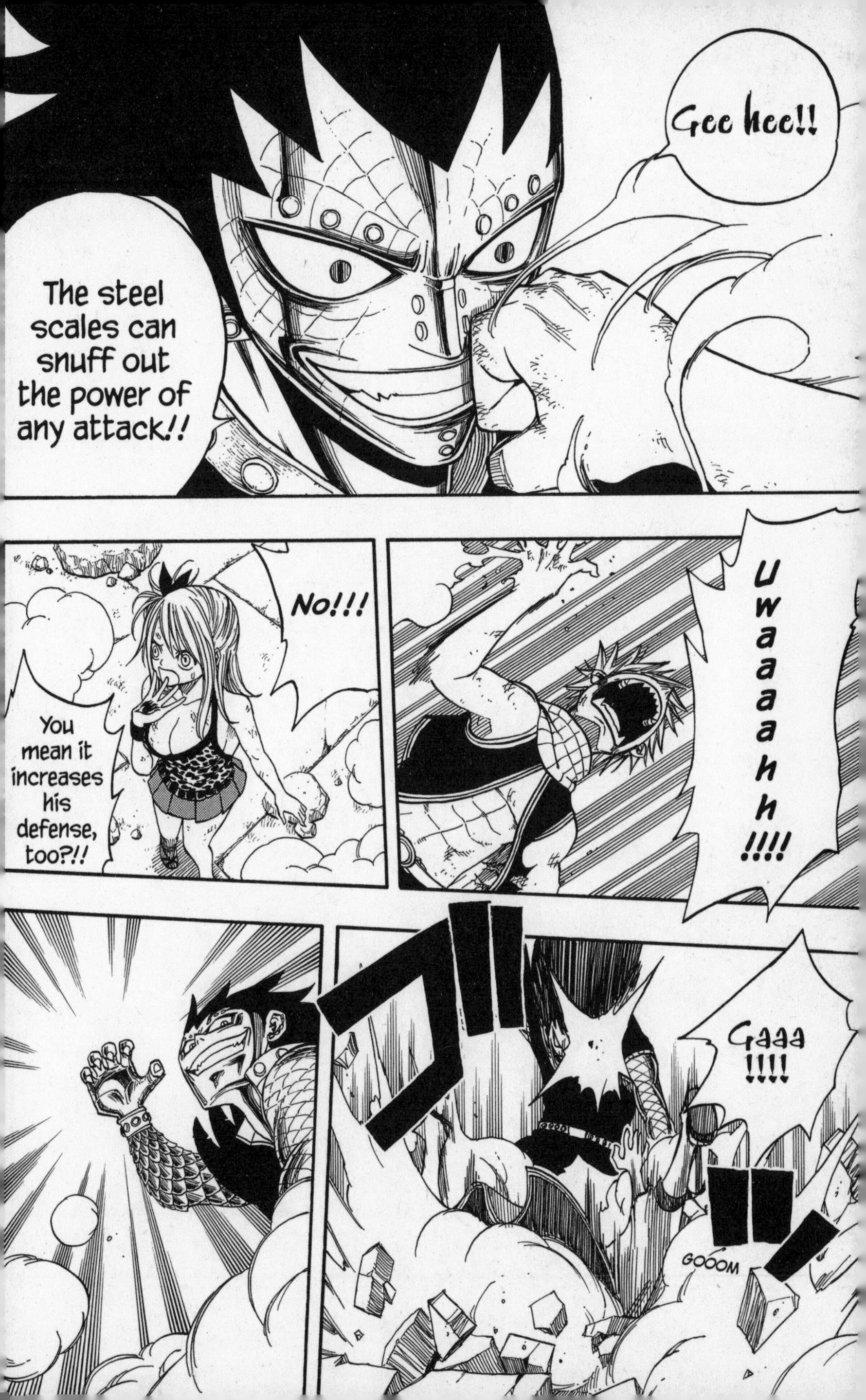
Gee hee!!
The steel scales can snuff out the power of any attack!!
Uwaaaaahh!!!!
No!!!
You mean it increases his defense, too?!!
Gaaa!!!!
GOOOM

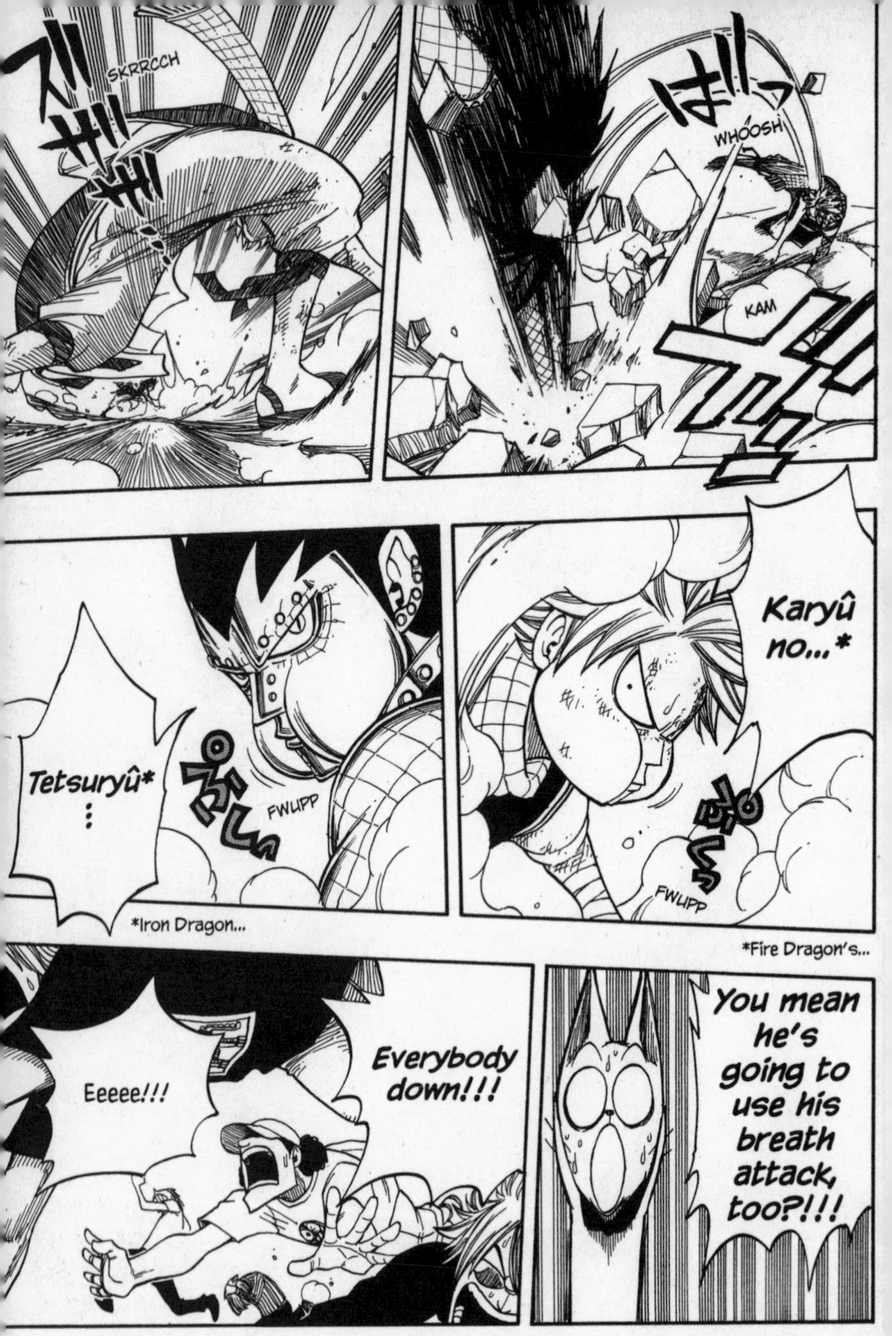
WHOOSH
KAM
SKRRCCH
Karyû no...*
FWUPP
*Fire Dragon's...
Tetsuryû* ...
FWUPP
*Iron Dragon...
You mean he's going to use his breath attack, too?!!!
Everybody down!!!
Eeeee!!!

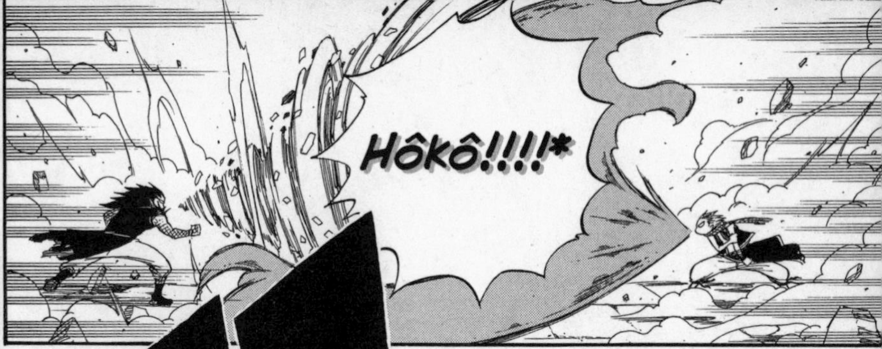
Hôkô!!!!*

*Roar!!!!

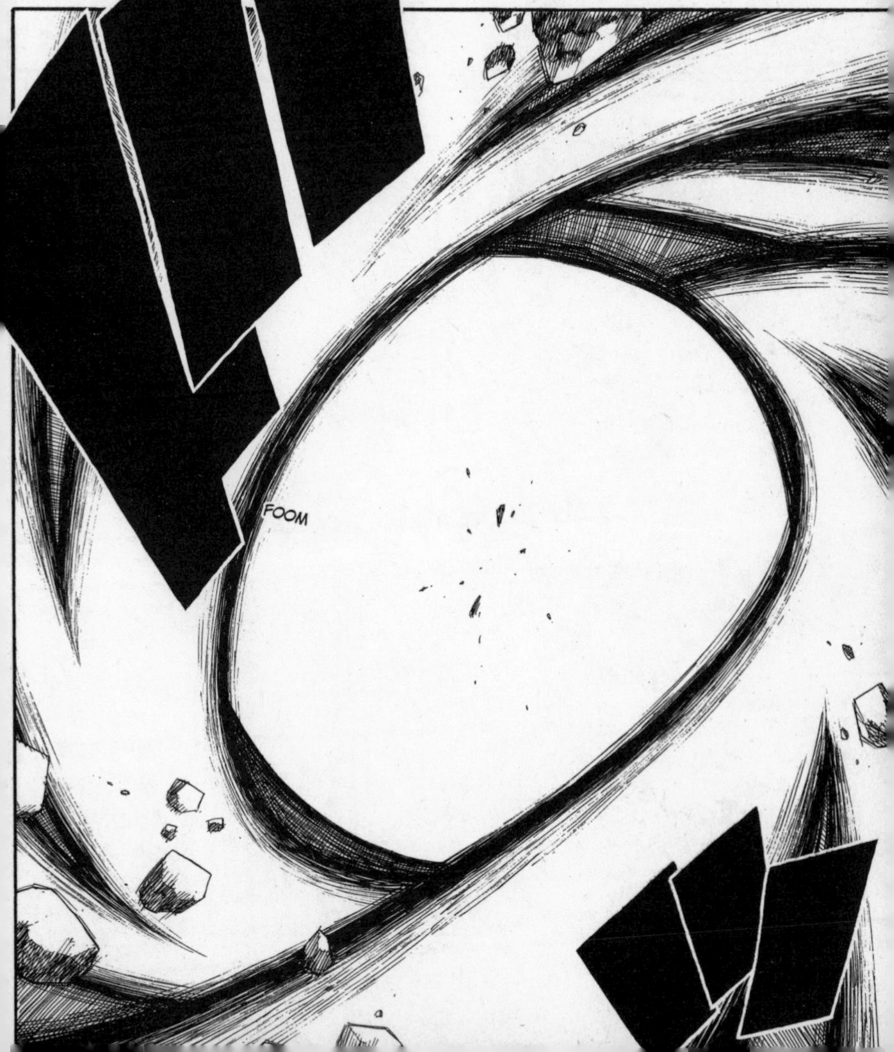
FOOM

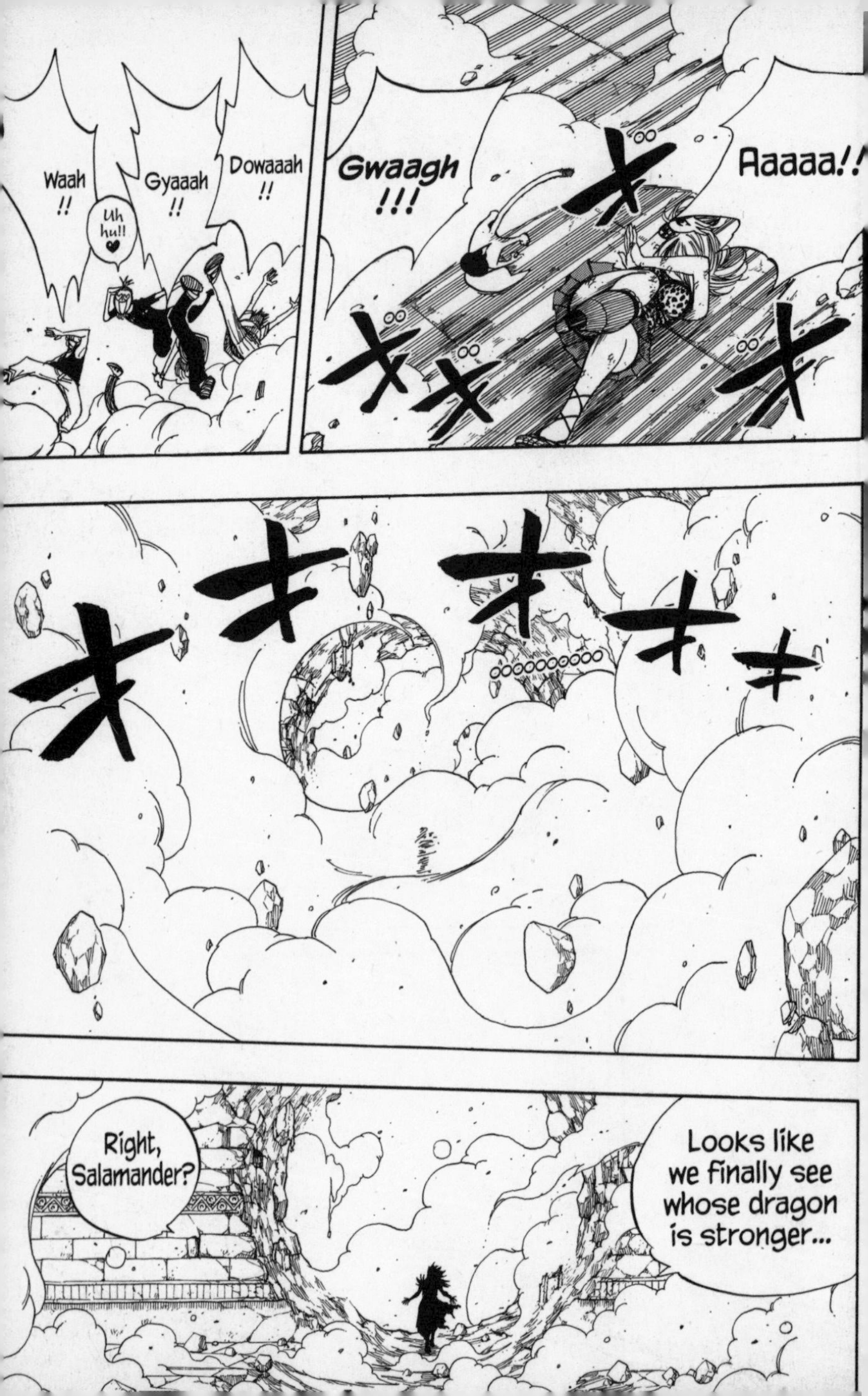
Aaaaa!!
Gwaagh !!!
Dowaaah !!
Gyaaah !!
Uh hu!!
Waah !!
Looks like we finally see whose dragon is stronger...
Right, Salamander?

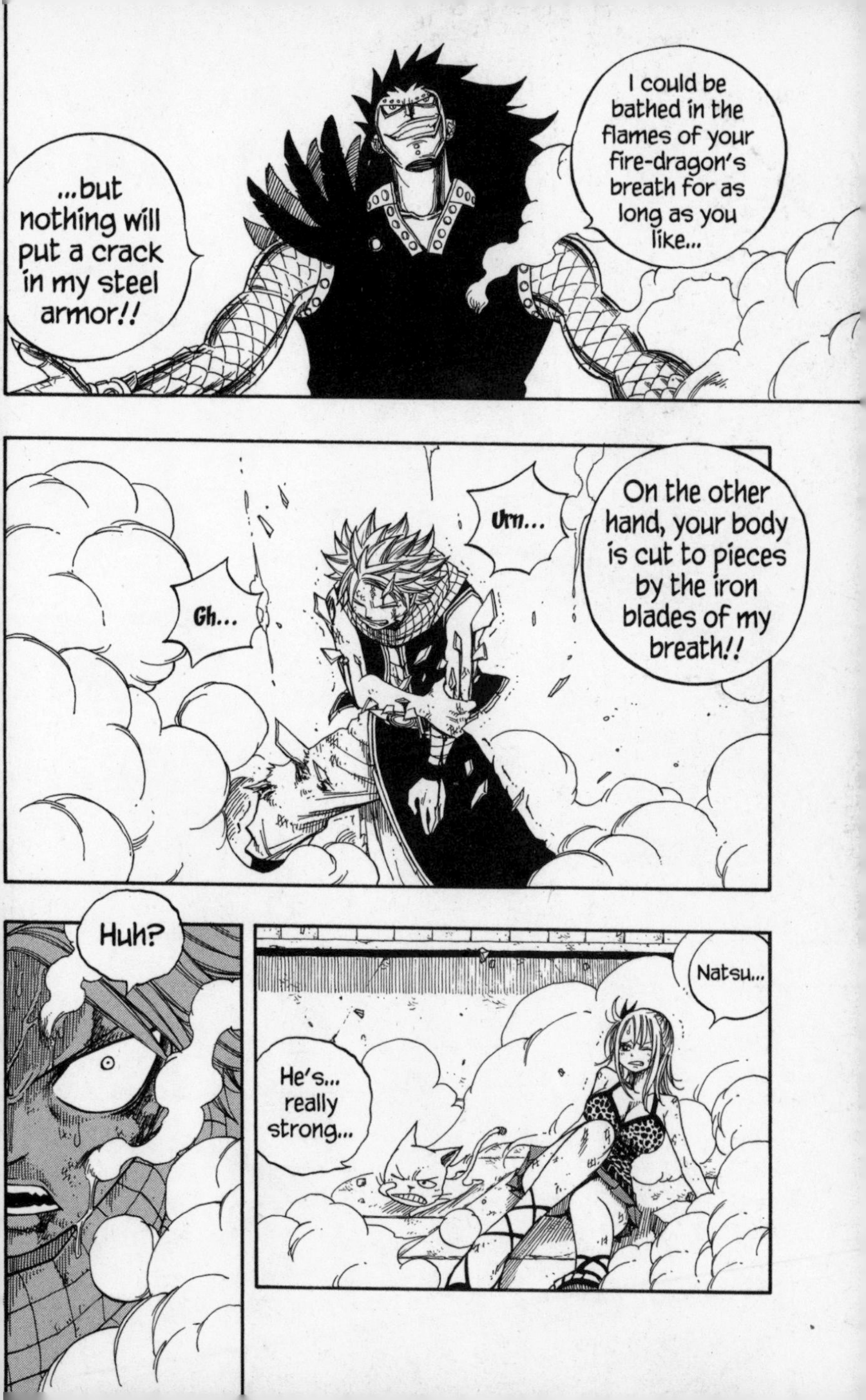
I could be bathed in the flames of your fire-dragon's breath for as long as you like...
...but nothing will put a crack in my steel armor!!
On the other hand, your body is cut to pieces by the iron blades of my breath!!
Urn...
Gh...
Natsu...
He's... really strong...
Huh?

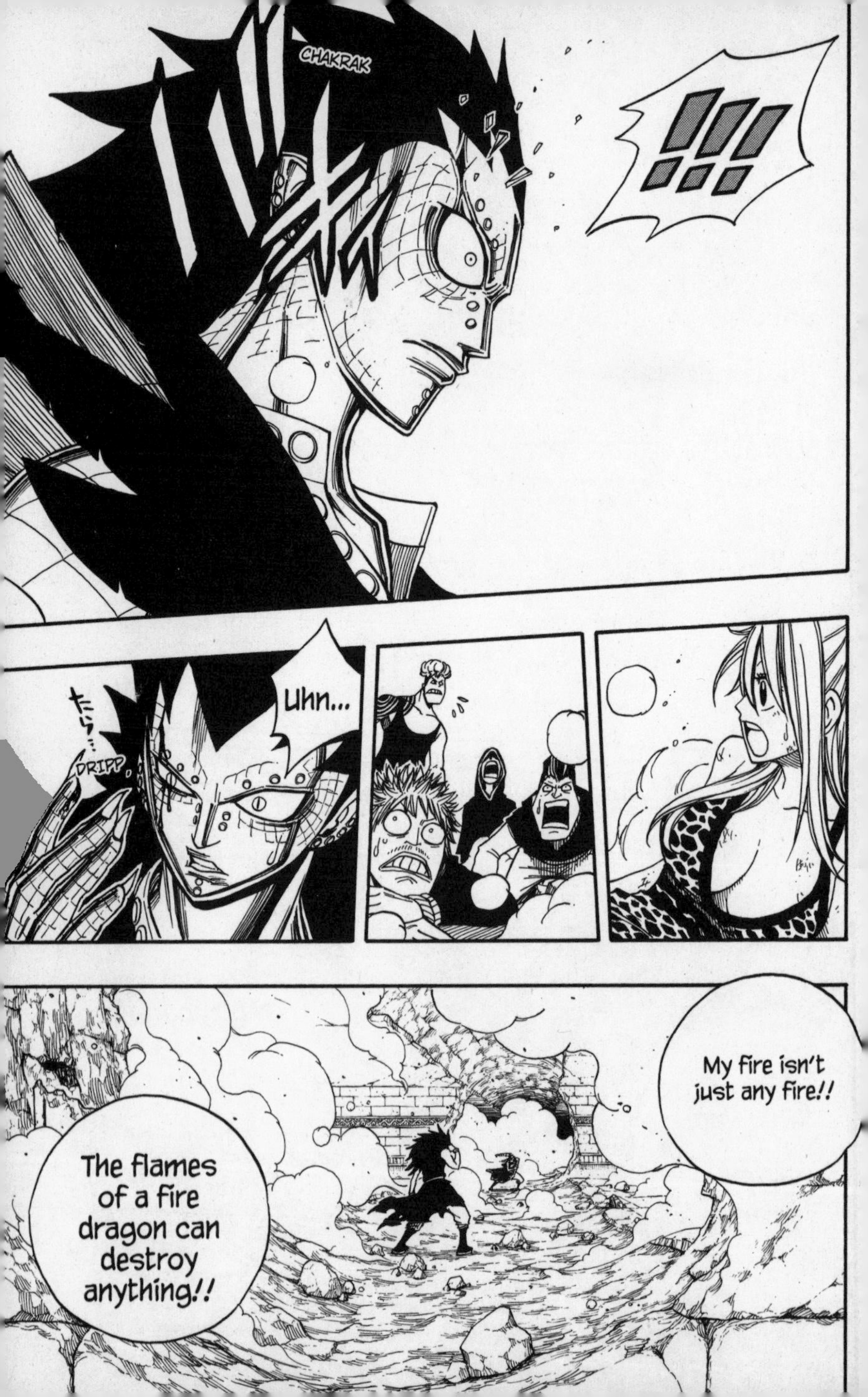
!!!
CHAKRAK
Uhn...
DRIPP
My fire isn't just any fire!!
The flames of a fire dragon can destroy anything!!

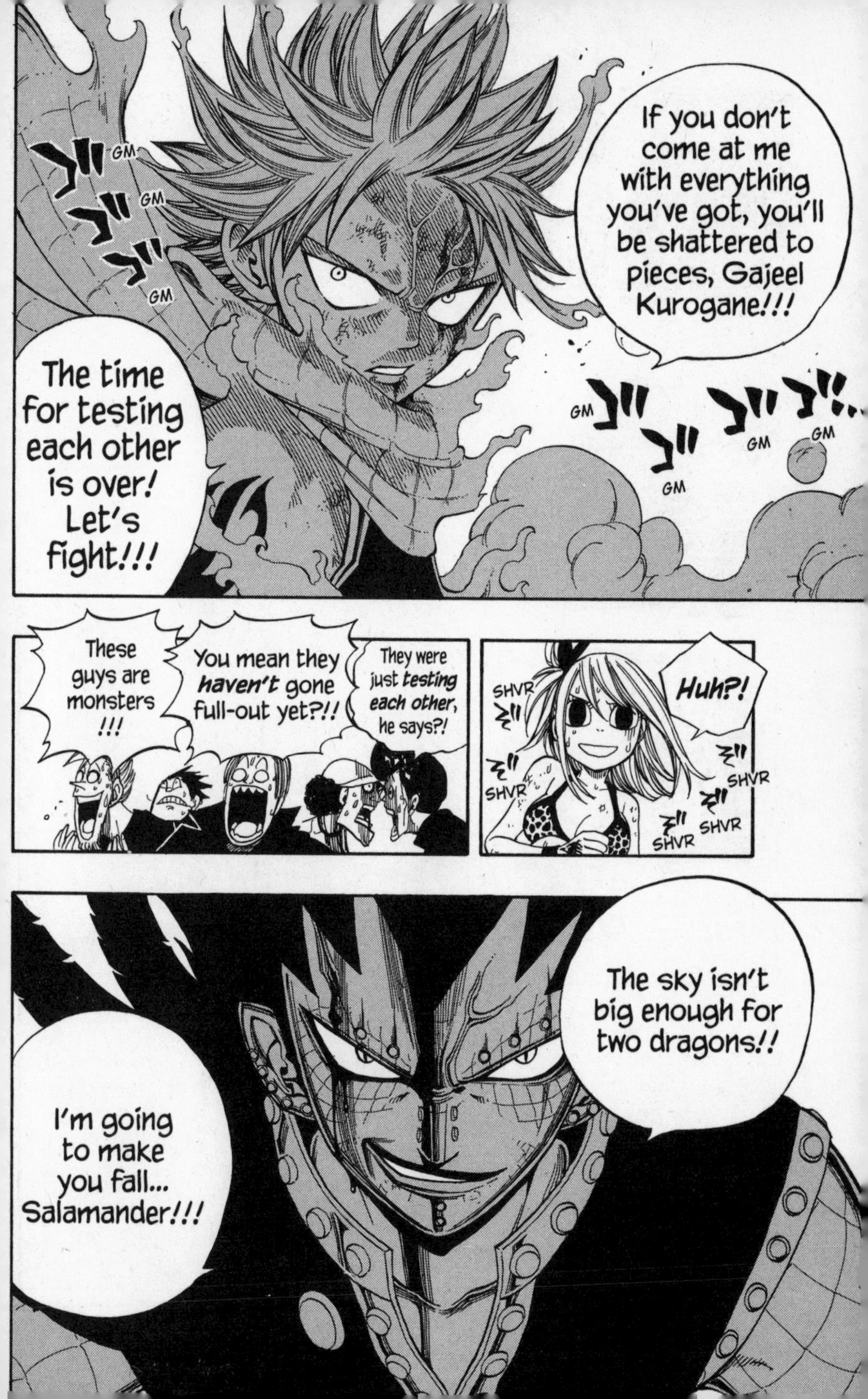

If you don't come at me with everything you've got, you'll be shattered to pieces, Gajeel Kurogane!!!
GM
GM
GM
GM
GM
GM
GM
The time for testing each other is over! Let's fight!!!
Huh?!
SHVR
SHVR
SHVR
SHVR
SHVR
They were just testing each other, he says?!
You mean they haven't gone full-out yet?!!
These guys are monsters!!!
The sky isn't big enough for two dragons!!
I'm going to make you fall... Salamander!!!

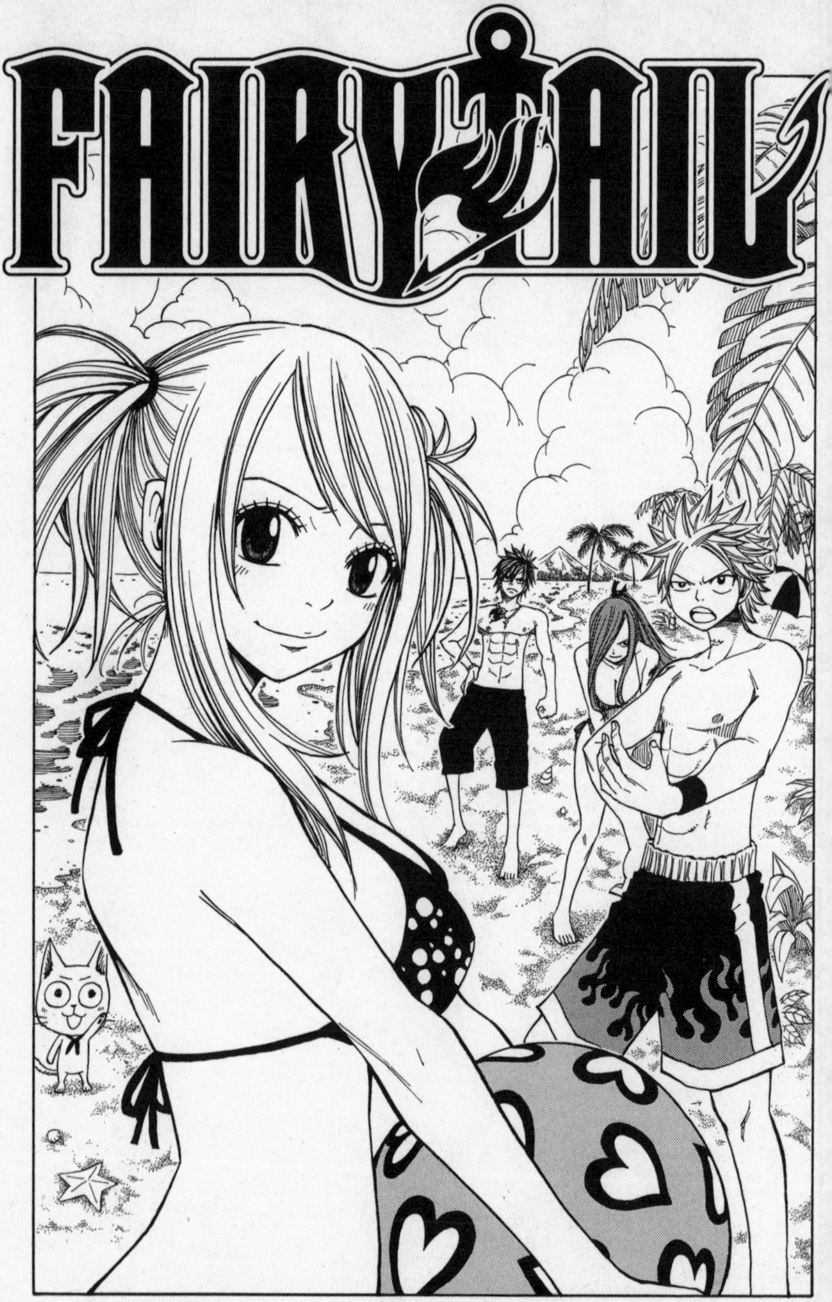
FAIRY TAIL

Chapter 62: When the Fairy Fell

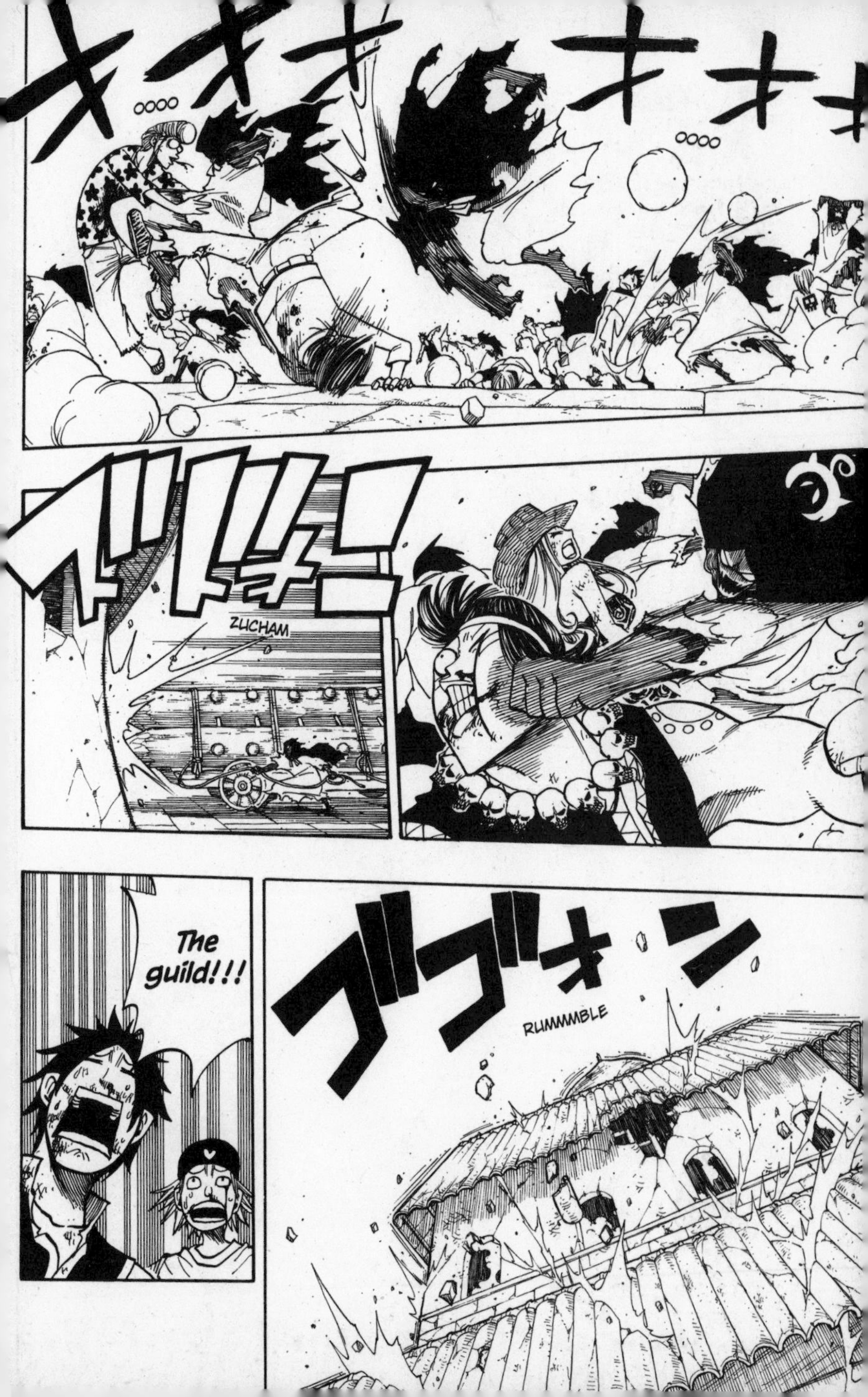
oooo
oooo
ZUCHAM
RUMMMBLE
The guild!!!

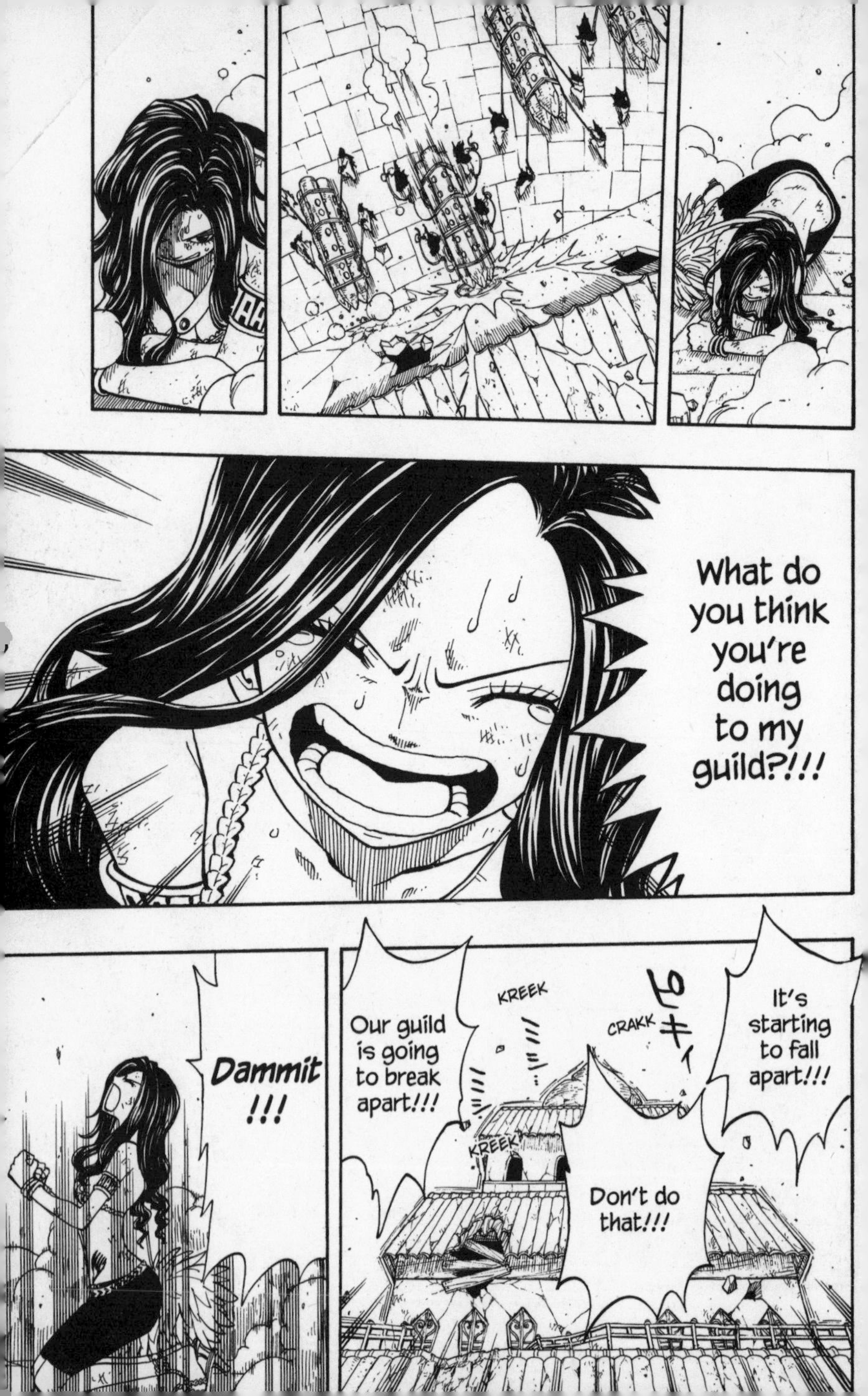
What do you think you're doing to my guild?!!!
It's starting to fall apart!!!
CRAKK
KREEK
Our guild is going to break apart!!!
KREEK
Don't do that!!!
Dammit!!!

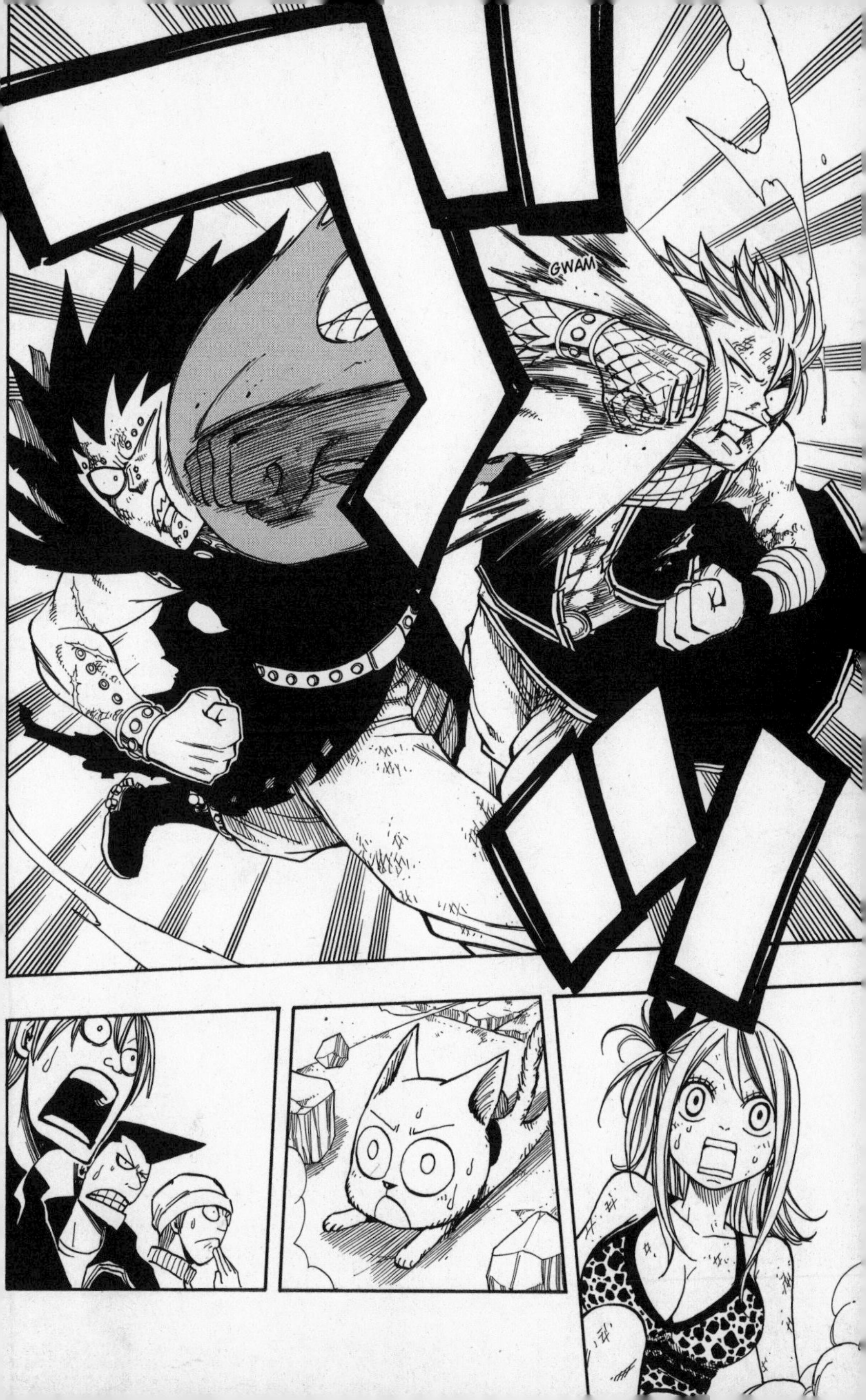
GWAM

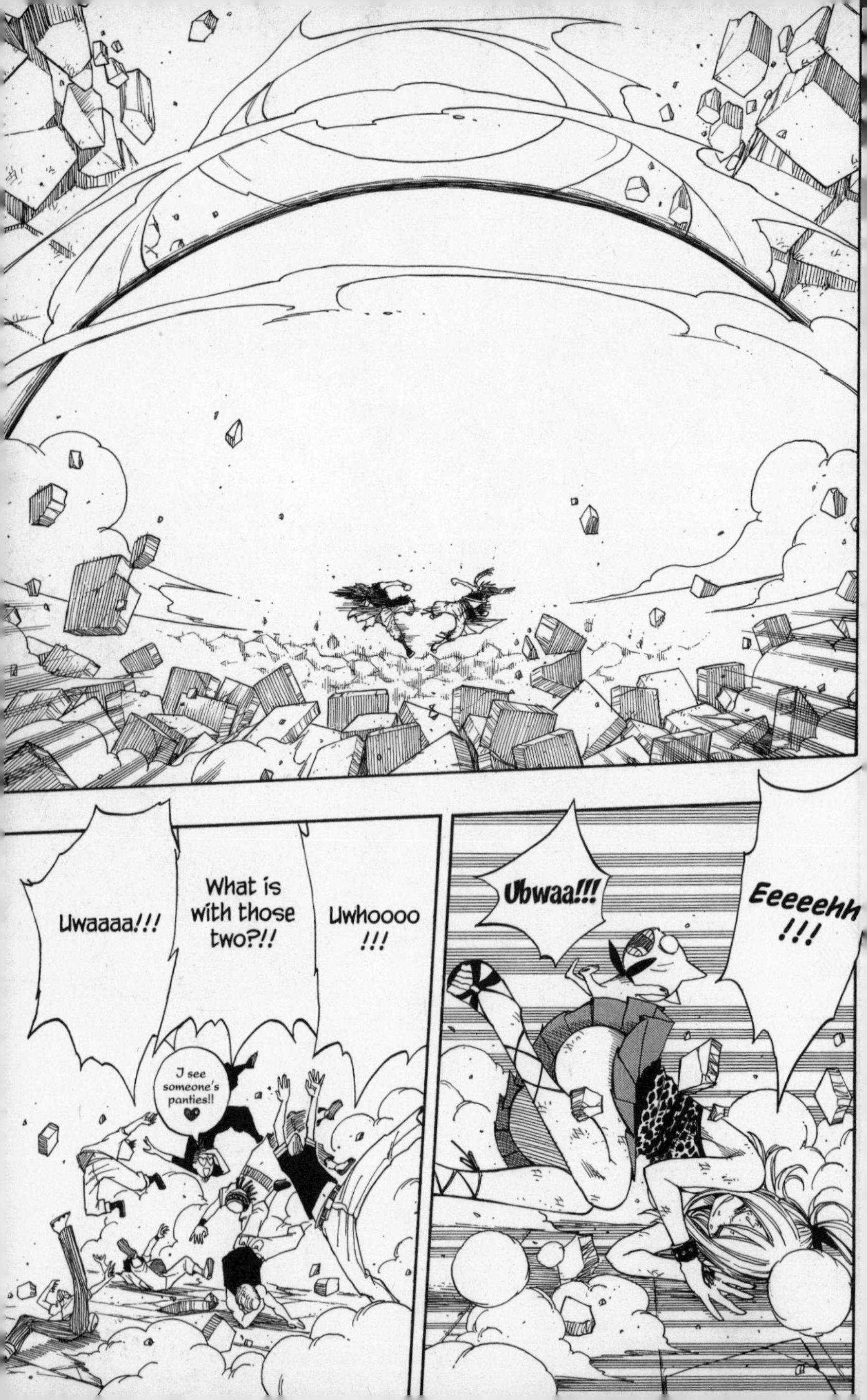
Eeeeehh !!!
Ubwaa!!!
Uwhoooo !!!
What is with those two?!!
Uwaaaa!!!
I see someone's panties!! ♥

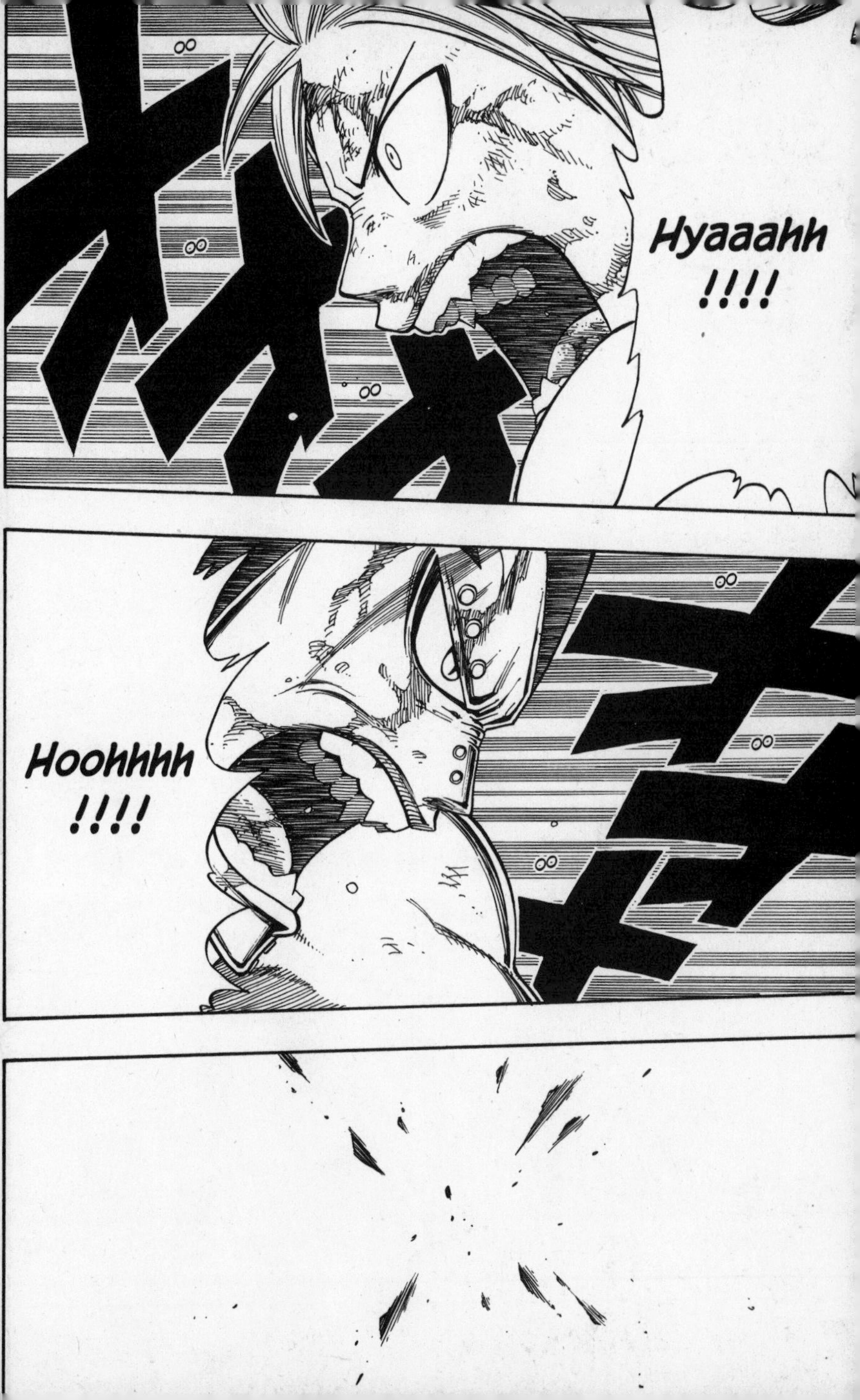
Hyaaahh !!!!
Hoohhhh !!!!

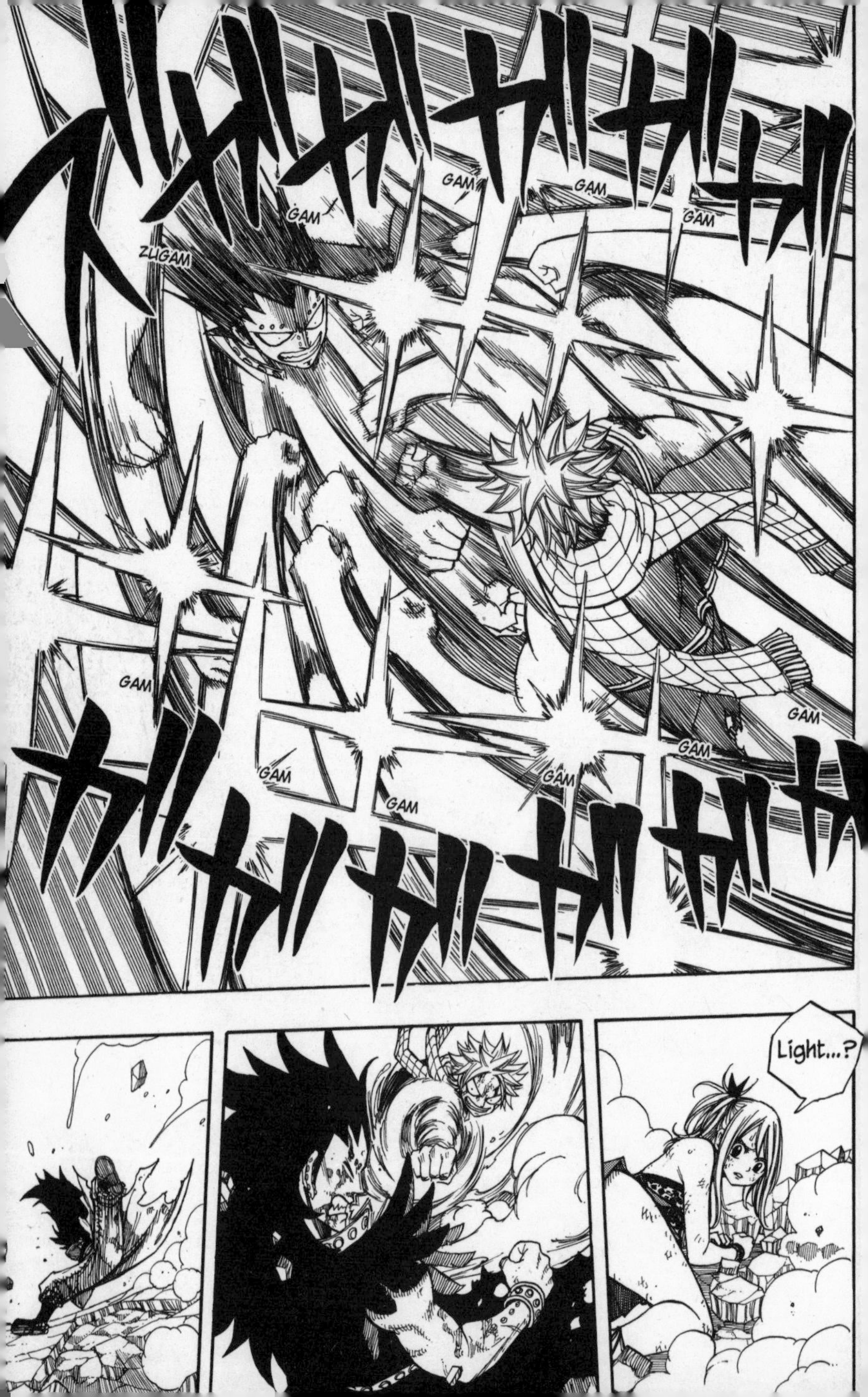
GAM
GAM
GAM
GAM
ZUGAM
GAM
GAM
GAM
GAM
GAM
GAM
Light...?

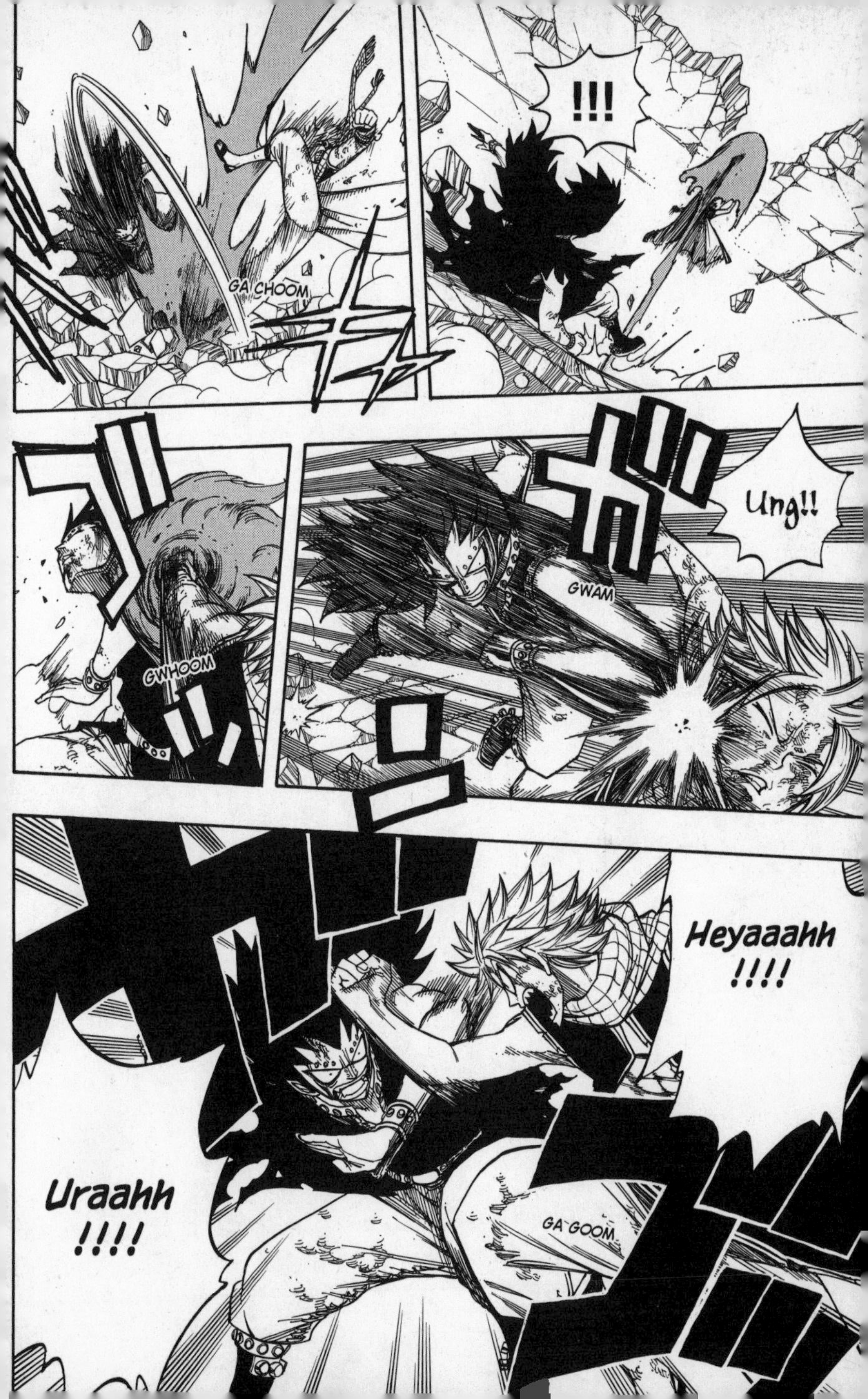
!!!
GA CHOOM
Ung!!
GWAM
GWHOOM
Heyaaahh !!!!
Uraahh !!!!
GA GOOM

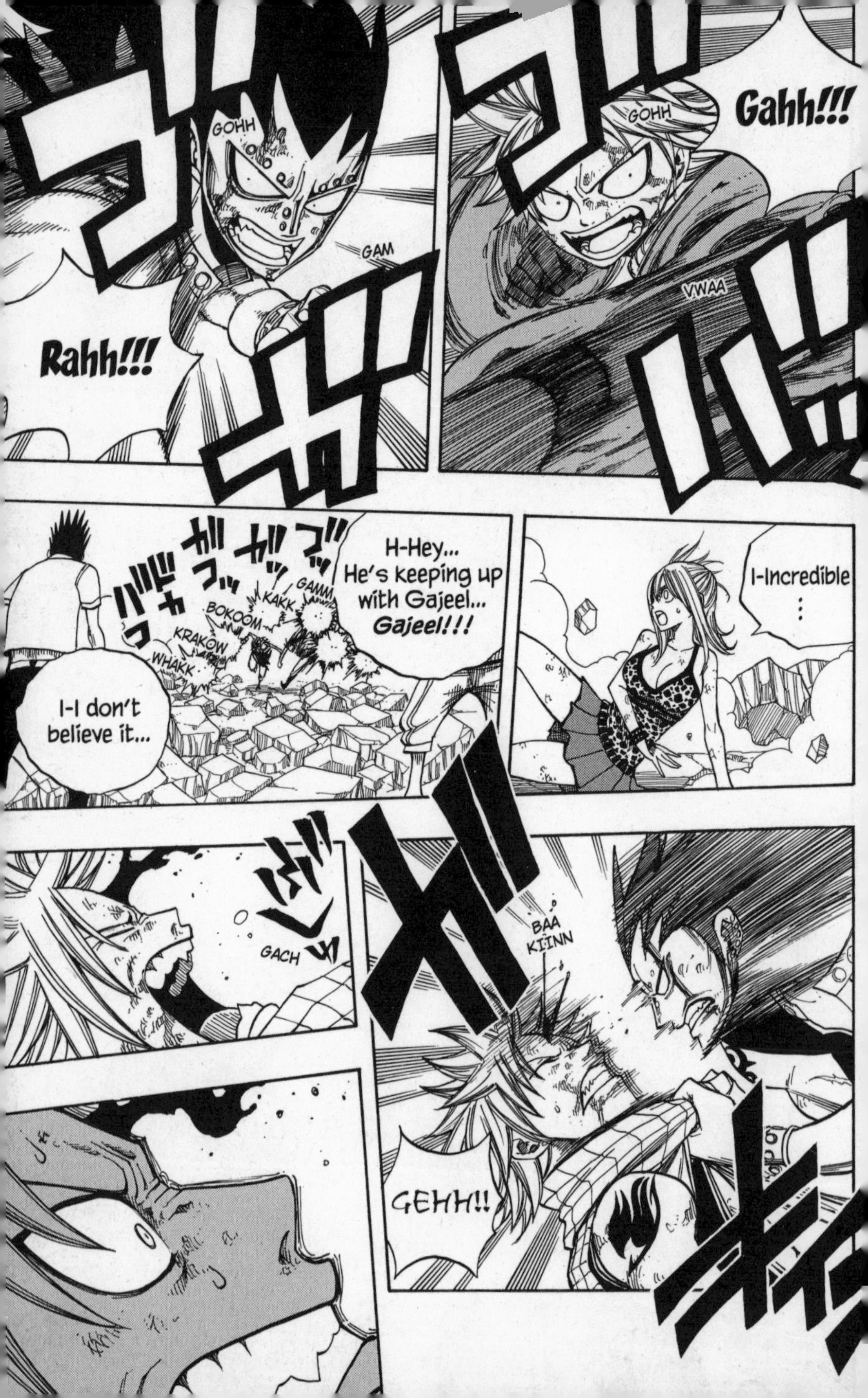
GOHH
Gahh!!!
VWAA
GOHH
GAM
Rahh!!!
I-Incredible
...
H-Hey... He's keeping up with Gajeel... *Gajeel!!!*
GAMM
KAKK
BOKOOM
KRAKOW
WHAKK
I-I don't believe it...
BAA KIINN
GEHH!!
GACH

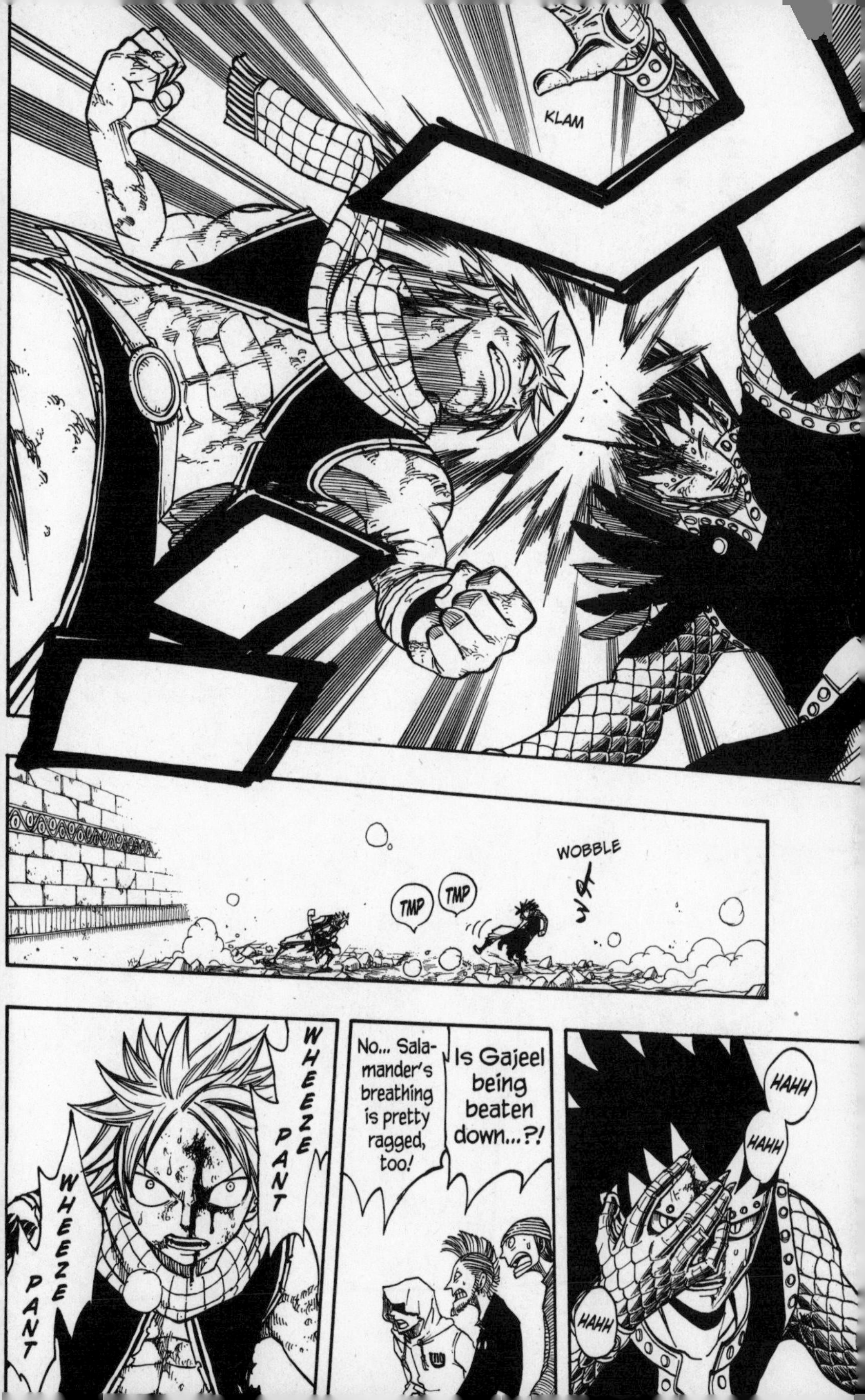
KLAM
WOBBLE
TMP
TMP
HAHH
HAHH
HAHH
Is Gajeel being beaten down...?!
No... Salamander's breathing is pretty ragged, too!
WHEEZE PANT
WHEEZE PANT

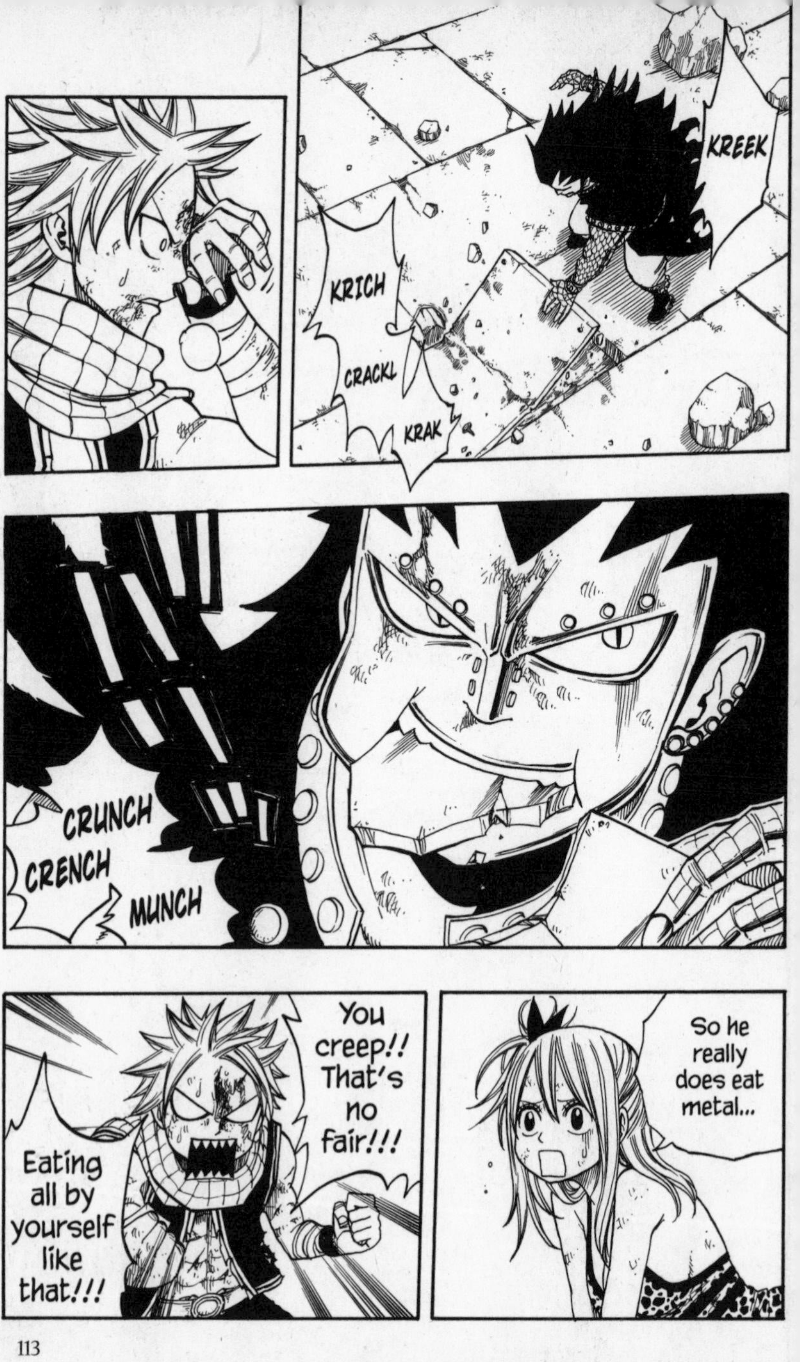
KREEK
KRICH
CRACKL
KRAK
CRUNCH
CRENCH
MUNCH
So he really does eat metal...
You creep!! That's no fair!!!
Eating all by yourself like that!!!

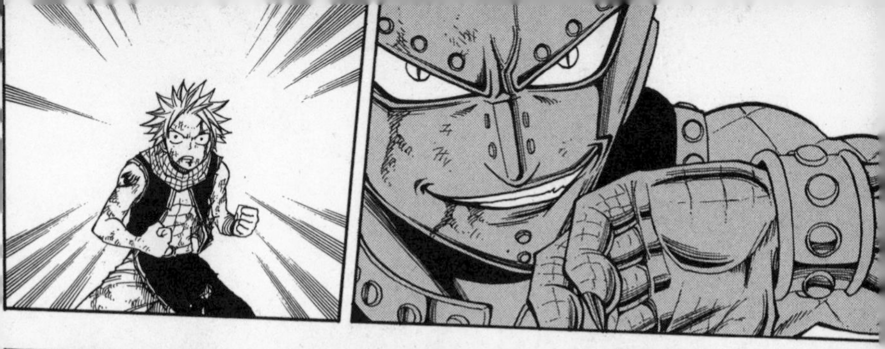

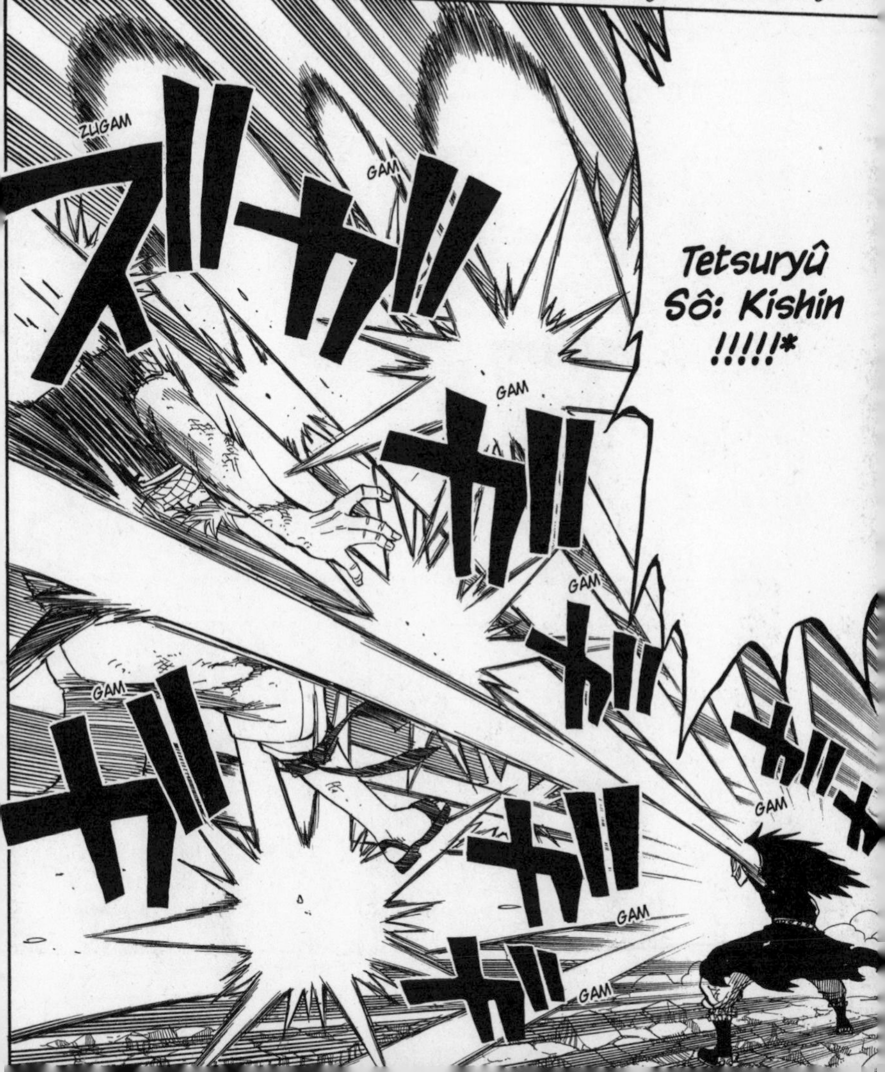
Tetsuryû
Sô: Kishin
!!!!!*
ZUGAM
GAM
GAM
GAM
GAM
GAM
GAM
GAM

*Iron Dragon Lance: Demon Logs

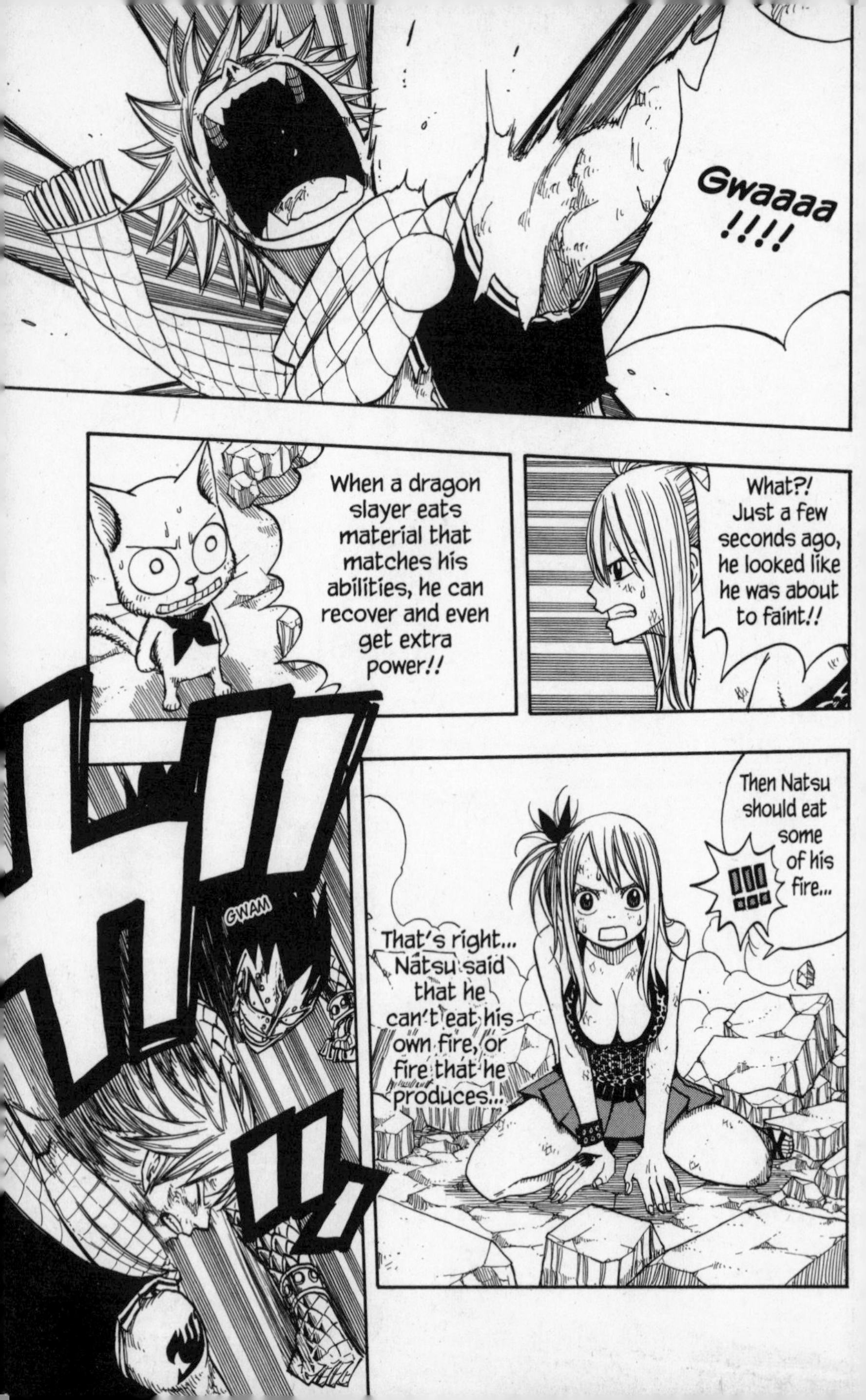
Gwaaaa!!!!
What?! Just a few seconds ago, he looked like he was about to faint!!
When a dragon slayer eats material that matches his abilities, he can recover and even get extra power!!
Then Natsu should eat some of his fire...
That's right... Natsu said that he can't eat his own fire, or fire that he produces...
GWAM

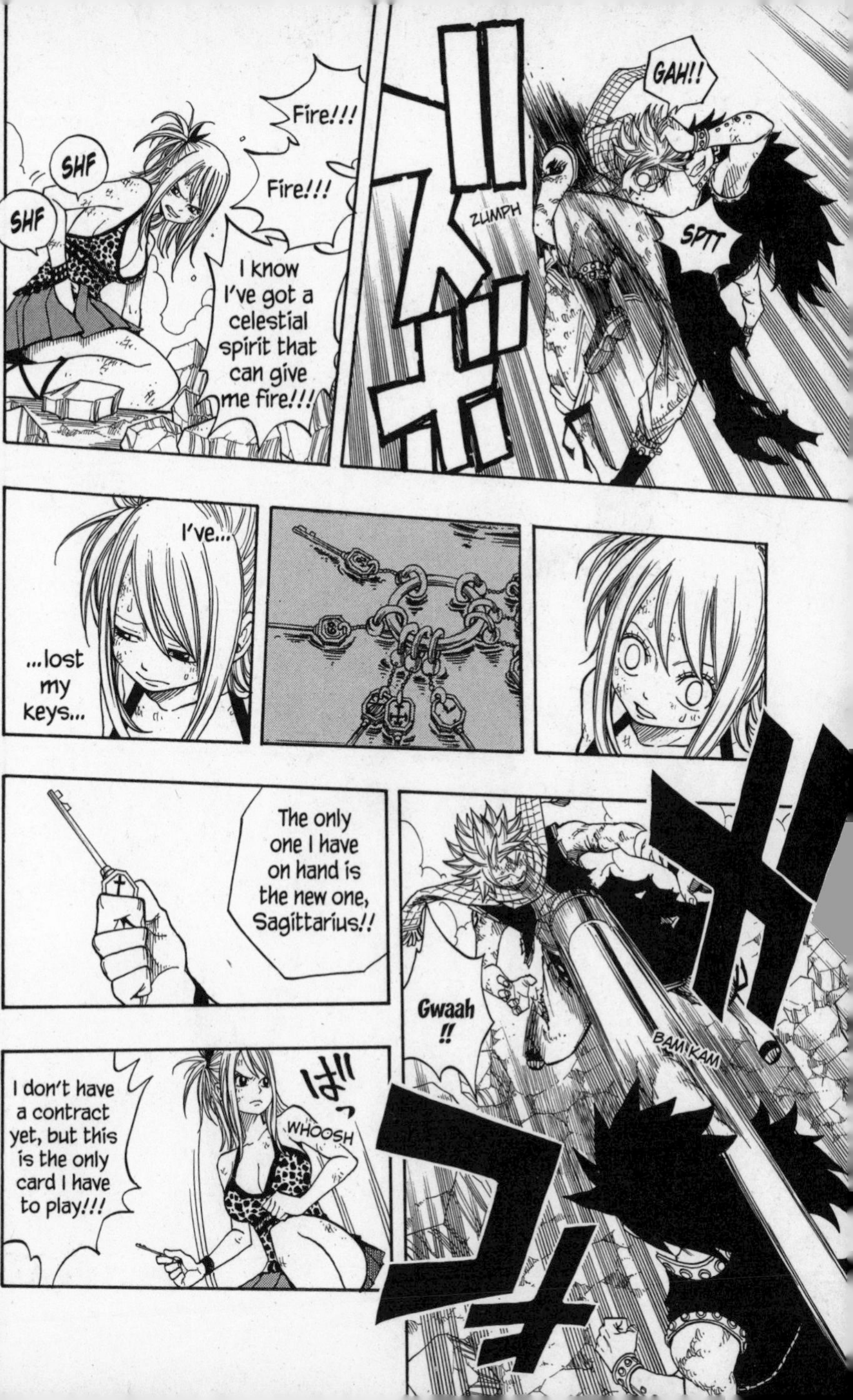
GAH!!
ZUMPH
SPTT
Fire!!!
Fire!!!
SHF
SHF
I know I've got a celestial spirit that can give me fire!!!
I've...
...lost my keys...
Gwaah!!
BAM KAM
The only one I have on hand is the new one, Sagittarius!!
ばっ
WHOOSH
I don't have a contract yet, but this is the only card I have to play!!!

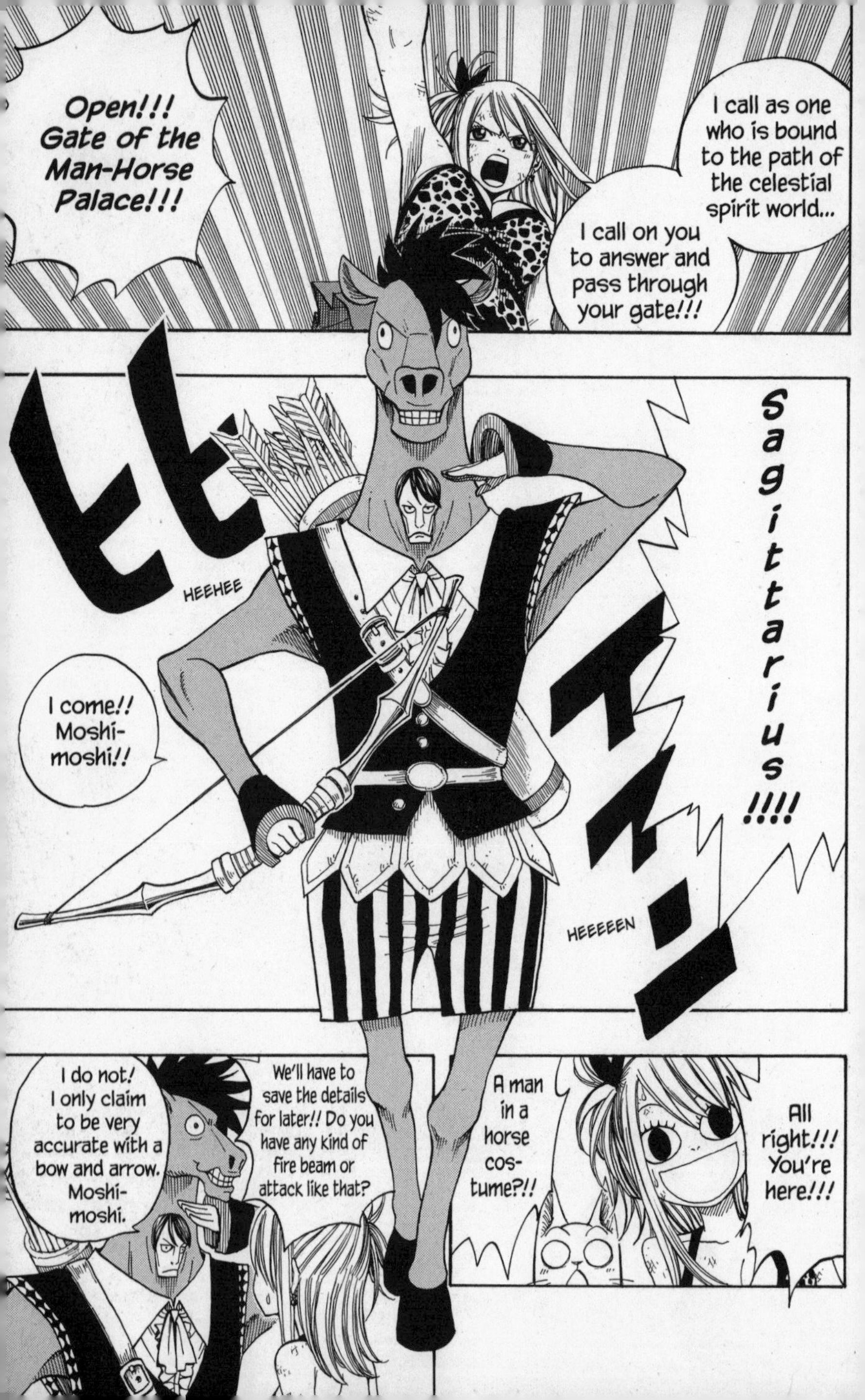
I call as one who is bound to the path of the celestial spirit world...
I call on you to answer and pass through your gate!!!
Open!!! Gate of the Man-Horse Palace!!!
Sagittarius!!!!
HEEEEEN
I come!! Moshi-moshi!!
HEEHEE
All right!!! You're here!!!
A man in a horse costume?!!
We'll have to save the details for later!! Do you have any kind of fire beam or attack like that?
I do not! I only claim to be very accurate with a bow and arrow. Moshi-moshi.

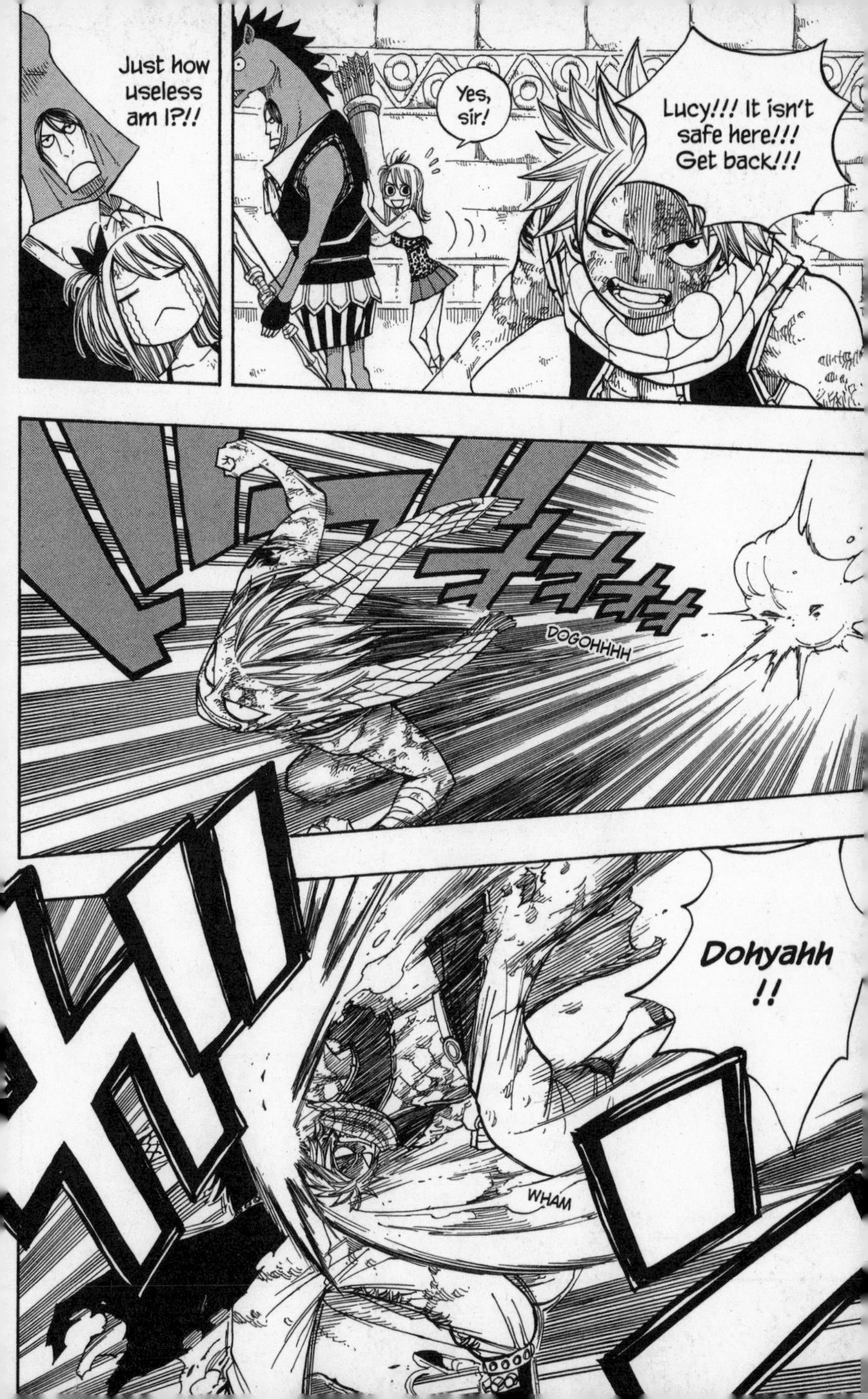
Lucy!!! It isn't safe here!!! Get back!!!
Yes, sir!
Just how useless am I?!!
DOGOHHHH
Dohyahh !!
WHAM

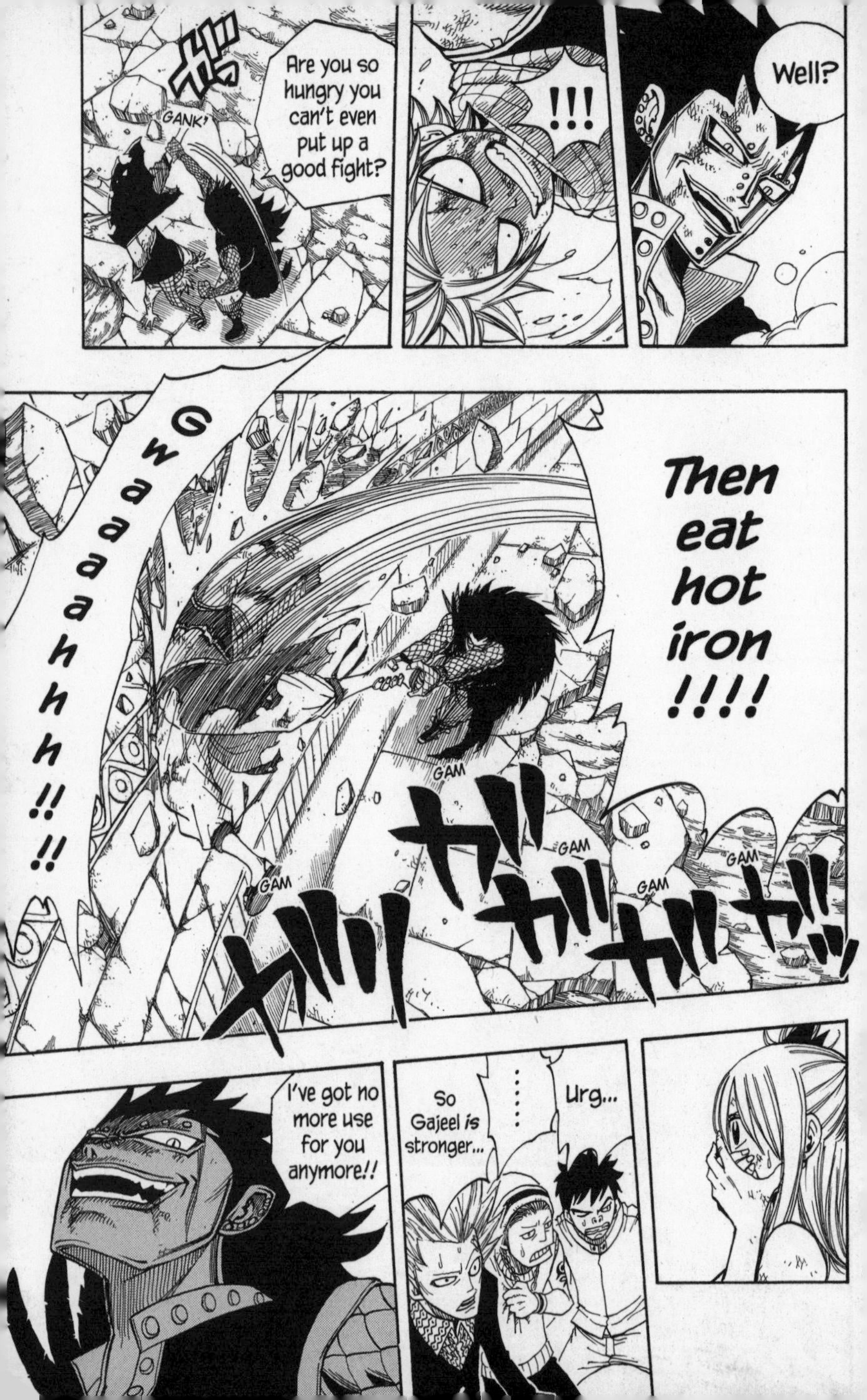

Well?
!!!
Are you so hungry you can't even put up a good fight?
GANK
Then eat hot iron!!!!
Gwaaaaahhh!!!!
GAM
GAM
GAM
GAM
GAM
Urg...
......
So Gajeel *is* stronger...
I've got no more use for you anymore!!

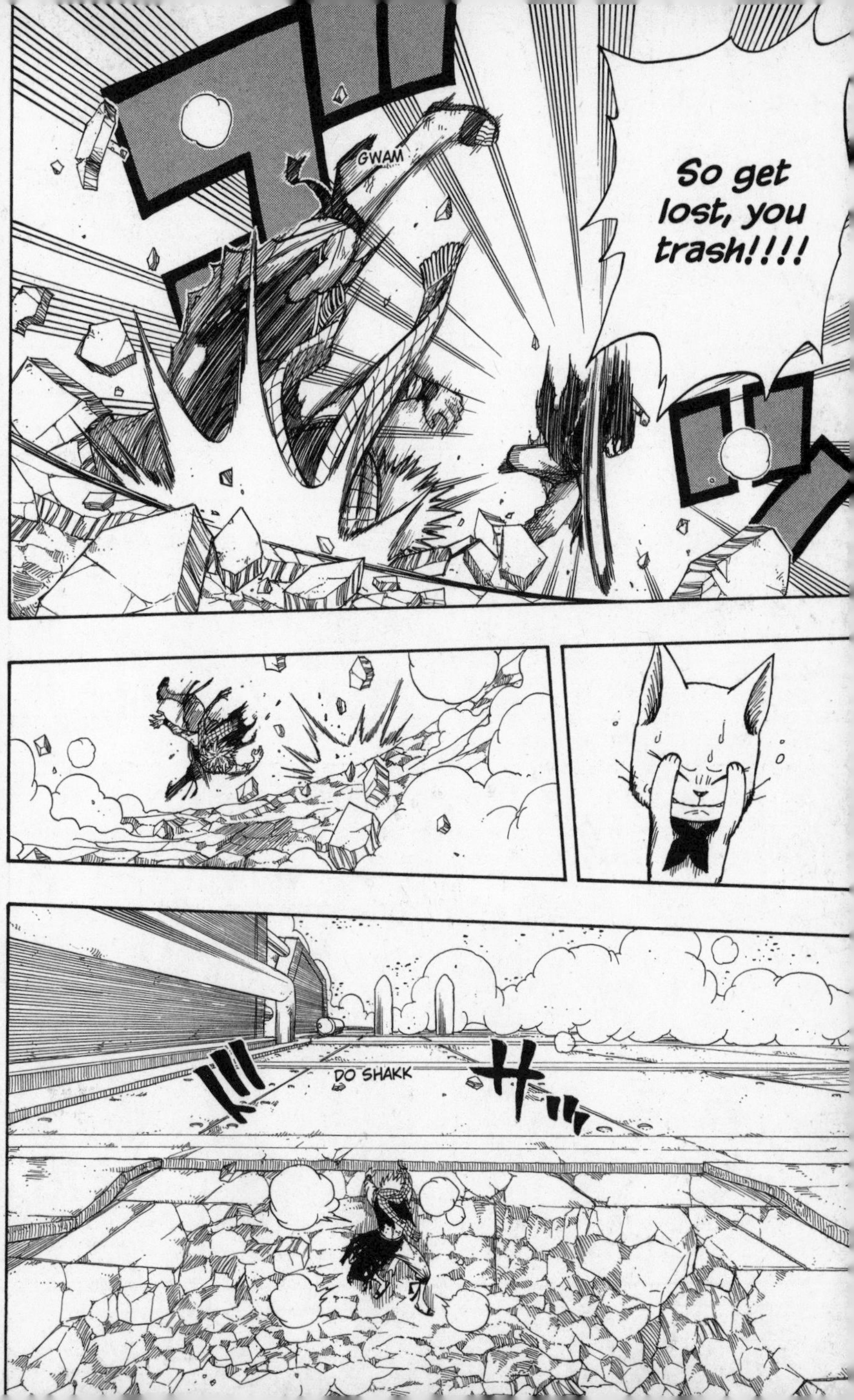
So get lost, you trash!!!!
GWAM
DO SHAKK

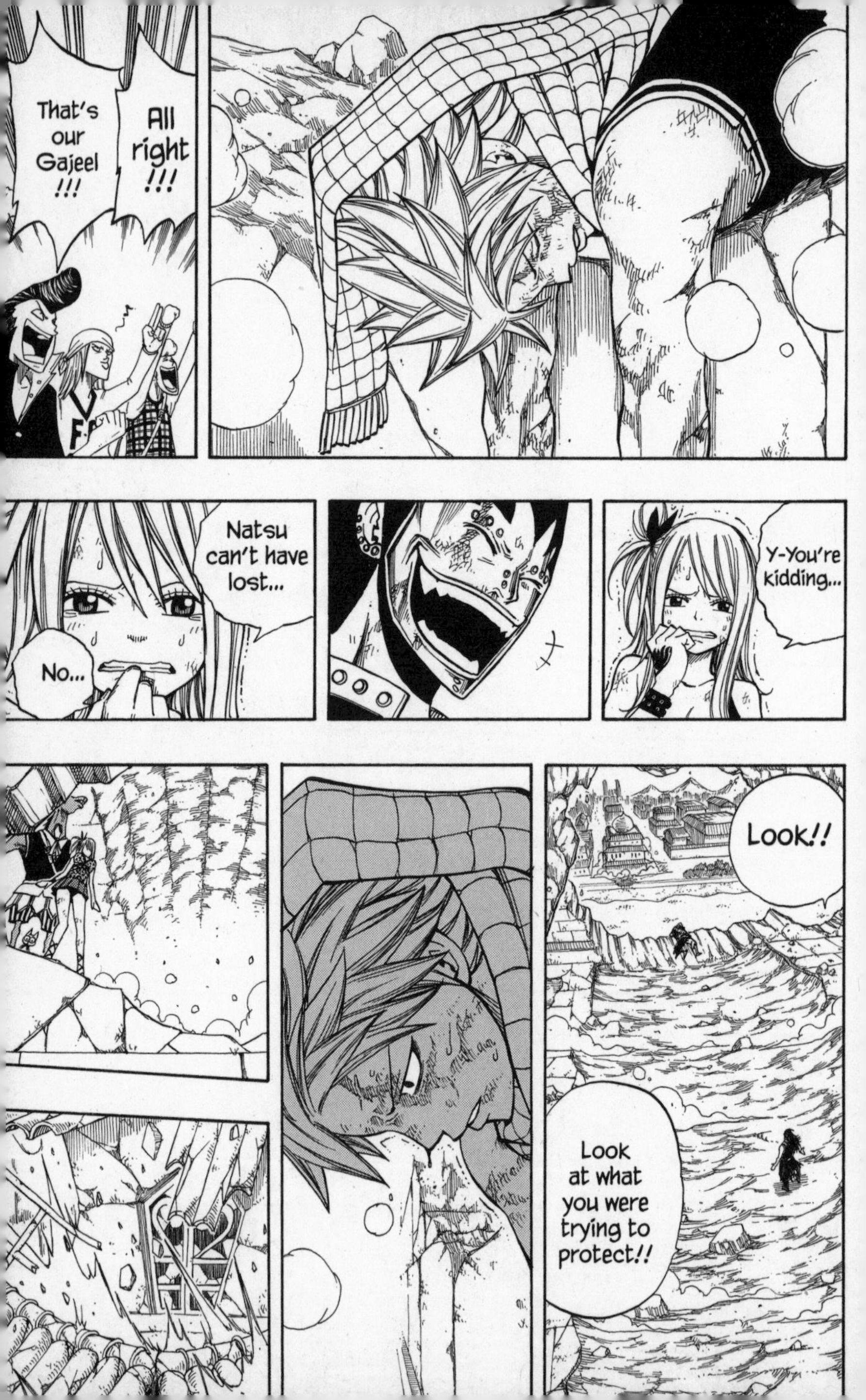
All right!!!
That's our Gajeel!!!
Y-You're kidding...
Natsu can't have lost...
No...
Look!!
Look at what you were trying to protect!!

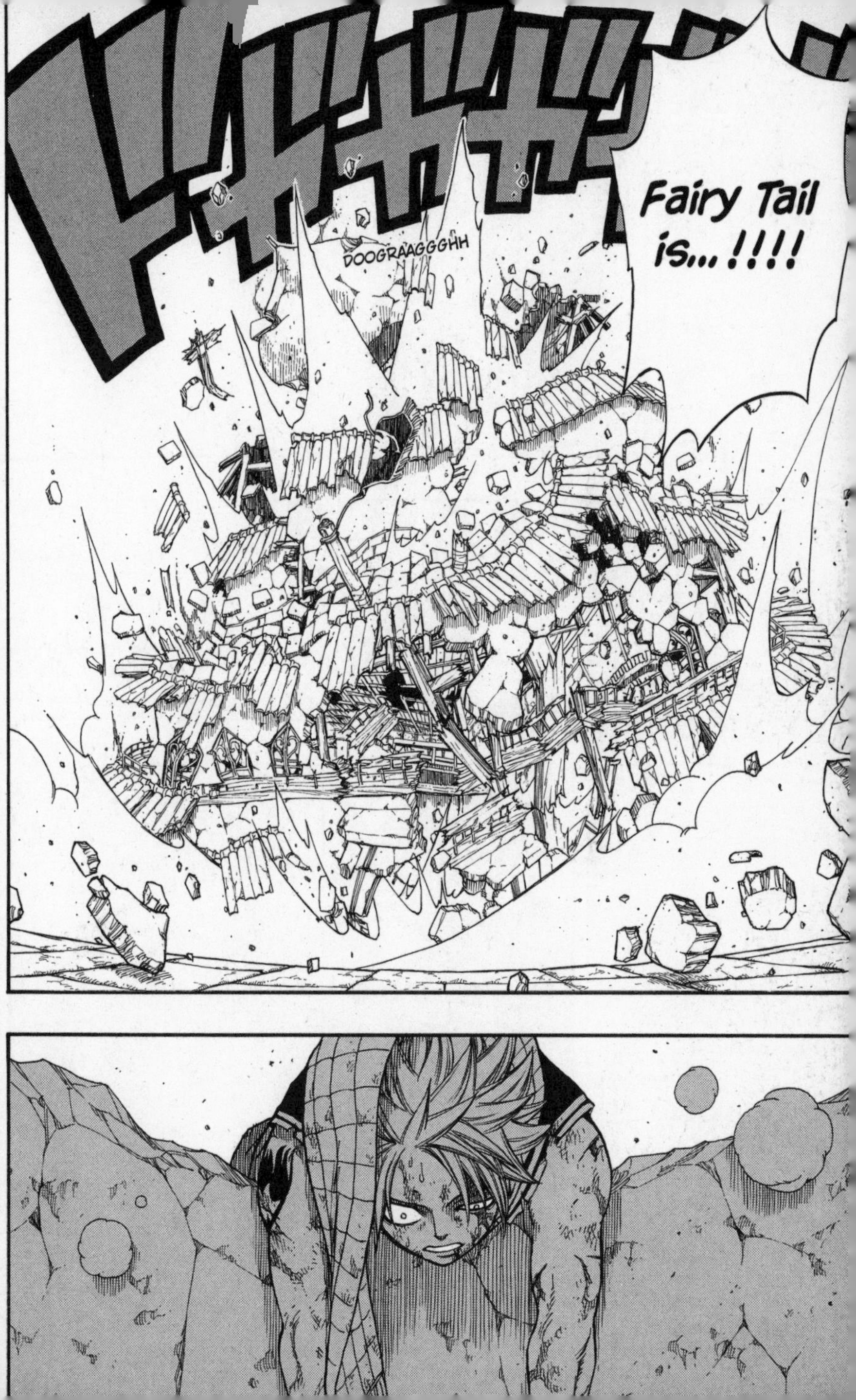
Fairy Tail is...!!!!
DOOGRAAGGGHH

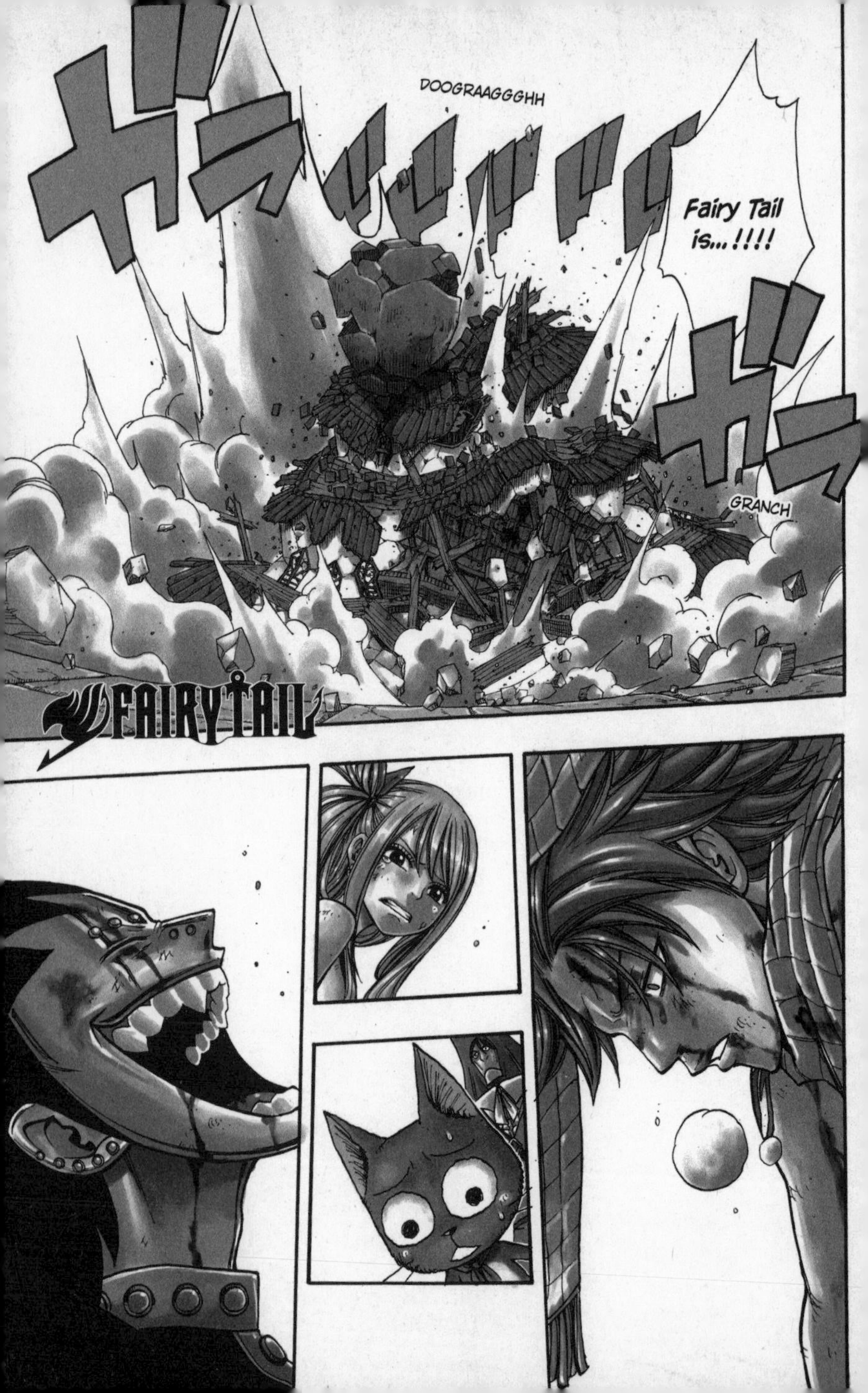
DOOGRAAGGGHH
Fairy Tail is...!!!!
GRANCH
FAIRY TAIL

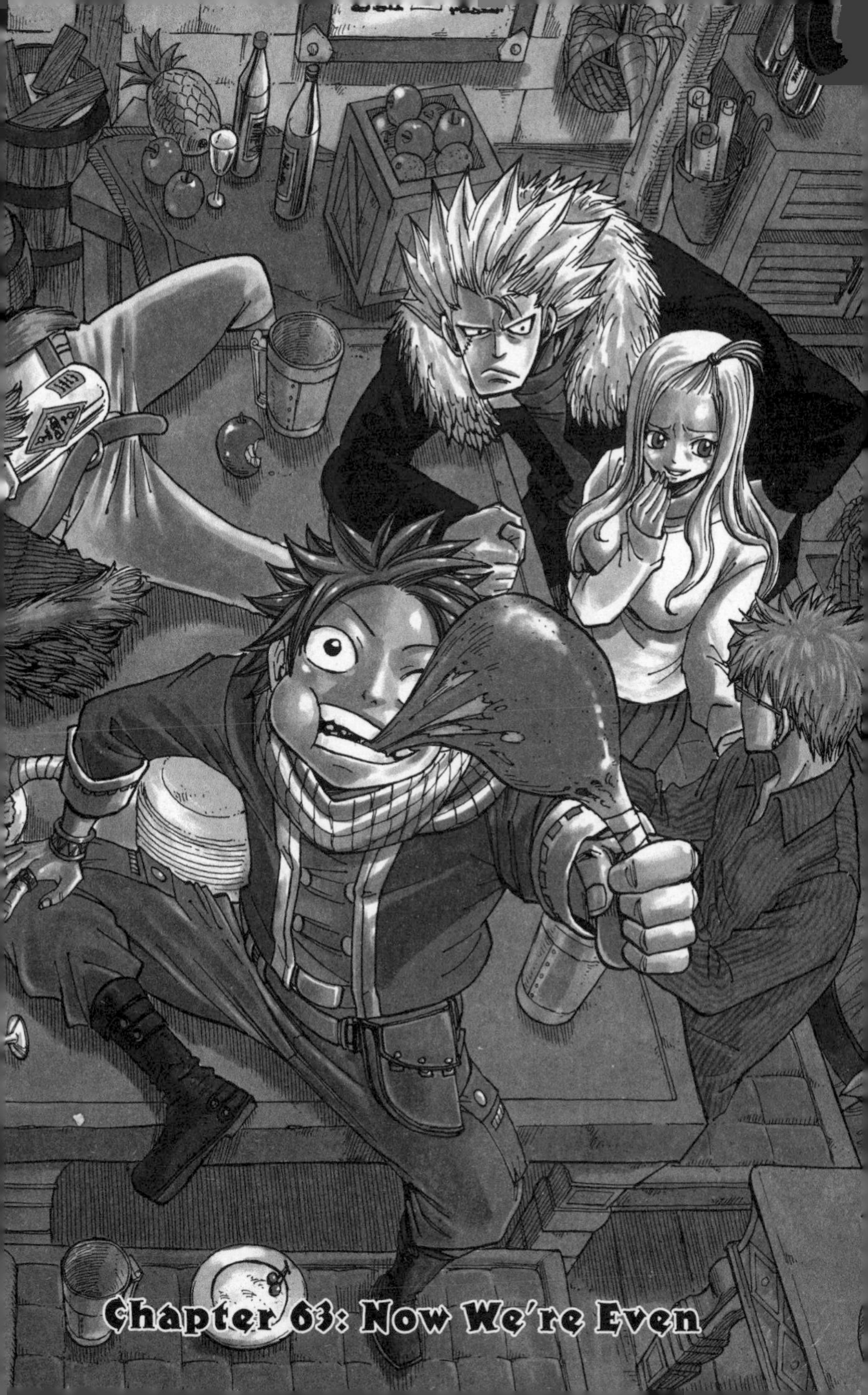

Chapter 63: Now We're Even

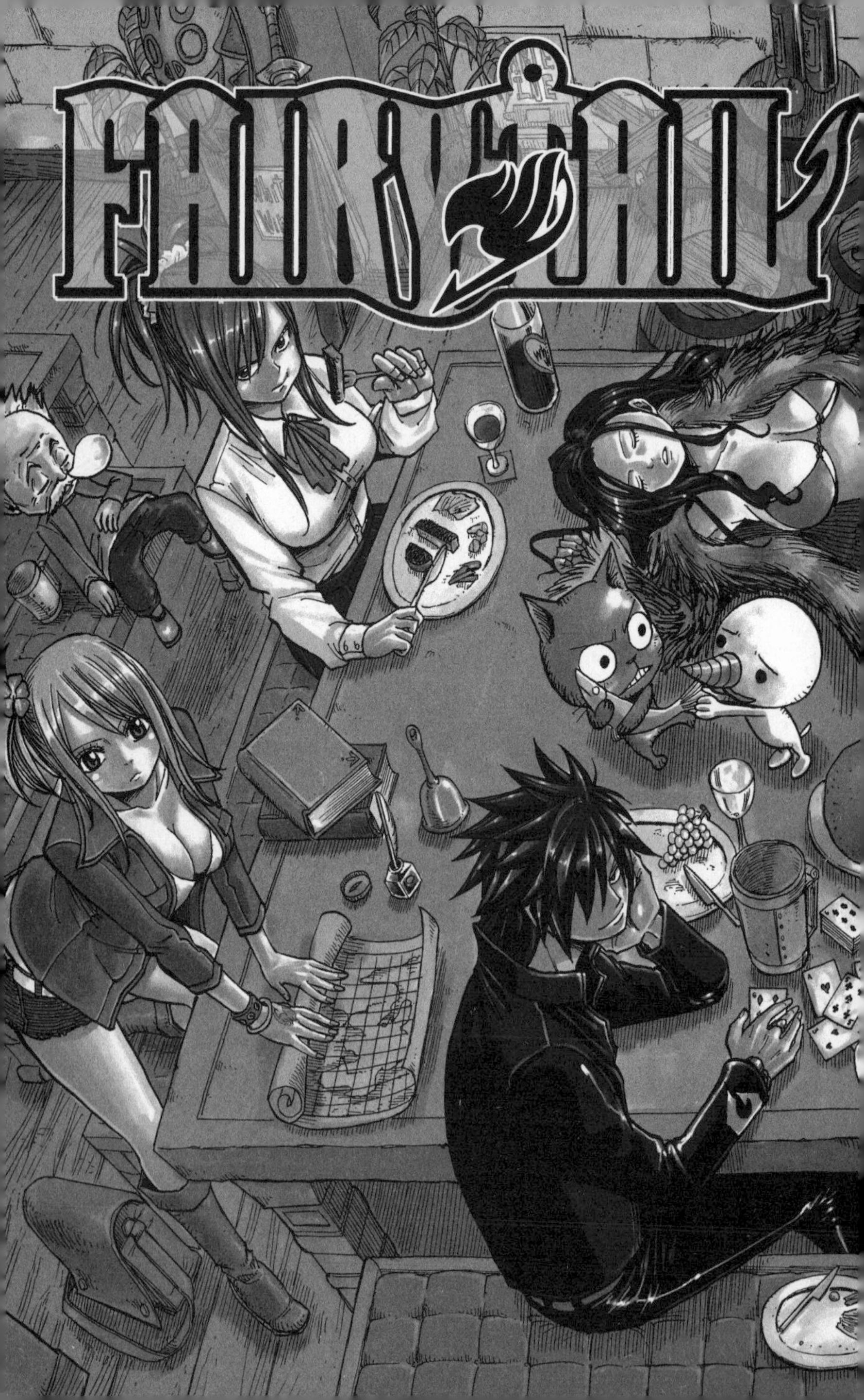
FAIRY TAIL

FAIRY TAIL

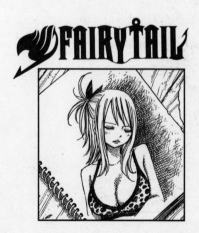

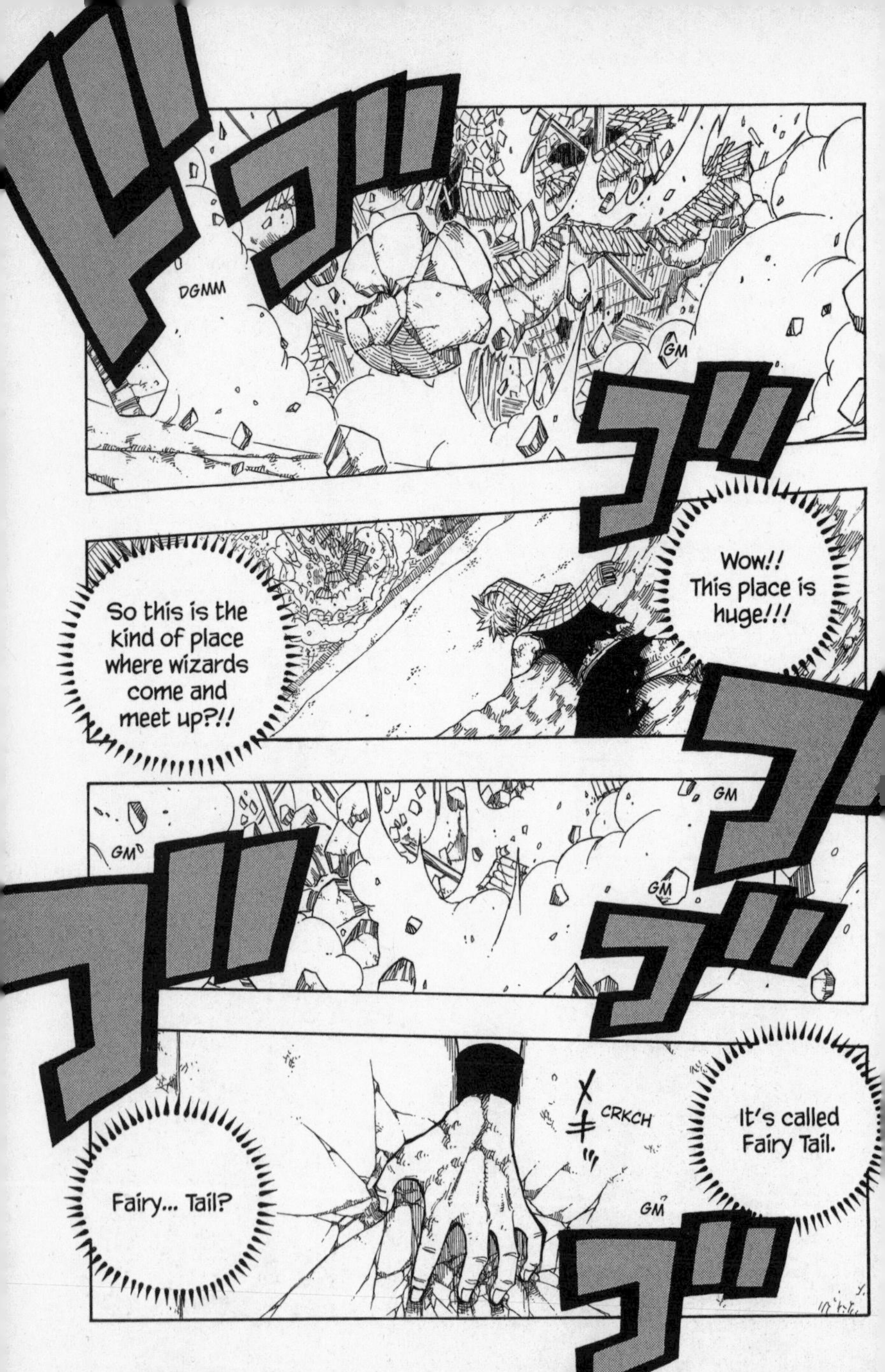
DGMM
GM
Wow!! This place is huge!!!
So this is the kind of place where wizards come and meet up?!!
GM
GM
GM
It's called Fairy Tail.
CRKCH
GM
Fairy... Tail?

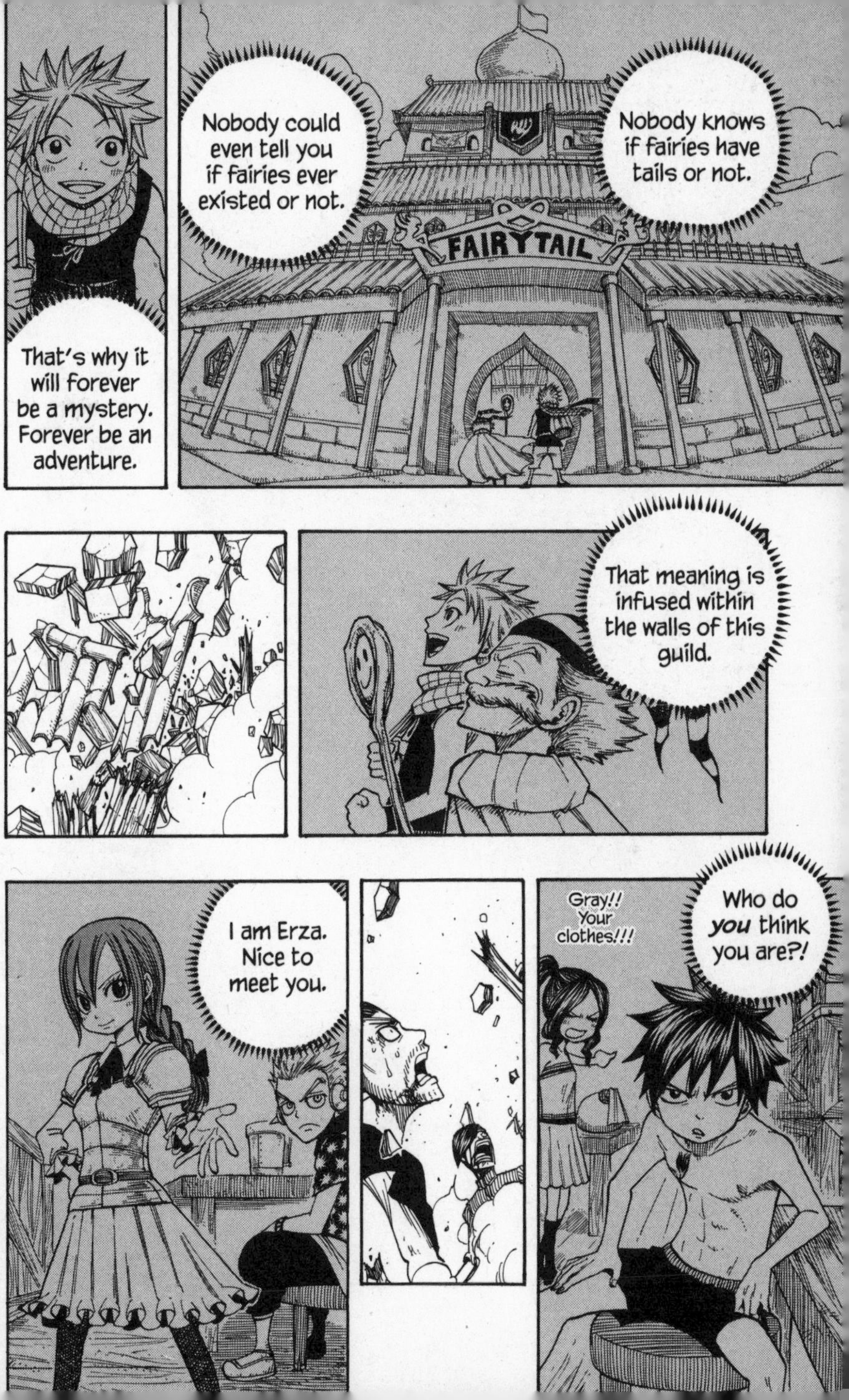
Nobody knows if fairies have tails or not.
Nobody could even tell you if fairies ever existed or not.
FAIRY TAIL
That's why it will forever be a mystery. Forever be an adventure.
That meaning is infused within the walls of this guild.
Who do *you* think you are?!
Gray!! Your clothes!!!
I am Erza. Nice to meet you.

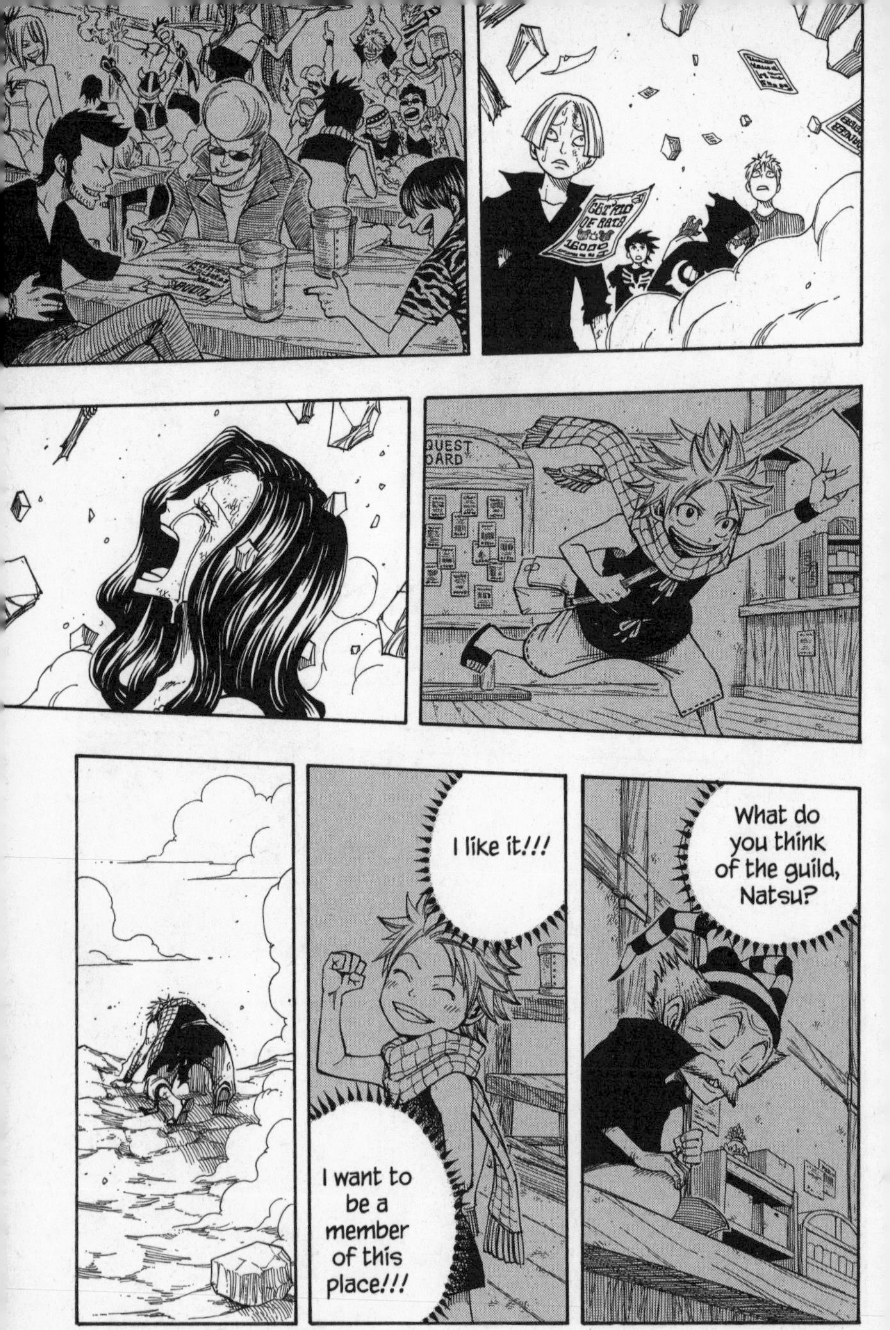
What do you think of the guild, Natsu?
I like it!!!
I want to be a member of this place!!!

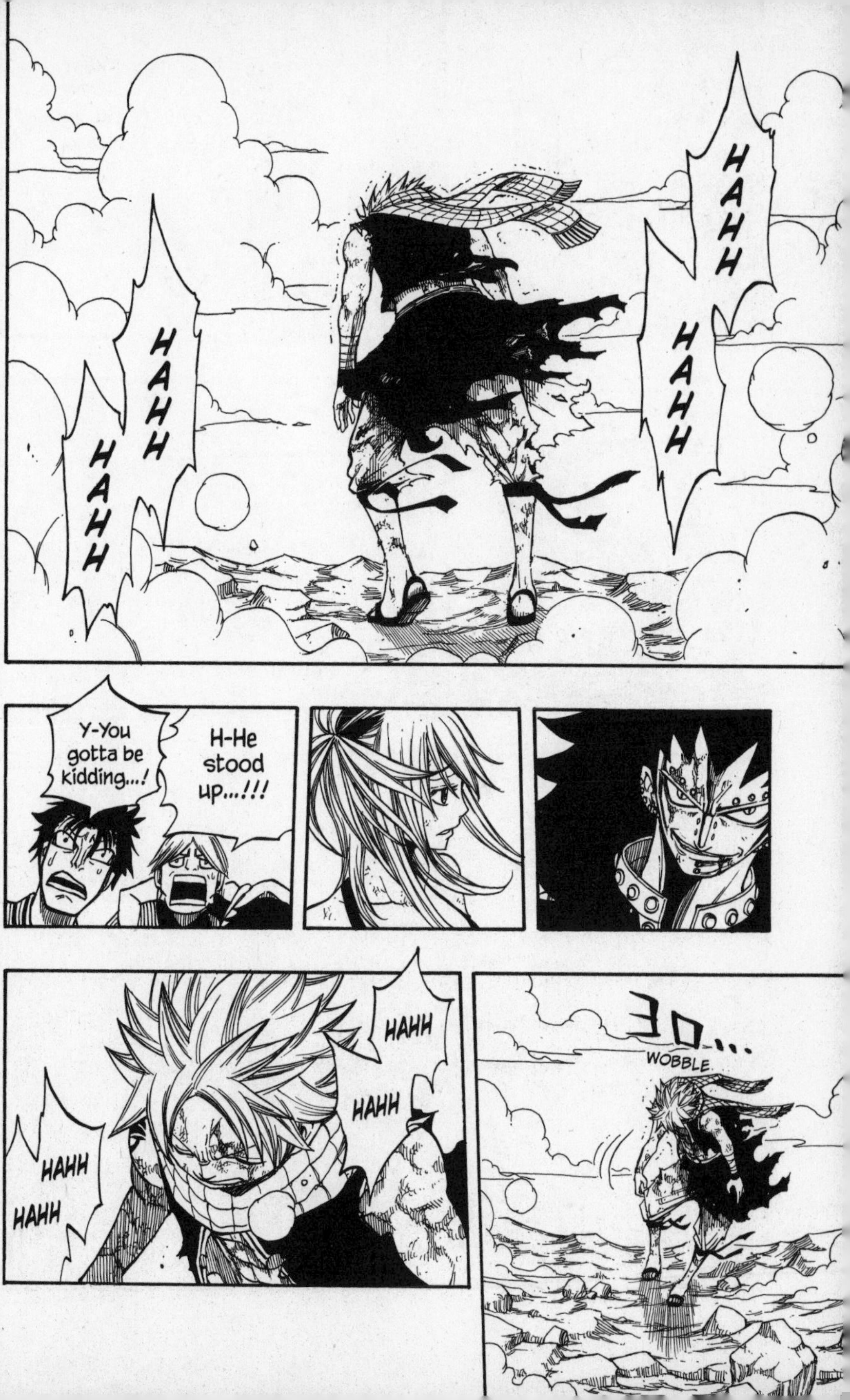
HAHH
HAHH
HAHH
HAHH
H-He stood up...!!!
Y-You gotta be kidding...!
WOBBLE
HAHH
HAHH
HAHH
HAHH

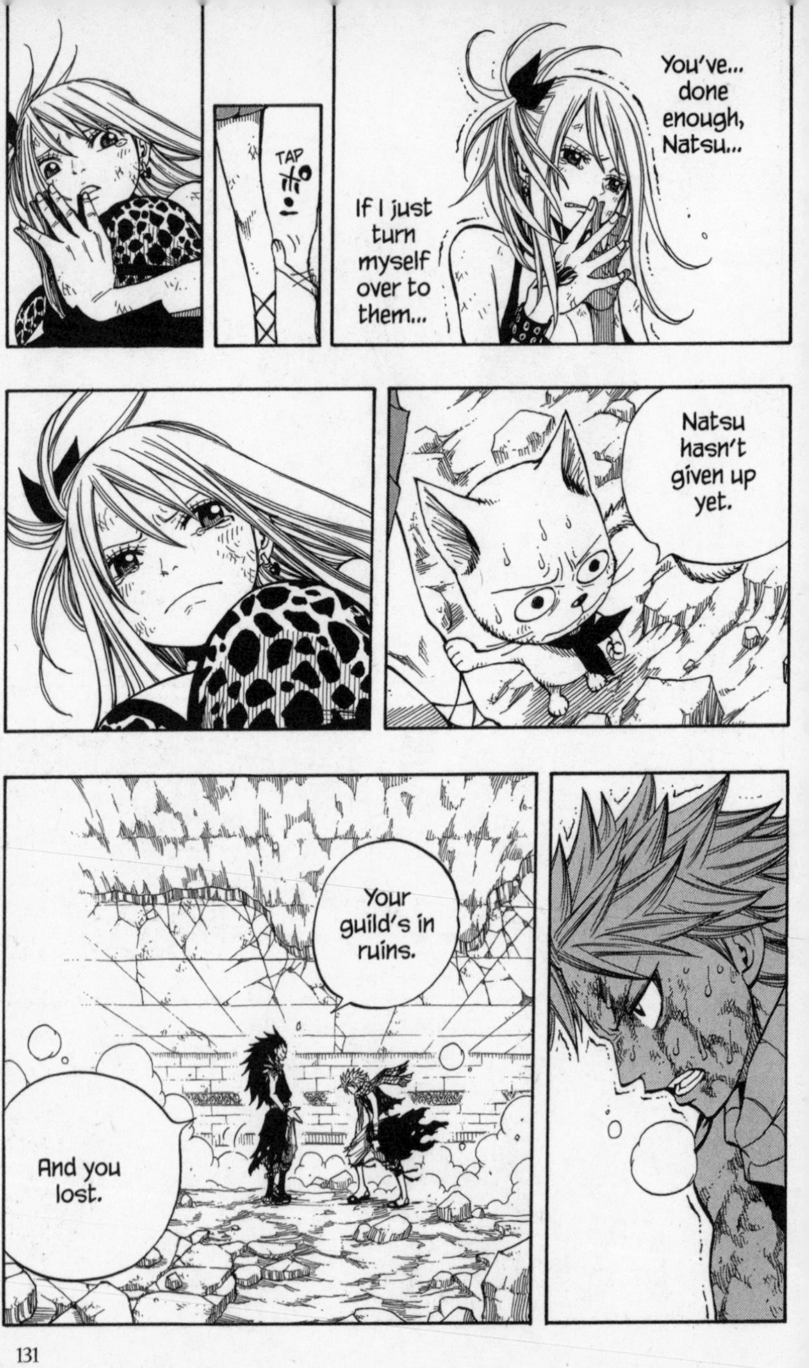
You've... done enough, Natsu...
If I just turn myself over to them...
TAP
Natsu hasn't given up yet.
Your guild's in ruins.
And you lost.

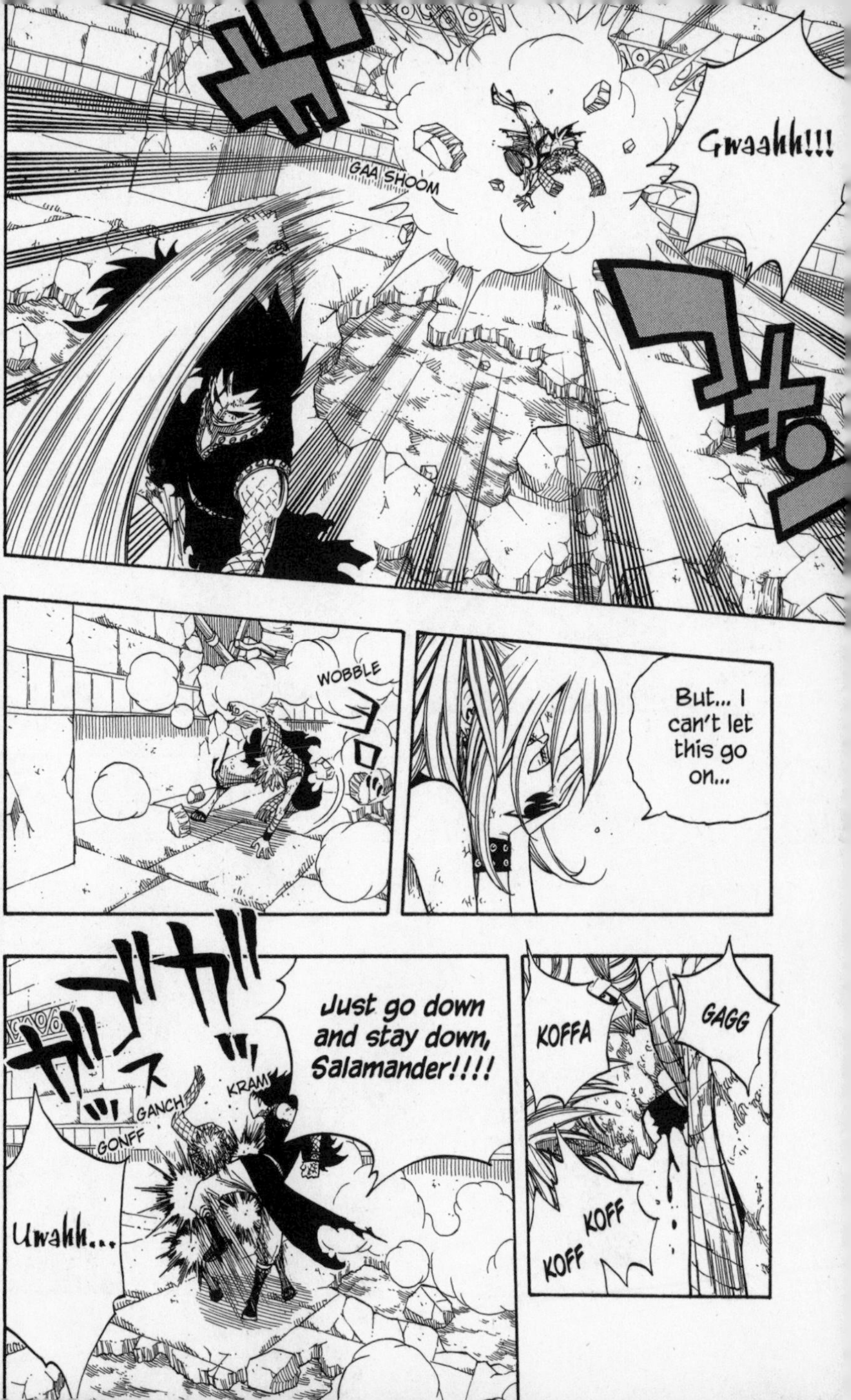
Gwaahh!!!
GAA SHOOM
But... I can't let this go on...
WOBBLE
GAGG
KOFFA
KOFF
KOFF
Just go down and stay down, Salamander!!!!
KRAM
GANCH
GONFF
Uwahh...

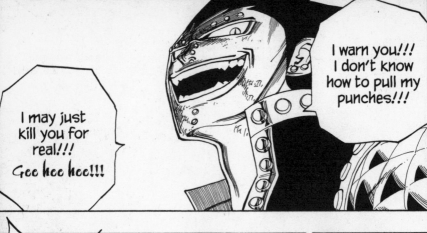

I warn you!!! I don't know how to pull my punches!!!
I may just kill you for real!!! Gee hee hee!!!
He destroyed Jupiter, and he took on your Element Four!!!
He's used up his magical powers!!!
If he could only eat some fire, Natsu would never lose!!!
......
!
Now I see...
SST
It seems we've had a bit of a miscommunication between us. Moshi-moshi.
GRN GRN

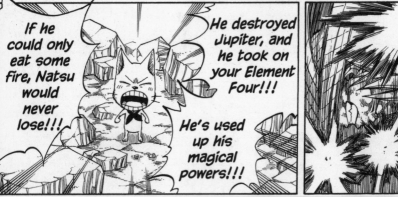

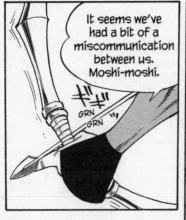

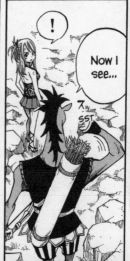

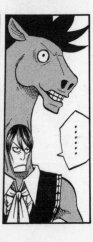

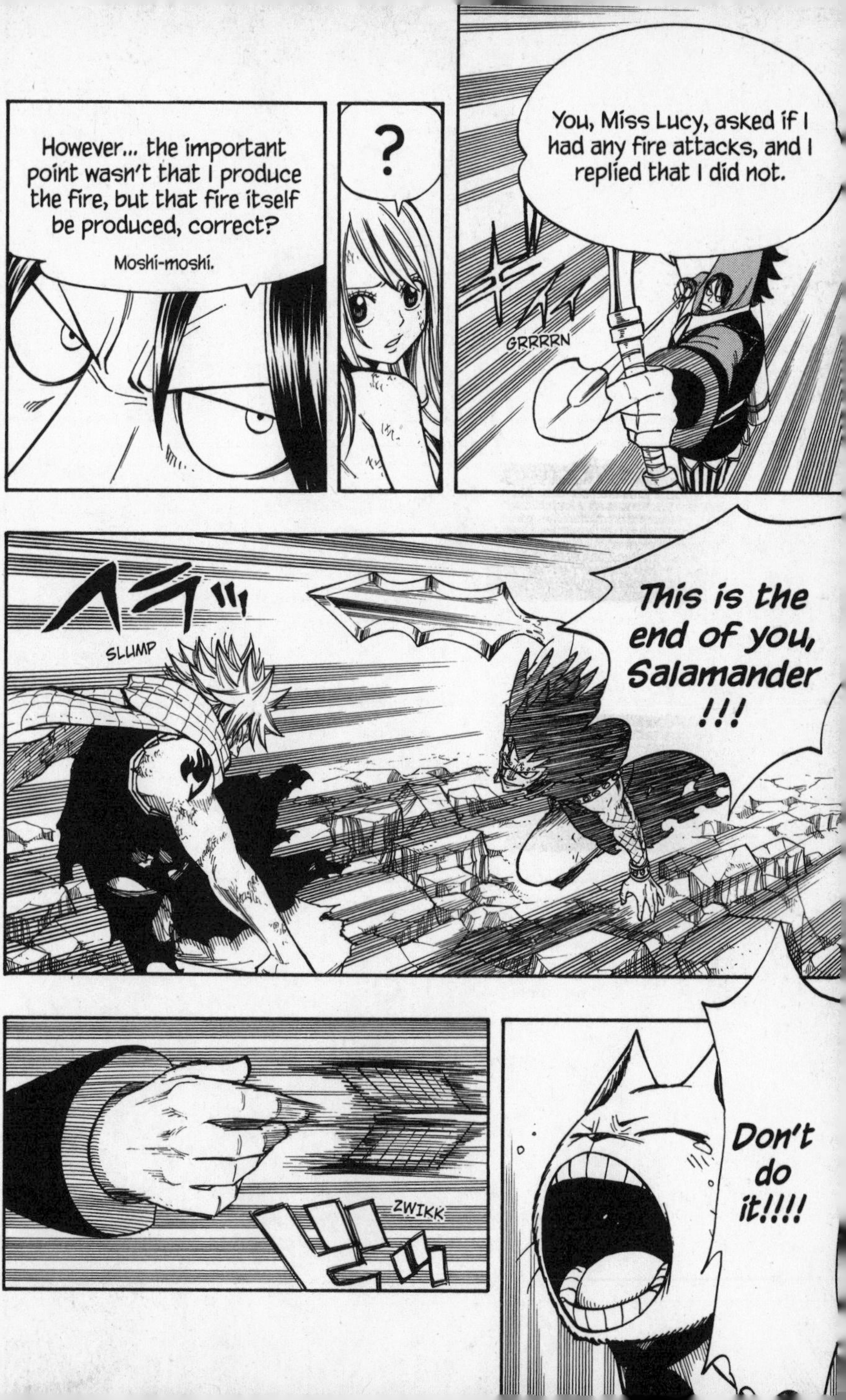
You, Miss Lucy, asked if I had any fire attacks, and I replied that I did not.
GRRRRN
?
However... the important point wasn't that I produce the fire, but that fire itself be produced, correct?
Moshi-moshi.
This is the end of you, Salamander !!!
SLUMP
Don't do it!!!!
ZWIKK

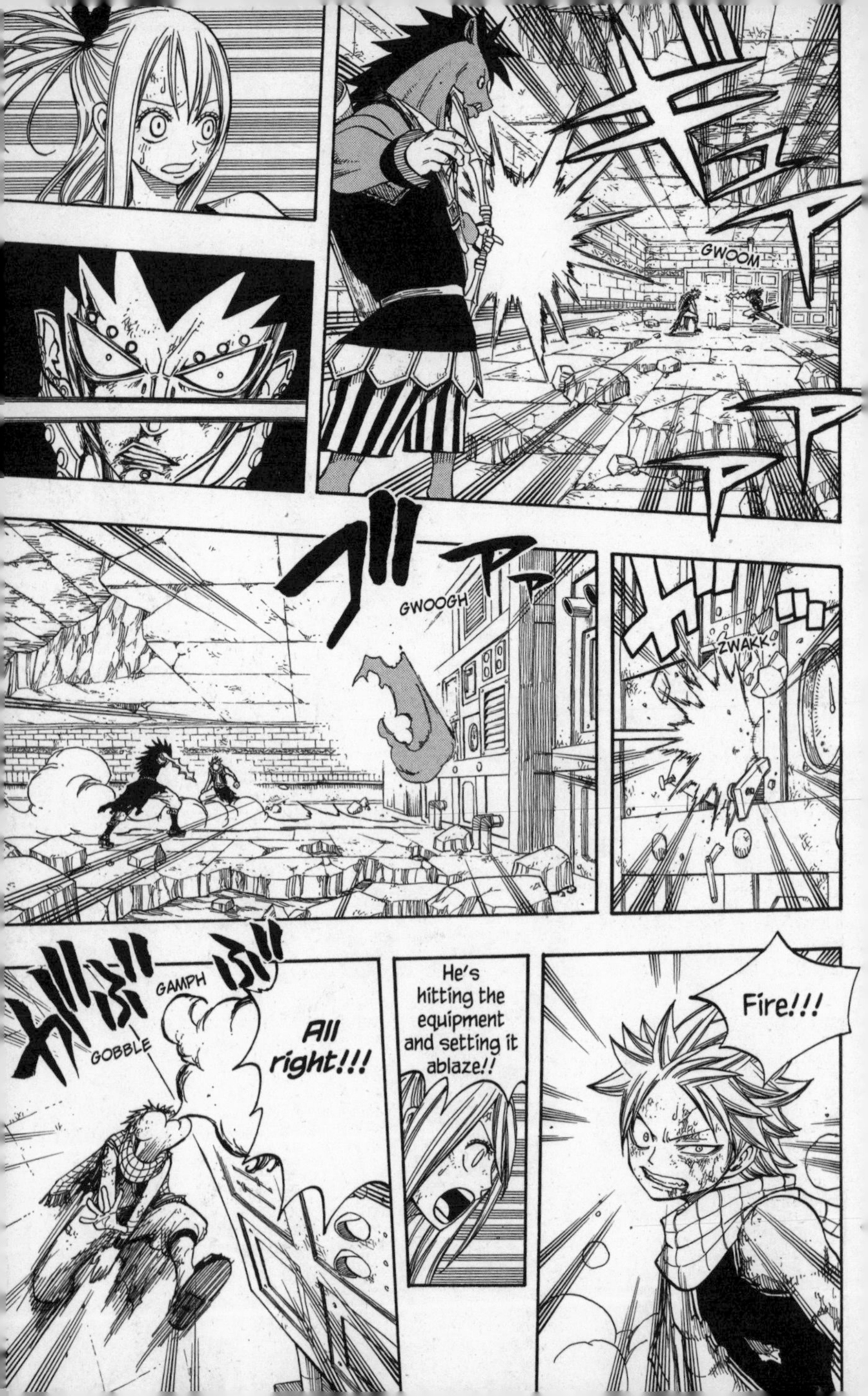
GWOOM
ZWAKK
GWOOGH
Fire!!!
He's hitting the equipment and setting it ablaze!!
All right!!!
GAMPH
GOBBLE

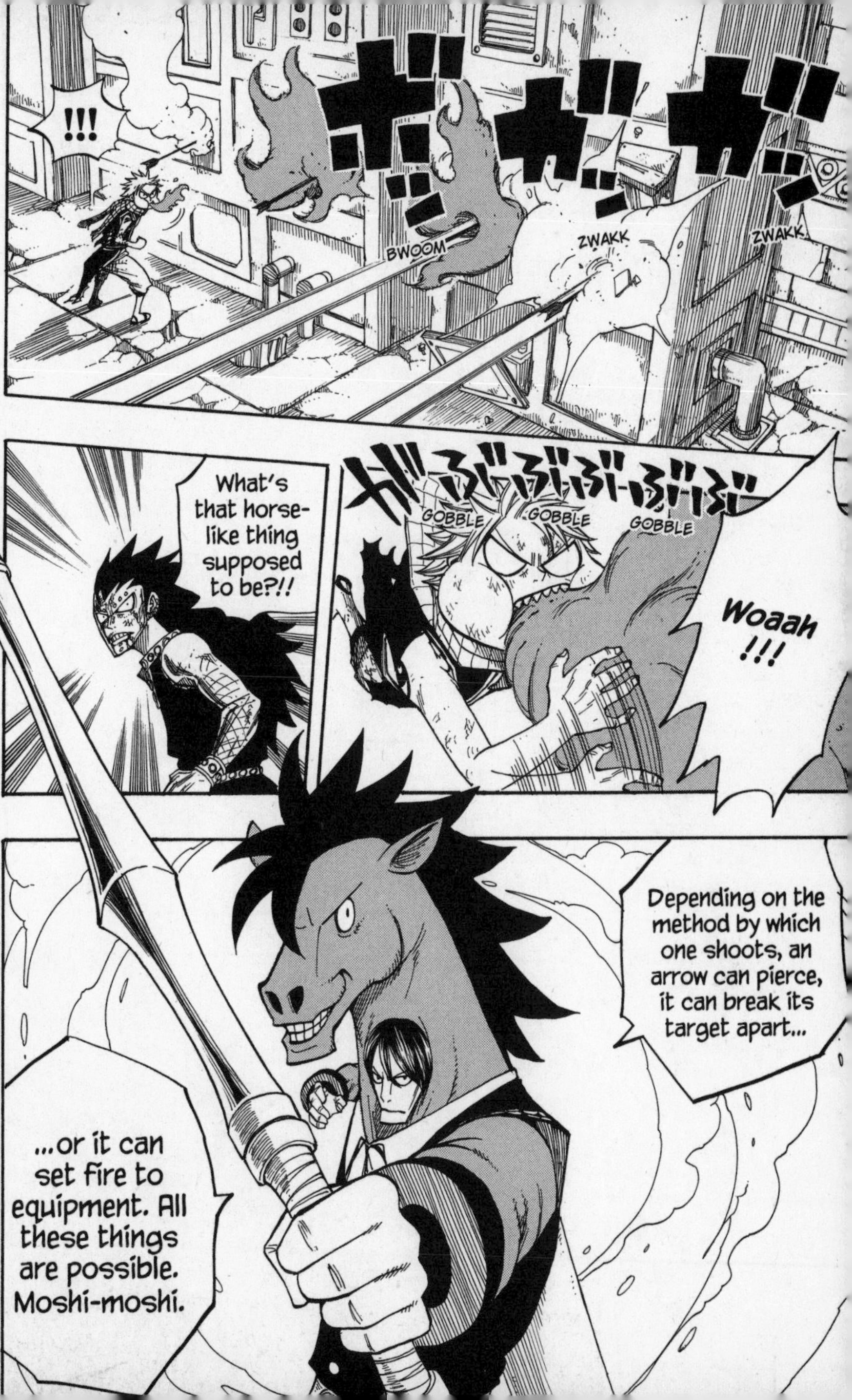
ZWAKK
ZWAKK
BWOOM
!!!
GOBBLE GOBBLE GOBBLE
Woaah !!!
What's that horse-like thing supposed to be?!!
Depending on the method by which one shoots, an arrow can pierce, it can break its target apart...
...or it can set fire to equipment. All these things are possible. Moshi-moshi.

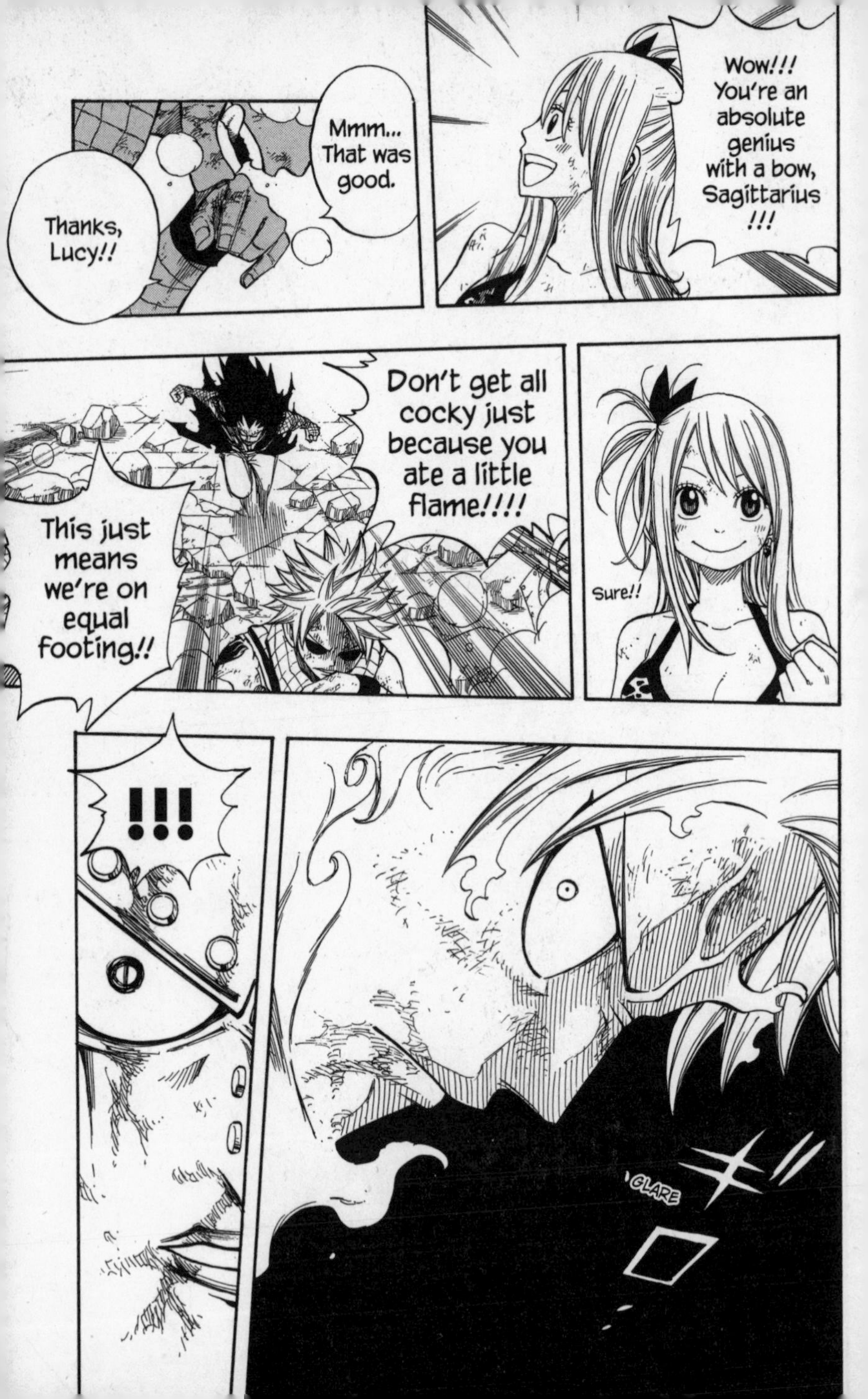
Wow!!! You're an absolute genius with a bow, Sagittarius !!!
Mmm... That was good.
Thanks, Lucy!!
Sure!!
Don't get all cocky just because you ate a little flame!!!!
This just means we're on equal footing!!
GLARE
!!!

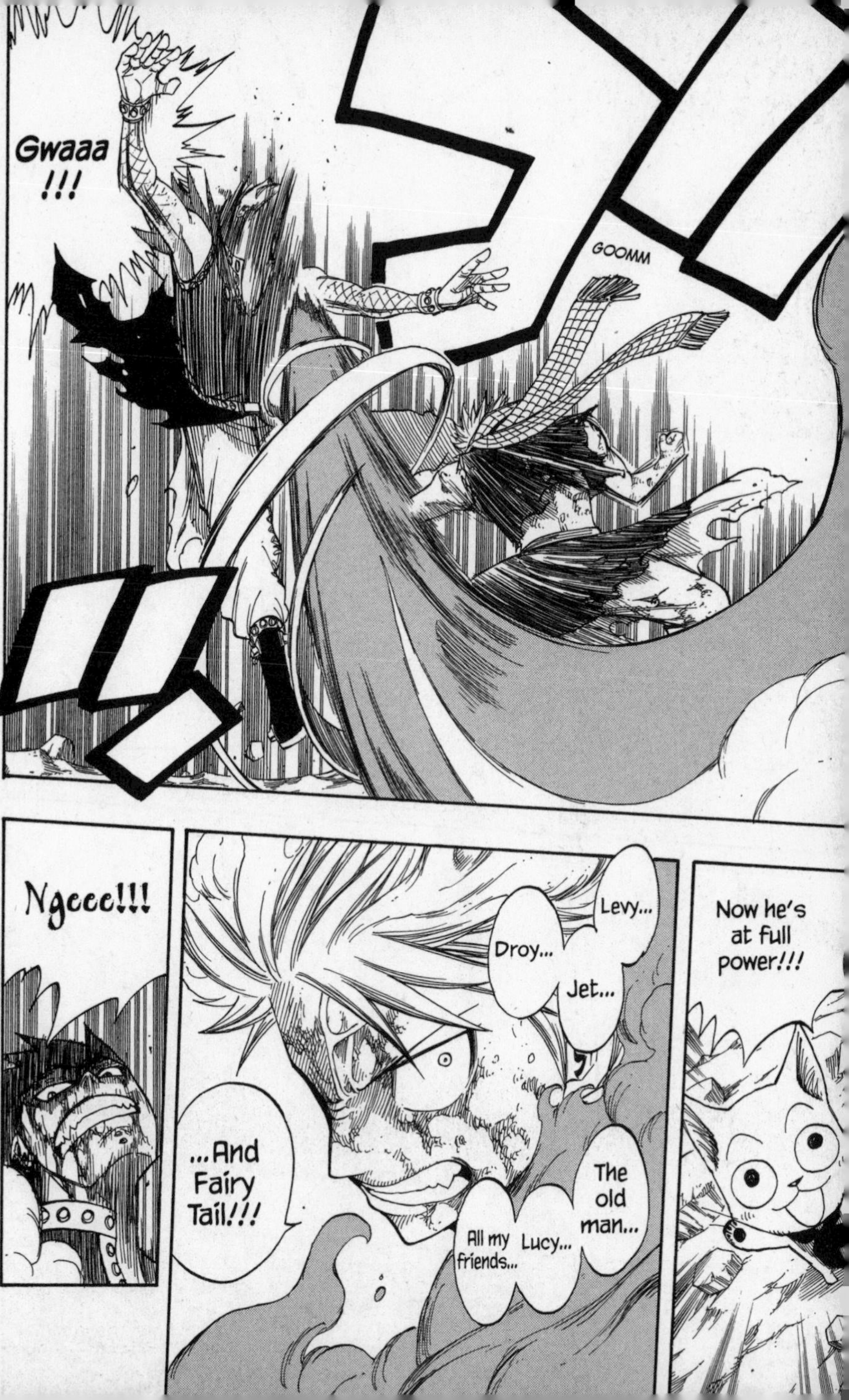
GOOMM
Gwaaa!!!
Now he's at full power!!!
Levy...
Droy...
Jet...
The old man...
Lucy...
All my friends...
...And Fairy Tail!!!
Ngeee!!!

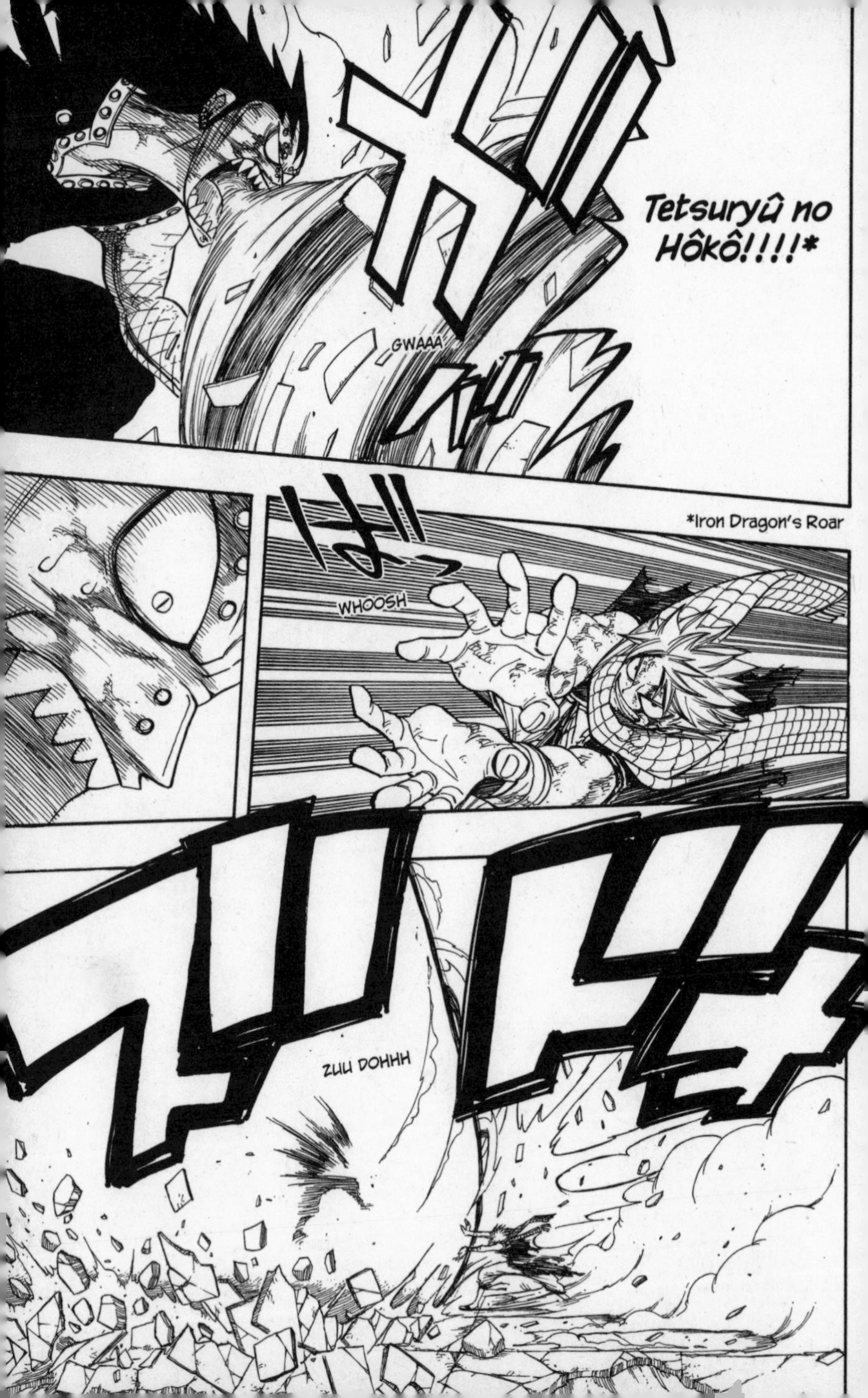
Tetsuryû no Hôkô!!!!*
GWAAA
WHOOSH
ZUU DOHHH

*Iron Dragon's Roar

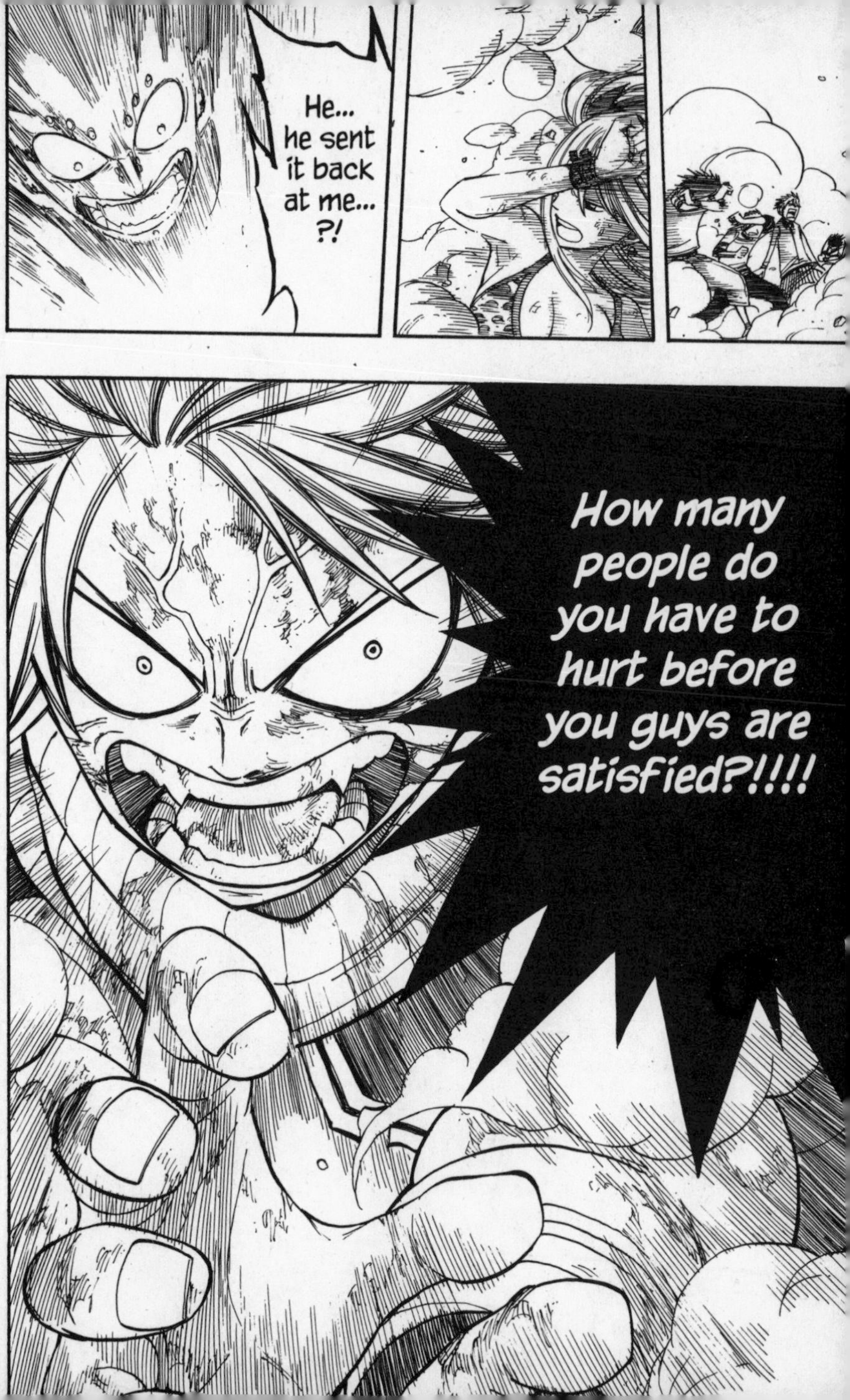
He... he sent it back at me...?!
How many people do you have to hurt before you guys are satisfied?!!!!

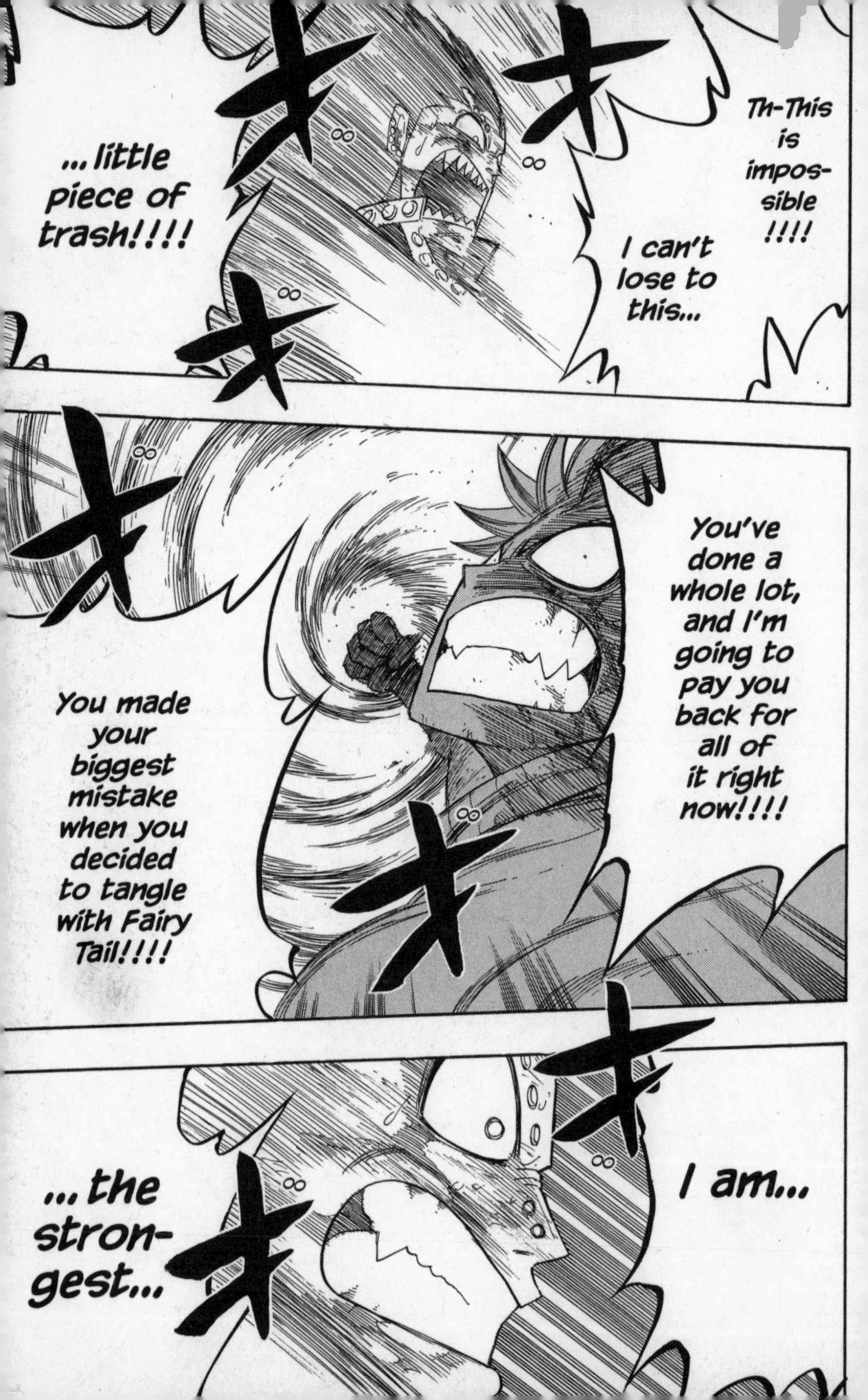
Th-This is impos-sible!!!!
I can't lose to this...
...little piece of trash!!!!
You've done a whole lot, and I'm going to pay you back for all of it right now!!!!
You made your biggest mistake when you decided to tangle with Fairy Tail!!!!
I am...
...the stron-gest...

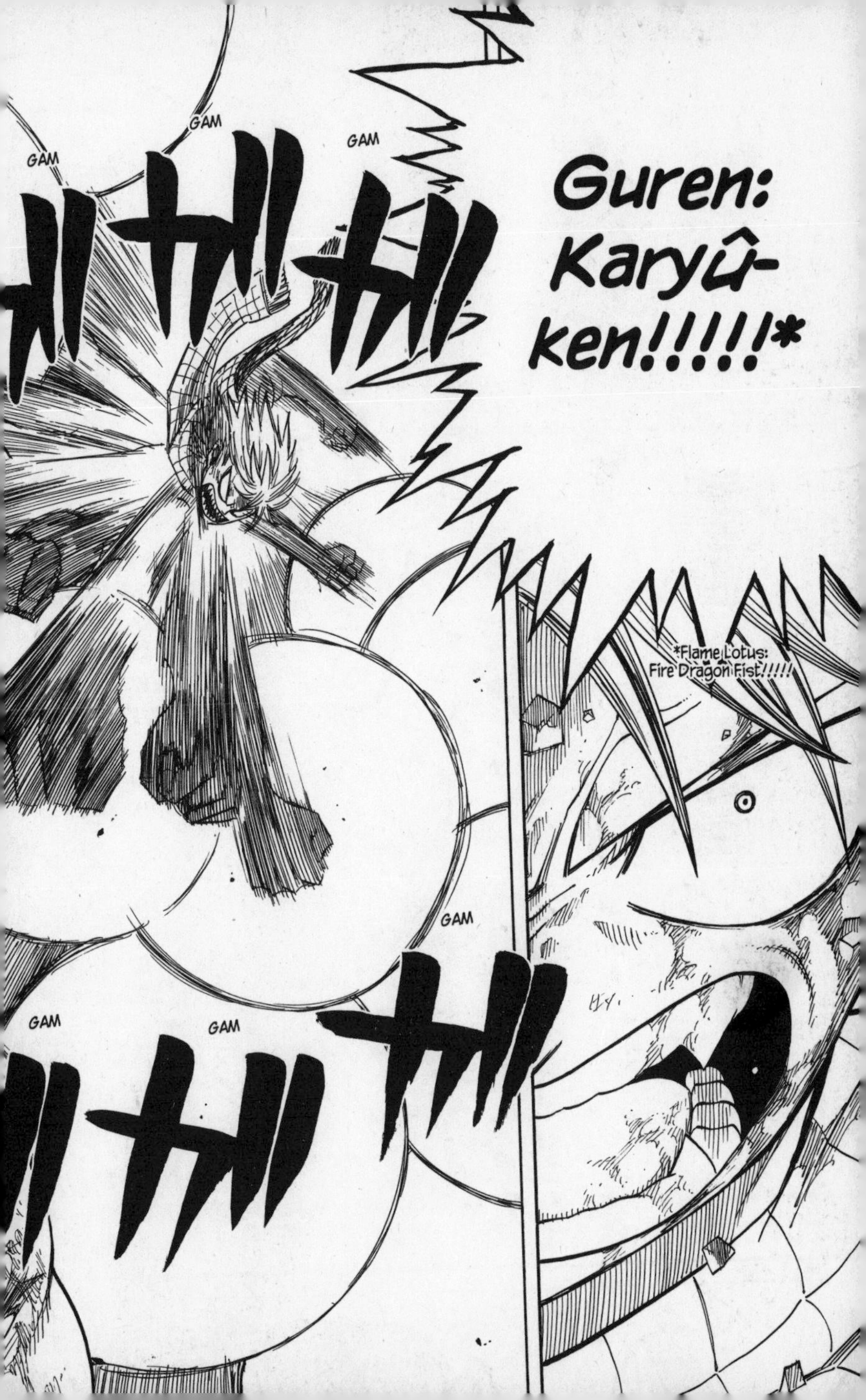

Guren: Karyû-ken!!!!!*
*Flame Lotus: Fire Dragon Fist!!!!!
GAM
GAM
GAM
GAM
GAM
GAM

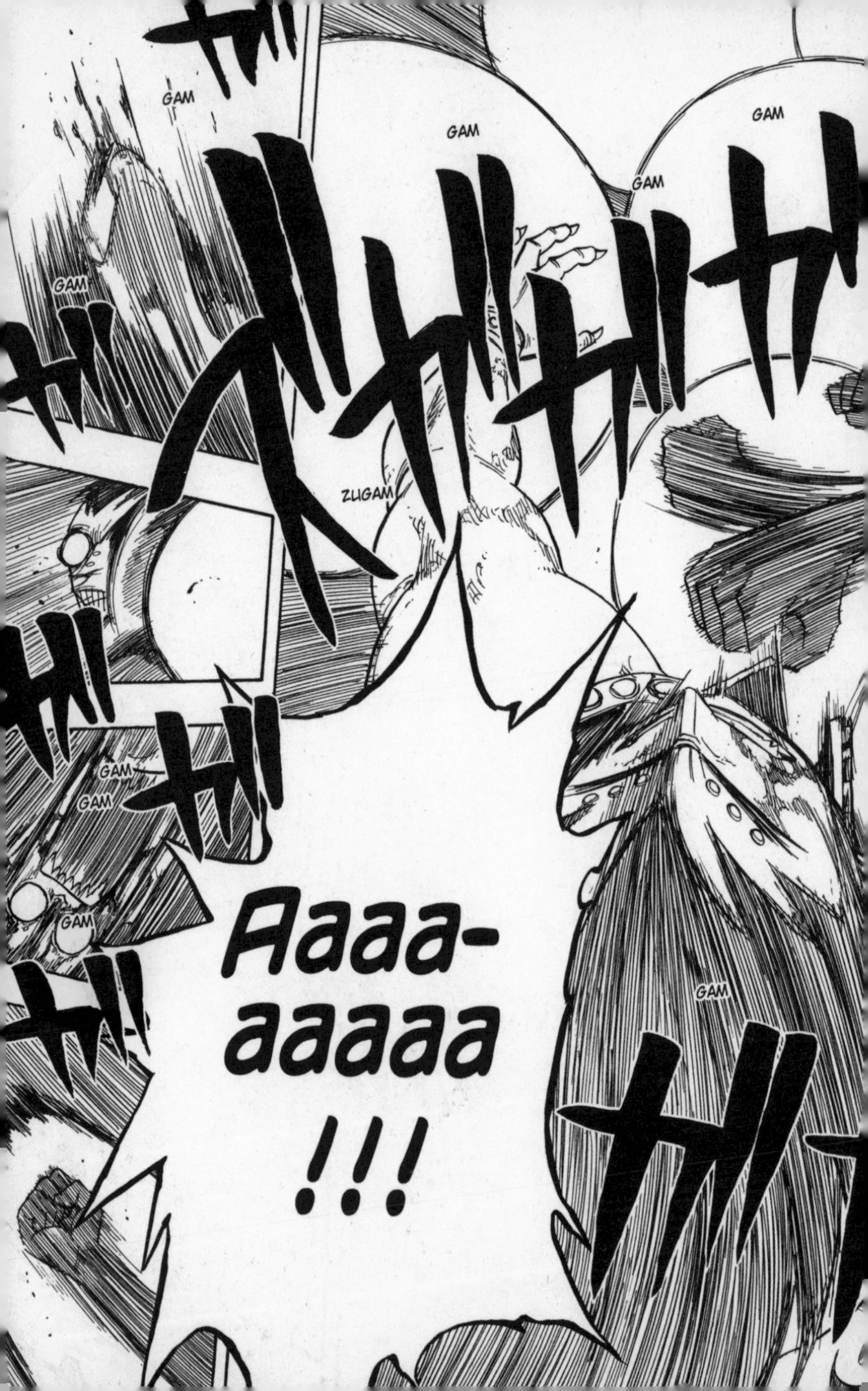
GAM
GAM
GAM
GAM
GAM
ZUGAM
GAM
Aaaa-aaaaaa!!!
GAM
GAM
GAM

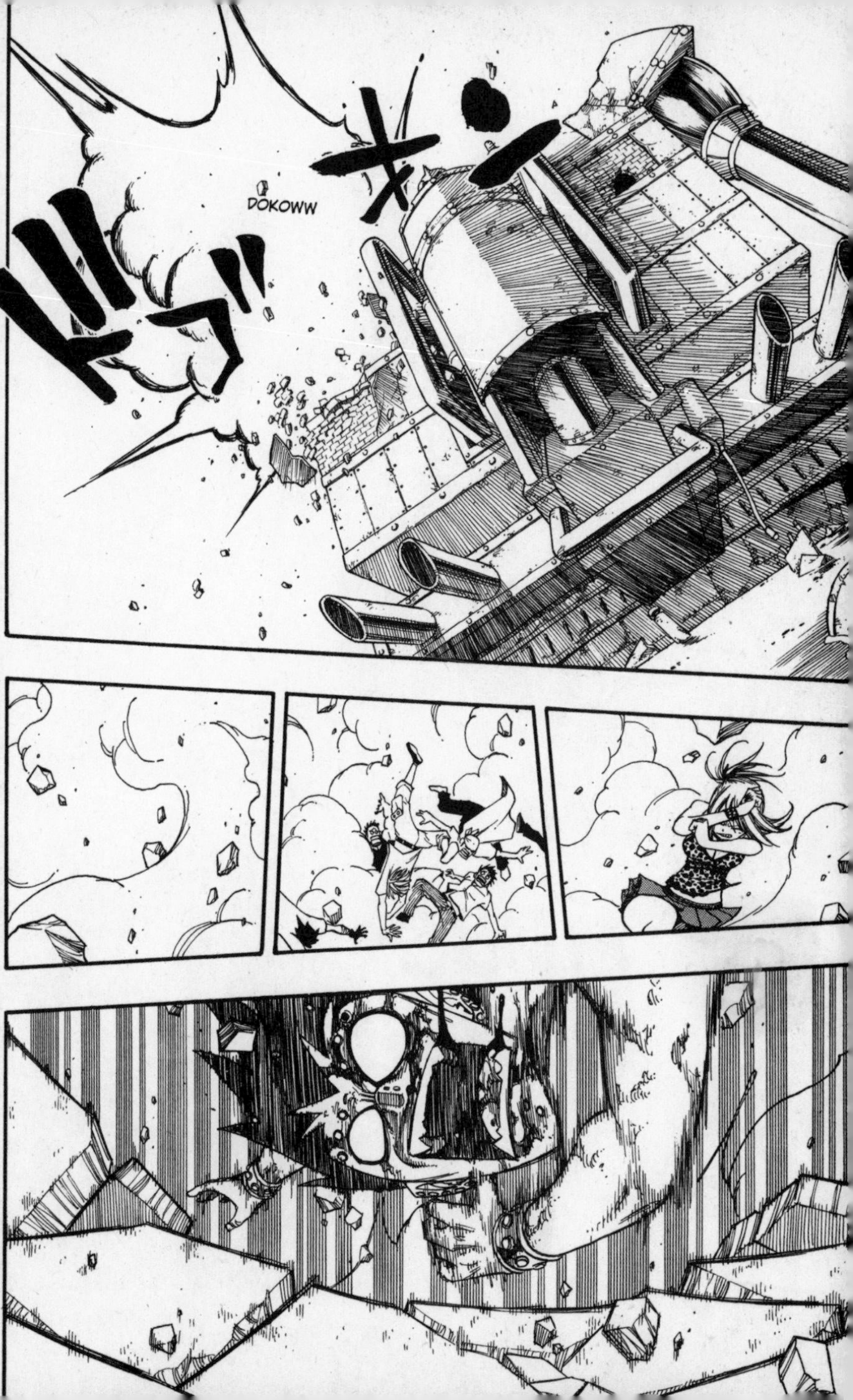
DOKOWW

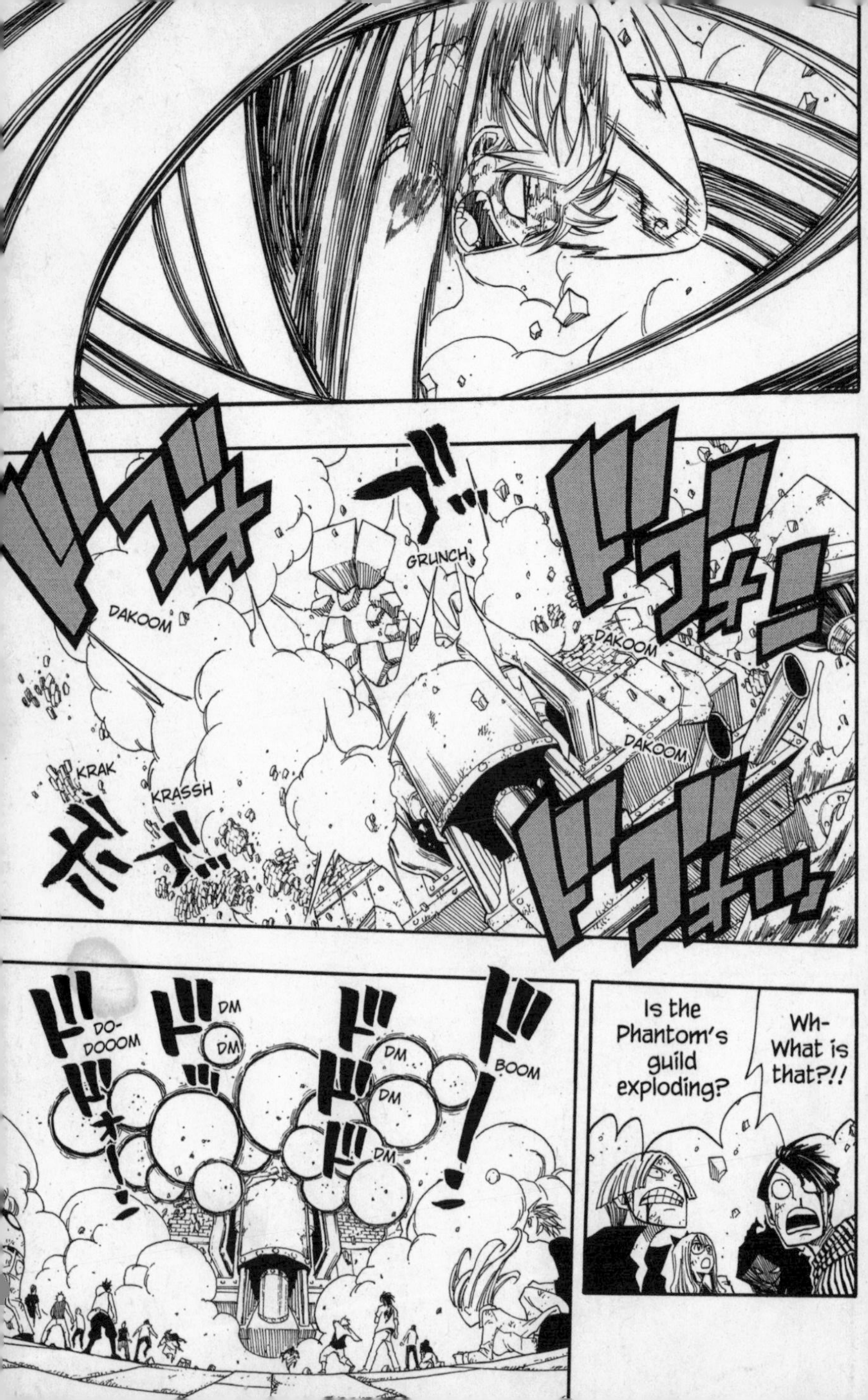
DAKOOM
DAKOOM
GRUNCH
DAKOOM
KRASSH
KRAK
Wh- What is that?!!
Is the Phantom's guild exploding?
BOOM
DM
DM
DM
DM
DM
DO-DOOOM

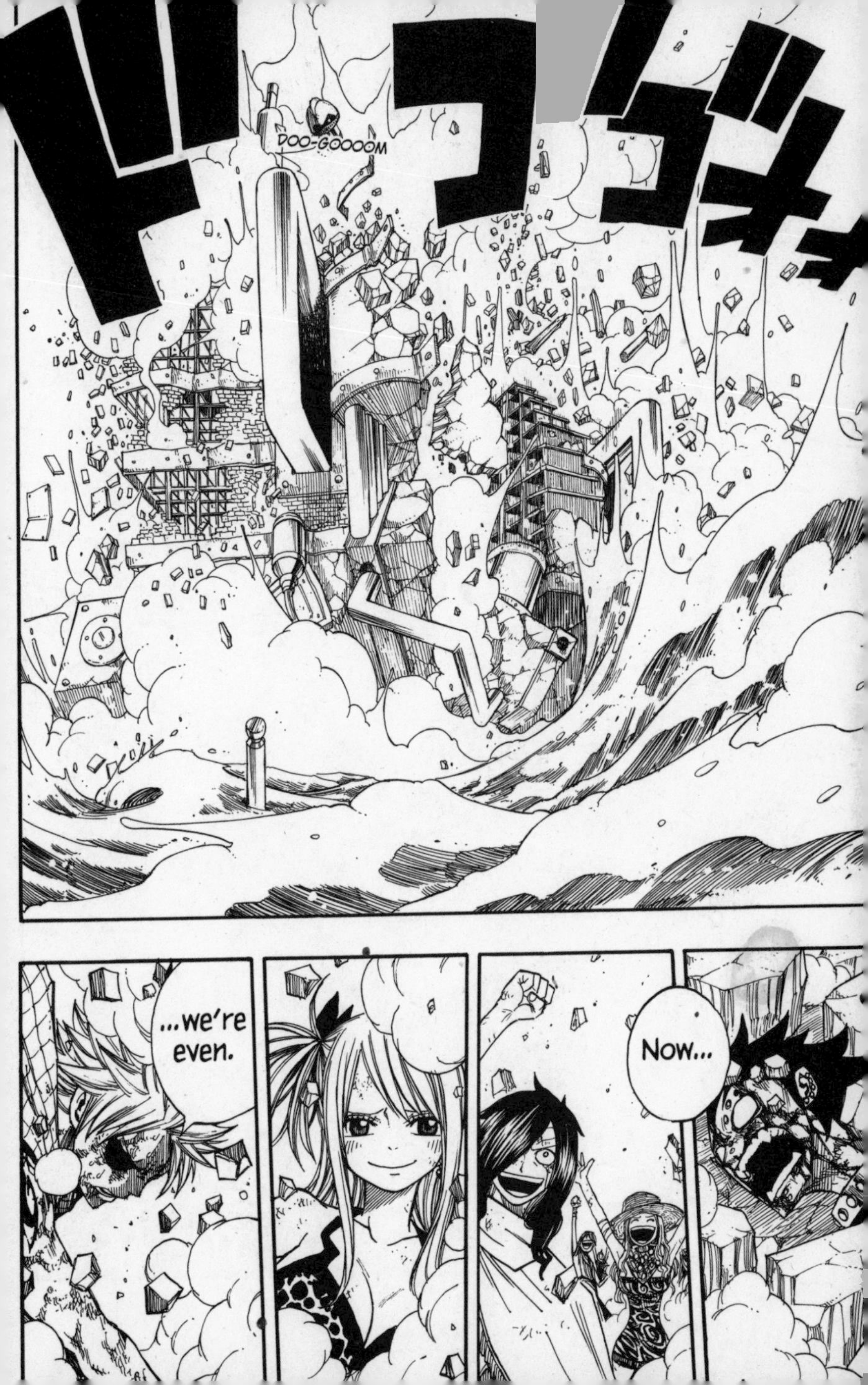
DOO-GOOOOM
Now...
...we're even.

FAIRY TAIL

Chapter 64: The Best Guild

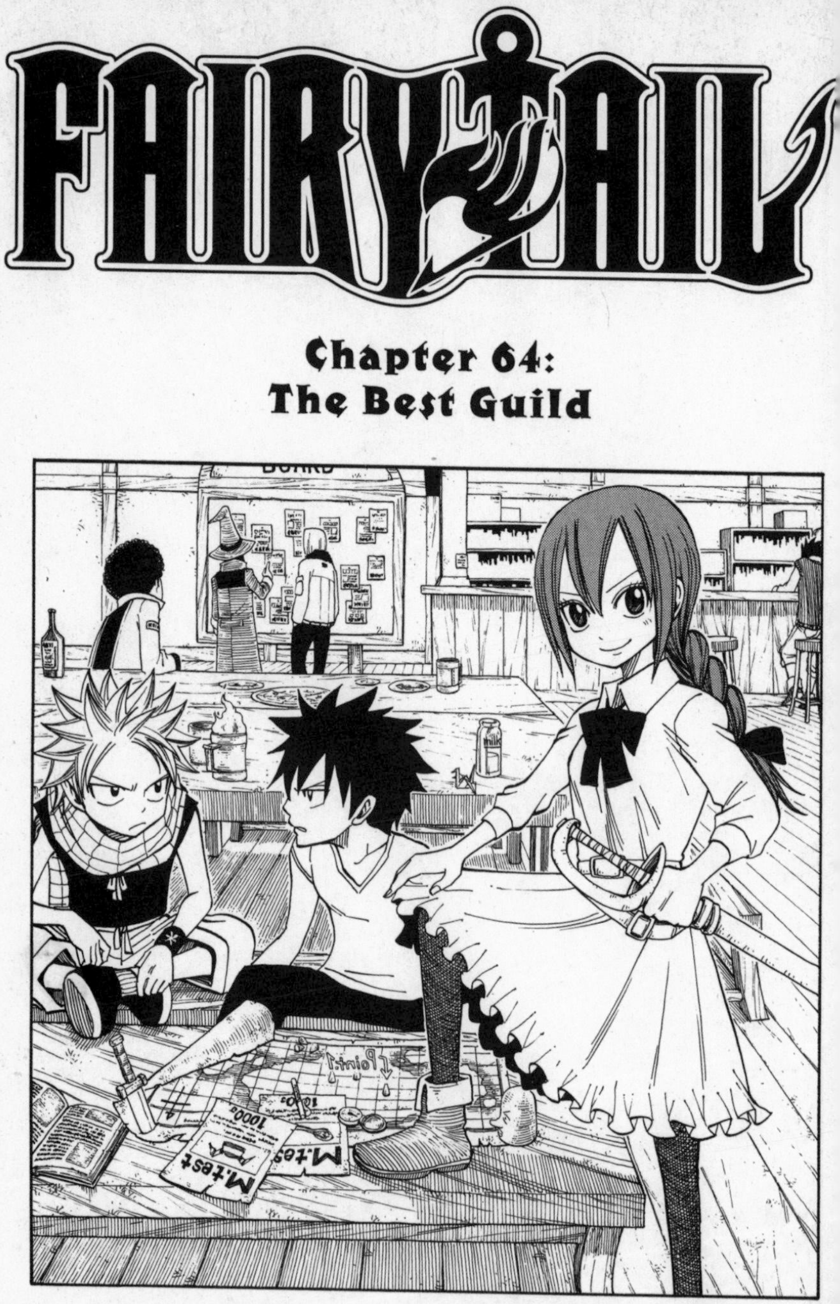

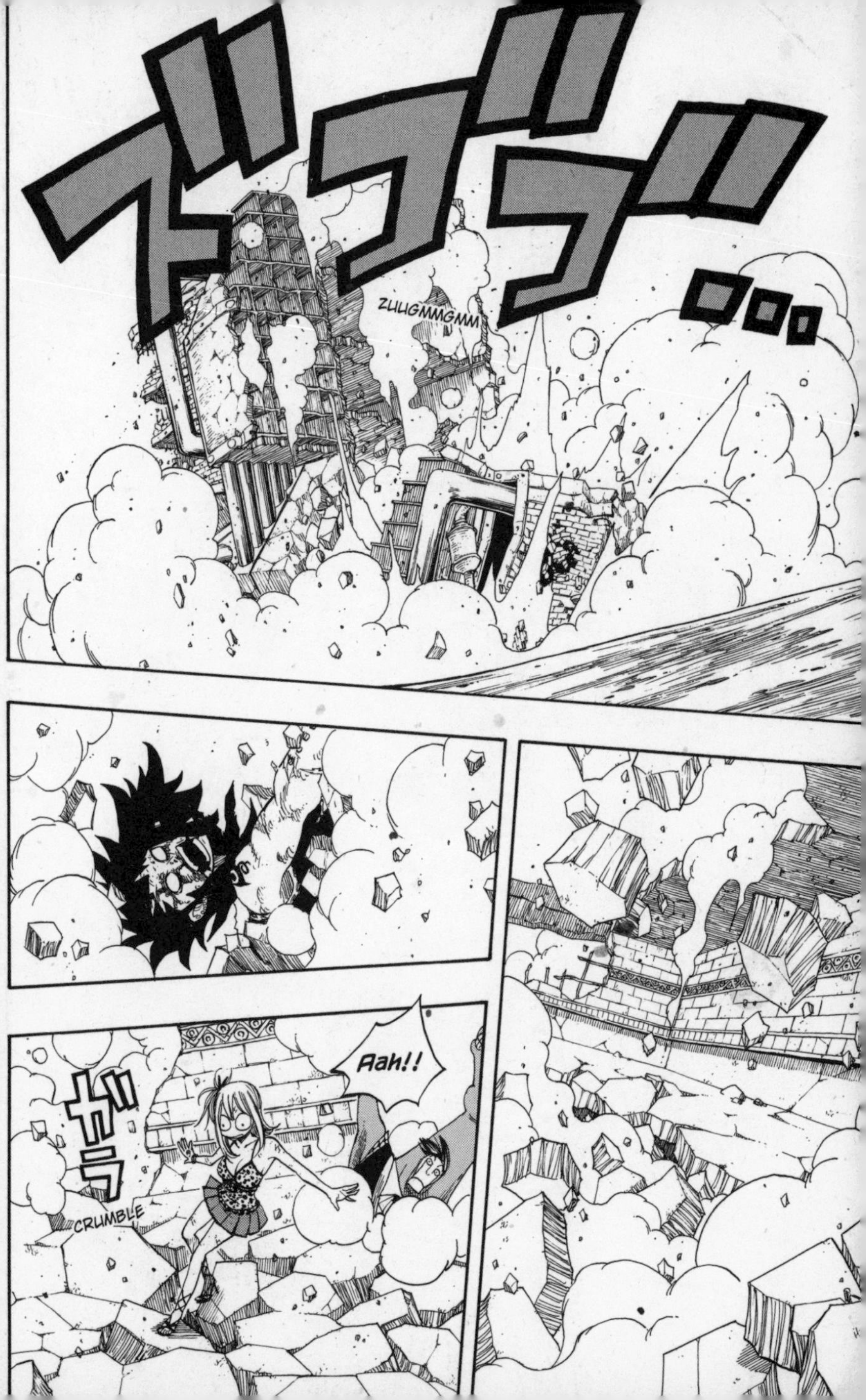
ズゴゴ…
ZUUGMMMGMM
Aah!!
ガラ
CRUMBLE

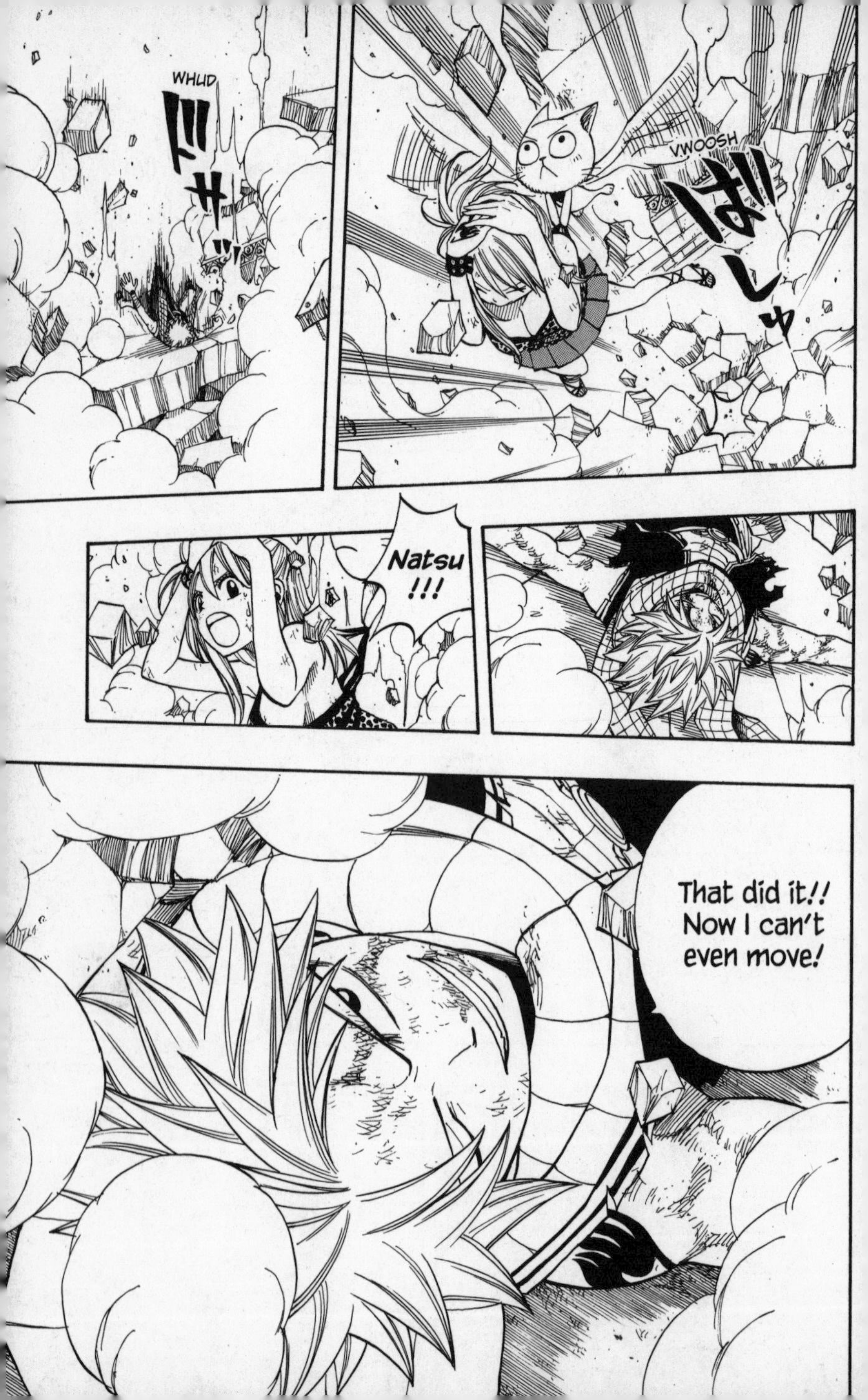
VWOOSH
ばしゅ
WHUD
ドサッ
Natsu!!!
That did it!! Now I can't even move!

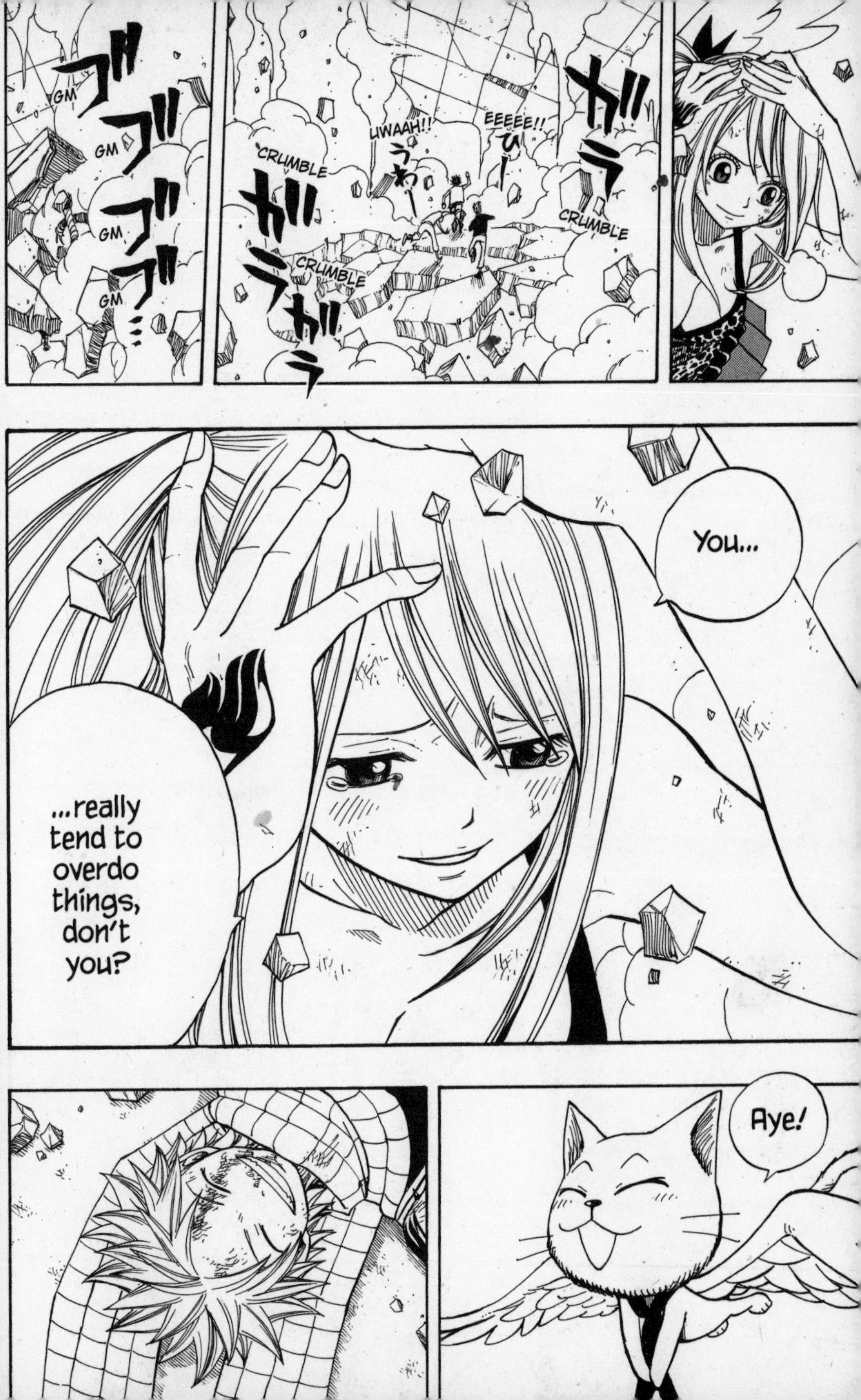
ガラ
CRUMBLE
EEEEEE!!
ひー
UWAAH!!
うわ
CRUMBLE
ガラ
CRUMBLE
ガラ
GM
ゴ
GM
ゴ
GM
ゴ
GM
ゴ...
You...
...really tend to overdo things, don't you?
Aye!

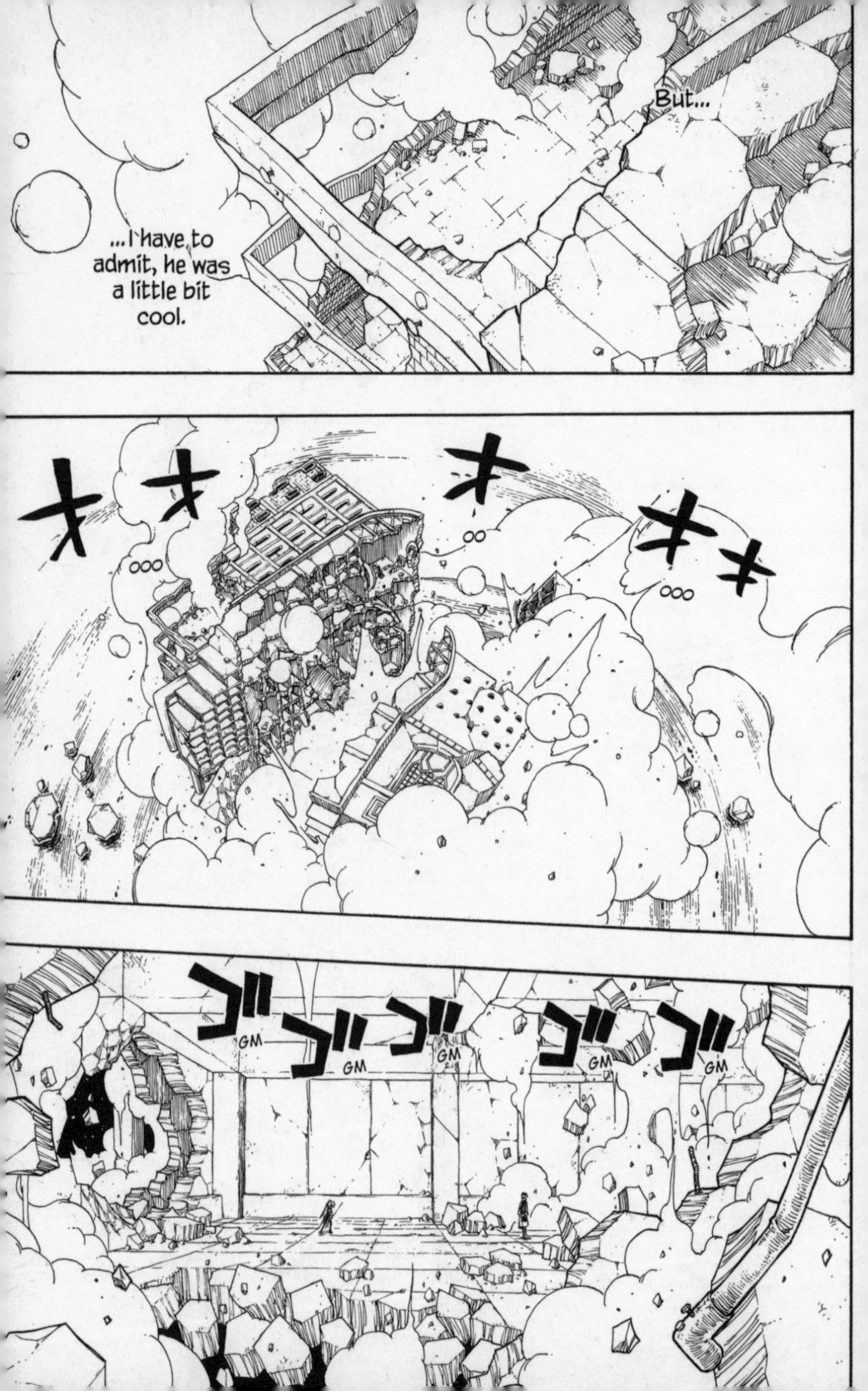
But...
...I have to admit, he was a little bit cool.
ooo
oo
ooo
GM
GM
GM
GM

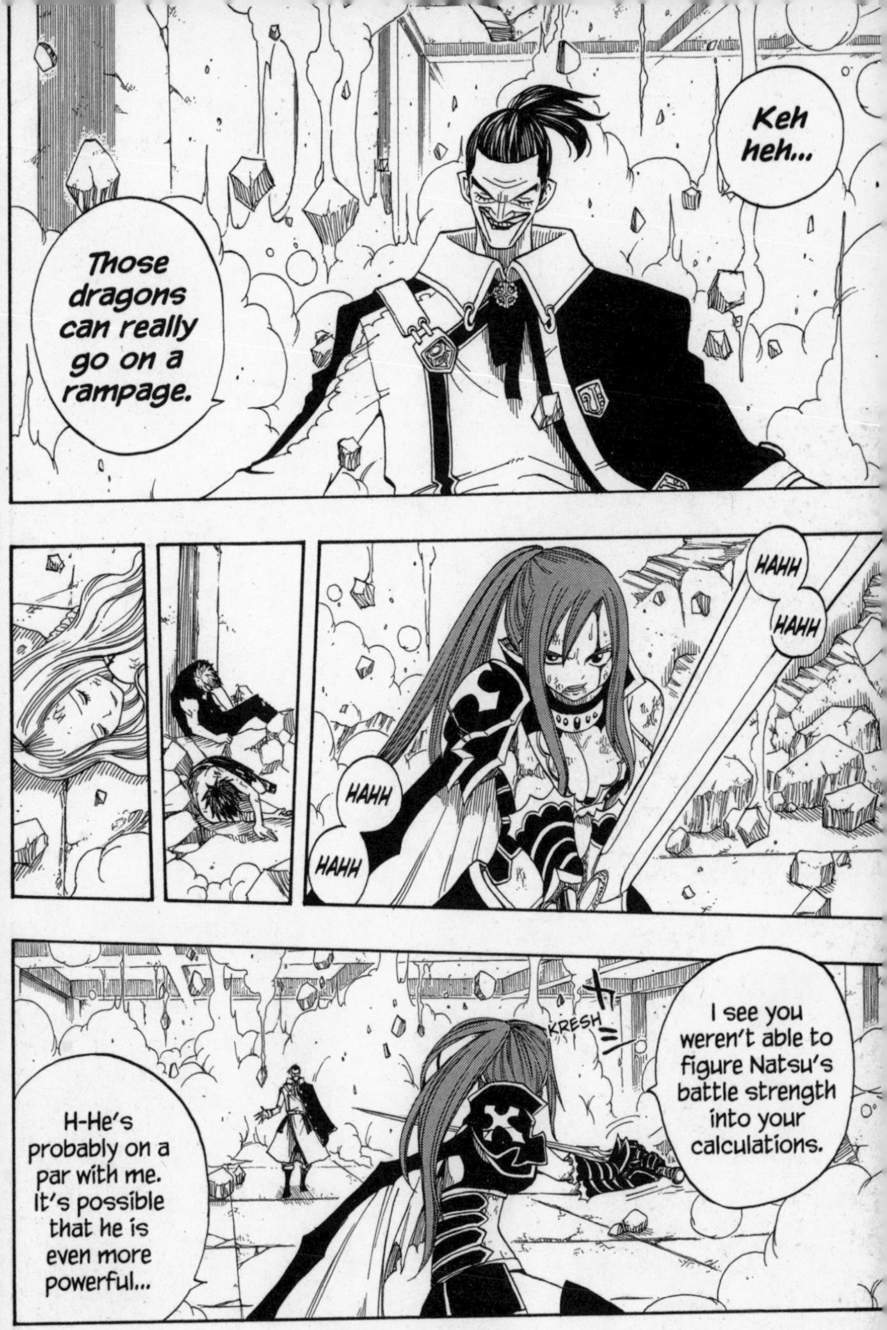
Keh heh...
Those dragons can really go on a rampage.
HAHH HAHH
HAHH HAHH
I see you weren't able to figure Natsu's battle strength into your calculations.
KRESH
H-He's probably on a par with me. It's possible that he is even more powerful...

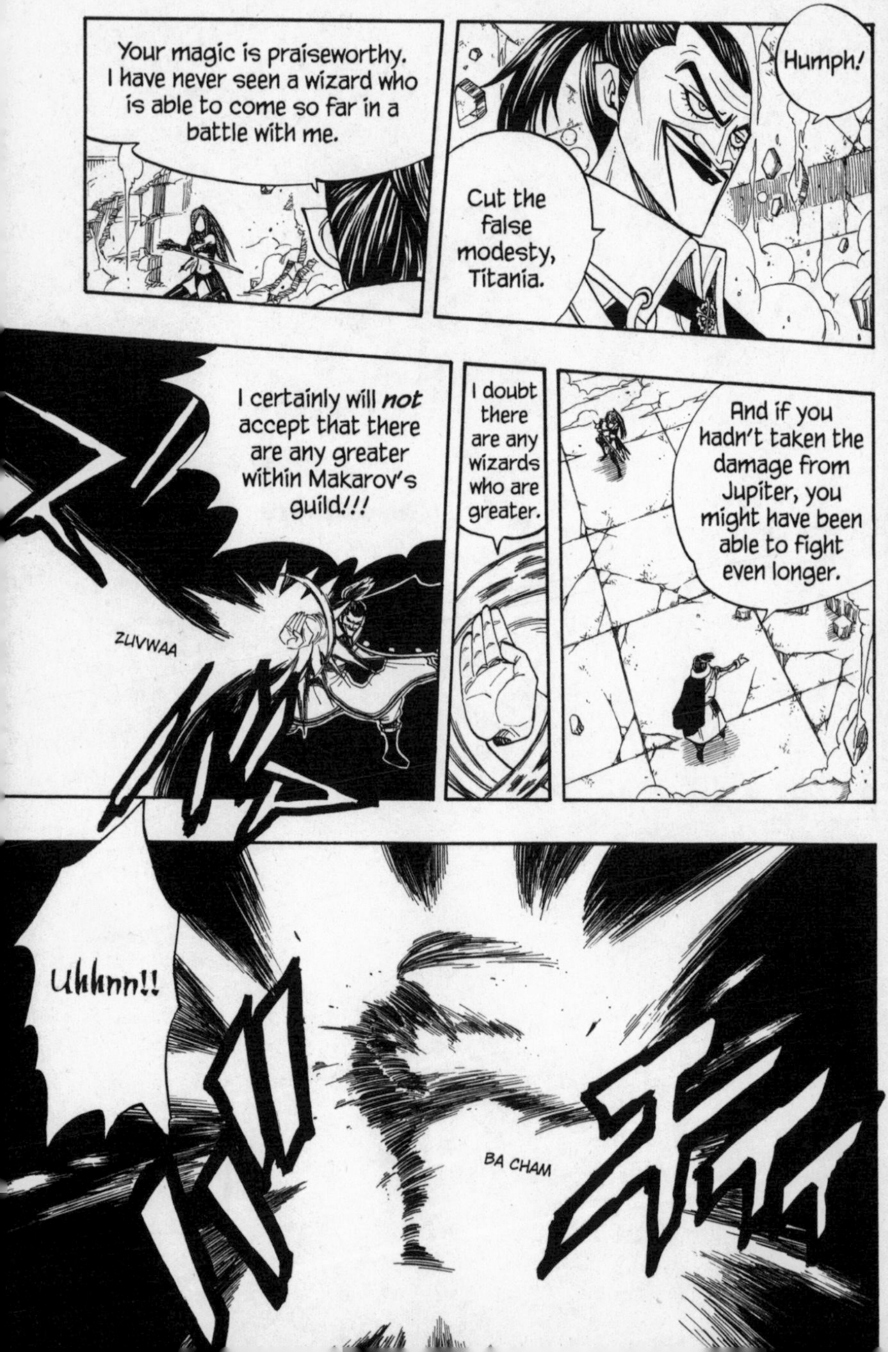
Humph!
Cut the false modesty, Titania.
Your magic is praiseworthy. I have never seen a wizard who is able to come so far in a battle with me.
And if you hadn't taken the damage from Jupiter, you might have been able to fight even longer.
I doubt there are any wizards who are greater.
I certainly will *not* accept that there are any greater within Makarov's guild!!!
ZUVWAA
Uhhnn!!
BA CHAM

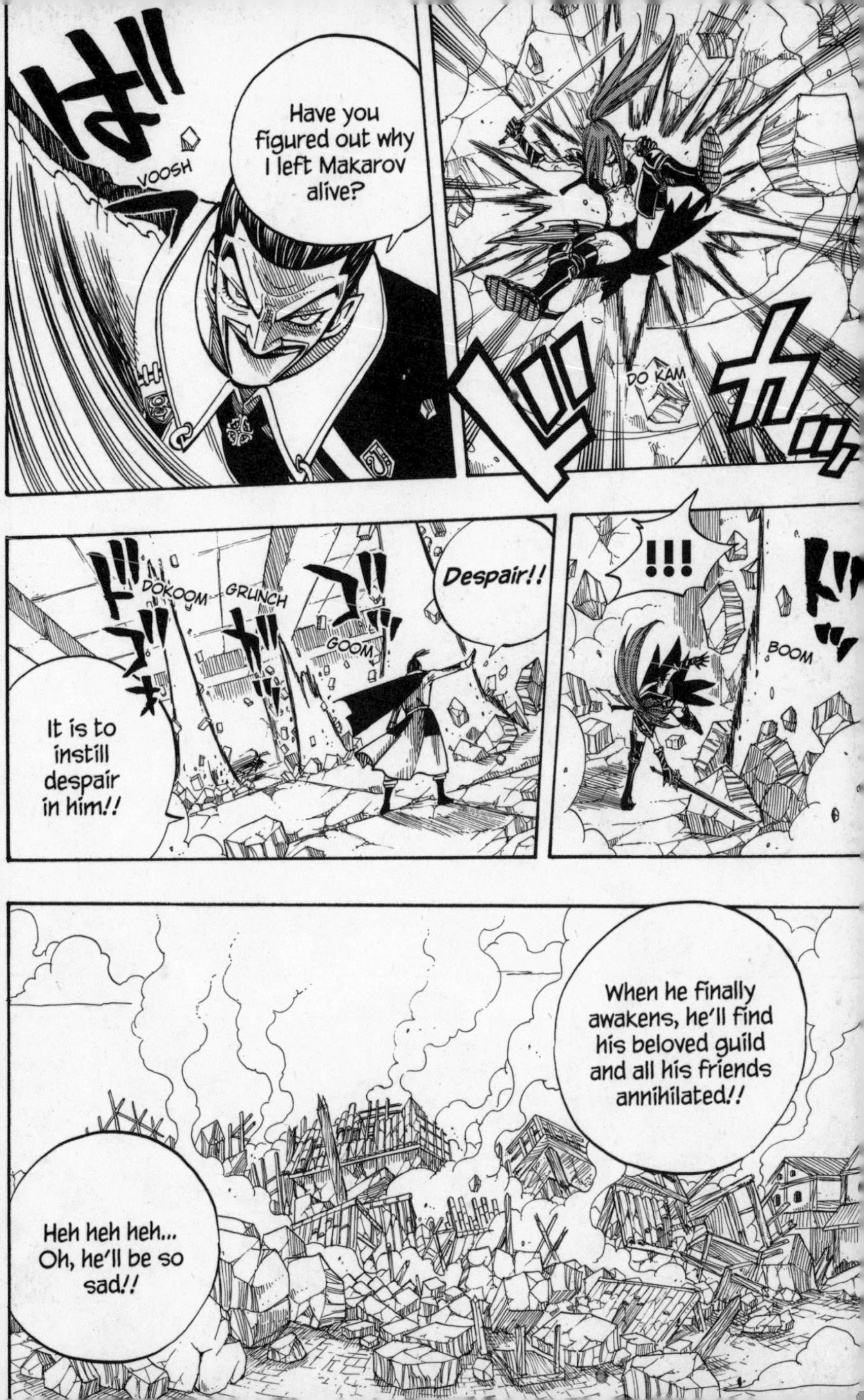
DO KAM
Have you figured out why I left Makarov alive?
VOOSH
!!!
BOOM
Despair!!
GOOM
GRUNCH
DOKOOM
It is to instill despair in him!!
When he finally awakens, he'll find his beloved guild and all his friends annihilated!!
Heh heh heh... Oh, he'll be so sad!!

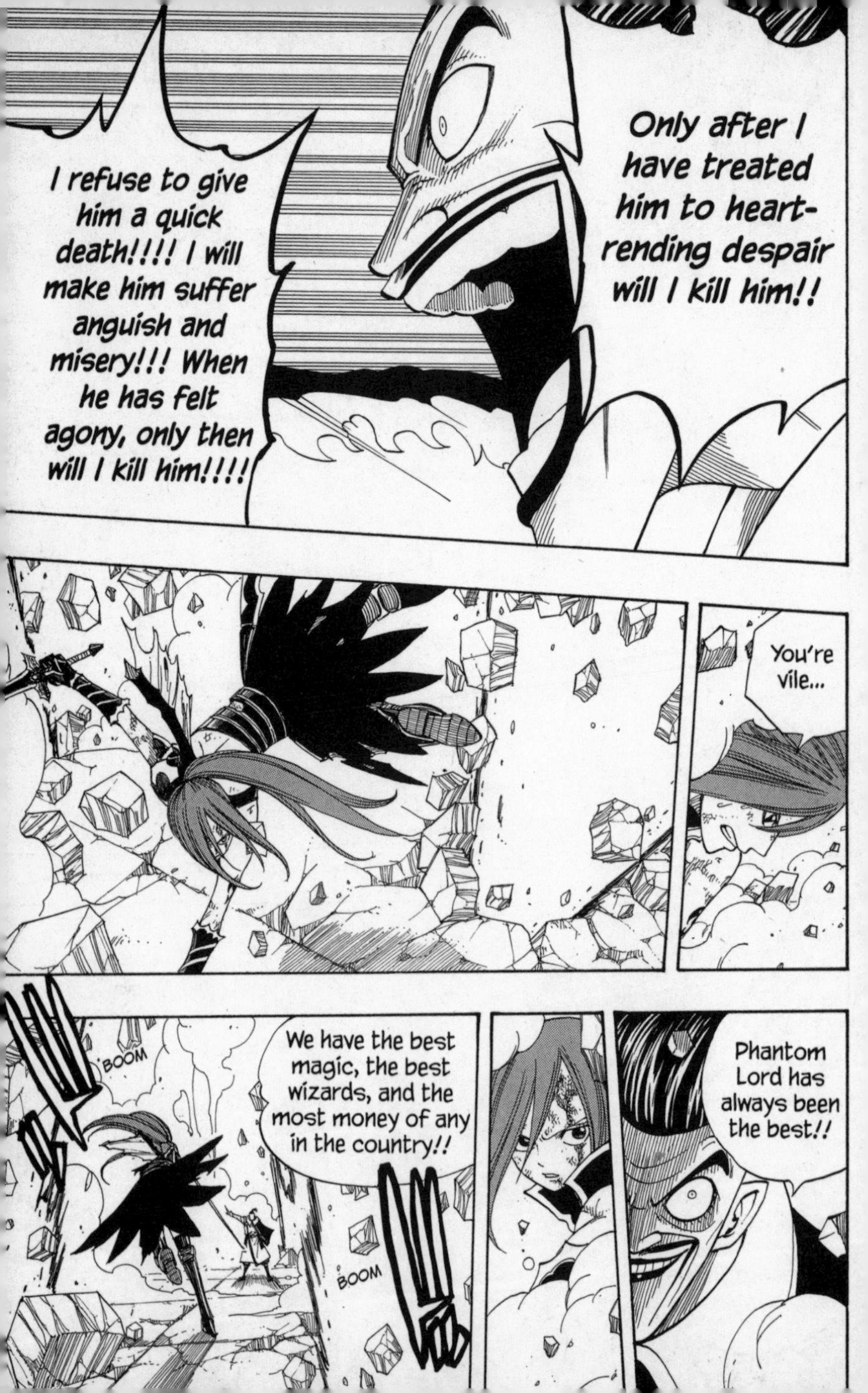
Only after I have treated him to heart-rending despair will I kill him!!
I refuse to give him a quick death!!!! I will make him suffer anguish and misery!!! When he has felt agony, only then will I kill him!!!!
You're vile...
Phantom Lord has always been the best!!
We have the best magic, the best wizards, and the most money of any in the country!!
BOOM
BOOM

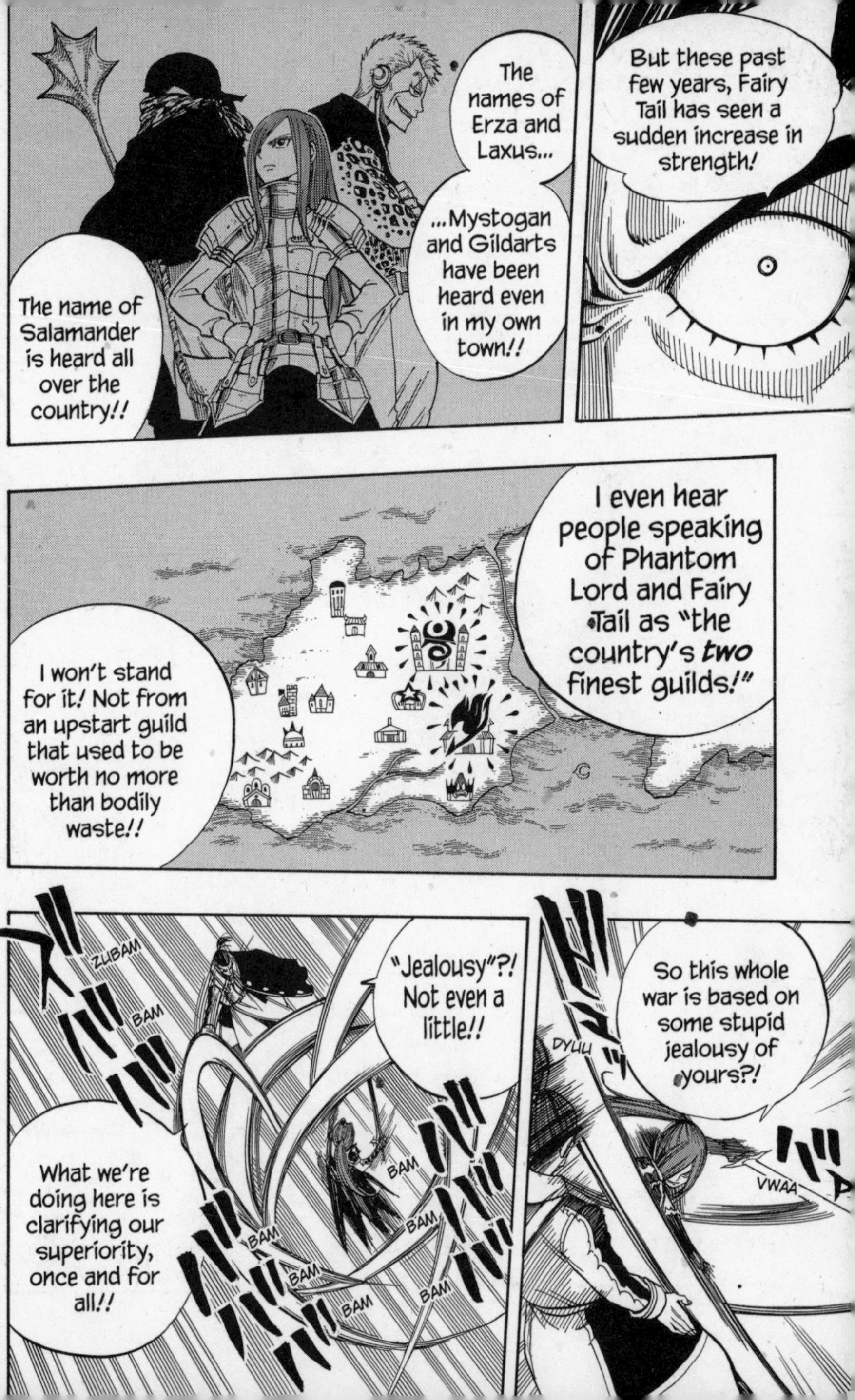
But these past few years, Fairy Tail has seen a sudden increase in strength!
The names of Erza and Laxus...
...Mystogan and Gildarts have been heard even in my own town!!
The name of Salamander is heard all over the country!!
I even hear people speaking of Phantom Lord and Fairy Tail as "the country's *two* finest guilds!"
I won't stand for it! Not from an upstart guild that used to be worth no more than bodily waste!!
So this whole war is based on some stupid jealousy of yours?!
DYUU
VWAA
"Jealousy"?! Not even a little!!
ZUBAM
BAM
BAM
BAM
BAM
BAM
BAM
BAM
What we're doing here is clarifying our superiority, once and for all!!

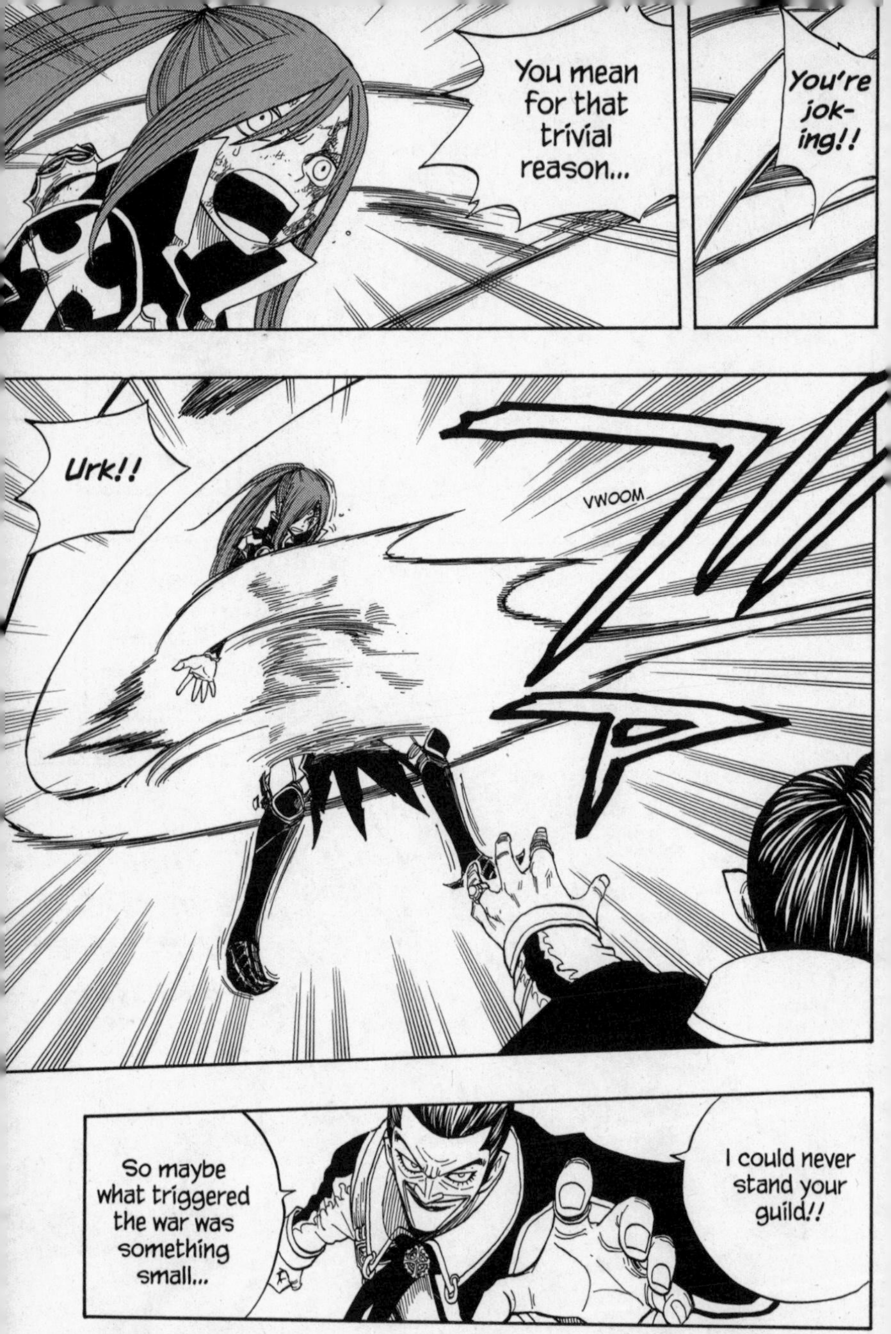
You're jok-ing!!
You mean for that trivial reason...
Urk!!
VWOOM
I could never stand your guild!!
So maybe what triggered the war was something small...

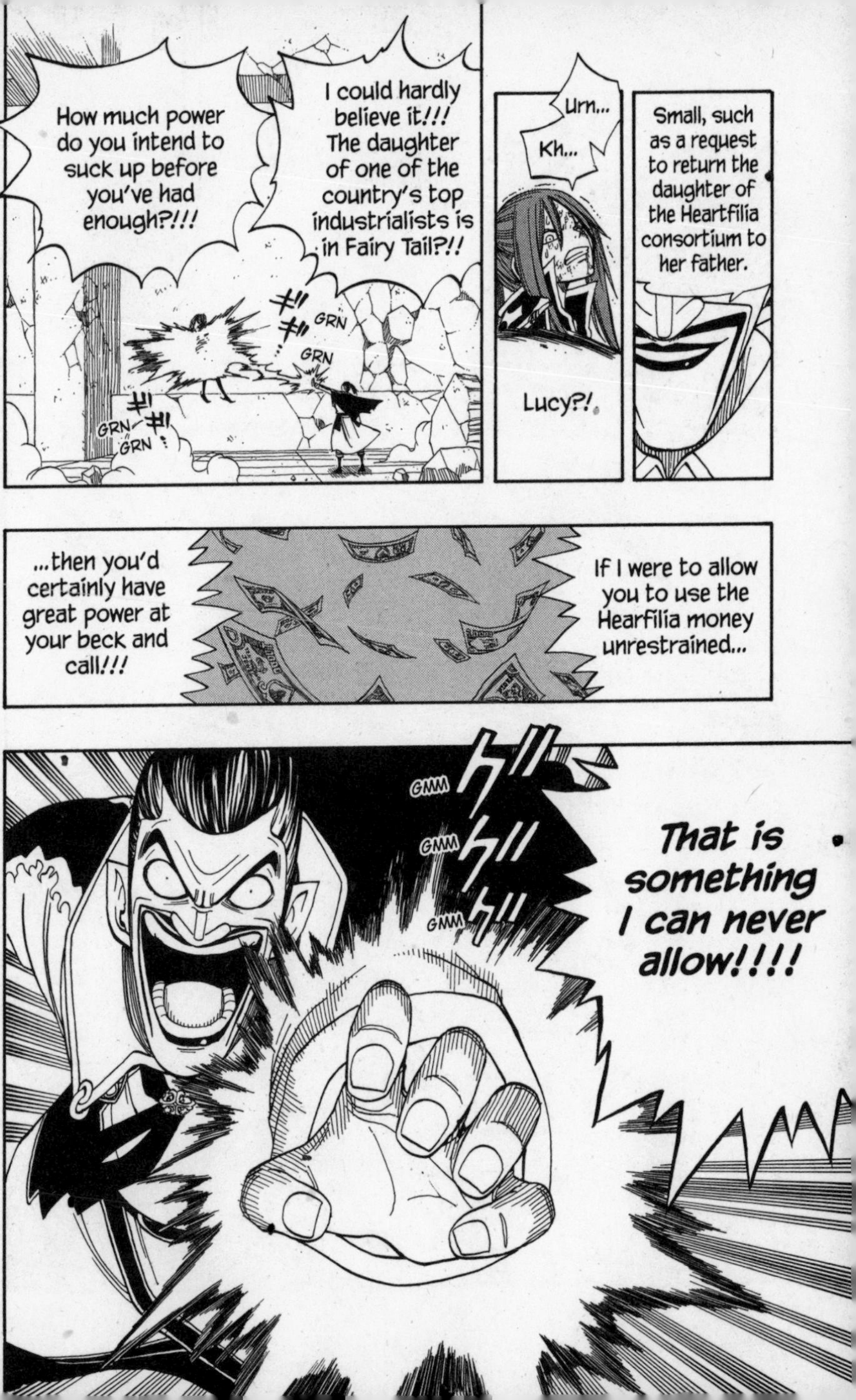
Small, such as a request to return the daughter of the Heartfilia consortium to her father.
Urn...
Kh...
Lucy?!
I could hardly believe it!!! The daughter of one of the country's top industrialists is in Fairy Tail?!!
How much power do you intend to suck up before you've had enough?!!!
GRN
GRN
GRN
GRN
If I were to allow you to use the Hearfilia money unrestrained...
...then you'd certainly have great power at your beck and call!!!
GMM
GMM
GMM
That is something I can never allow!!!!

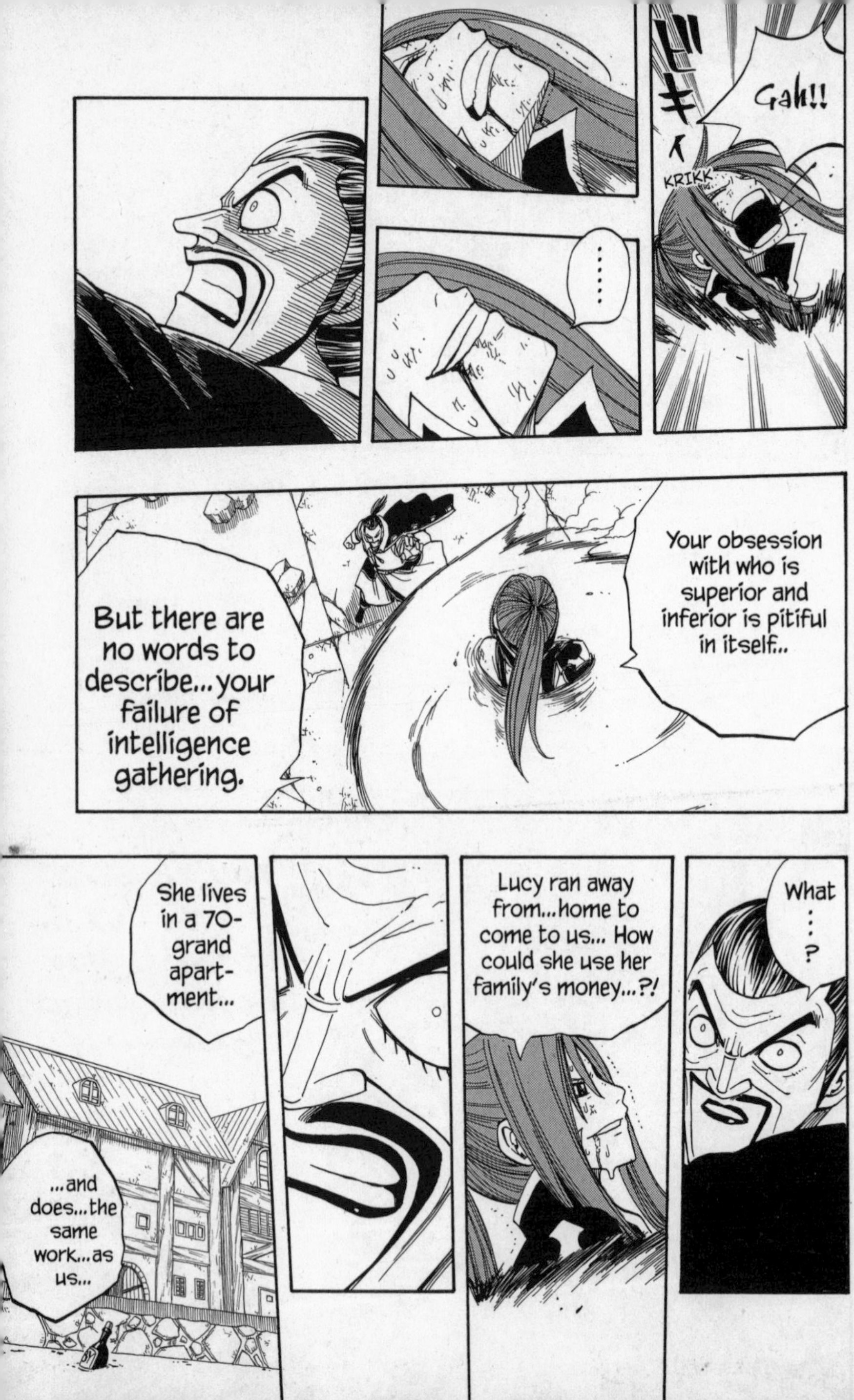
Gah!!
KRIKK
......
Your obsession with who is superior and inferior is pitiful in itself..
But there are no words to describe...your failure of intelligence gathering.
What...?
Lucy ran away from...home to come to us... How could she use her family's money...?!
She lives in a 70-grand apartment...
...and does...the same work...as us...

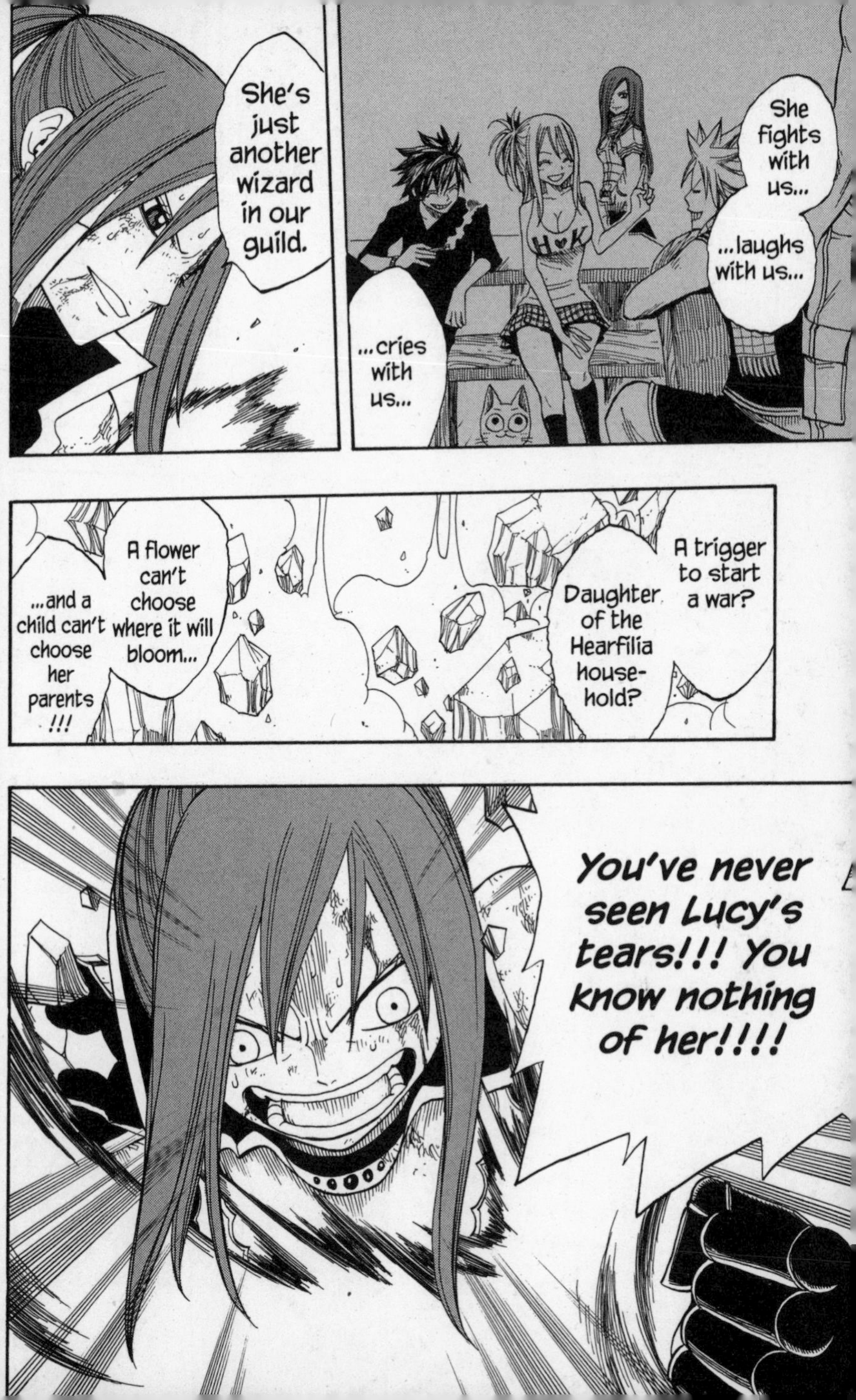
She fights with us...
...laughs with us...
...cries with us...
She's just another wizard in our guild.
A trigger to start a war?
Daughter of the Hearfilia house-hold?
A flower can't choose where it will bloom...
...and a child can't choose her parents!!!
You've never seen Lucy's tears!!! You know nothing of her!!!!

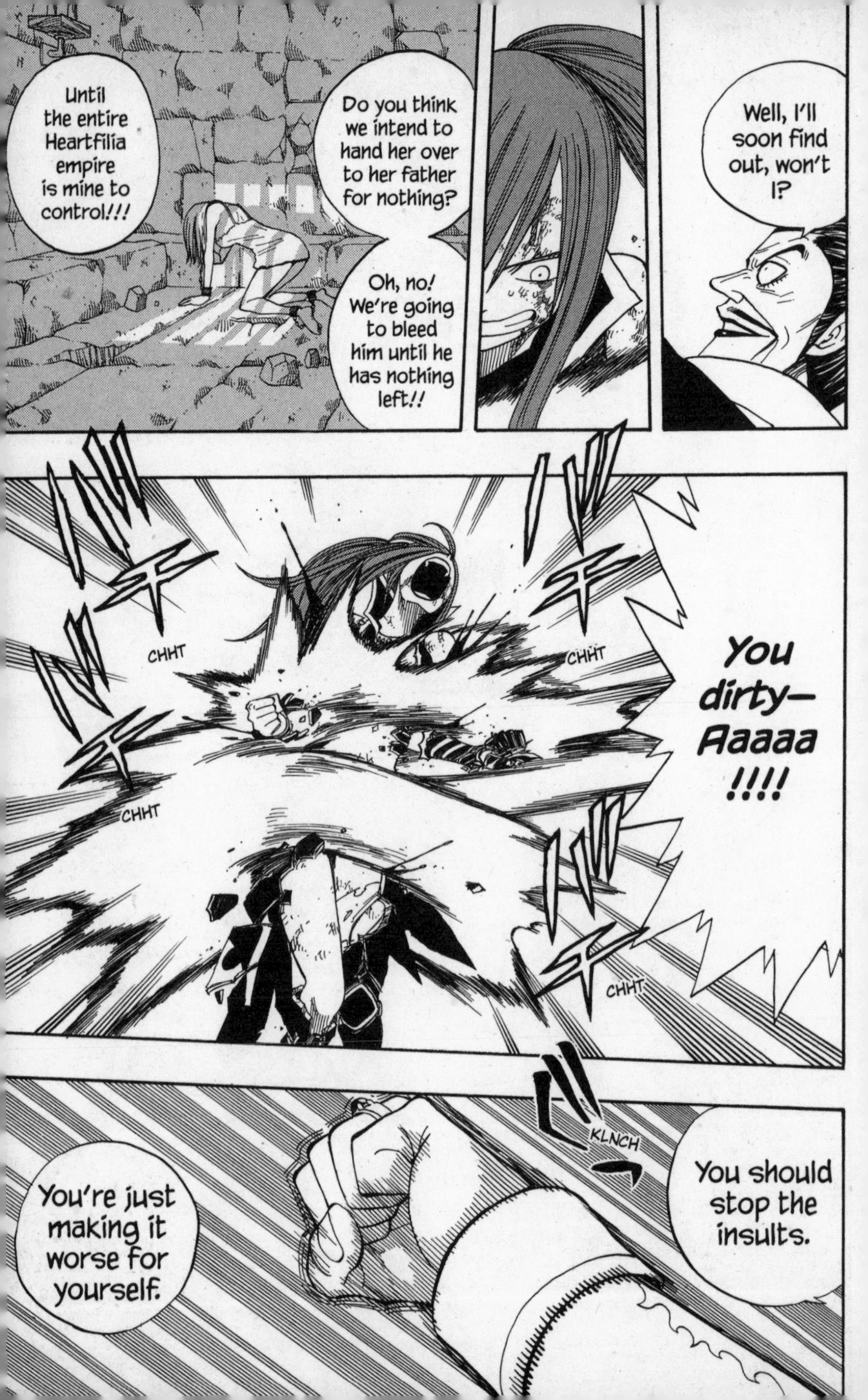
Well, I'll soon find out, won't I?
Do you think we intend to hand her over to her father for nothing?
Oh, no! We're going to bleed him until he has nothing left!!
Until the entire Heartfilia empire is mine to control!!!
You dirty— Aaaaa!!!!
CHHT
CHHT
CHHT
CHHT
KLNCH
You should stop the insults.
You're just making it worse for yourself.

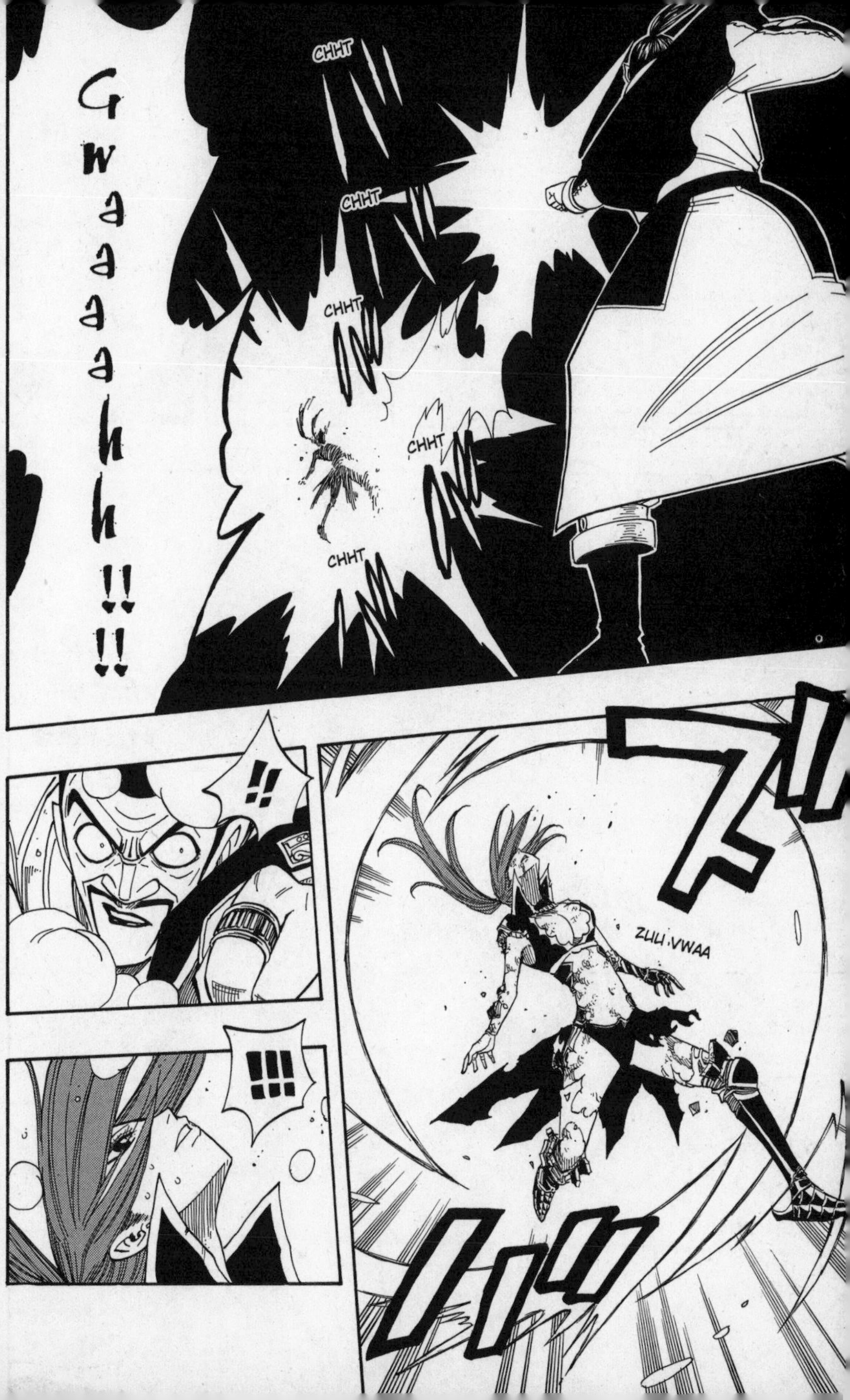
CHHT
CHHT
CHHT
CHHT
CHHT
Gwaaaahh!!!!
ZUU VWAA
!!
!!!!

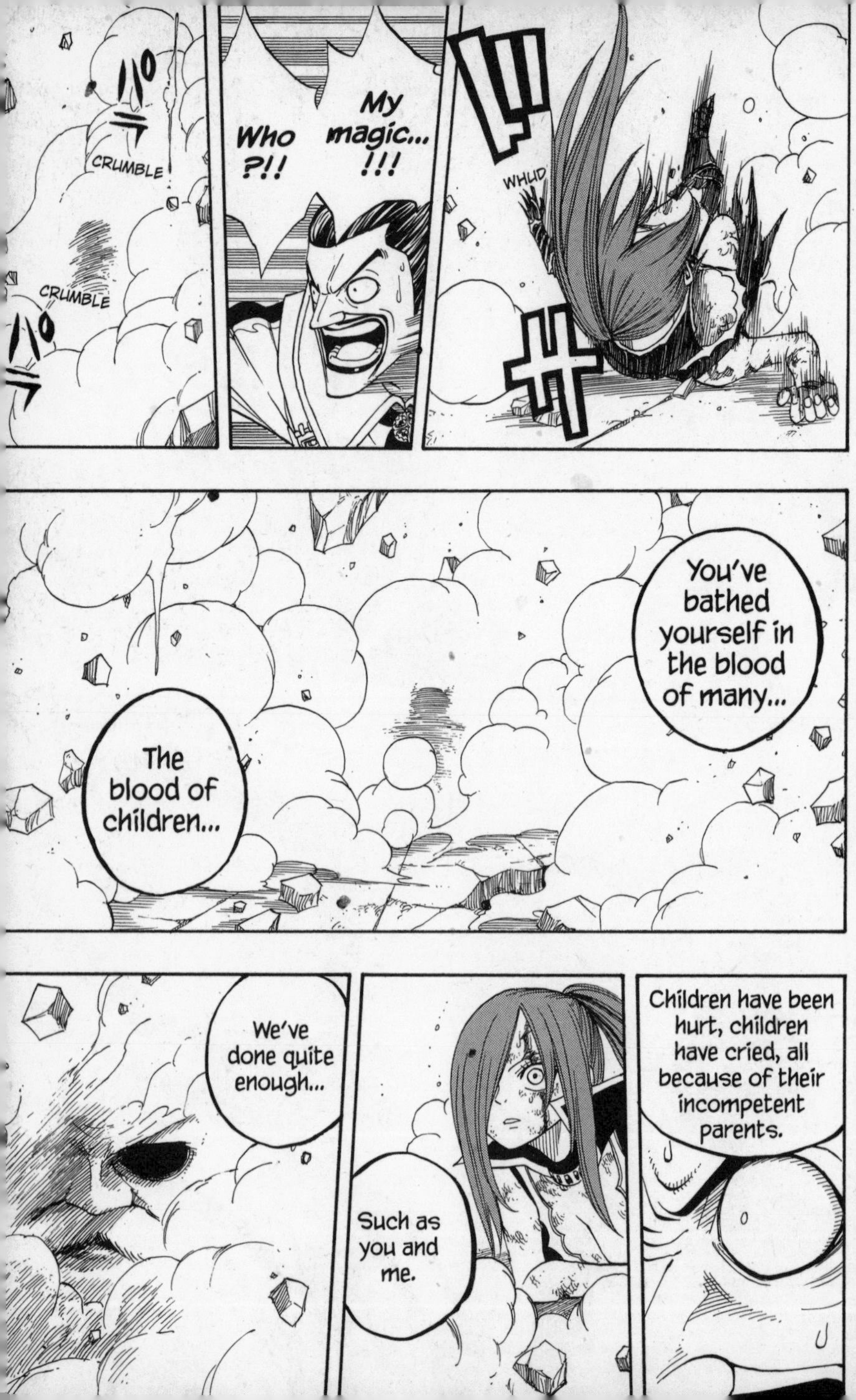
WHUD
My magic... !!!
Who ?!!
CRUMBLE
CRUMBLE
You've bathed yourself in the blood of many...
The blood of children...
Children have been hurt, children have cried, all because of their incompetent parents.
Such as you and me.
We've done quite enough...

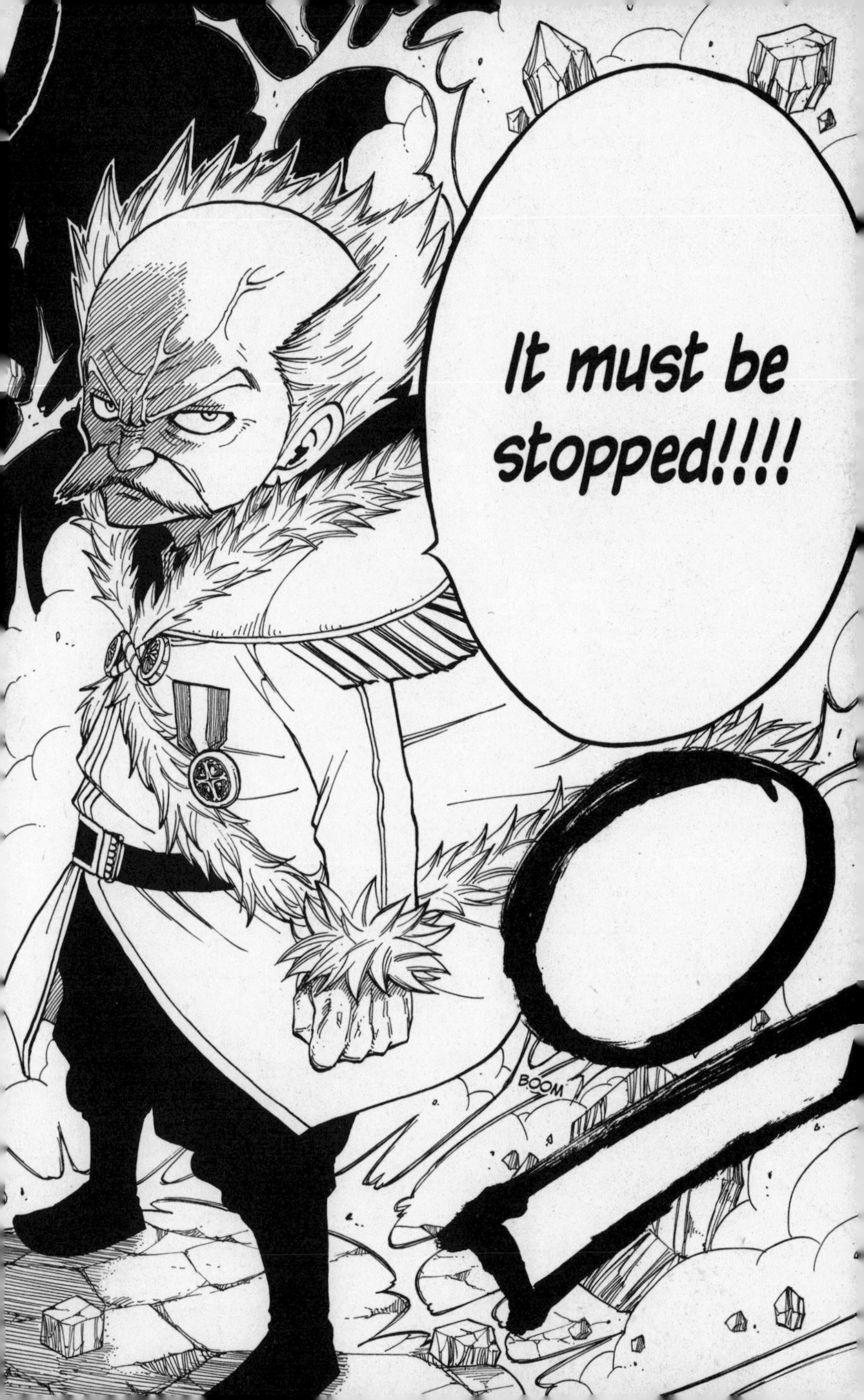
It must be stopped!!!!
BOOM

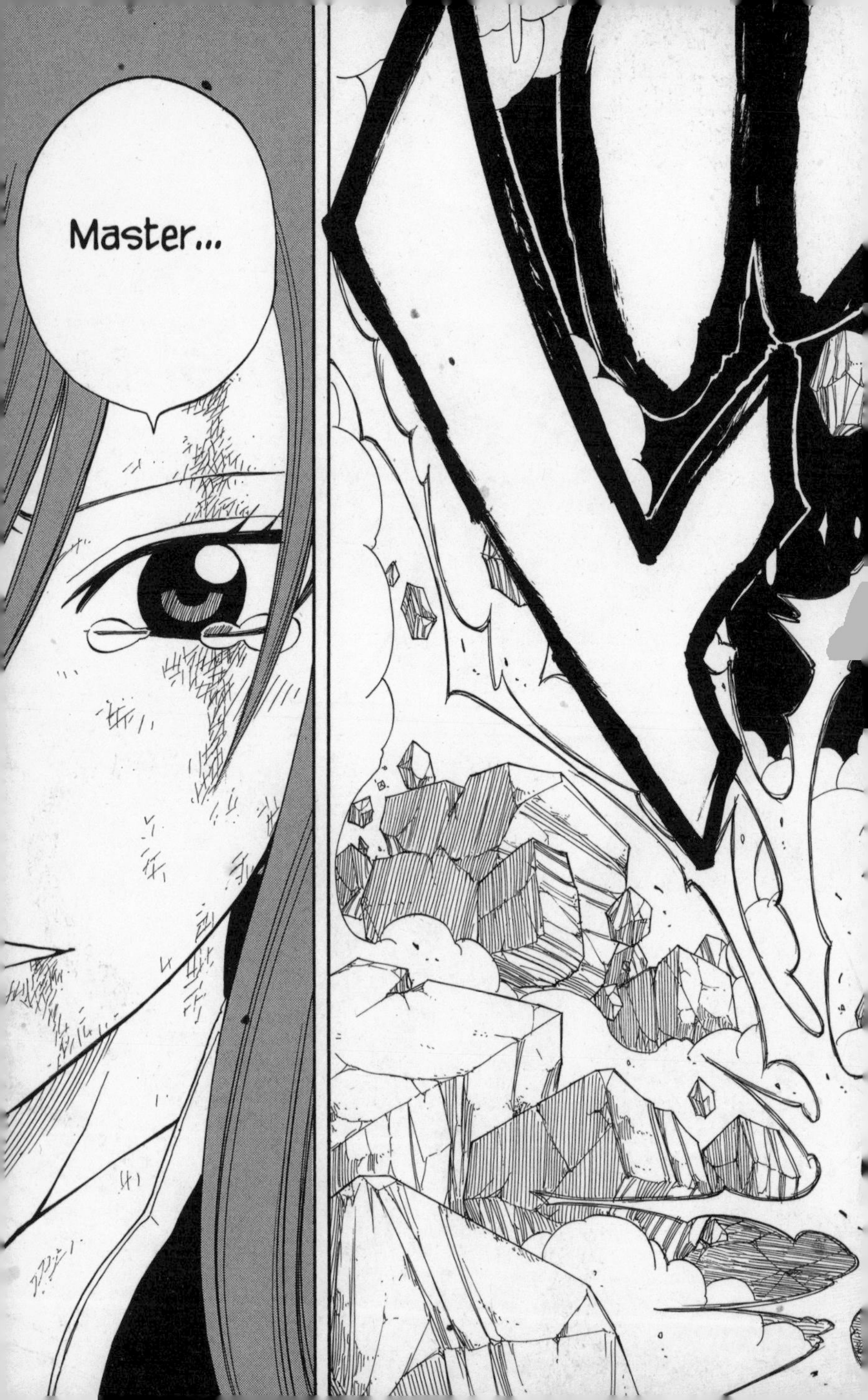
Master...

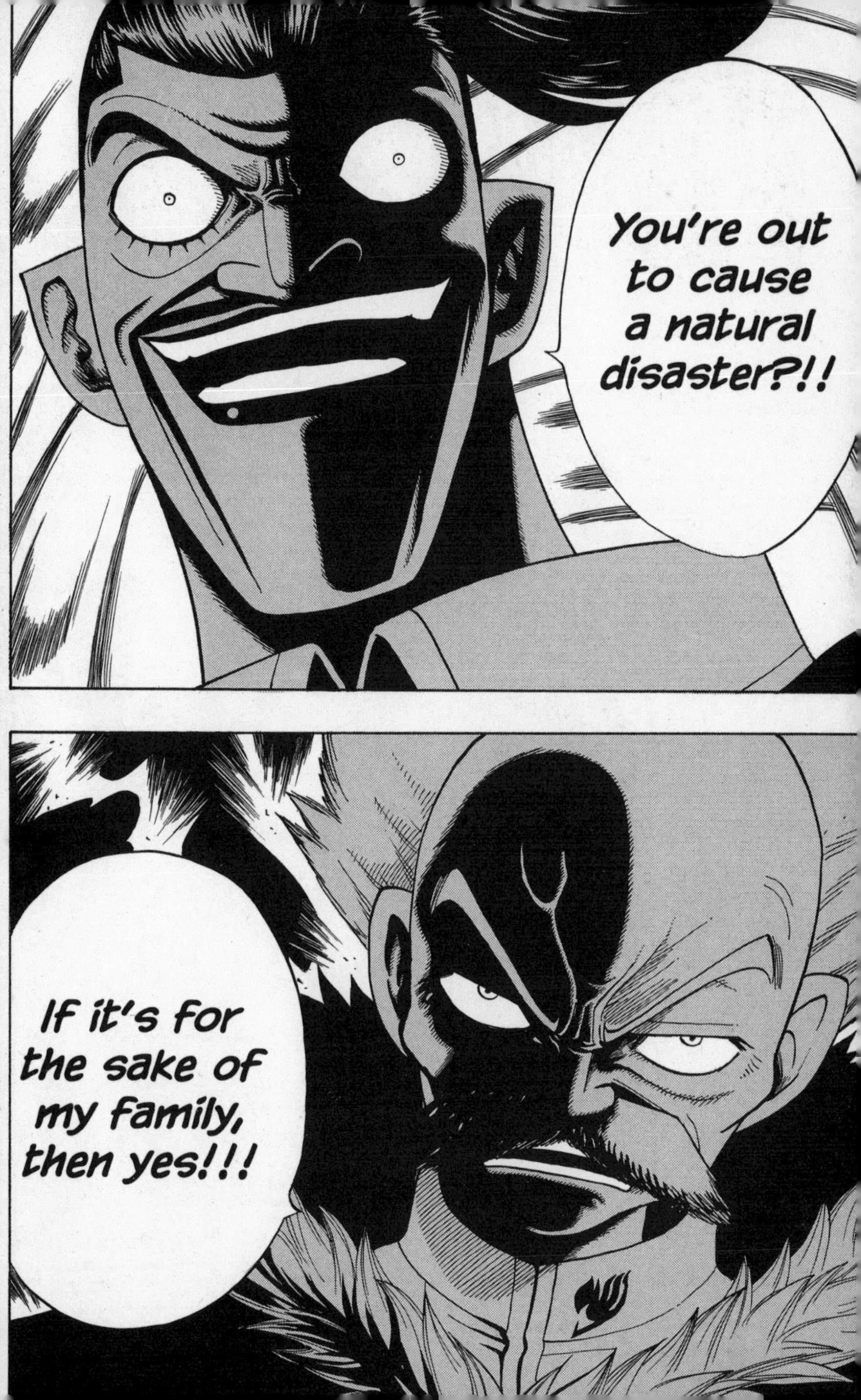
You're out to cause a natural disaster?!!
If it's for the sake of my family, then yes!!!

FAIRY TAIL

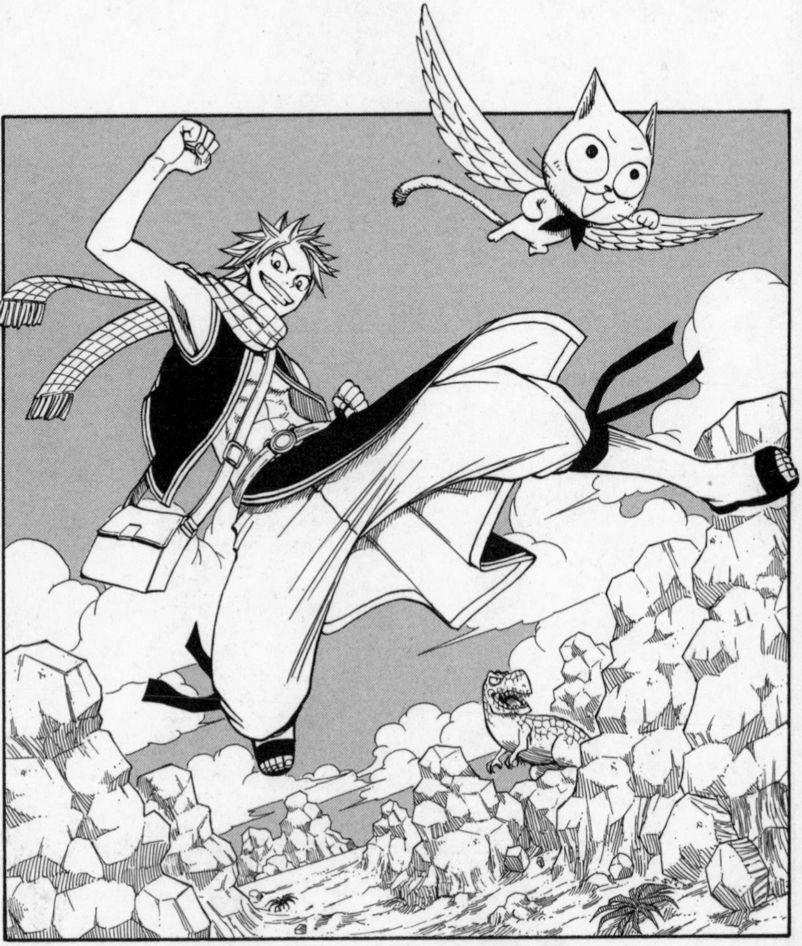

Chapter 65: Fairy Law

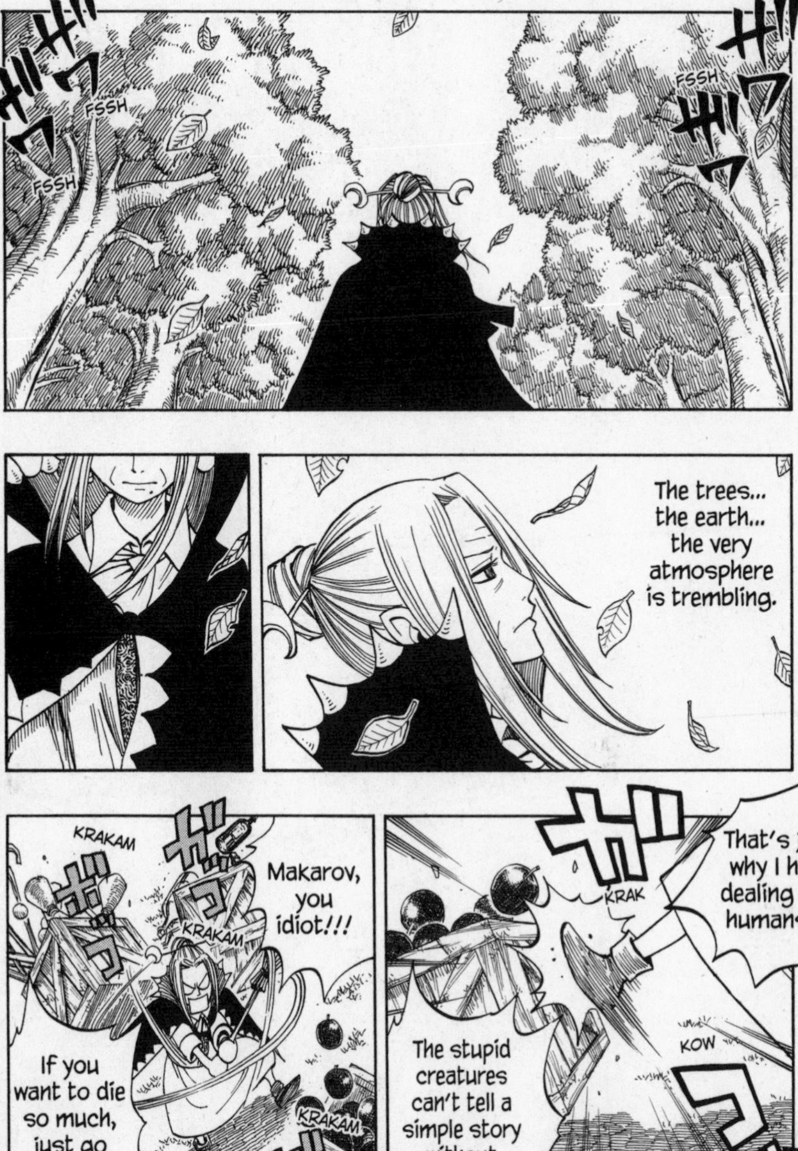
FSSH
FSSH
FSSH
FSSH
The trees... the earth... the very atmosphere is trembling.
That's just why I hate dealing with humans!!!
KRAK
The stupid creatures can't tell a simple story without turning it into a war!!!
KOW
Makarov, you idiot!!!
KRAKAM
KRAKAM
If you want to die so much, just go ahead and do it!!!
KRAKAM

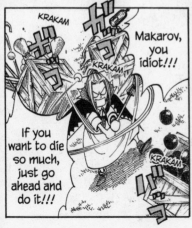

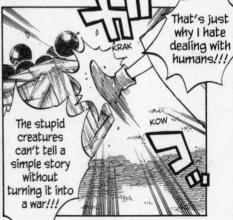

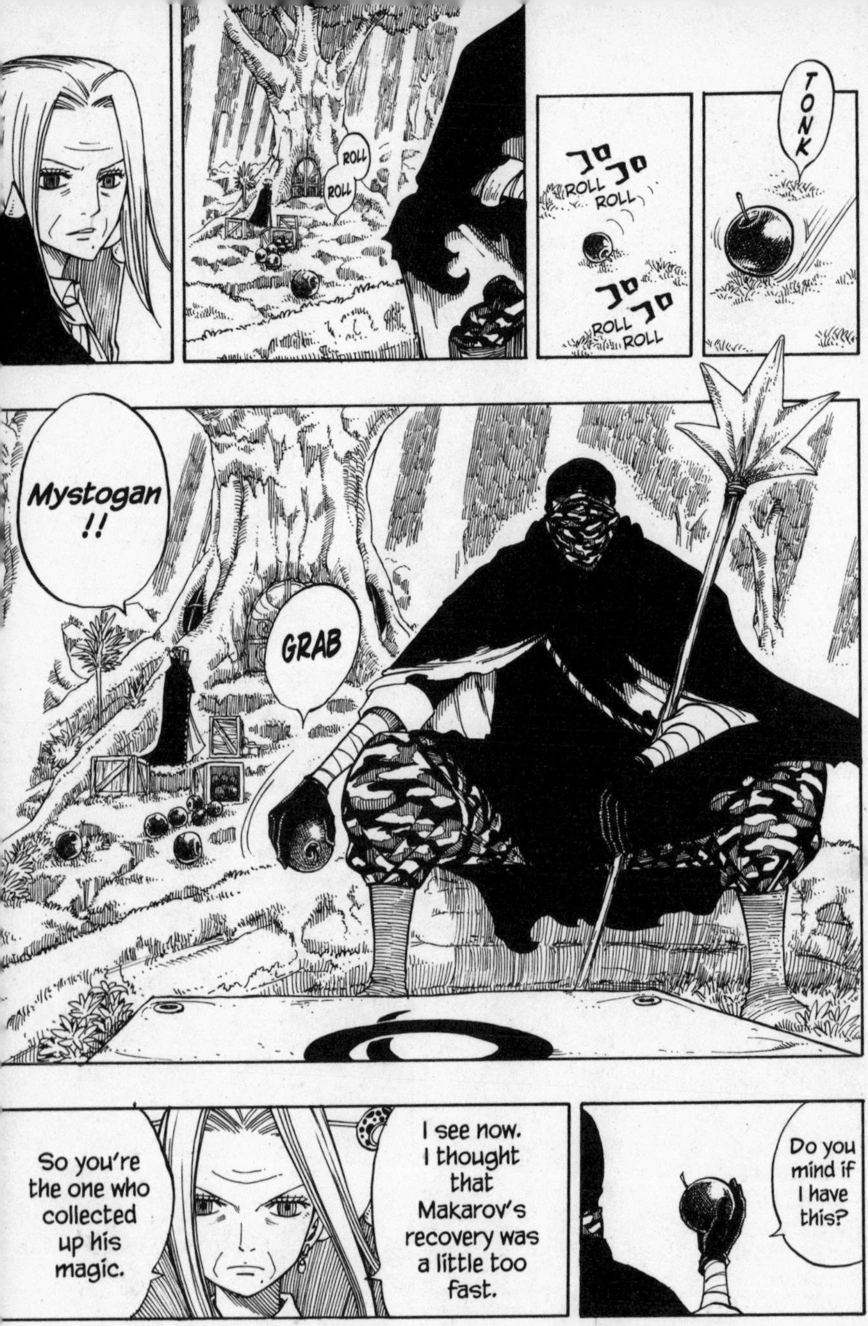
TONK
コロコロ
ROLL ROLL
コロコロ
ROLL ROLL
ROLL
ROLL
Mystogan !!
GRAB
Do you mind if I have this?
I see now. I thought that Makarov's recovery was a little too fast.
So you're the one who collected up his magic.

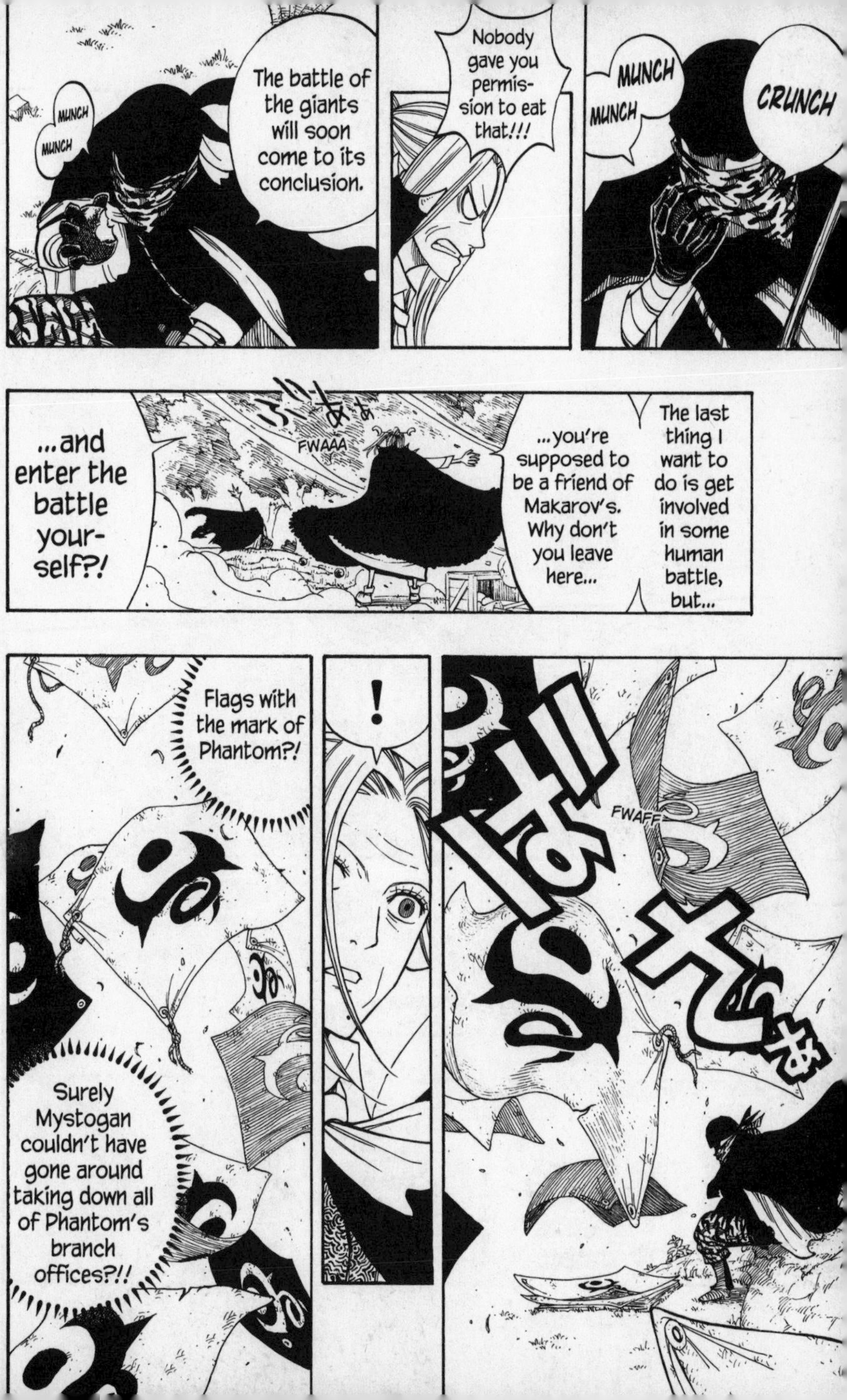
CRUNCH
MUNCH
MUNCH
Nobody gave you permis-sion to eat that!!!
The battle of the giants will soon come to its conclusion.
MUNCH
MUNCH
The last thing I want to do is get involved in some human battle, but...
...you're supposed to be a friend of Makarov's. Why don't you leave here...
FWAAA
...and enter the battle your-self?!
FWAFF
!
Flags with the mark of Phantom?!
Surely Mystogan couldn't have gone around taking down all of Phantom's branch offices?!!

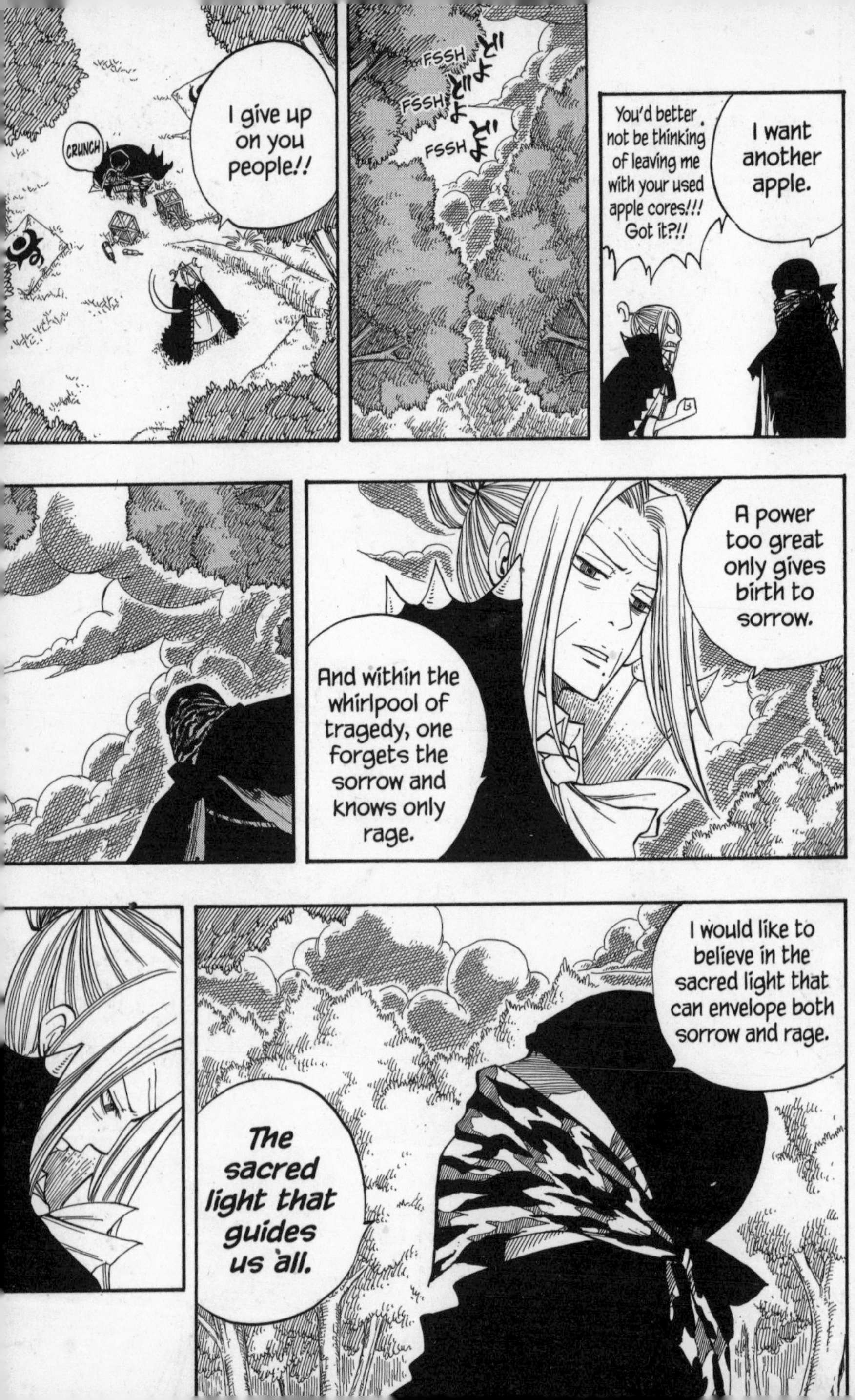
I want another apple.
You'd better not be thinking of leaving me with your used apple cores!!! Got it?!!
FSSH
FSSH
FSSH
I give up on you people!!
CRUNCH
A power too great only gives birth to sorrow.
And within the whirlpool of tragedy, one forgets the sorrow and knows only rage.
I would like to believe in the sacred light that can envelope both sorrow and rage.
The sacred light that guides us all.

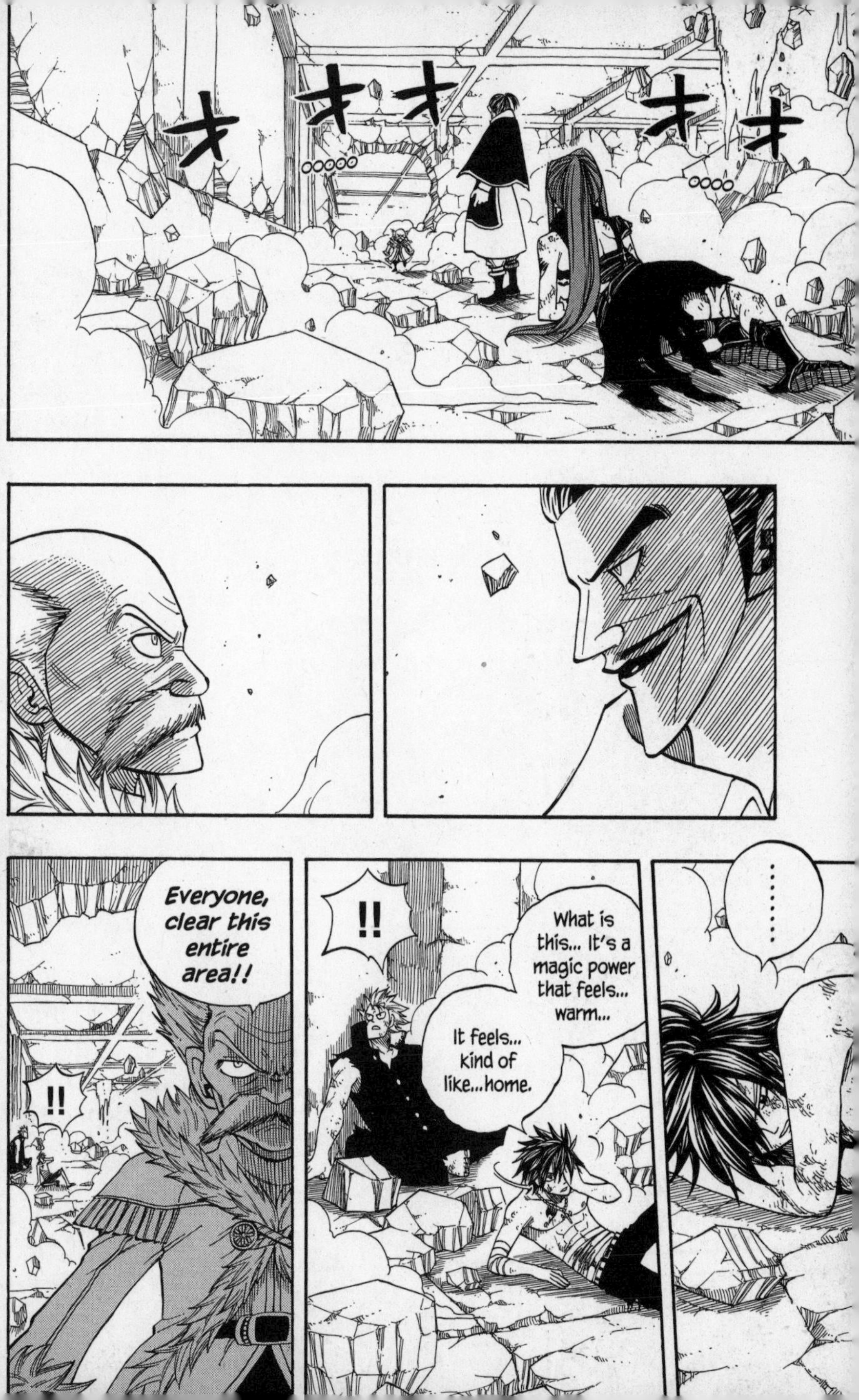

オオ
oooo
オオオ
ooooo
......
!!
What is this... It's a magic power that feels... warm...
It feels... kind of like...home.
Everyone, clear this entire area!!
!!

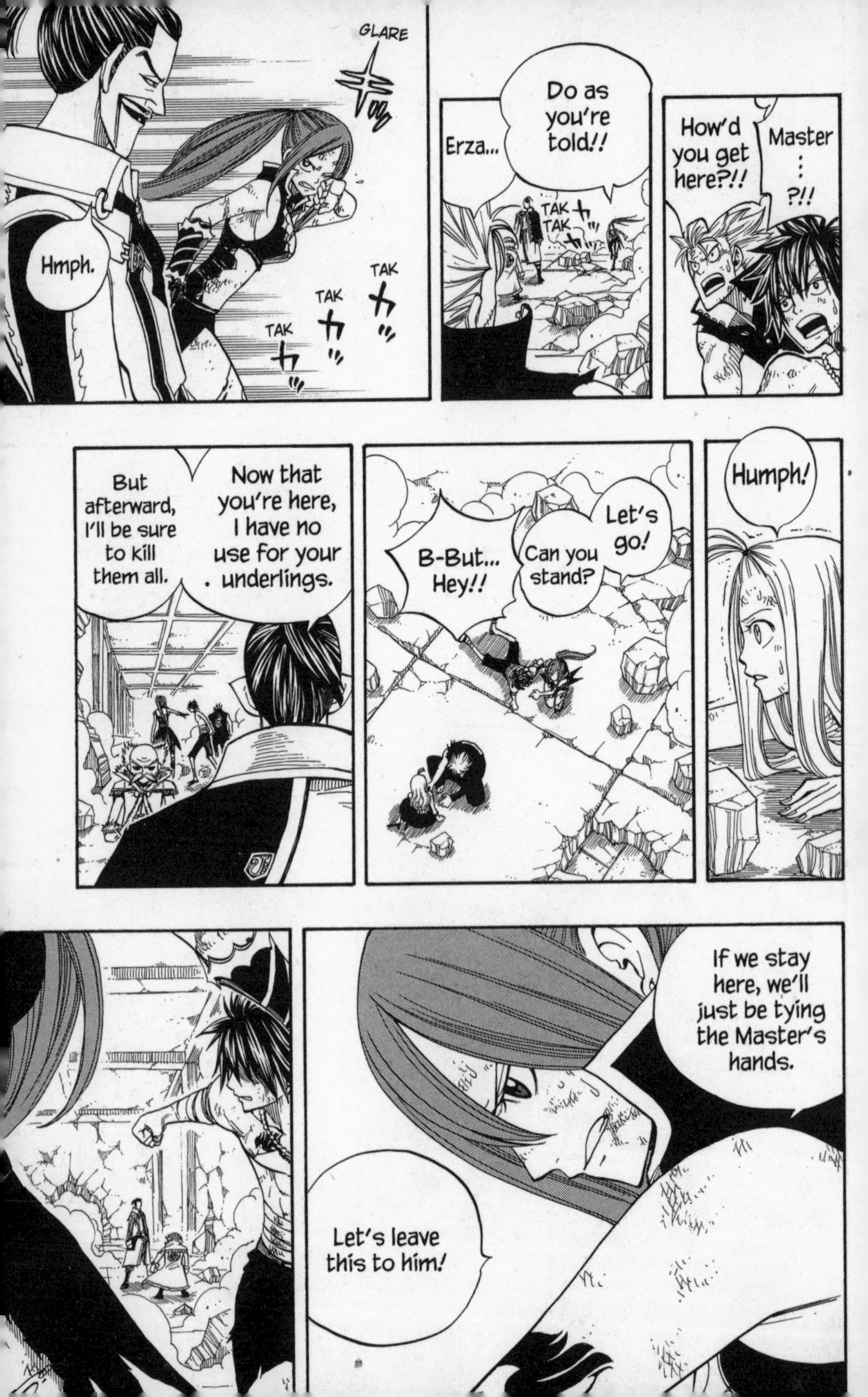
Master ... ?!!
How'd you get here?!!
Do as you're told!!
Erza...
TAK TAK
GLARE
TAK TAK TAK
Hmph.
Humph!
Let's go!
Can you stand?
B-But... Hey!!
Now that you're here, I have no use for your underlings.
But afterward, I'll be sure to kill them all.
If we stay here, we'll just be tying the Master's hands.
Let's leave this to him!

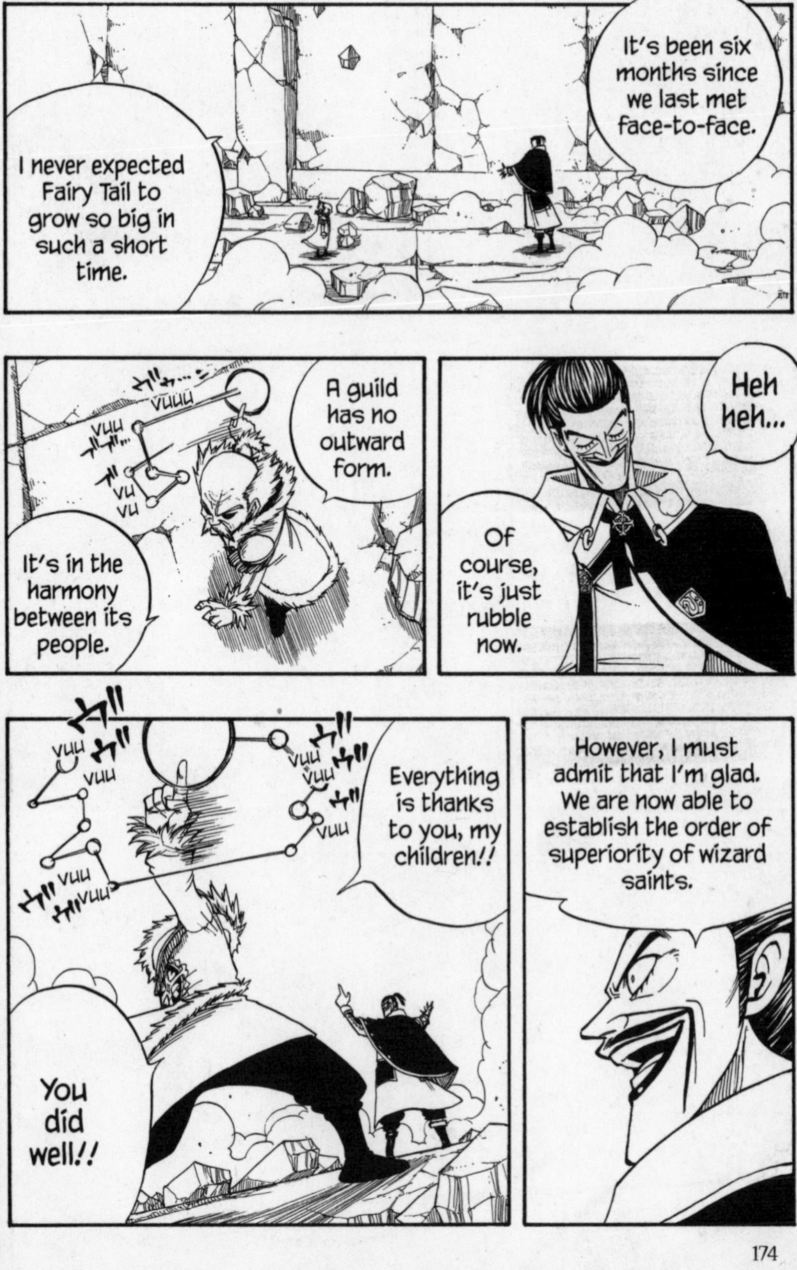
It's been six months since we last met face-to-face.
I never expected Fairy Tail to grow so big in such a short time.
Heh heh...
Of course, it's just rubble now.
A guild has no outward form.
VUUU
VUU
VU
VU
It's in the harmony between its people.
However, I must admit that I'm glad. We are now able to establish the order of superiority of wizard saints.
Everything is thanks to you, my children!!
VUU
VUU
VUU
VUU
VUU
VUU
VUU
You did well!!

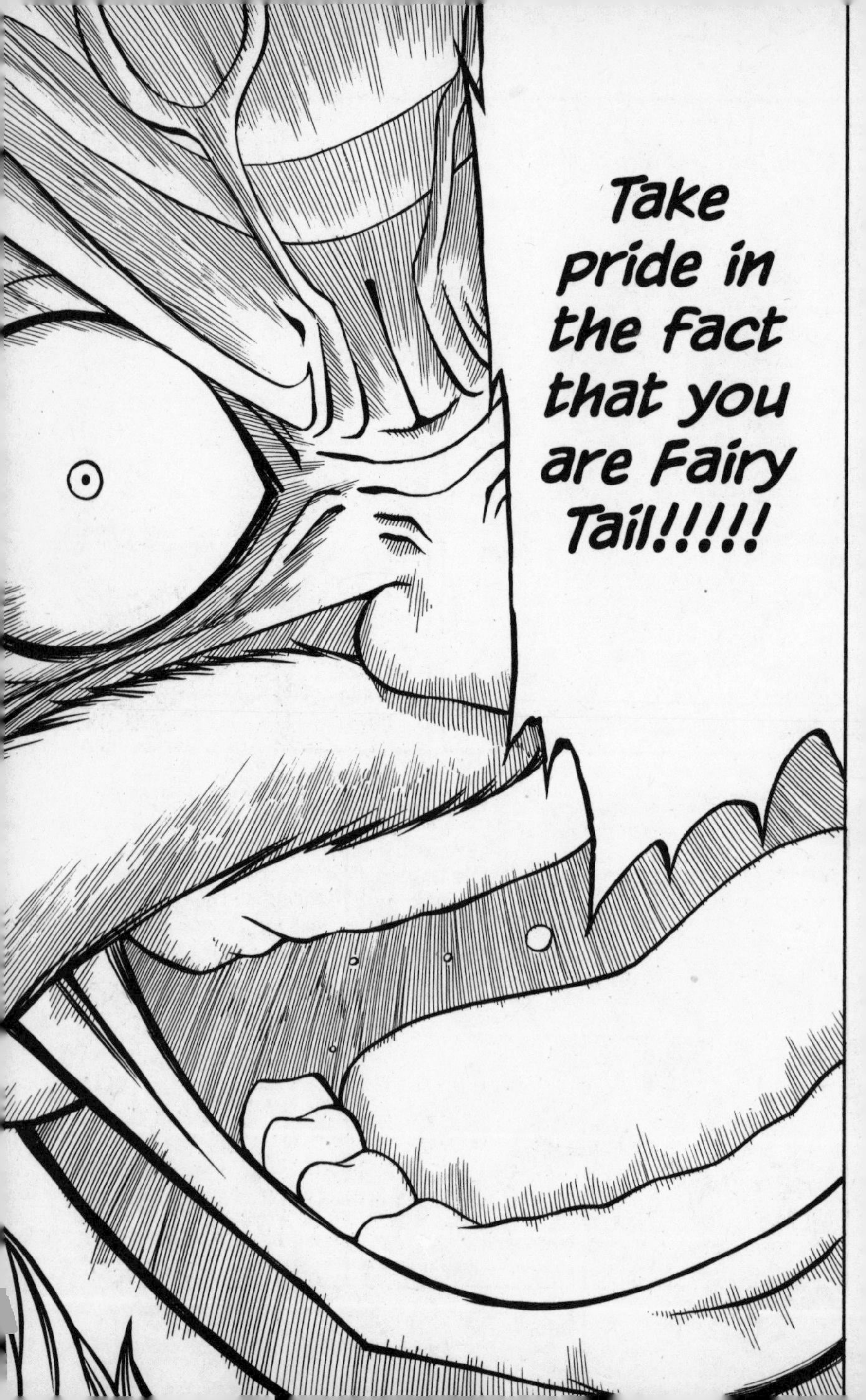
Take pride in the fact that you are Fairy Tail!!!!!

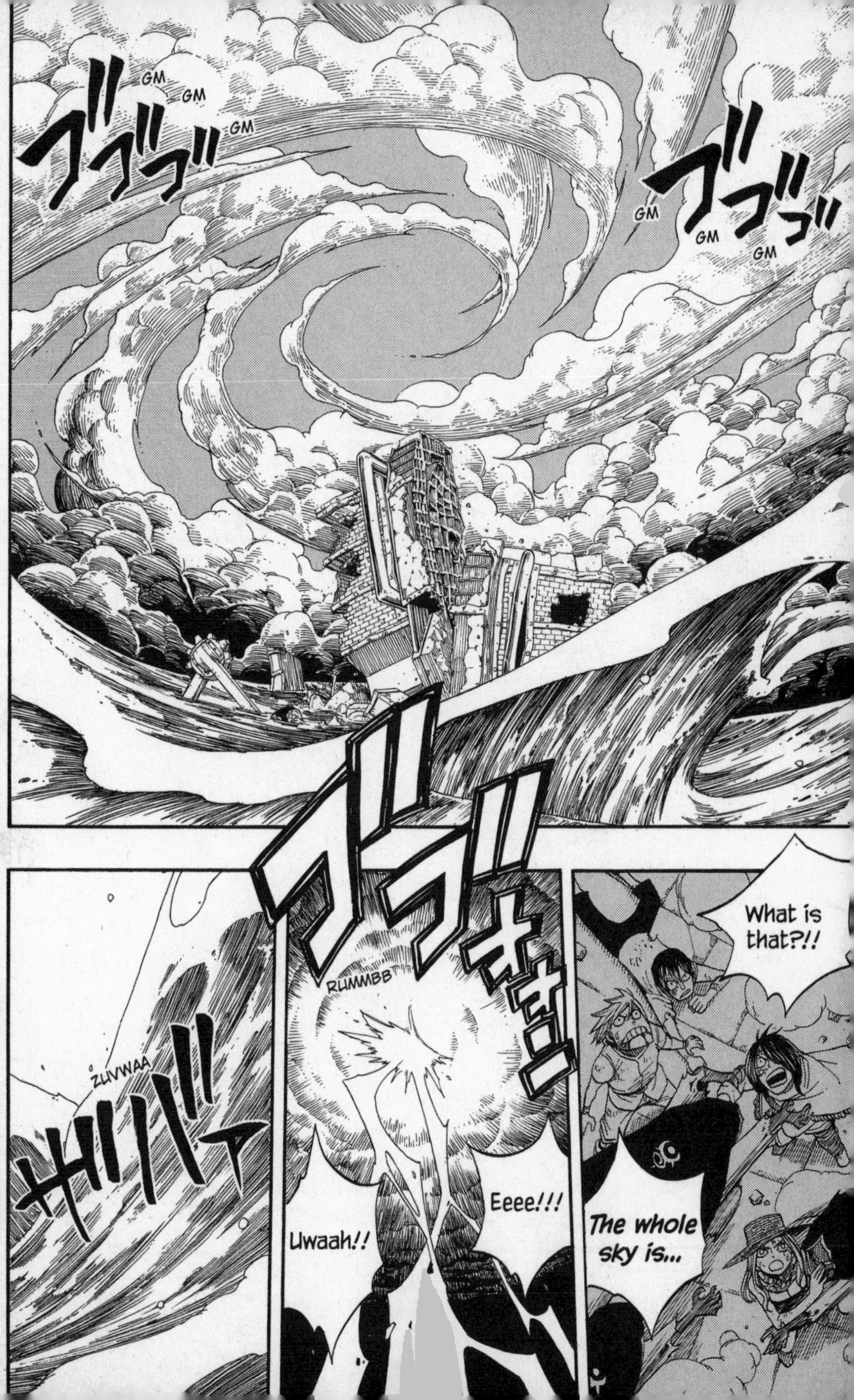
GM
GM
GM
GM
GM
GM
What is that?!!
The whole sky is...
RUMMBB
Eeee!!!
Uwaah!!
ZUVWAA

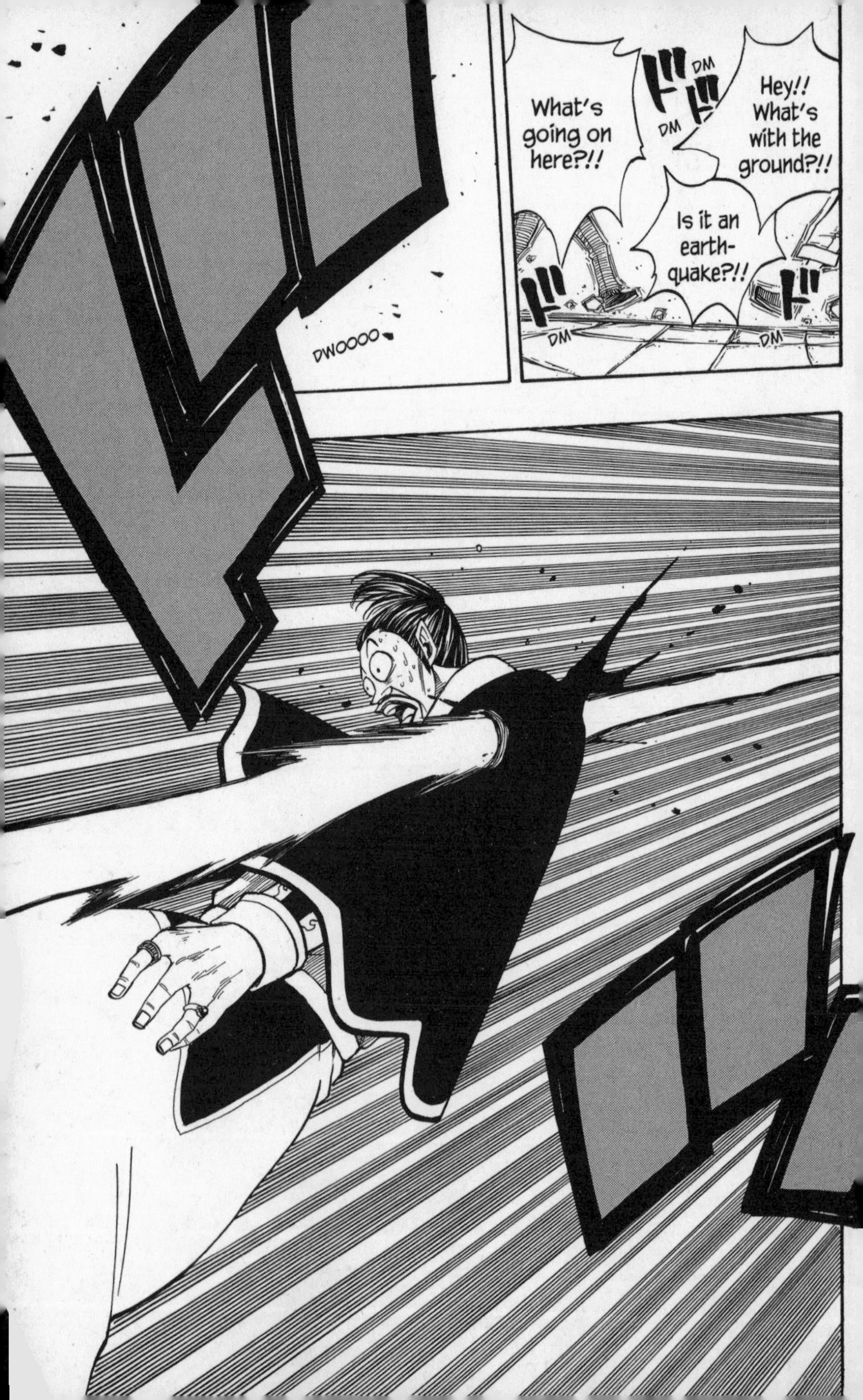
Hey!! What's with the ground?!!
DM
DM
What's going on here?!!
Is it an earth-quake?!!
DM
DM
DWOOOO

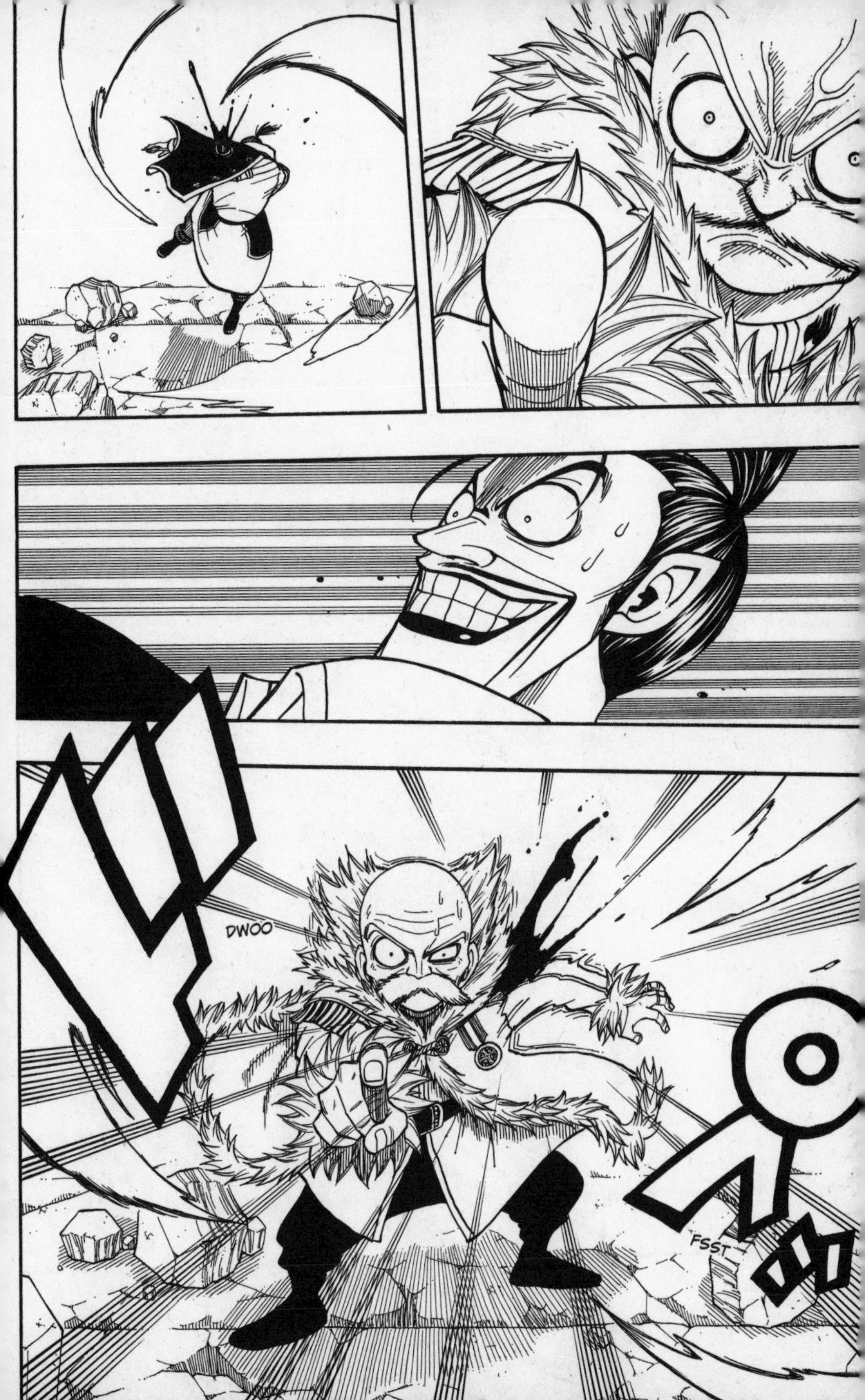
FSST
DWOO

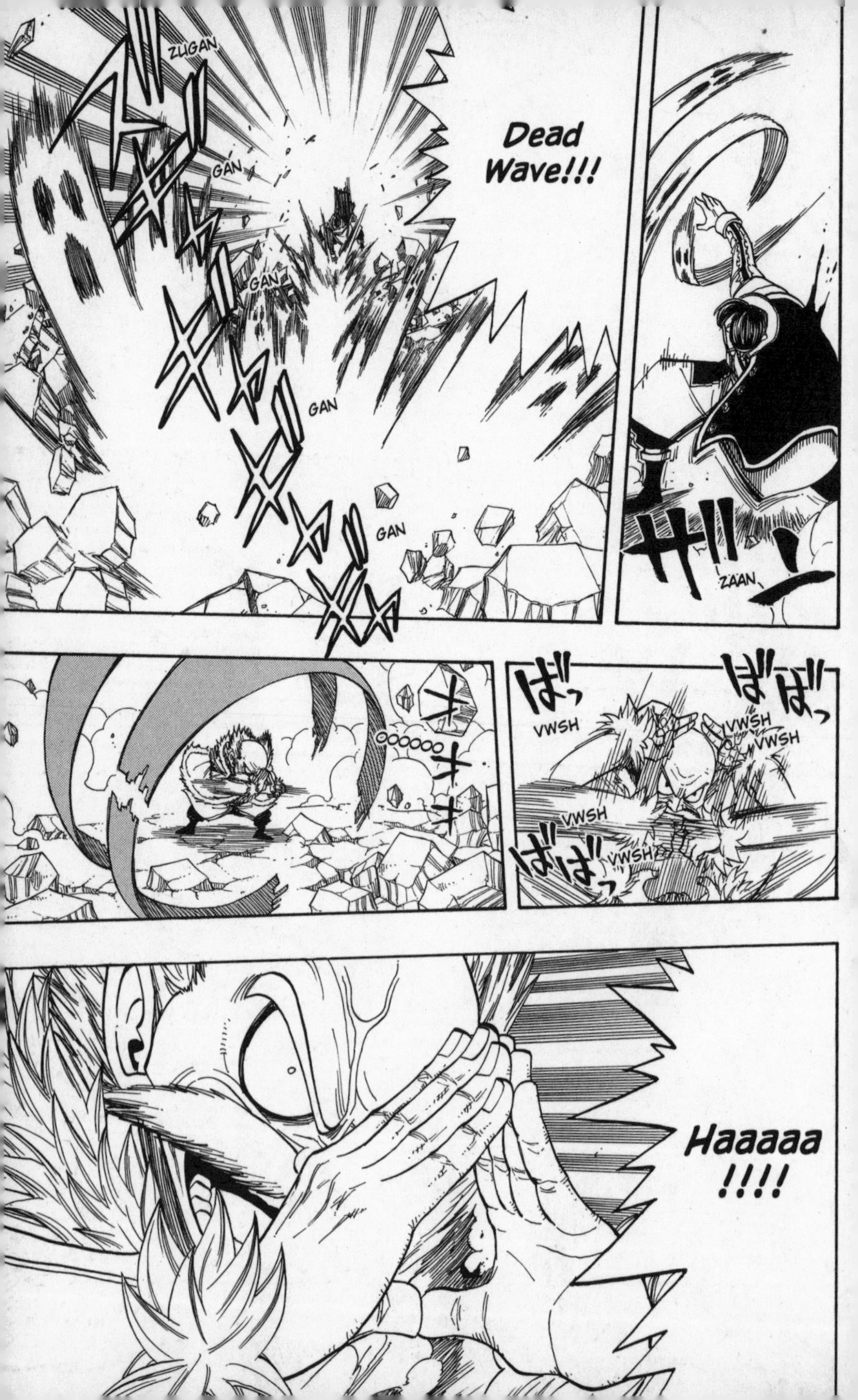
ZAAN
Dead Wave!!!
ZUGAN
GAN
GAN
GAN
GAN
ばばっ
VWSH
VWSH
ばっ
VWSH
VWSH
ばばっ
VWSH
OOOOOO
Haaaaa !!!!

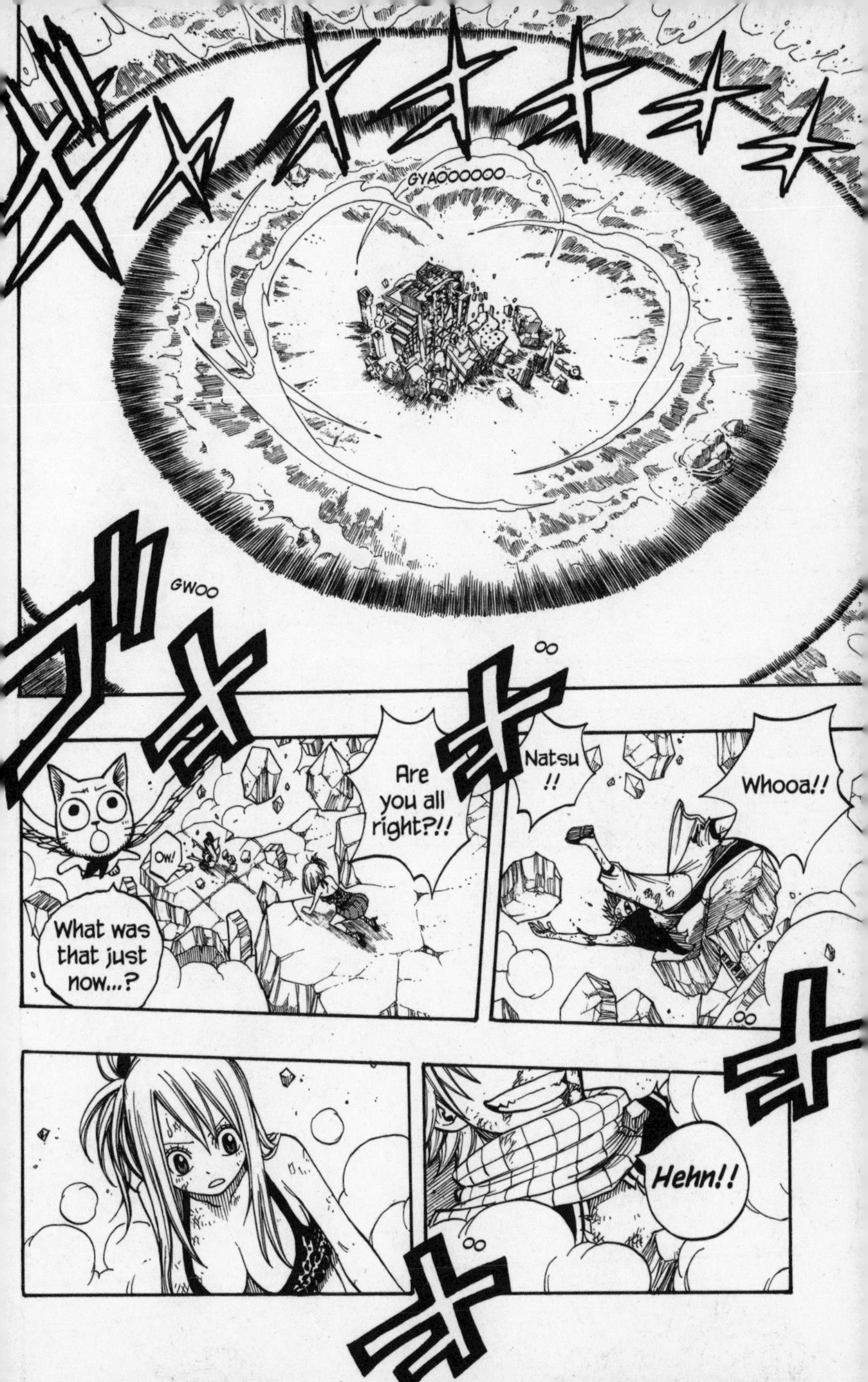
GYAOOOOOO
GWOO
Whooa!!
Natsu !!
Are you all right?!!
Ow!
What was that just now...?
Hehn!!

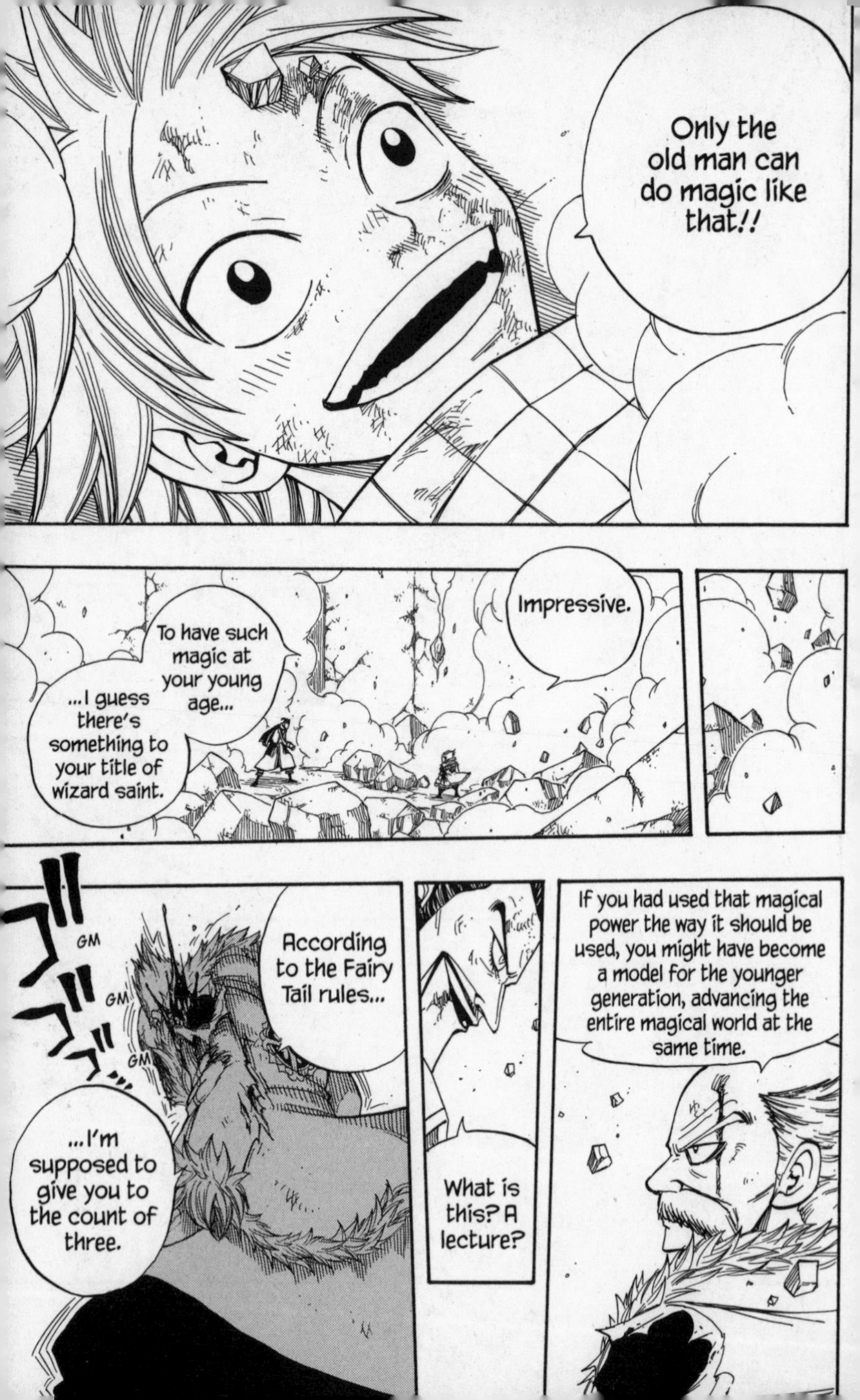
Only the old man can do magic like that!!
Impressive.
To have such magic at your young age...
...I guess there's something to your title of wizard saint.
If you had used that magical power the way it should be used, you might have become a model for the younger generation, advancing the entire magical world at the same time.
What is this? A lecture?
GM GM GM
According to the Fairy Tail rules...
...I'm supposed to give you to the count of three.

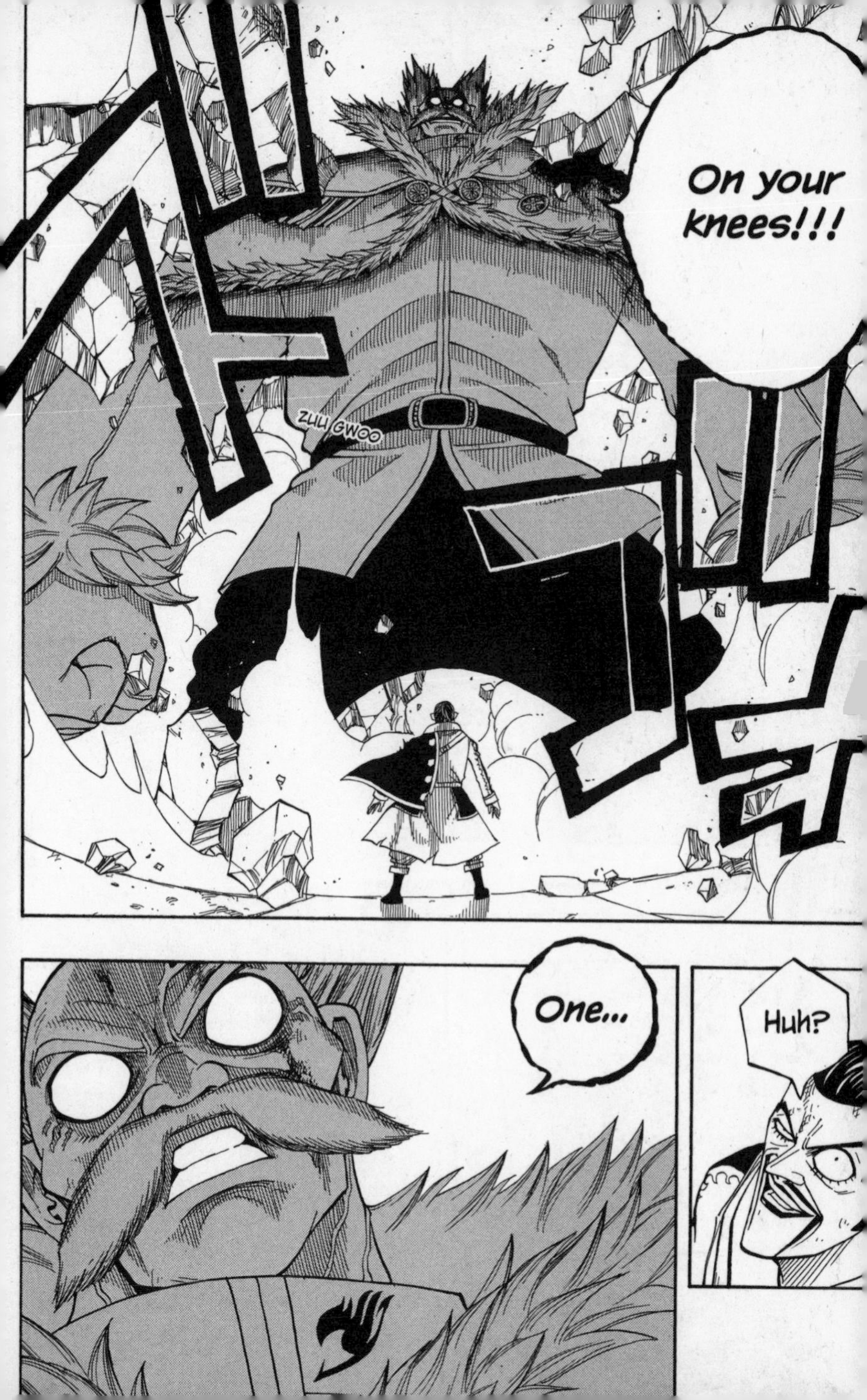
On your knees!!!
ZUU GWOO
Huh?
One...

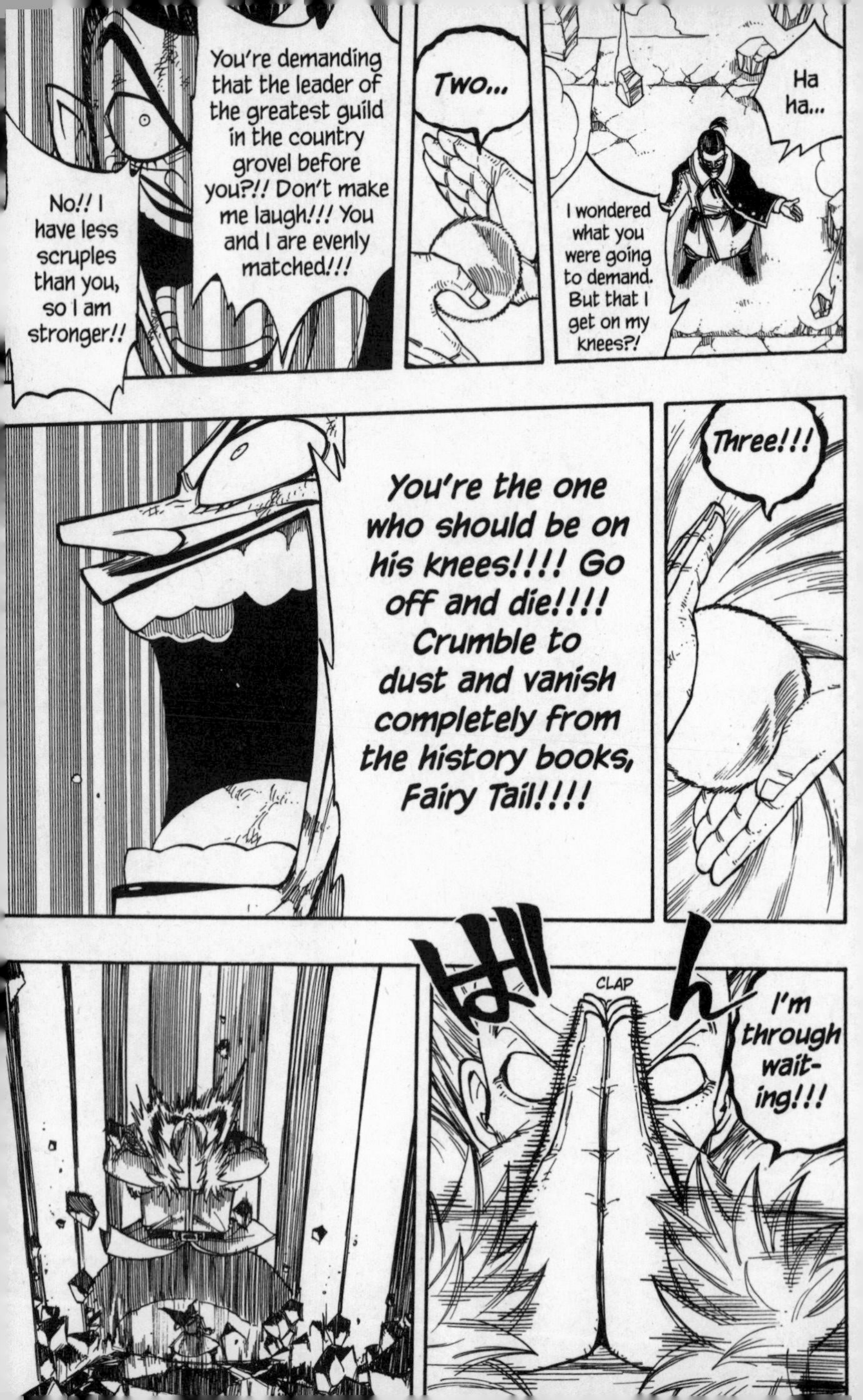
Ha ha...
I wondered what you were going to demand. But that I get on my knees?!
Two...
You're demanding that the leader of the greatest guild in the country grovel before you?!! Don't make me laugh!!! You and I are evenly matched!!!
No!! I have less scruples than you, so I am stronger!!
Three!!!
You're the one who should be on his knees!!!! Go off and die!!!! Crumble to dust and vanish completely from the history books, Fairy Tail!!!!
CLAP
I'm through wait-ing!!!

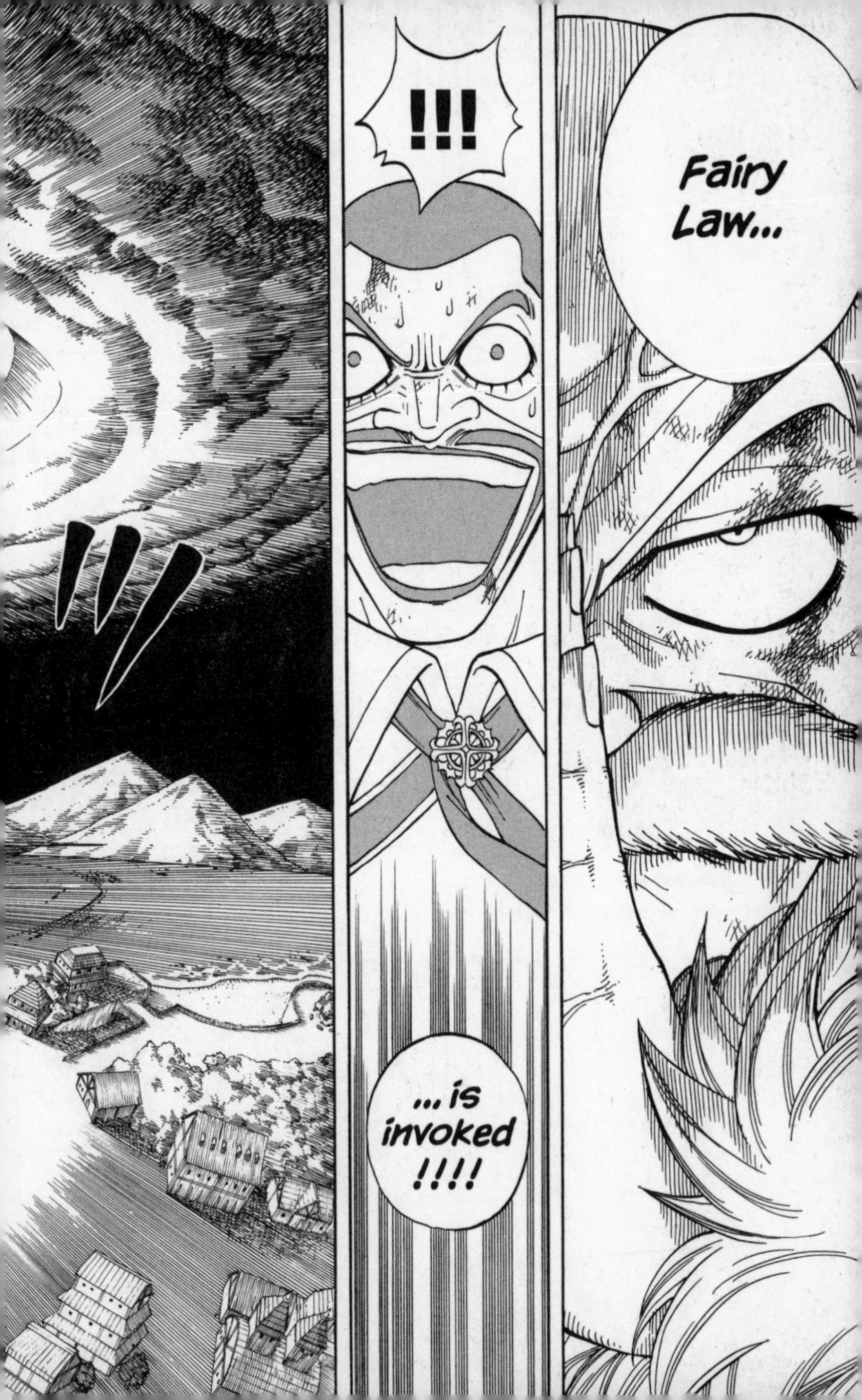
Fairy Law...
!!!
...is invoked!!!!

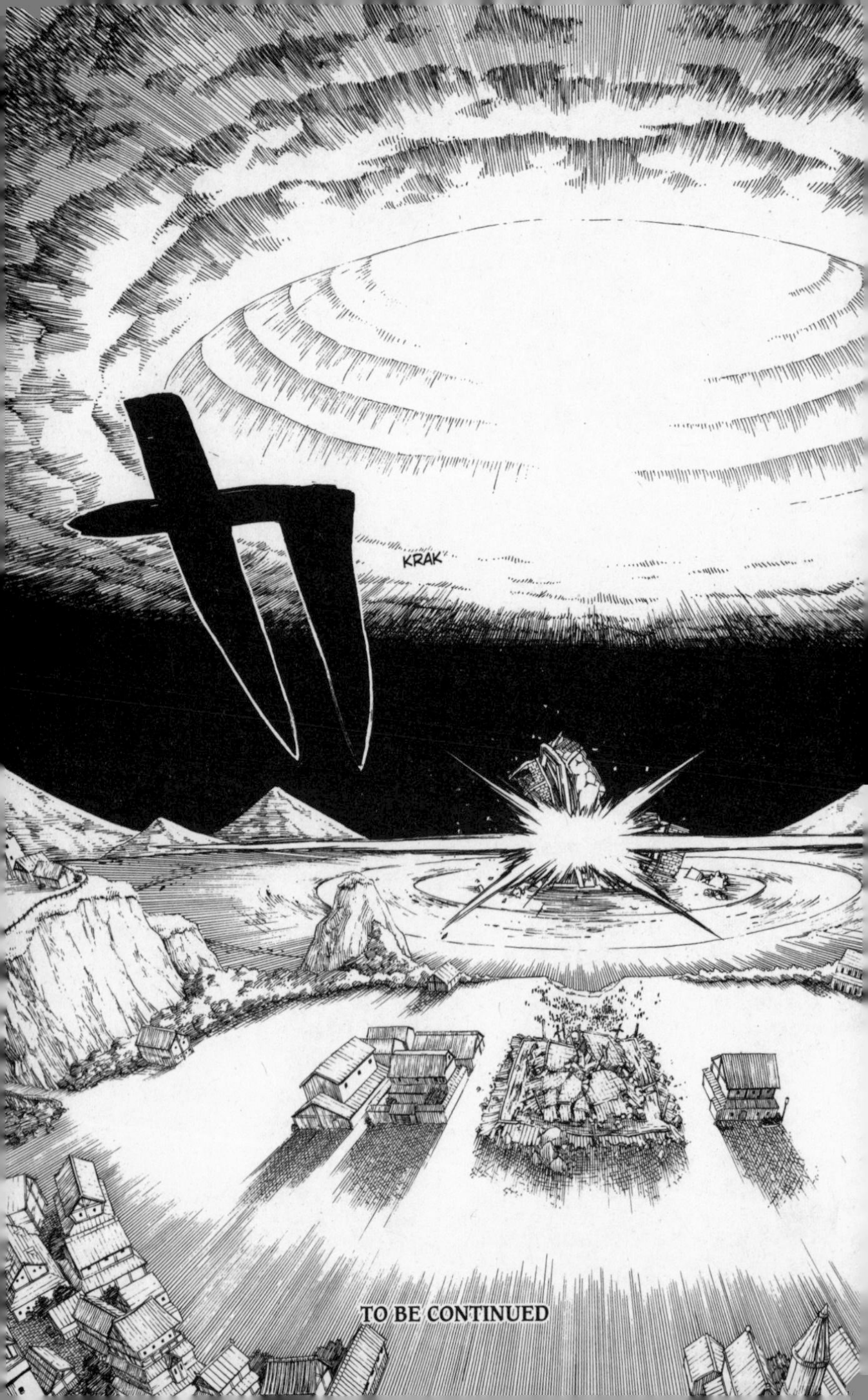
KRAK
TO BE CONTINUED

Continued from the left-hand page ⬇

***Mira*:** Shall we read the next question?

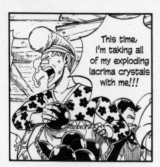

This time, I'm taking all of my exploding lacrima crystals with me!!!

What's a lacrima?

***Lucy*:** It's a magical crystal. A magic item that even normal humans can use.
***Mira*:** That's right. I think for people living in the world these questions are coming from, you should picture a lighter in your minds. Even if you can't do magic, you can make fire with a lighter, right? In the same way, there are magical items in our world that have made their way into people's everyday lives.
***Lucy*:** "Lacrima"...that means "tear," right?
***Mira*:** Yep! But if lacrima are distributed too widely, then our work as wizards might dry up! I think that's why the creator gave it such a masochistic-sounding name.

: Is...that...right...?

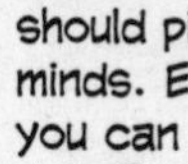

***Mira*:** And now, our final question.
***Lucy*:** All right!! Now we hit the sea!!
***Mira*:** It's a question *about* the sea.
***Lucy*:** Huh?

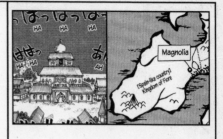

Magnolia
[Spain-like country] Kingdom of Fiore
HA HA HA
HA HA
AH

In some scenes, the Fairy Tail guild is shown right in front of a huge sea, but on the map, the guild seems to be pretty far inland...?

***Mira*:** ....
***Lucy*:** ....

:Why don't we go swimming, Lucy?

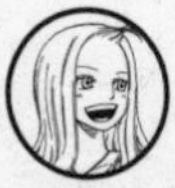

***Lucy*:** Sure! ♥ But what is the meaning of this?!
***Mira*:** You've got to give the reader credit. He's pretty sharp.
***Lucy*:** I'm sure the author is putting on a face that says, "Oops!" right now.
***Mira*:** Actually, that's a lake.
***Lucy*:** Don't you think it might be a little too big for a lake?

: Let's just say it's a lake and let it go at that, okay?

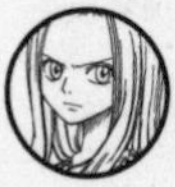

***Lucy*:** I-I...guess...it's okay...
***Mira*:** Fine! Now, let's go swimming.

: With a lake that close, I don't have any idea why we came all the way to the seaside to swim, though.

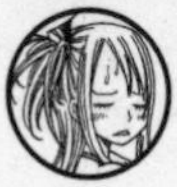

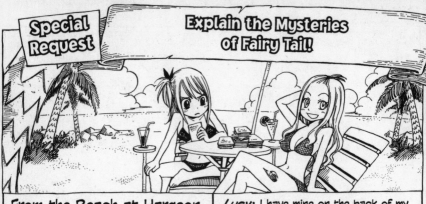

Special Request

Explain the Mysteries of Fairy Tail!

From the Beach at Hargeon

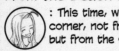

 : This time, we bring you this corner, not from the guild, but from the seaside! ♥

: We're at the beach! We should be having fun!! Why do we have to do this?!!

Mira: Because the artist doesn't really think his stories through, so there are a lot of postcards from the readers with questions.

Lucy: Then let's get this over with fast, so we can go swimming!! Come on, Mira-san!!

Mira: Okay, here's our first question.

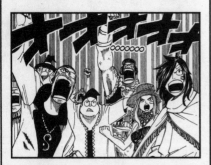

Does every member of Fairy Tail have the symbol somewhere on their bodies?

Lucy: Normally, it's in a place you can't see.

Mira: Yes, of course everybody does.

Lucy: I have mine on the back of my hand. It's on Natsu's right shoulder. It's on Erza's left arm.

Mira: As you can see ↑, it's on my left thigh.

 : Wow!! So that's where you have it?

 : Loke has it on his **ck.

 : His **ck?!!!!

Mira: That's right. His **ck.

Lucy: Mira-san...Um...Uh...Is that...okay?

Mira: Of course! It's a magic stamp! Not a tattoo!!

Lucy: No, I don't mean that. I mean...is it okay to talk about things like that here...?

Mira: Huh? Why would talking about his B-A-C-K not be okay?

Lucy: His... b... ack...?

Mira: Of course. His **ck.

 Lucy: Y-You know, in my opinion, there's no reason to censor that.

Continued on the right-hand page

TAIL d'ART

The *Fairy Tail* Guild d'Art is an explosion of fan art! Please send in your black-and-white art on large postcard stock!! Those chosen to be published will get a signed mini poster!♪ Make sure you write your real name and address on the back of your postcard!

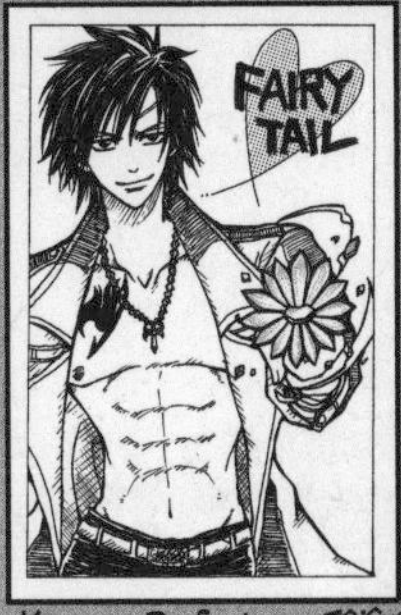
FAIRY TAIL

Kagawa Prefecture, Tôjûrô

▼ Whoa! He's cool!! It looks like Gray's popularity isn't slipping in the slightest! (How does a guy that shy and retiring do it?)

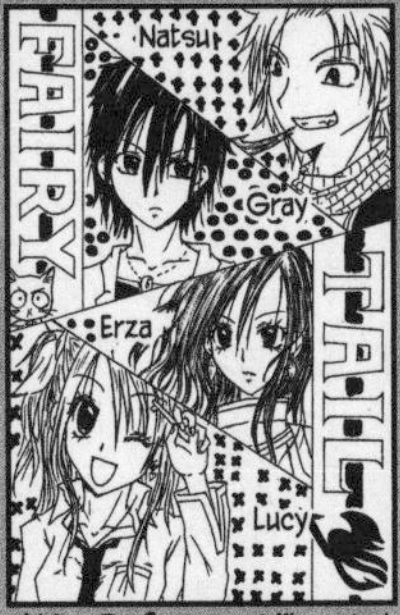
Natsu
FAIRY
Gray
TAIL
Erza
Lucy

Akita Prefecture, Mikan-bako

▼ I especially like Erza and the odd way that she shines.

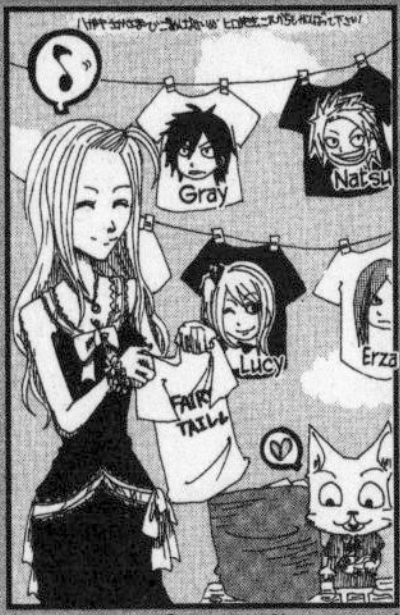
Gray
Natsu
Lucy
Erza
FAIRY TAIL

Shizuoka Prefecture, Chawanmushi

▼ I think that Mira-chan actually does everybody's laundry, too!

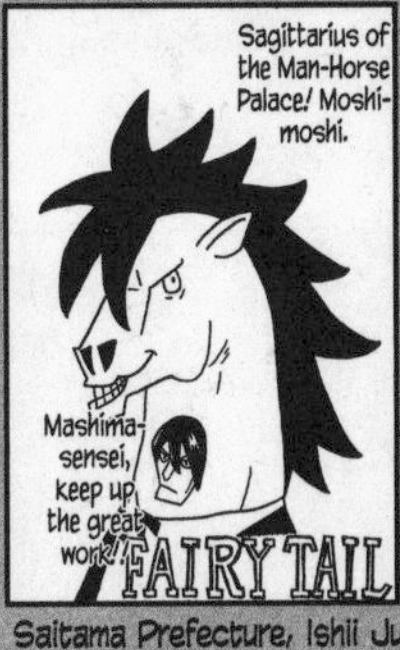
Sagittarius of the Man-Horse Palace! Moshi-moshi.
Mashima-sensei, keep up the great work!
FAIRY TAIL

Saitama Prefecture, Ishii Jun

▼ Here's our "rare-character" fan art for this time. I never expected it to be *this character*!!

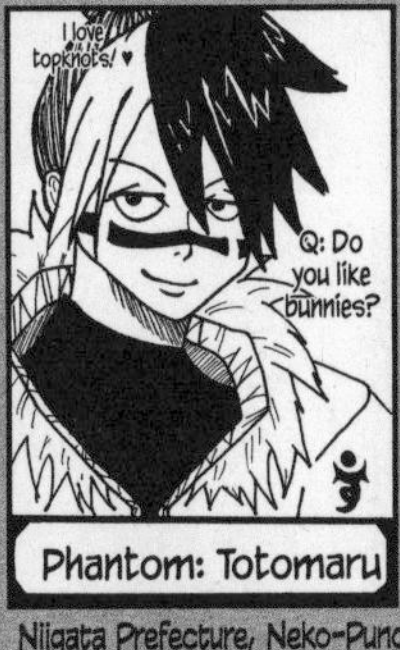
I love topknots! ♥
Q: Do you like bunnies?
Phantom: Totomaru

Niigata Prefecture, Neko-Punch

▼ So you like bunnies? I have to say that is...pretty normal.

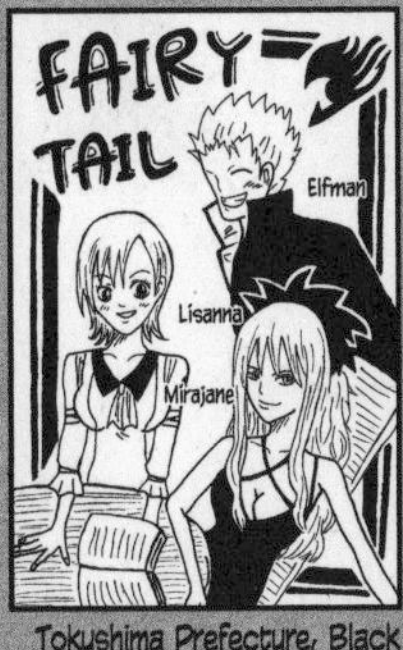
FAIRY TAIL
Elfman
Lisanna
Mirajane

Tokushima Prefecture, Black

▼ The story of these three isn't over yet! I'm going to draw the next chapter someday!

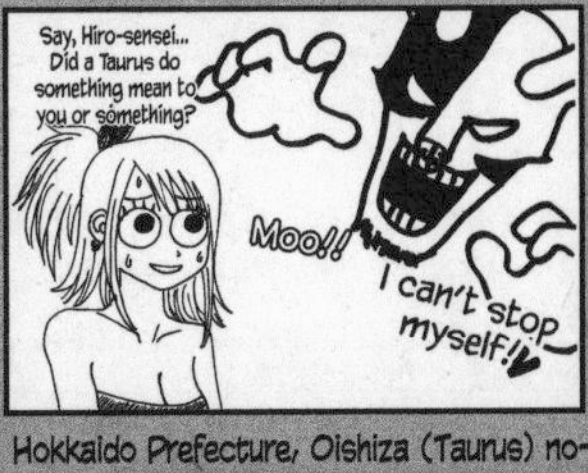
Say, Hiro-sensei... Did a Taurus do something mean to you or something?
Moo!!
I can't stop myself!! ♥

Hokkaido Prefecture, Oishiza (Taurus) no-i

▼ Actually, I'm a Taurus myself! So I draw him with the utmost loving attention! ♥

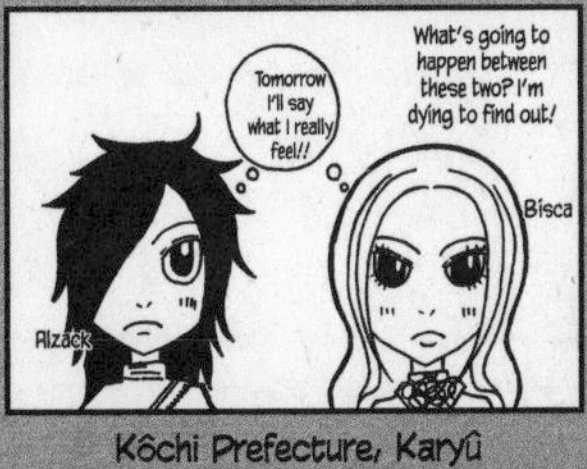
What's going to happen between these two? I'm dying to find out!
Tomorrow I'll say what I really feel!!
Bisca
Alzack

Kôchi Prefecture, Karyû

▼ Thanks for rooting for the simple love story! Now, what will happen between them?

Send to Hiro Mashima, Kodansha Comics
451 Park Ave. South, 7th Floor New York, NY 10016

FAIRY GUILD

Any letters and postcards you send with your personal information, such as your name, address, postal code, and other information, will be handed over, as is, to the author. When you send mail, please keep that in mind.

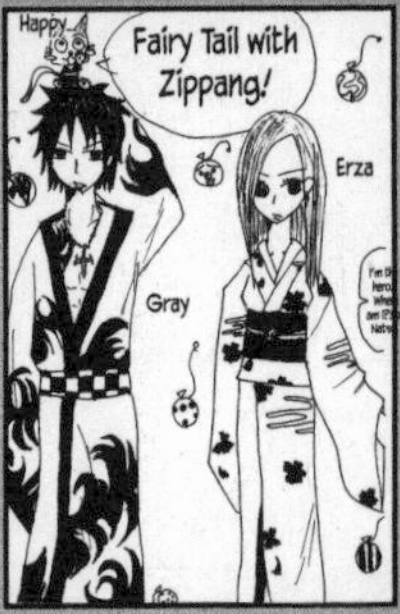
Happy
Fairy Tail with Zippang!
Erza
Gray
Aichi Prefecture, Nakane Chisato

▼ Hey, I like this kind of picture, too! I really like the slender Erza!!

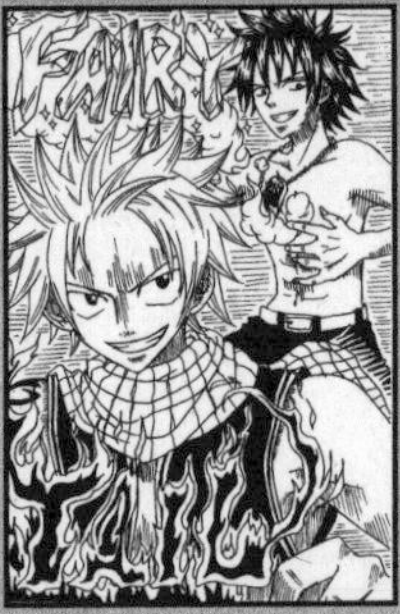
Kyoto, Sachiko

▼ This artist did the logo as fire and ice!! I never thought of that!

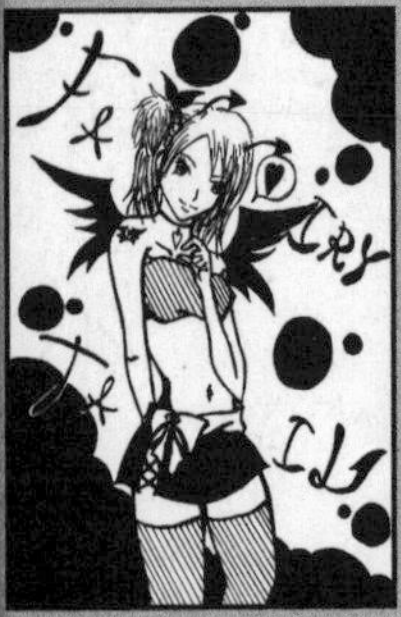
Ibaragi Prefecture, Namikaze

▼ A little devil Lucy. Hm... You already knew that I was a sucker for sexy illustrations, didn't you?

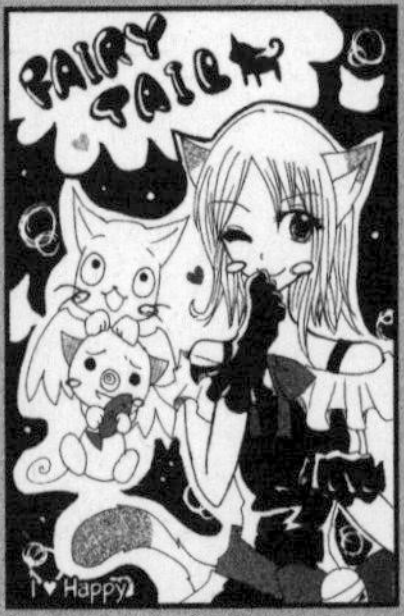
FAIRY TAIL
I ♥ Happy
Aichi Prefecture, Happy Love2

▼ These are what people call "nekomimi" (cat's ears). I think *zōmimi* (elephant ears) are going to be the next big thing!

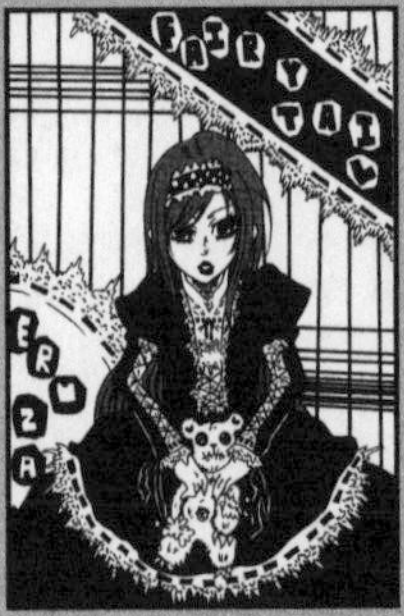
FAIRY TAIL
ERZA
Gunma Prefecture, Ishijima Tomoka

▼ Goth Erza, and so well done!! I'm really bad at drawing clothes like that!! (Just look at Sherry!)

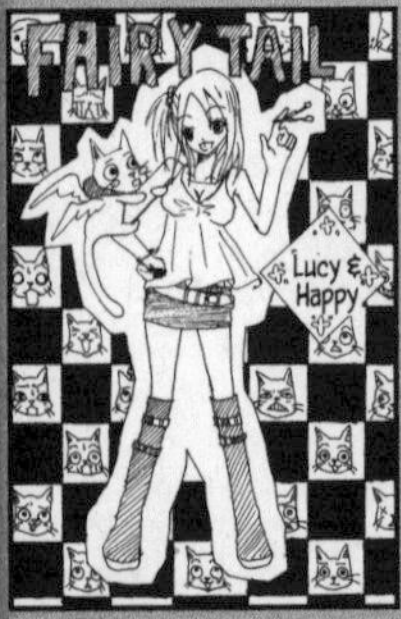
FAIRY TAIL
Lucy & Happy
Saitama Prefecture, Ajisai

▼ There are a ton of Happys in the background all making great faces!!

Rejection Corner

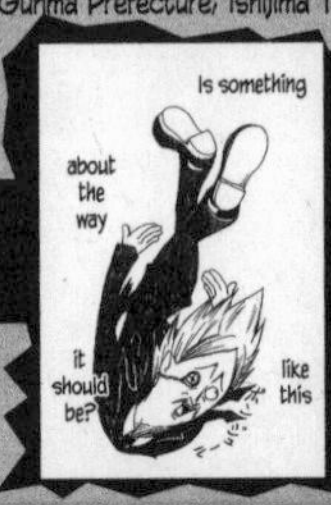
Is something
about the way
it should be?
like this

◀ Well... Sure, why wouldn't it be? Whatever that means.
Kyoto, Hirorin Sumiyabazaru

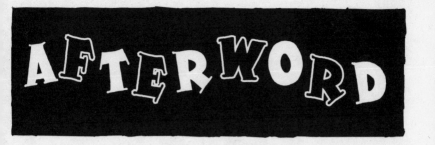

AFTERWORD

Once I set on the idea of doing a dragon slayer, I knew that other dragon slayers would show up. And after a long wait, the one who showed up was Gajeel-kun (at work, we all call him Gajeel-kun (♠♠)). As Natsu's rival, he was extremely scary right from the start. Actually, there was a fight scene planned between Gajeel-kun on one side and Loke (guy with glasses) and Reedus (big guy) on the other, but with the way the episode shaped up, it had to be cut. Still, instead we got a pretty hot fight between him and Natsu, so we'll call it a good thing. Right at the very beginning, some characters called the dragon-slaying magic "Dragon Slayer," but in point of fact, dragon slayers are the people who use dragon-slaying magic. Sorry for all the confusion. This wasn't a mistake. It's just such an old form of magic that the characters don't understand the term anymore. As time went on, people had trouble differentiating between the magic and the users of that magic. But I didn't get that across to the readers very well, huh?(♠)

By the way, there are even more dragon slayers in this world. They may appear over the course of the story, but then again, they may not. The dragon Igneel passed on the techniques for slaying dragons and then disappeared. Hmm…A weird story. But I have my reasons for it, and those reasons may become key information later on. But then again, they may not. Hmm…I sort of forgot what I was trying to say, so I'm just going to end this here.

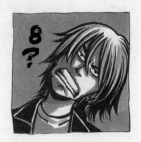

It happened so fast! My original goal of ten volumes is already in sight. Before I started, I thought that my previous work was so long (thirty-five volumes) that this time, I'd limit it to only about ten volumes. But it turned out to be much more fun drawing *FT* than I originally thought it would be. It looks like I can make this story a lot longer than planned! So root for me as I continue on…at least to volume 11!!

—Hiro Mashima

Translation Notes

Japanese is a tricky language for most Westerners, and translation is often more art than science. For your edification and reading pleasure, here are notes on some of the places where we could have gone in a different direction in our translation of the work, or where a Japanese cultural reference is used.

General Notes:
Wizard

In the original Japanese version of *Fairy Tail*, you'll find panels in which the English word "wizard" is part of the original illustration. So this translation has taken that as its inspiration and translated the word *madôshi* as "wizard." But *madôshi*'s meaning is similar to certain Japanese words that have been borrowed by the English language, such as judo (the soft way) and kendo (the way of the sword). *Madô* is the way of magic, and *madôshi* are those who follow the way of magic. So although the word "wizard" is used in the original dialogue, a Japanese reader would be likely to think not of traditional Western wizards such as Merlin or Gandalf, but of martial artists.

Names

Hiro Mashima has graciously agreed to provide official English spellings for just about all of the characters in *Fairy Tail*. Because this version of *Fairy Tail* is the first publication of most of these spellings, there will inevitably be differences between these spellings and some of the fan interpretations that may have spread throughout the Web or in other fan circles. Rest assured that the spellings contained in this book are the spellings that Mashima-sensei wanted for *Fairy Tail*.

Fair-Weather Charm, page 3

The Japanese have a popular charm that is supposed to avert rain: the *teru-teru bôzu*, where *teru* means "to shine" as in sunshine, and *bôzu* means a Buddhist priest or monk. To make one, a white tissue, napkin, or cloth is wrapped around a ball and tied off at the "neck" making a head with the rest of the cloth or paper trailing off as robes. Usually a smiley face is drawn on it (see page 15 for a slightly clumsy example). It is called a "*bôzu*" because it has a round, bald head much like Buddhist monks or priests do. Once the charm is made, it is usually hung under the roof's rafters as a charm to stop the rain. If it is hung upside down, it is supposed to encourage the rain to fall.

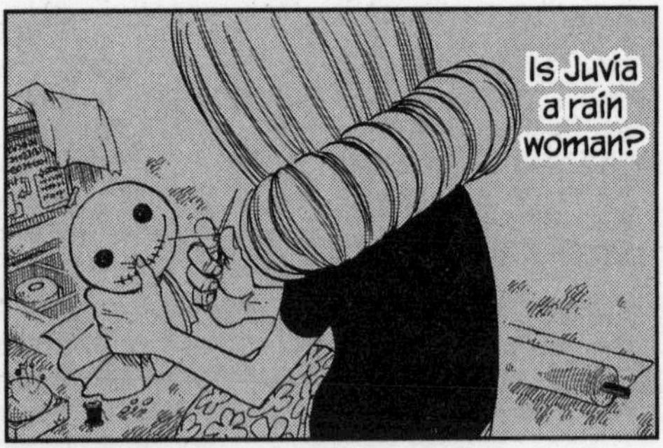
Is Juvia a rain woman?

Rain Woman, page 15

Rain Women (*Ame onna* in Japanese) are a recurrent theme in Japanese folklore, and later, much used in manga and anime. In ancient Japan's agrarian culture, the rain women were called upon to help rain fall on the crops, and some worshipped *Ame onna* as deities. In more recent depictions they tend to be tragic figures who bring nonstop rain wherever they go, shunned and ostracized for something they cannot control.

Nattô, page 63

There are foods in nearly every culture that are generally loved by those within the culture and abhorred by almost anyone coming to the culture from the outside. Hawaii has *poi*, the Inuit have *muqtuq* blubber, and the Japanese have *nattô*. *Nattô* is a strong-smelling fermented soybean dish in which beans are connected by a viscous, stringy, slimy fluid. The dish is very nutritious, containing *nattokinase*, a fibrinolytic enzyme that is said to prevent clotting in the arteries. However, despite the benefits, most non-Japanese can't palate it. Of course, there are some Western lovers of *nattô*, and a large number of Japanese who do not eat it—in other words, there are always exceptions—but the rule is, Japanese love *nattô* and foreigners can't stand the stuff.

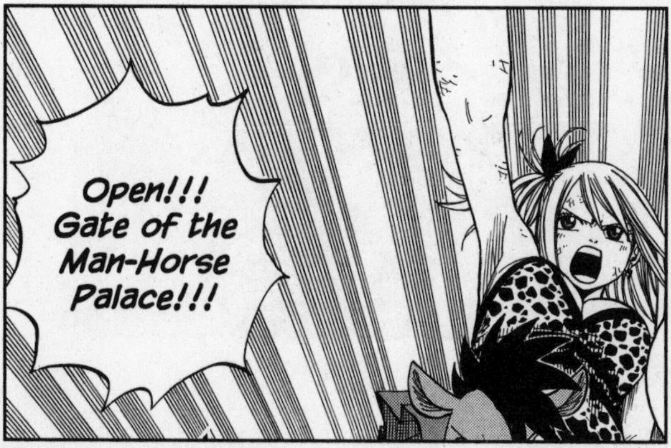
Open!!! Gate of the Man-Horse Palace!!!

Man-Horse Palace, page 117

Sagittarius is Latin for "Archer," and that is how it is referred to in astrology, but in Greek mythology, Sagittarius is Chiron, the Centaur. Chiron was unlike the other, bestial centaurs, and instead was a wise and learned hunter and healer. In this version, Mashima-sensei makes a joke of the man-horse by presenting it in an unusual way. However, if I had translated the palace as the "Centaur Palace," Mashima's version of the man-horse wouldn't follow logically as it does with the more literal translation of "Man-Horse Palace."

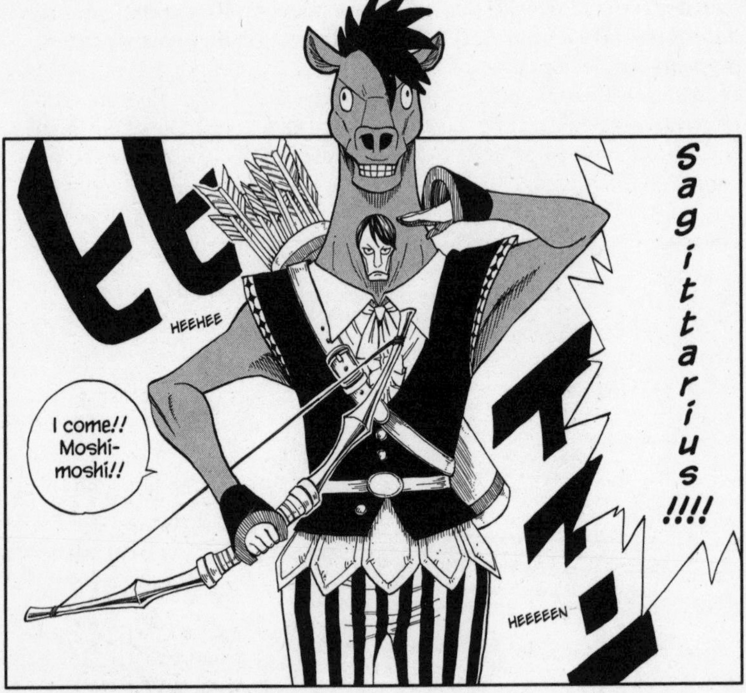
Sagittarius!!!!
I come!! Moshi-moshi!!
HEEHEE
HEEEEEN

Moshi-moshi, page 117

At first, I thought Sagittarius's "moshi-moshi," was a Japanese horse sound, but I could find no incidents of horses using that sound in my research. (If you know of examples, let me know!) I just have to assume that it is a cute sentence-ending sound much like Cancer's "-ebi" at the end of his sentences (see the note in volume 2). By the way, the phrase, "moshi-moshi" is generally used as the English "hello" is used when answering the phone or when tentatively trying to get someone's attention. That doesn't seem to be Sagittarius's meaning when using the phrase here, though.

Topknots, page 188

Most samurai-movie fans recognize the classic samurai hairstyle of a shaved forehead and a topknot (an oiled ponytail that comes forward over the top of the head). It is called in Japanese a *chonmage*. Totomaru doesn't have the samurai style of topknot, but he does have a rather punk-style topknot.

Honorifics Explained

Throughout the Kodansha Comics books, you will find Japanese honorifics left intact in the translations. For those not familiar with how the Japanese use honorifics and, more important, how they differ from American honorifics, we present this brief overview.

Politeness has always been a critical facet of Japanese culture. Ever since the feudal era, when Japan was a highly stratified society, use of honorifics—which can be defined as polite speech that indicates relationship or status—has played an essential role in the Japanese language. When addressing someone in Japanese, an honorific usually takes the form of a suffix attached to one's name (example: "Asuna-san"), is used as a title at the end of one's name, or appears in place of the name itself (example: "Negi-sensei," or simply "Sensei").

Honorifics can be expressions of respect or endearment. In the context of manga and anime, honorifics give insight into the nature of the relationship between characters. Many English translations leave out these important honorifics and therefore distort the feel of the original Japanese. Because Japanese honorifics contain nuances that English honorifics lack, it is our policy at Kodansha not to translate them. Here, instead, is a guide to some of the honorifics you may encounter in Kodansha Comics.

-**san**:   This is the most common honorific and is equivalent to Mr., Miss, Ms., or Mrs. It is the all-purpose honorific and can be used in any situation where politeness is required.

-**sama**:   This is one level higher than "-san" and is used to confer great respect.

-**dono**:   This comes from the word "tono," which means "lord." It is an even higher level than "-sama" and confers utmost respect.

-kun: This suffix is used at the end of boys' names to express familiarity or endearment. It is also sometimes used by men among friends, or when addressing someone younger or of a lower station.

-chan: This is used to express endearment, mostly toward girls. It is also used for little boys, pets, and even between lovers. It gives a sense of childish cuteness.

Bozu: This is an informal way to refer to a boy, similar to the English terms "kid" and "squirt."

Sempai/
Senpai: This title suggests that the addressee is one's senior in a group or organization. It is most often used in a school setting, where underclassmen refer to their upperclassmen as "sempai." It can also be used in the workplace, such as when a newer employee addresses an employee who has seniority in the company.

Kohai: This is the opposite of "sempai" and is used toward underclassmen in school or newcomers in the workplace. It connotes that the addressee is of a lower station.

Sensei: Literally meaning "one who has come before," this title is used for teachers, doctors, or masters of any profession or art.

-[blank]: This is usually forgotten in these lists, but it is perhaps the most significant difference between Japanese and English. The lack of honorific means that the speaker has permission to address the person in a very intimate way. Usually, only family, spouses, or very close friends have this kind of permission. Known as *yobisute*, it can be gratifying when someone who has earned the intimacy starts to call one by one's name without an honorific. But when that intimacy hasn't been earned, it can be very insulting.

Preview of Volume 9

We're pleased to present you with a preview from volume 9, now available from Kodansha Comics. See our Web site (www.kodanshacomics.com) for more details!

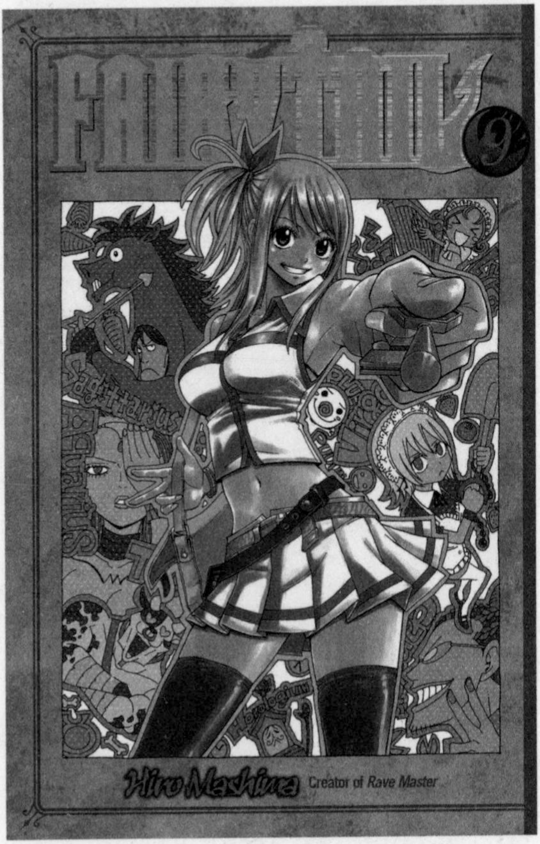
FAIRY TAIL
9
Sagittarius
Aquarius
Virgo
Horologium
Hiro Mashima Creator of Rave Master

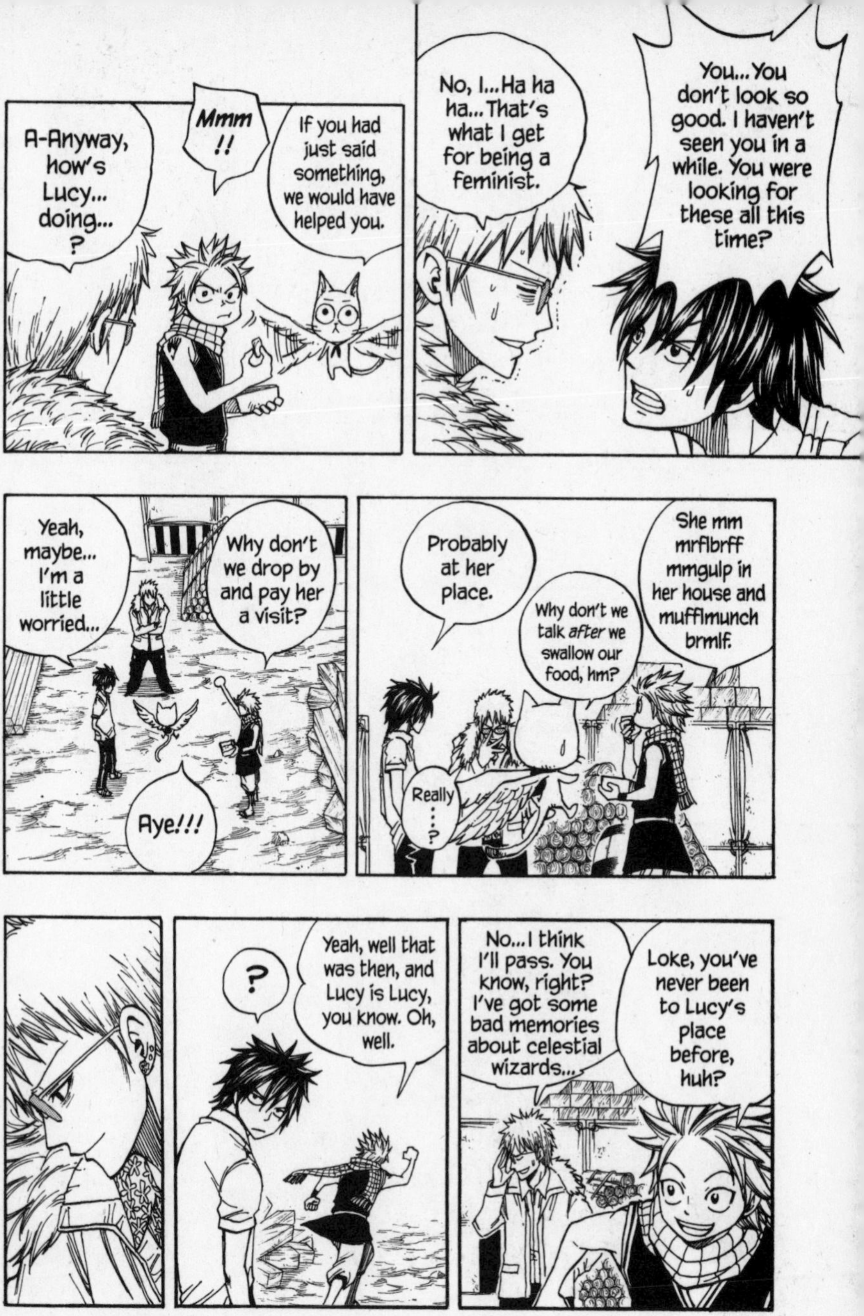
You...You don't look so good. I haven't seen you in a while. You were looking for these all this time?
No, I...Ha ha ha...That's what I get for being a feminist.
If you had just said something, we would have helped you.
Mmm !!
A-Anyway, how's Lucy... doing... ?
She mm mrflbrff mmgulp in her house and mufflmunch brmlf.
Why don't we talk *after* we swallow our food, hm?
Probably at her place.
Really...?
Why don't we drop by and pay her a visit?
Yeah, maybe... I'm a little worried...
Aye!!!
Loke, you've never been to Lucy's place before, huh?
No...I think I'll pass. You know, right? I've got some bad memories about celestial wizards...
Yeah, well that was then, and Lucy is Lucy, you know. Oh, well.
?

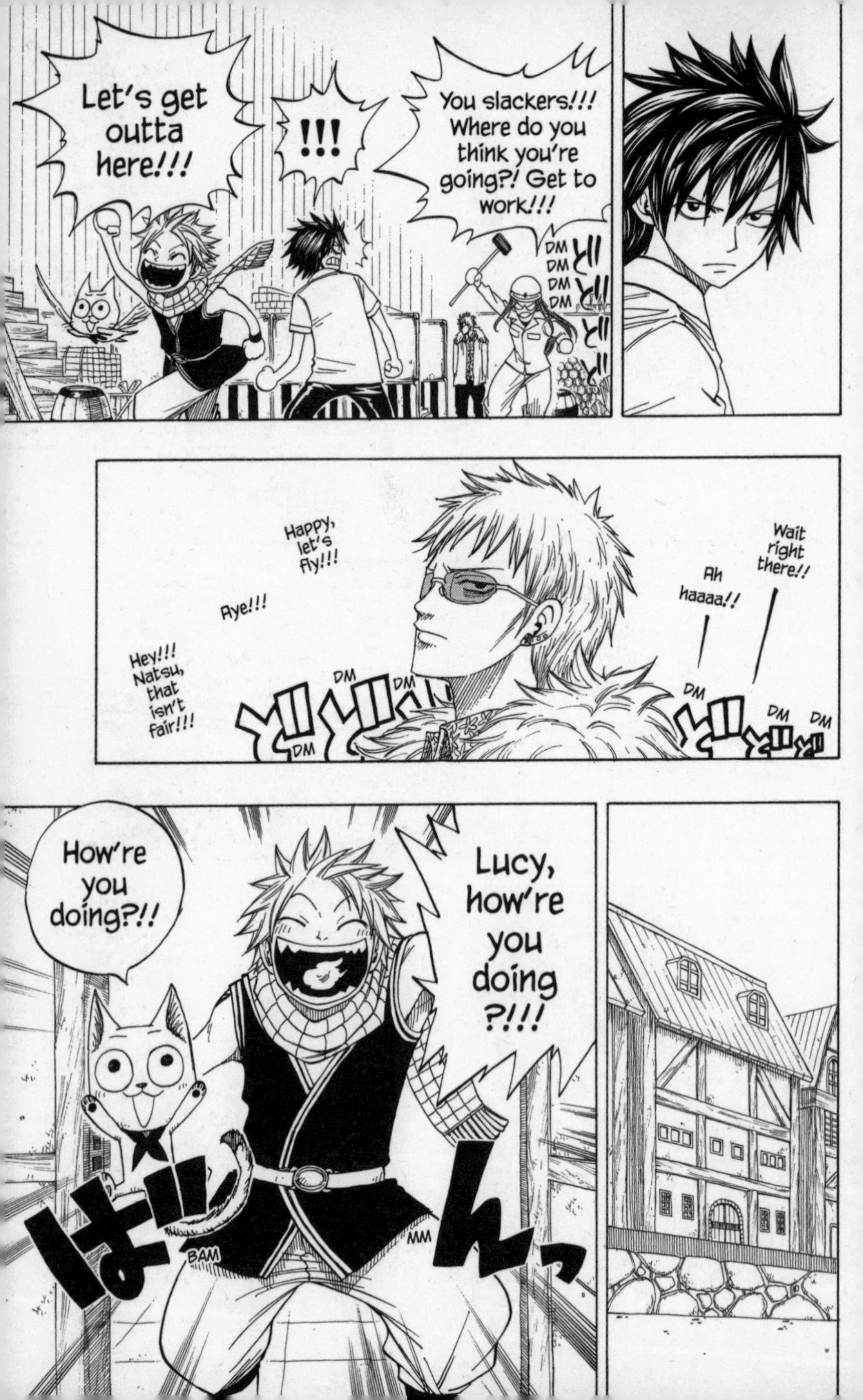
You slackers!!! Where do you think you're going?! Get to work!!!
DM DM DM DM
!!!
Let's get outta here!!!
Wait right there!!
Ah haaaa!!
DM DM DM
Happy, let's fly!!!
Aye!!!
DM DM
Hey!!! Natsu, that isn't fair!!!
DM
Lucy, how're you doing?!!!
How're you doing?!!
MM
BAM

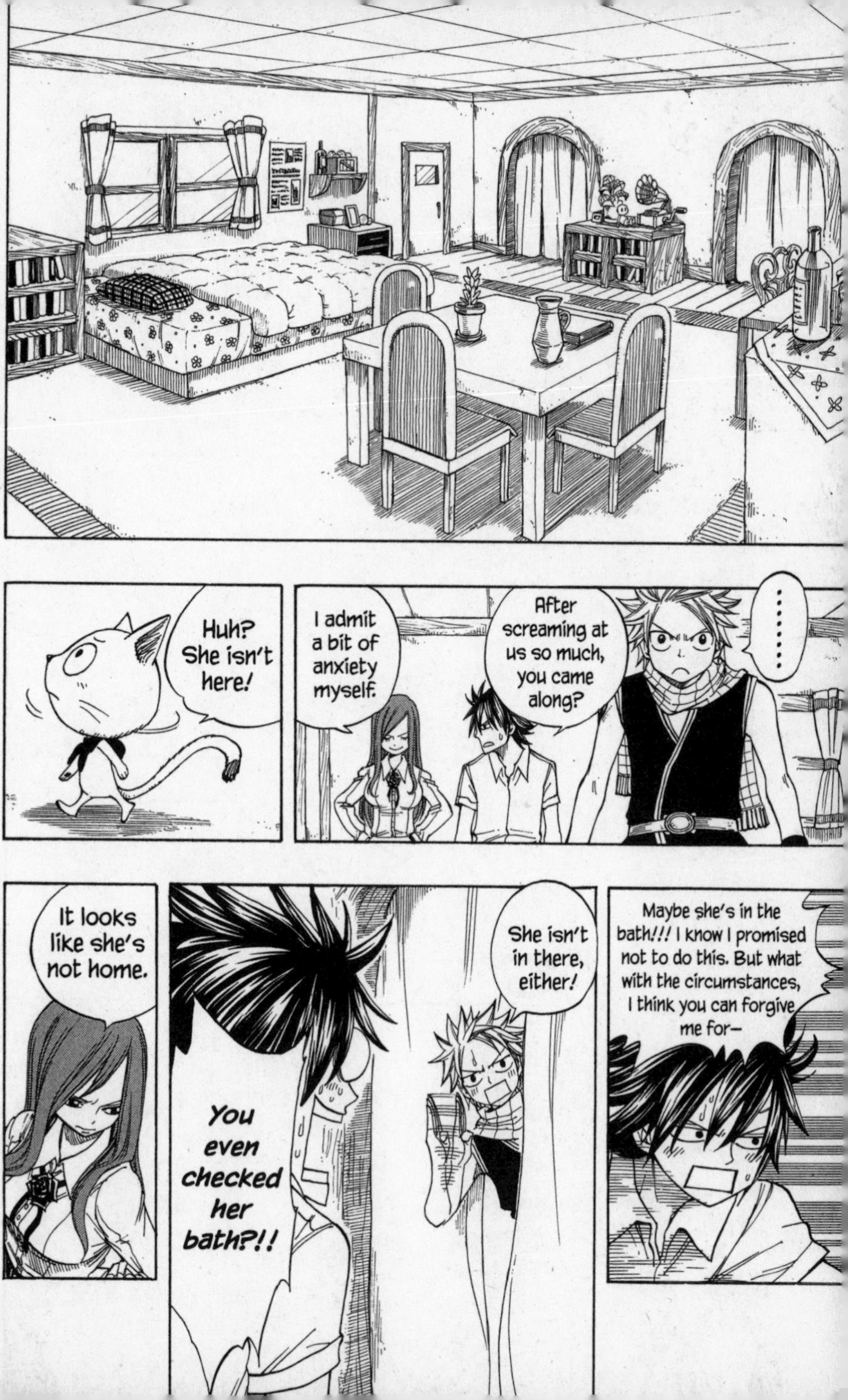
......
After screaming at us so much, you came along?
I admit a bit of anxiety myself.
Huh? She isn't here!
Maybe she's in the bath!!! I know I promised not to do this. But what with the circumstances, I think you can forgive me for—
She isn't in there, either!
You even checked her bath?!!
It looks like she's not home.

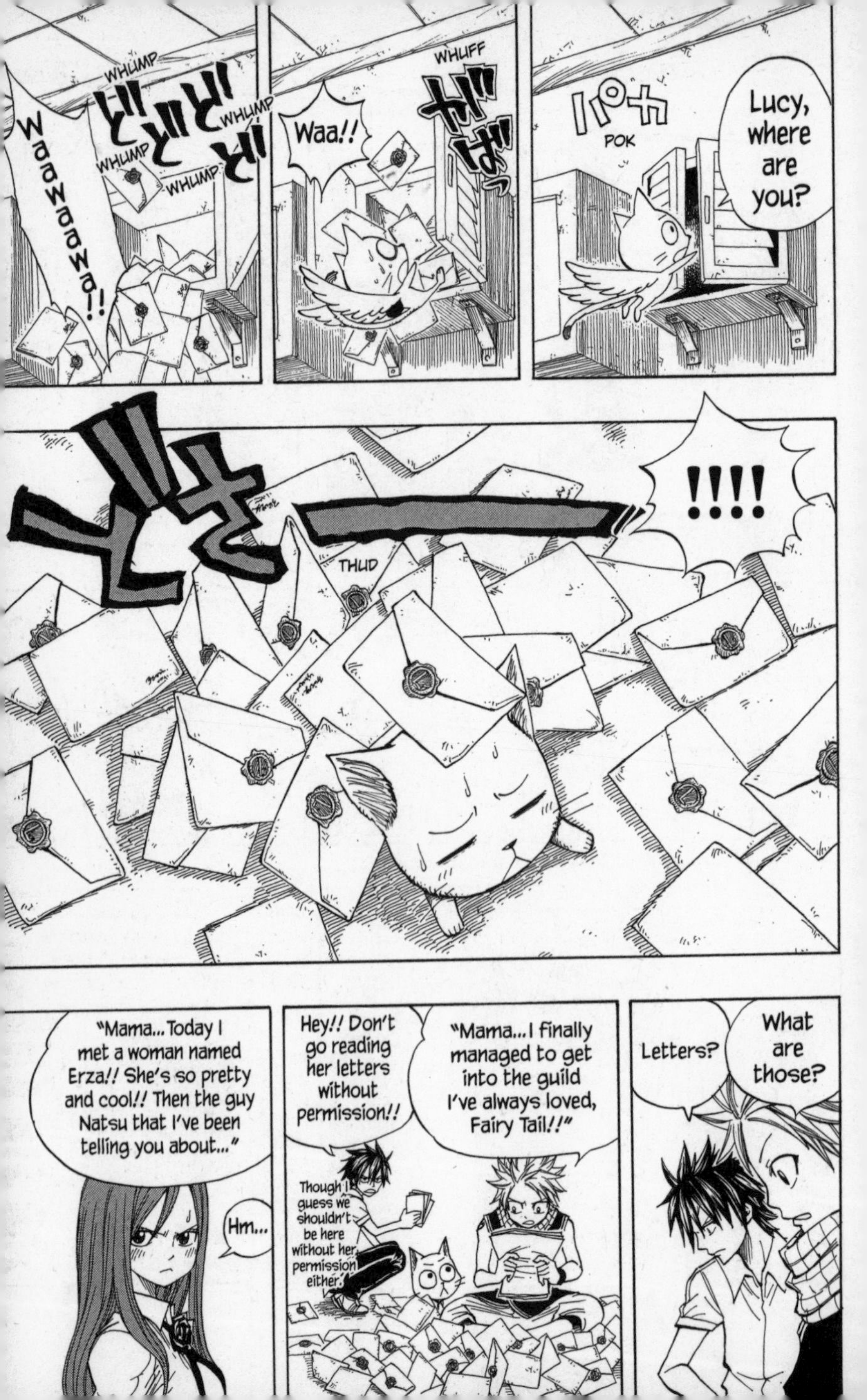
POK
Lucy, where are you?
WHUFF
Waa!!
WHUMP
WHUMP
WHUMP
WHUMP
Waawaawaawa!!
!!!!
THUD
What are those?
Letters?
"Mama...I finally managed to get into the guild I've always loved, Fairy Tail!!"
Hey!! Don't go reading her letters without permission!!
Though I guess we shouldn't be here without her permission either.
"Mama...Today I met a woman named Erza!! She's so pretty and cool!! Then the guy Natsu that I've been telling you about..."
Hm...

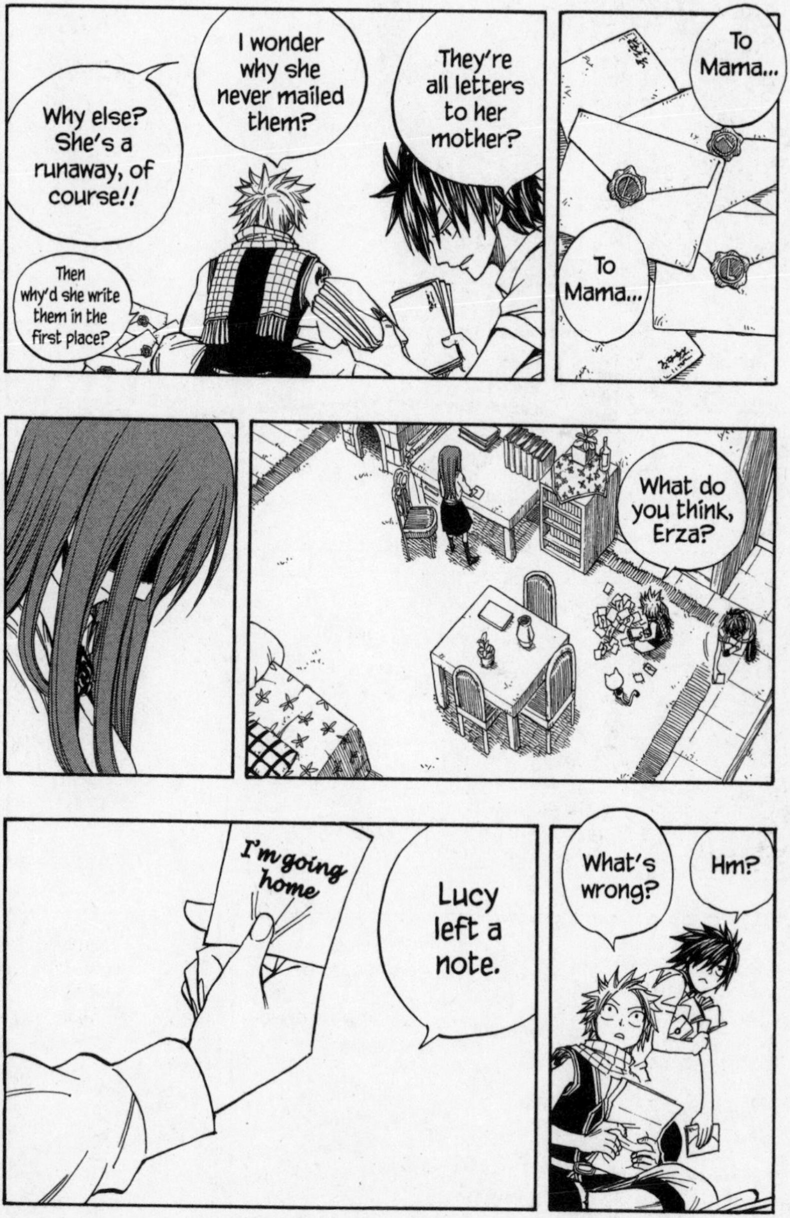
To Mama...
To Mama...
They're all letters to her mother?
I wonder why she never mailed them?
Why else? She's a runaway, of course!!
Then why'd she write them in the first place?
What do you think, Erza?
Hm?
What's wrong?
Lucy left a note.
I'm going home

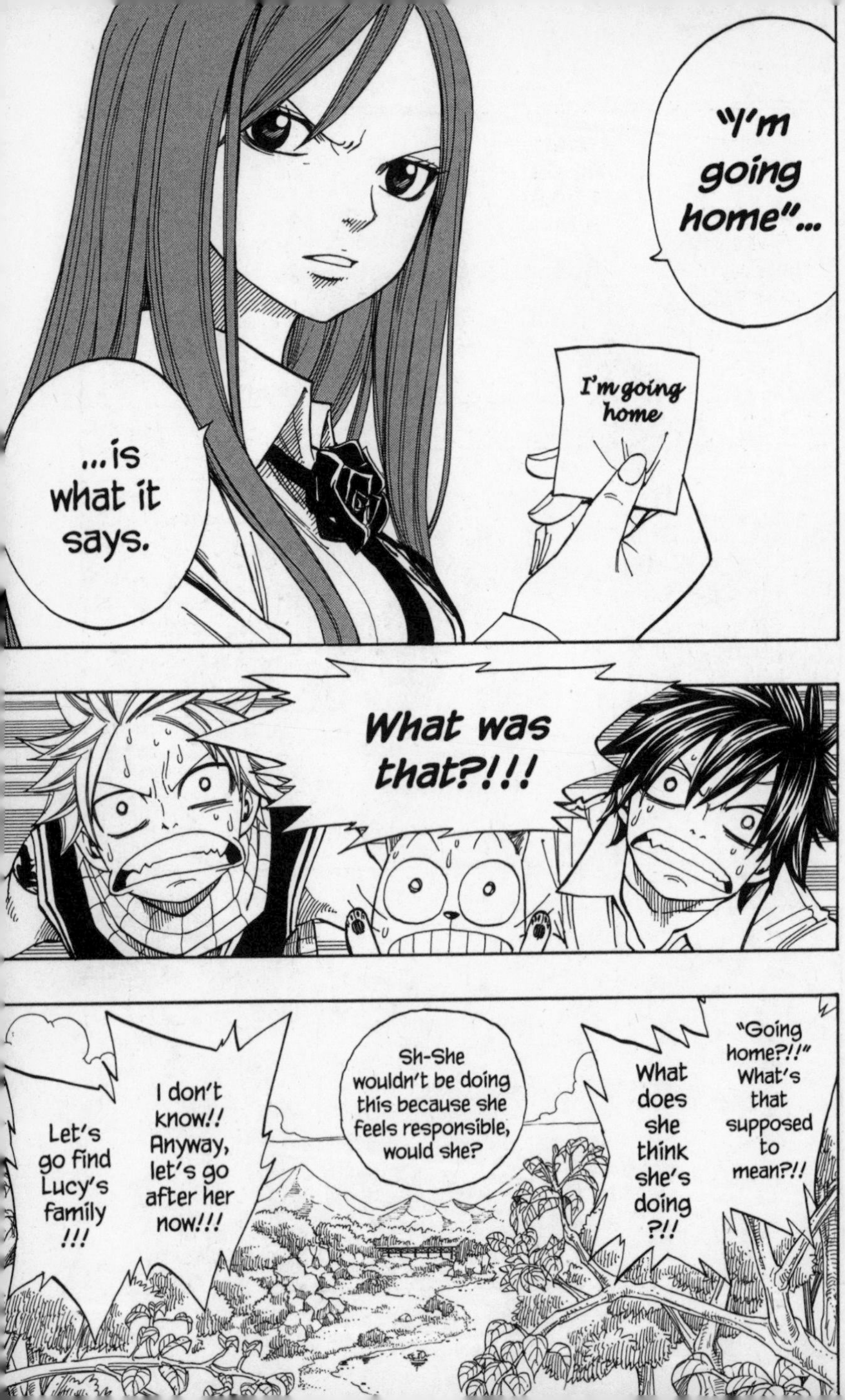
"I'm going home"...
I'm going home
...is what it says.
What was that?!!!
"Going home?!!" What's that supposed to mean?!!
What does she think she's doing?!!
Sh-She wouldn't be doing this because she feels responsible, would she?
I don't know!! Anyway, let's go after her now!!!
Let's go find Lucy's family!!!

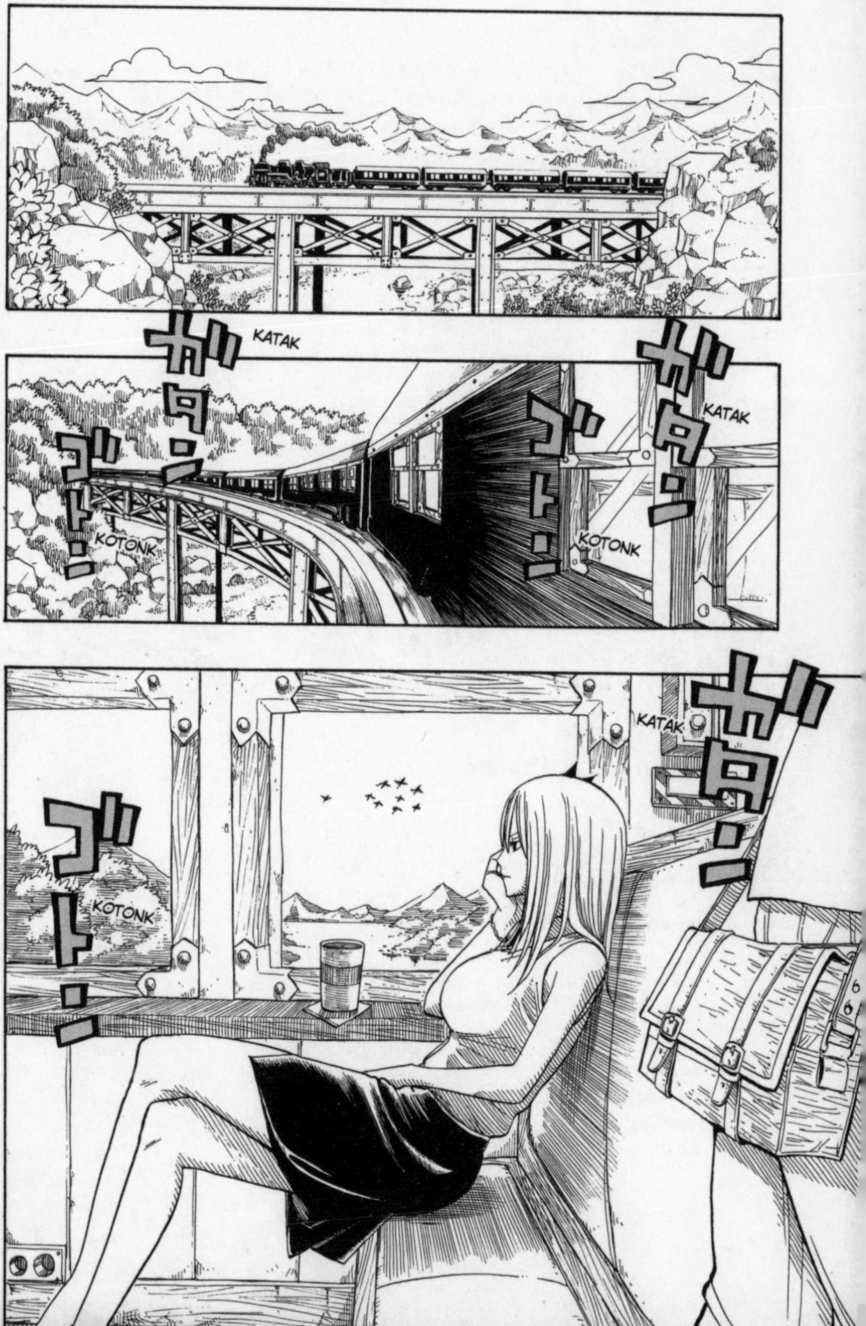
ガタン
KATAK
ゴトン
KOTONK
ガタン
KATAK
ゴトン
KOTONK
ガタン
KATAK
ゴトン
KOTONK

Fairy Tail volume 8 is a work of fiction. Names, characters, places, and incidents are the products of the author's imagination or are used fi ctitiously. Any resemblance to actual events, locales, or persons, living or dead, is entirely coincidental.

A Kodansha Comics Trade Paperback Original.

Published in the United States by Kodansha Comics, an imprint of Kodansha USA Publishing, LLC., New York.

Publication rights for this English edition arranged through Kodansha Ltd., Tokyo.

First published in Japan in 2008 by Kodansha Ltd., Tokyo

ISBN 978-1-61262-101-2

Printed in the United States of America

www.kodanshacomics.com

9 8 7 6 5 4

Translator/Adapter: William Flanagan
Lettering: North Market Street Graphics

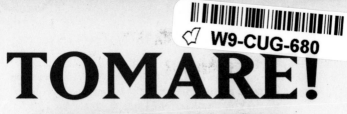

TOMARE!

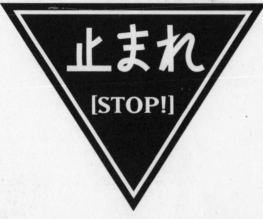

止まれ

[STOP!]

You're going the wrong way!

Manga is a completely different type of reading experience.

To start at the *beginning*, go to the *end*!

That's right! Authentic manga is read the traditional Japanese way—from right to left, exactly the opposite of how American books are read. It's easy to follow: Just go to the other end of the book and read each page—and each panel—from right side to left side, starting at the top right. Now you're experiencing manga as it was meant to be!